ONCE UPON A TIME IN
IRAQ

ONCE UPON A TIME IN
IRAQ

JAMES BLUEMEL & DR RENAD MANSOUR

1 3 5 7 9 10 8 6 4 2

BBC Books, an imprint of Ebury Publishing
20 Vauxhall Bridge Road,
London SW1V 2SA

BBC Books is part of the Penguin Random House group of companies
whose addresses can be found at global.penguinrandomhouse.com

Copyright © James Bluemel and Renad Mansour

James Bluemel and Renad Mansour have asserted their right to be identified
as the authors of this Work in accordance with the Copyright, Designs
and Patents Act 1988

This book is published to accompany the television series entitled *Once Upon A Time in Iraq* first broadcast on BBC Two in 2020.

Once Upon A Time in Iraq is a Keo Films production.

First published by BBC Books in 2020
Paperback edition published by BBC Books in 2021

www.penguin.co.uk

Editor: Steve Tribe

A CIP catalogue record for this book is available from the British Library

ISBN 9781785944574

Printed and bound in Italy by Grafica Veneta S.p.A.

The authorised representative in the EEA is Penguin Random House Ireland,
Morrison Chambers, 32 Nassau Street, Dublin D02 YH68.

Penguin Random House is committed to a sustainable future for
our business, our readers and our planet. This book is made
from Forest Stewardship Council® certified paper.

Contents

Preface vii
Introduction xiii

Chapter 1. Decisive Force 1
  9/11 9
  Critical Mass 14
  Operation Iraqi Freedom 26
  The Statue Falls 49
  City on Fire 56
  Mission Accomplished 67

Chapter 2. How to Build an Insurgency 75
  'Taste of Freedom' 83
  The Village People Operation 103
  The Spider Hole 118
  The Road to Fallujah 141

Chapter 3. The Killing Machine 151
  'We Have to Respond' 157
  The 4,000-Mile Screwdriver 166
  Abu Ghraib 176

'They Were Ghosts'	179
The Minaret	203
'The Rest is Up to Allah'	221
Chapter 4. A False Dawn	225
'We Called Him Saddam'	231
'Only for Presidents'	236
The Defendant	251
'That's the End of Him'	263
Just and Fair	276
Chapter 5. 'Those Who Are Wet Aren't Scared of the Rain'	279
'If You Only Smile'	285
The New Bogeyman	306
The Awakening and the Surge	322
Withdrawal	332
A New Law in Town	346
'We Are Life'	357
A Clean Mirror	367
Contributors	375
Index	381

Preface

Back in 2003, nobody really understood the extraordinary gamble taken by America and Britain when they invaded Iraq. Most people expected an easy victory. That was a grave mistake. This book is about that mistake and the ramifications it continues to have for people in Iraq and the West, still living in its tumultuous aftermath.

All the main political players and their advisers have already gone on record with their version of events, and their excuses. There is nothing new to say about any of that. This book takes a different approach. It focuses on the stories of the soldiers, civilians and journalists who were caught up in the war. It looks at how the war changed them as individuals and also, by extension, how it went on to change the world.

Some of the people interviewed were in the military. Others were ordinary civilians. All of them lived through the horrors of the war, and their actions were dictated by the extreme situation they found themselves in. Almost half the people I spoke to were Iraqi. Their perspective is fascinating, vital and, until now, rarely heard in the West.

As with Berlin after the fall of the Wall, the recent events of Baghdad encapsulate a moment of history which is somehow bigger than the city itself. Baghdad had once been a cosmopolitan and liberal city. Old film footage shows neatly laid-out streets, delicate and intricate architecture, cafés, open spaces and public gardens carefully planted with flowers. These are not the images that spring to mind today when you mention Baghdad. Today, the scenes that form in our collective imagination are filled with violence, shattered and broken buildings, car bombs tearing the city and its people apart. We imagine a broken and bleeding city freshly wounded by war. This is the version of Baghdad that emerged after the fall of Saddam Hussein.

I spent six weeks in Baghdad in the winter of 2018 during a rare period of calm in a city still ravaged by conflict. It felt as if the city was slowly re-emerging from the horrors of the past 15 years. There was a tentative sense of optimism on the streets. It was readable on people's faces, but especially on that of Ammar, my Iraqi fixer. Proud to be showing me around his home city, he pointed out with relief and excitement the many roads that had until recently been blocked to the public by huge slabs of concrete and old blast walls. These monolithic barriers littered the city, blocking both traffic and pedestrians. There were many roads like this in Baghdad, that could not be used, forcing the rest of the city to suffer and suffocate under the strain of the extra congestion that these barriers created. Their removal was not just symbolic of safer times but, as Ammar said, 'It has given new air to the city, we can breathe again.'

I had first visited Iraq in 2016, when I was halfway through a three-year project documenting the refugee crisis in Europe. At the time ISIS were in Mosul, and I wanted to meet Yezidi refugees in the northern city of Duhok. My team and I handed out dozens of mobile phones to migrants and refugees attempting to travel to Europe. We asked them to film the bits of their journeys which no other camera crews could access: the perilous boat crossings from Turkey to Greece, the lawless desert runs across the Sahara to Libya, the lorry-jumpers breaking into the Eurostar terminal in Calais, the people fleeing ISIS.

We produced six hours of television for BBC Two, in a series called *Exodus*. It told the stories of some of the migrants and refugees, who were all seeking a better life in Europe, in their own words. It was at times harrowing, of course, but there were many surprising and life-affirming moments. I was prepared for and expecting to witness upsetting scenes, to hear horrific stories of

PREFACE

death, destruction and sadness. And I did see and hear all of that. But what I was not expecting was the hope, humour and undeniable resilience of the human spirit.

At the end of that project, I felt the need to try and make sense of the world we are living in today; a world where it has become normal for millions of people to flee their countries in the Middle East because of escalating conflicts, prolonged war, economic ruin and the rise of Islamic terrorism. Where did this all start? Following the domino trail of cause and effect back from the present, I arrived at an interesting and provocative juncture in history which I believe holds the key to understanding our current times: the decision to remove Saddam Hussein from power. The ramifications of that decision have been shaping our world ever since.

There are many places at which to start this story. For some, it might begin in 1979, when Saddam Hussein became president of Iraq. One of his first acts as president was to execute anyone in the Ba'ath party whom he considered disloyal. Anyone who has seen the grainy black-and-white video of this event, showing people being dragged from their seats, taken outside and shot, will understand the sense of theatre Saddam employed in conjuring the spectre of fear that he relied on to rule. For some the story might start later, with the indiscriminate chemical attack in Halabja, a town in Iraqi Kurdistan. Mustard gas along with other nerve agents was used on the town, killing nearly 5,000 people, most of them civilians, many of them children. For others, it might be the collective punishment he threw at the Shia after the 1991 uprising, which killed thousands and displaced many others. This list could go on and on. There are countless events of cruelty, torture and murder which took place in Saddam's Iraq, any of which would be cause enough to wish for the dictator's removal.

In the West, the journey for many starts with 9/11, when al-Qaeda purposefully crashed two planes into the World Trade Center in New York, killing thousands of American civilians. Iraq should not be connected to 9/11, but it is. There was no evidence linking Saddam Hussein to the attacks, but a theoretical link was proposed and repeated by the Bush administration. This theorising may have stopped short of a definitive statement of fact, but only just. For many Americans, the repeated utterance of a link between the attacks and Saddam cemented a connection, and gave a much-needed target for blame and a focus for revenge.

The idea of removing Saddam Hussein from power had been kicked around various American administrations since the late 1980s, but it was only after 9/11 that it was finally acted upon and the case for war was made. We were told that, by removing Saddam, the world would become a safer place. We were told that he was evil and addicted to weapons of mass destruction. We were told that an invasion of Iraq would stop this evil tyrant, who had already gassed thousands of his own people. We were told that removing the despot would stop him fulfilling his dream of turning his evil intentions towards the West. We were told that a pre-emptive strike on Iraq was the only way to halt Saddam's plans to unleash a huge armoury of nuclear, chemical and biological weapons that were primed and aimed, ready to fire at the West. We were told that a war in Iraq would stop his plans to collaborate with al-Qaeda to unleash ever more deadly terrorist attacks against our freedom and democracy. We were told that Saddam's removal would release Iraqis from his tyrannical rule and create a democratic and free Iraq, a grateful and helpful partner in the Middle East.

The plan might have been great on paper. The reality was anything but great. It is one of the significant ironies of the invasion of Iraq that a pre-emptive strike on a country, to stamp out a possible terrorist threat, ended up creating the perfect breeding ground for terrorism.

People may think they know the story of the Iraq War, but I believe that, by focusing on ordinary people's lives, there is a chance to bring empathy and understanding to a situation in which empathy and understanding are both in short supply. This book is the result of over 100 hours of conversations I had with a broad range of people across seven different countries. I met with working-class Iraqi families who had watched as their country erupted into civil war; with American and British soldiers, who had struggled to comprehend their orders or understand their enemy; with Iraqis who had taken up arms against what they saw as foreign oppressors; and with American families dealing with the grief of losing a son or a daughter in a war that made no sense to them.

Through listening to individual accounts and experiences, from a wide range of people directly involved in one way or another, it became clear that the Iraq War was a war of many different truths. It is these voices, though, which cumulatively tell the real story of what happened... Once upon a time, in Iraq.

James Bluemel

Introduction

On 2 May 2003, standing in front of a giant banner that read 'Mission Accomplished' aboard the USS *Abraham Lincoln* in the Persian Gulf, President George W. Bush declared that 'major combat operations' in Iraq had ended. 'In the battle of Iraq, the United States and our allies have prevailed,' he told a crowd of American sailors, a little over a month after the US-led invasion had begun. 'And now our coalition is engaged in securing and reconstructing that country [...] The battle of Iraq is one victory in a war on terror.'

Rather than defeating terror and transforming Iraq into a free and prosperous democracy, however, the Iraq War unleashed violent cycles of conflict, affecting the lives of millions of people inside and outside the country. The 2003 war led to the rise of Salafi-jihadist groups like al-Qaeda in Iraq and the so-called Islamic State, the flow of millions of refugees towards Europe and North America, and the escalation of violence throughout the region. Every few years, the US and its allies would be back in Iraq fighting to liberate the country. Fifteen years after Bush famously announced victory, another US president, Donald Trump, would again declare victory after defeating ISIS in 2018.[1]

For many Iraqis, Saddam's 25 years as president were marked by conflict and oppression. Coming into office in 1979, he initiated an eight-year war of attrition against neighbouring Iran, then

---

[1] https://www.realclearpolitics.com/video/2017/12/12/trump_signs_national_defense_authorization_act_we_need_military_to_be_perfecto.html

invaded Kuwait in 1990. This evoked a regional and international response that saw very few countries stand with Iraq, and was followed by a decade of hard sanctions in the 1990s. Saddam used chemical weapons against the Kurds in the north in the late 1980s and violently brought down Shia opposition movements in the south in the early 1990s. The Iraq that Saddam inherited as president was not the Iraq that he left behind in 2003.

At the time, most Iraqis supported the 2003 invasion, a fact that can be easy to forget. On the eve of the US-led invasion, according to a Gallup public opinion poll, only 23 per cent of Iraqis believed that the war was a mistake. Three-quarters believed the war was a good idea.[2] Immediately following the invasion, Iraqis celebrated the overthrow of Saddam and his Ba'ath regime. They cheered and danced, toppling the dictator's statues and throwing shoes at the hundreds of portraits that he had erected throughout the country. Iraqis celebrated the end of a tyrant.

I was one of these Iraqis. I grew up in an exiled family that dreamed that one day Saddam Hussein would be no longer be in power. Our biggest fear was not only that Saddam would stay, but that he would be succeeded by his sons, and many more decades of tyranny. Throughout the 1990s, as Saddam became international public enemy number one, we watched as the Clinton administration occasionally bombed Iraq and called for the end of Saddam's rule. We hoped that Washington would one day get the job done.

During these years, my father worked as a journalist for the Arabic press. Like many Iraqi journalists, he was also political. He joined the Iraqi opposition that emerged in the early 1990s and began lobbying foreign governments to bring down Saddam Hussein. He would go to opposition meetings in London, New York and elsewhere. Sometimes, I accompanied him, where I met the political figures who were planning to fix Iraq. They told me that the end of Saddam's rule would usher in democracy and a better Iraq. At the time, I believed them.

---

[2] https://news.gallup.com/poll/1633/iraq.aspx

INTRODUCTION

When that day came in March 2003, we celebrated. We all returned to Iraq: political opposition figures and my father. However, it soon became clear that the promises and assurances of a better life after Saddam were falling apart, amid civil unrest and civil war. Had I been naive to believe that this group of exiled political leaders, the friends of my father, genuinely wanted to rebuild Iraq?

These questions drove me to study politics – much to my family's dismay (Iraqis are meant to study medicine or engineering). But I wanted to understand what went wrong.

*

Sixteen years after the invasion, Iraqis are still without the basics of daily life. Electricity cuts and unclean or contaminated water make the hot summer months unbearable. In recent years, the gross national income per capita (GNI) has decreased, meaning that Iraqis are less well off. Unemployment is high. The government in Baghdad since 2003 has not been able to sufficiently provide any essential services. The education system has deteriorated.

Many point to sectarianism as the reason for Iraqis' woes. They question whether Iraqi society – a mix of Shia, Sunni, Kurdish and other minorities – can function as one country. Conflict in Iraq is often framed as a competition between the different ethnosectarian groups in Iraqi society. Yet the problems they endure are not specific to any one group. Everyone suffers.

Reeling from these societal challenges, the country falls back into civil war every few years. Iraqis have grown accustomed to Islamist radicals terrorising their families, foreign militaries invading and bombarding their homes, and a corrupt political class fattening its wallets by stealing the national wealth. Yet, despite the repeated failures, the very same leaders and political parties continue to govern the country.

A growing nostalgia among Iraqis across the political and sectarian sector (including those who were victimised by Saddam) has led many to romanticise the prior period, forgetting or ignoring life under Saddam and even yearning for his return. Many Iraqis today say *Allah yerhamo Saddam Hussein*, Arabic for 'God rest the soul of Saddam Hussein'. This is not to say that Iraqis want a dictator or that Iraqis prefer authoritarian rule. On the contrary, most prefer a leader who is elected from free and fair elections. However, they have not seen such a process since 2003. Instead, their lives have been made less stable. They want predictability more than anything else. The failures of the post-2003 leaders, who became wealthy in a system marred by endemic corruption at the expense of everyday Iraq, have brought us to this point. Iraqis from all walks of life have said to me, 'We used to have one Saddam, but today we have hundreds of Saddams.'

Fifteen years after George W. Bush declared 'mission accomplished', the story of the Iraq War and its aftermath is far from over.

*

The term 'regime change' – the practice of changing a country's leadership or executive administration while maintaining the institutions of the state – is primarily affiliated with the Iraq War. (It was during the days leading up to the invasion that I recall first hearing the cliché, 'cut off the head of the snake'.) But regime change has actually been integral to US foreign policy since the Second World War. America's intervention in the war itself was under the strategy to change regimes in Germany and Japan. By the second half of the twentieth century, the US was engaging in regime change in several South American countries, including Panama, Honduras, Mexico, Haiti, Nicaragua and the Dominican Republic. Washington also pursued regime change in the Philippines and Korea. They even helped bring down the regime of Iranian president Mohammad Mosaddegh in 1953.

In 2003, the Bush administration's plan for the invasion of Iraq was sold primarily as an exercise in regime change, and it wasn't the first such change in the modern history of Iraq. Over the twentieth century the country went through several, including the 1958 overthrow of the Hashemite monarchy, the 1963 coup d'état and the 1968 Ba'athist revolution (known as the 17 July Revolution). Each instance was accompanied by massive bloodshed and targeting of old regime figures.

However, what happened in 2003 was different. The US and its allies of Iraqi political exiles not only removed the old leadership, but they enacted policies that went further in destroying the key institutions of the state – something that the previous revolutionaries never thought to do during their coup d'états. Immediately after the invasion, the US established the Coalition Provisional Authority (CPA), headed by Paul Bremer. From May 2003 until the handover of power in June 2004, Bremer was the highest civilian authority in Iraq and as such the country's new sovereign leader.

In its first order, which became known as de-Ba'athification, the CPA removed several layers of Ba'ath Party membership from their positions and prohibited them from future employment in the public sector. This order also targeted individuals who held positions in the top three layers of administration in every government ministry, affiliated corporations and other organisations such as universities and hospitals. All these individuals were removed from their jobs, and often became the subject of criminal investigations. In a single order, just over a page long, Paul Bremer wiped out the institutional framework of the Iraqi state.

The ripples of this decision are continuing to be felt in Iraq today. Its government ministries and public sector universities and hospitals have been unable to rebuild. Those civil servants and technocrats who knew how the system functioned were removed overnight. All institutional memory vanished. The new civil servants had nothing to work from, and have since been unable to revamp these state institutions.

Bremer's second order as sovereign of Iraq was to disband the country's security institutions, including the army, air force, navy, police, emergency response forces, intelligence agencies and border guards. This complete abandonment of native security institutions created a massive power vacuum. Iraqis took advantage of the chaos, looting from state institutions and further weakening state capacity. The US and its allies – now representing the only security force in the country – stood idly by as people stole equipment and fixtures, destroyed state institutions, and burned critical archives of legal documents and libraries.

This destruction laid the foundation for protracted conflict in Iraq, and sheds some light on why Iraq fell victim to cycles of violence. After all, who was there to rebuild the state? It was a relationship between officials within the Bush administration and a group of Iraqi exiled elites seeking to supplant the Saddam Hussein regime. These Iraqi allies were part of the Iraqi opposition, which primarily included the Iraqi National Congress (INC) led by Ahmad Chalabi; two major Kurdish parties – the Kurdistan Democratic Party (KDP) and the Patriotic Union of Kurdistan (PUK); Shia Islamist parties like the Supreme Council for the Islamic Revolution in Iraq (SCIRI); and a secular party, the Iraqi National Accord (INA). After 2003, another major Shia Islamist party, the Islamic Dawa Party, would become part of this leadership. These Iraqi leaders all returned to Iraq after decades of exile. Because they lacked strong constituencies inside the country, they focused on identity, stressing Kurdishness or Shi'ism as a way for them to garner support in Baghdad and other parts of Iraq where they had been largely absent for decades. US policymakers and internationals found dividing Iraqis this way to be an easy path to understanding the complexities of the country.

Western coverage of the Iraq War has often focused on the role of the Bush administration. However, Iraqis were advising and at times pushing their US patrons. And although it was the US intervention that brought about the destruction of the state, it is Iraq's leaders who, after over almost a decade-and-a-half, have been unable to rebuild a viable successor state. The Americans have left, but these Iraqis are still in power with no end in sight and foreign interference, including the US-Iran conflict, continue to impede any stabilisation or democratisation process.

*

INTRODUCTION

Today, it is easy to assume that the mixed nature of Iraqi society – which includes Shia Arabs, Sunni Arabs, Kurds, Christians, Yezidis, Turkmen, Shabak and other minority groups – would naturally lead to sectarianism. This was not always the case. Sectarianism was not always a formal part of the Iraqi political system. The seeds of today's sectarianism were sown in the early 1990s.

In 1990 Saddam Hussein invaded Kuwait, and turned himself from a regional ally to a pariah leader in the eyes of the US. Tariq Aziz, who would serve as the Ba'ath regime's main international face throughout this period, would many years later, while under house arrest, say that the invasion of Kuwait was Saddam's biggest mistake and the turning point. From this point, the US and its allies began calling for regime change. These calls would not stop until 2003, when the US finished its mission.

In the 1990s, after Saddam had led the Anfal genocide (using chemical weapons to kill between 50,000 and 182,000 Kurds in the north), the US, the UK and France set up a no-fly zone in northern Iraq to protect the Kurds from Saddam. The West also initiated tough sanctions that crippled Iraq's economy. Sensing an opportunity, and encouraged by the CIA, Iraqi opposition leaders began plotting for a possible future after Saddam. They sought to create the grounds for regime change, and Washington provided significant financial support for the initiative. The opposition leaders convened several meetings throughout the 1990s, when the primary actors to emerge were the Kurdish nationalist and Shia Islamist groups. This group elected a 26-member board and called itself the Iraqi National Congress (INC). Its leader, Ahmad Chalabi, worked closely with US allies to topple the Saddam Hussein regime. From this point until 2003, the US would send over a hundred million dollars to the INC.

The Kurdish nationalist parties and the Shia Islamist parties, along with their American backers, would become the builders of the new Iraqi state, and they sought a system based on ethno-sectarian identities for a number of reasons. These leaders were guided by the legacies of Saddam's dictatorship, which they saw as based on a minority Sunni identity that oppressed both Kurds and Shias, who made up the majority of Iraq. More critically, these groups had spent decades in exile. They lacked a strong constituency inside Iraq. They relied on identity as a way to build imagined communities which they could lead. This move would help them get – and keep – their seats at the table.

Iraq's new leaders established a scheme for power-sharing that would become known as *muhassasa*. Under this arrangement, all of Iraq's government positions, from ministers down to civil servants, are split along a rough quota system based on ethnic or sectarian identities. This system allowed the post-2003 political parties, based on ethnic and sectarian communities, to fill these positions with their proxies and as such build patronage networks within the state. Lost in this system, however, were many ordinary Iraqis who were not part of the political party patronage system. As a result, a protest movement would later emerge denouncing *muhassasa* as the symbol of the post-2003 corrupt order.

The invasion of Iraq provided an opportunity to implement the plans sketched out in the early 1990s. The exiled political parties that made up the INC returned with their American-led liberators to pick up the mantle from the fallen Saddam Hussein regime. Many of these leaders had not set foot in Iraq for decades. So much of their home country had changed. Some of these leaders told me that they barely recognised Baghdad. Nonetheless, they arrived and were poised to lead its people.

Muhassasa was formalised in the pivotal year of 2005, when Iraqis went to the polls twice. In January, they voted for a committee that would draft the national constitution and in December they voted for their first parliament. The main competitors in this election were the Shia Islamist and Kurdish nationalist parties. To monopolise the process, all major Shia Islamist parties came together to form one electoral block, which they called the United Iraqi Alliance (*al-itilaf al-Iraqi al-muwahad*, or UIA). The Kurdish nationalist groups also came together to form one electoral block, which they called the Kurdistan Alliance (*al-tahaluf al-Kurdistani*, or KA).

INTRODUCTION

However, many Iraqis did not fit into this neat identity-based structure. Mixed Sunni-Shia marriages were quite common, and others preferred to engage in politics along ideological lines. (I remember a leftist once telling me, 'I wanted to enter politics. But I didn't know which party to join. All the big parties were either Shia, Kurdish or Sunni. I had to check if I was more Shia or more Sunni.') Those Iraqis seeking a life in politics, but unable to neatly fit along the ethno-sectarian divide, were left out of the process. Their ideology mattered less in this new game. They had to join *muhassasa*.

In the aftermath of the invasion, the CPA argued it was too soon for an election. However, Grand Ayatollah Ali al-Sistani, the top Shia cleric, pushed for elections as soon as possible. Sistani believed that the Americans should not keep ruling Iraq. He also contended that without elections, Iraq would be at risk of returning to a leader who did not represent the majority. For many Iraqi Shias, the 'majority' meant their sect, which had always been at the behest of minority-Sunni leaders.

Unsurprisingly, many Iraqi Sunni groups felt left out of this process. They didn't have a political party in the same way the Kurds and Shia did. A large Sunni boycott in the pivotal year of 2005 meant that Sunnis would have very little say in drafting the constitution, and minimal representation in Iraq's first post-2003 elected government. Following the dissolution of the Ba'ath party, the Sunnis were not as prepared for political representation as the Kurds and Shias, who had parties stemming back several decades. Nonetheless, several individual Sunni leaders would take part in the political process throughout the years.

As the story goes, Iraqi politics became a game of sharing power and wealth with a group of political leaders and parties formed along identity lines. Iraqis call it the great 'splitting of the cake' (*taqsim al-kake*). Under *muhassasa*, every Iraqi government thereafter would include a mix of mainly Shia and Kurdish officials, but also Sunni and minority leaders. No single ethnic group or sect was excluded in this form of representation. These leaders all sat in Baghdad's Green Zone – a ten square kilometre area in central Baghdad that was separated from the rest of the city to protect the government from violence.

*

The story of sectarianism seemed to perfectly fit the civil war that erupted in 2006 and lasted until 2008. In each year of this bloody civil war, over one thousand Iraqis died. On one side, a group of Sunni insurgents – linked to the Salafi-jihadi group al-Qaeda in Iraq, the Mujahideen Shura Council and former Ba'ath commanders – launched a resistance campaign against both the invading Western forces and the Shia Islamist groups that had taken power in post-2003 Iraq. On the other side, Shia militias formed to fight off the American occupation and the Sunni insurgency. The most notorious Shia militia was the Mahdi Army (Jaysh al-Mahdi) led by Muqtada al-Sadr.

The trigger came in February 2006, when a group of Sunni insurgents bombed one of the holiest Shia sites, the al-Askari Mosque in Samarra. In response, groups of disgruntled Shia fighters mobilised in armed groups, primarily linked to the Mahdi Army, and sought revenge. They became notorious for running so-called death squads, which began with kidnapping and brutally torturing Sunnis, at times drilling holes in the prisoner's feet before finally executing them. Some of these executions were conducted in public squares, and even included beheadings.

During the civil war, the rhetoric turned explicitly sectarian. Competing for Iraqi identity, each side referred to the other as outsiders; Shias argued that the Sunnis were Wahhabis coming from Saudi Arabia, while Sunnis argued that the Shias were Safavids coming from Persia (or Iran). However, there was also significant internal struggle within the sect-based communities themselves. Despite those who sought to partition, Iraq did not neatly break into identity-based pieces. Neither the Sunni nor the Shia blocks were monolithic at any point after 2003. When US General David

INTRODUCTION

Petraeus wanted to bring down the Sunni insurgency, he looked to Sunnis who opposed al-Qaeda, a process that became known as the Sunni Awakening, which successfully brought in important Sunni tribal leaders to defeat the Sunni insurgency. Similarly, the Shia Mahdi Army included many factions that did not necessarily follow the leader, Muqtada al-Sadr. Sadr would later say that these rogue figures within his own block were the main perpetrators of the sectarianism violence, which he claimed to be against. Then, shortly after the defeat of al-Qaeda and the end of the civil war, Iraqi prime minister Nouri al-Maliki – a Shia leader – waged a war against the Mahdi Army in what became known as Operation Charge of the Knights or the Battle of Basra. In this battle, Shia groups fought against Shia groups.

By the end of 2008, the civil war was over. The Sunnis and Shia had fought each other and themselves, and reached a temporary settlement. At this point, the situation in Iraq seemed promising. Sectarianism that seemingly marked the past few years had calmed down, the levels of violence and casualties were dwindling, and Iraq seemed on a path towards stabilisation and good governance.

Yet, only a few years later, Iraq fell into another bloody civil war as the Islamic State of Iraq and Syria (ISIS) took over one-third of Iraqi territory in a matter of months, with only a few thousand fighters. ISIS's narrative was similarly sectarian. It began targeting Shias. The most notorious instance of sectarian violence was the Camp Speicher massacre, where ISIS militants killed over 1,500 Shia cadets in training on 12 June 2014. Videos emerged of ISIS fighters shooting handcuffed young Shia men and throwing their dead bodies into the river.

In response, several Shia militias – the remnants of the Mahdi Army and some newcomers – mobilised to fight once more. This group became the Popular Mobilisation Units (*al-hashd al-shaabi* in Arabic). Some of its leaders at times using sectarian rhetoric again. For instance, Qais al-Khazali, a former Mahdi Army leader who had split from Muqtada to create a new group, the League of the Righteousness, claimed, 'the liberation of Mosul [from ISIS] will be the revenge against the killers of Hussein.' He was referring to the historic Battle of Karbala, where the Sunni Umayyad Caliphate defeated the Shia leader Hussein Ibn Ali. Although there were flashes of sectarianism during the civil war against ISIS, however, for the most part the killings associated with the first civil war did not occur from 2014 to 2017.

This narrative of sectarianism defined the story of Iraq after 2003, an explanation used in policy circles and the press to simplify the problem. However, it has led to an understanding of the Iraq War and its legacies that diverges from realities on the ground. The story of Iraq after 2003 has primarily focused on the leadership in Baghdad and in foreign capitals from Tehran to Washington DC. Because of this, the story has centred on the elite. These leaders are the ones who have politicised and at times militarised ethno-sectarian identities. Many of Iraq's post-2003 leaders came back to their country after decades in exile. Yet their families still live abroad. When these leaders or members of their family get ill, they go abroad for medical treatment because the healthcare system in Iraq is too weak. When these leaders have children, they send them abroad for schooling because the education system in Iraq is inadequate. These leaders have bank accounts in foreign countries from the United Arab Emirates to Beirut to London. In a way, since 2003, they have served more as political consultants who have been sent in to rebuild and who will leave as soon as their contract expires.[3] The new generation of leaders who are emerging in Iraq do the same.

Most Iraqis – the real victims of the violence for decades – have been largely voiceless in the debates that have surrounded their country since 2003. Unlike the Shia, Kurdish and Sunni leaders, who have become incredibly wealthy from Iraq's immense oil wealth, these people have been left behind. In Baghdad, most Iraqis have not even been allowed to enter the Green Zone (where the Shia, Kurdish and Sunni leaders live and work).

---

[3] Kanan Makiya, in his novel *The Rope*, refers to this elite as 'foreigner Iraqis'.

In recent times, these citizens have begun to voice their grievances. However, elections have not served as a way to channel their voices. As a result, each election year has seen lower and lower voter turnout. In 2018, many cities in southern Iraq had a real turnout at around 20 per cent – far from the first election in 2005, when some 80 per cent of Iraqis voted. Many Iraqis question the point of voting. This doesn't mean they are against democracy. However, they feel that they don't want an election with the same leaders who have always failed them, and that the lack of any alternative is not democracy. And they are right. Political parties in Iraq are less and less based on ideological foundations and more and more based on patronage networks.

Instead, Iraqis are turning to protests as the only way to have a say. Shia protesters in southern Iraq demonstrate against their own Shia leaders and reject the post-2003 *muhassasa* system. The largest scale of protests erupted in central and southern Iraq in 2015 – which also coincided with the peak of ISIS power. Although ISIS was a Sunni group targeting the Shias, many Iraqi Shias were not convinced that their own leaders could legitimately represent their interests. Some protesters said that the terrorist is the same as the corrupt. In 2018, in Basra, the protests turned violent, as demonstrators attacked and burned the political offices of all political parties across the board. In the Kurdistan region, Kurdish protesters have similarly begun to protest against their own Kurdish leaders. Sunni residents have also begun to speak out against their leaders. Clearly, the identity-based politics that was forced on the many by the new leadership after 2003 is being rejected. The Iraqi sociologist Faleh Abdul Jabar, before his passing in 2018, would be the first to write on these changes, arguing that his country is on the move from identity to issue-based politics.

Whether Iraq is on a genuine trajectory away from *muhassasa* and identity-based politics is still up for debate. However, the missing piece in the story of Iraq has been the people's voice. Most of these people are now realising that the post-2003 system has never legitimately represented their voices or interests. And they are speaking out in any way they can, from protests to social media to a thriving entrepreneurial scene.

This crucial imbalance is captured by James Bluemel and his team through both the BBC series and this book. Rather than the same old narratives that have marked coverage of the Iraq War since 2003, James's focus on the story of Iraq, as told by ordinary Iraqis – who did not live in secured compounds or the Green Zone but in the real Iraq – is one of the first to acknowledge the voiceless. As the story of Iraq continues, the gap between elite and citizen will continue to grow. And those telling the story become important to understanding the cycles of conflict, the flows of refugees, the eruption of protests and also the rise of armed groups, including Salafi-jihadi organisations such as ISIS. Better understanding the roots of the problem necessarily requires hearing from ordinary Iraqis, and not the elite who have failed them for the past decade and a half.

Renad Mansour
Senior Research Fellow, Middle East and
North Africa Programme, Chatham House

Chapter 1
Decisive Force

Timeline

11 September 2001   Al-Qaeda coordinates four terrorist attacks on the United States of America, destroying the Twin Towers of the Word Trade Center, damaging the Pentagon, injuring more than 6,000 people and killing almost 3,000.

16 September 2001   President George W. Bush announces a 'war on terrorism'.

20 September 2001   The USA publicly identifies Osama bin Laden as responsible for 9/11, issuing an ultimatum to the Taliban in Afghanistan to surrender all al-Qaeda leaders.

7 October 2001   Airstrikes targeting al-Qaeda and the Taliban herald the US-led NATO invasion of Afghanistan – Operation Enduring Freedom.

29 January 2002   In his State of the Union address, President Bush categorises Iran, Iraq and North Korea 'and their terrorist allies' as 'an axis of evil, arming to threaten the peace of the world'.

12 September 2002   President Bush formally presents the US case for an invasion of Iraq to the UN Security Council; the subsequent UN Resolution 1441 mandates the reopening of weapons inspections in Iraq.

16 October 2002	The US Congress passes a 'Joint Resolution to authorize the use of United States Armed Forces against Iraq'.
13 November 2002	Saddam Hussein unconditionally accepts UN Resolution 1441; weapons inspections resume in Iraq a fortnight later.
7 March 2003	UN weapons inspection chairman Hans Blix informs the UN Security Council that no evidence of a nuclear programme and no weapons of mass destruction have been found in Iraq, but that key questions about chemical and biological weapons remain unanswered.
17 March 2003	In an Address to the Nation, President Bush says that the UN Security Council 'has not lived up to its responsibilities, so we will rise to ours' and demands that Saddam Hussein and his sons leave Iraq within 48 hours: 'Their refusal to do so will result in military conflict, commenced at a time of our choosing. ... As our coalition takes away their power, we will deliver the food and medicine you need. We will tear down the apparatus of terror and we will help you to build a new Iraq that is prosperous and free.'
18 March 2003	The House of Commons votes heavily in favour of a government motion authorising the United Kingdom to participate in the invasion of Iraq.

20 March 2003	Operation Iraqi Freedom begins with airstrikes on Baghdad, with coalition forces moving into Iraq from Kuwait.
3 April 2003	US forces take Saddam International Airport in Baghdad.
6 April 2003	British forces take the city of Basra.
9 April 2003	US forces take Baghdad; the televised toppling of the statue of Saddam Hussein in Tahrir Square signals the end of his regime. Saddam himself makes his last public appearance before fleeing Baghdad, and an eight-month hunt for him begins.
13 April 2003	Saddam's home town, Tikrit, is taken by US forces.
15 April 2003	Coalition leaders declare major combat operations in Iraq 'now over'.
1 May 2003	Mission Accomplished: President Bush announces that US operations in Iraq 'have ended'.

Introduction

March 2003. The American and British armies have gathered on the southern border of Iraq. This is where the main invasion will start. Iraqis have known the invasion was coming since their president, Saddam Hussein, was linked by the Bush administration to the 9/11 terror attacks in New York. For some, the news of an invasion was welcome. For almost a quarter of a century, Saddam Hussein had ruled Iraq with absolute authority, holding it in a grip of fear and intimidation. He had led Iraq into protracted wars with its neighbours, and personally ordered the deaths of thousands of his own countrymen. Saddam demanded absolute loyalty from the Iraqi people. Those who were not loyal were often tortured or killed, or both. It is no wonder that many Iraqis secretly wished for his removal. However, there were also many Iraqis who loved Saddam, and who would go to any lengths to protect him and their country from an invading foreign force.

Waleed Nesyif was one of the Iraqis who was secretly wishing for Saddam's demise. Waleed was 18 years old in 2003, and fascinated by Western youth culture. When America promised to liberate Iraq from the tyranny of Saddam Hussein, Waleed hoped that his country would become one of the great countries of the world, a country perhaps like America. For Um Qusay, an illiterate woman from a rural village north of Baghdad, it was also with hope that she considered the impending invasion. But her desire was not so much ideological, as driven by revenge. Her father had been murdered by Saddam himself, making any justice therefore impossible to seek. Now, as one of the most powerful armies in the world gathered on Iraq's borders, Um Qusay wanted to witness the downfall of the once all-powerful leader. Others, however – like Issam Al Rawi, who came from the same tribe as the president and loved him dearly – guarded Saddam fiercely, with unwavering loyalty, in his final days in power. To Issam, Saddam was nothing short of divine.

For many of the American and British soldiers gathered on the border of Iraq, there was a clarity and an optimism about their mission. Staff Sergeant Rudy Reyes, a Recon Marine, had just returned from Afghanistan, where his division had helped deliver a definitive victory over the Taliban. Now it was time to liberate the Iraqi people. The overwhelming opinion held by the soldiers was that this new mission would also be successful. It was anticipated that Saddam would fall quickly, victory would be established, and they would be celebrating back at home by August.

It was a time that was defined by a hope and an enthusiasm that many of us today may have forgotten ever existed. But it was also then, in those very early days, that cataclysmic mistakes would be made. Although they may have felt small and insignificant at the time, they would later, like seeds sown in the earth, grow and envelop the entire project.

9/11

When al-Qaeda's operatives flew the planes into the Twin Towers, the atrocity was witnessed live on television by a worldwide audience. Journalist **Dexter Filkins** *was in New York at the time ...*

Iraq should not be connected to 9/11, but unfortunately it is. So, in that way, 9/11 was the kick-off. But for me it started even before then because I had been going to Afghanistan under the Taliban for three years before 9/11; I spent a lot of time out there. And I knew that there was a lot of storm clouds gathering. I didn't know what it was or where it was going, but I just kind of knew ...

... and CIA analyst **John Nixon** *was watching in his Washington office.*

I had worked very late the night before 9/11. I had come across a story in traffic that this man called Ahmed Shah Masood, who was head of the Northern Alliance in Afghanistan, had been assassinated by a film crew pretending to be journalists. He had been around for a really long time. He had been an ally of the US, and that's pretty big. What I didn't know at the time was that that was the kick-off. The Taliban had extracted that price in order to allow al-Qaeda to use their territory to plot and plan.

The next morning, I go into headquarters. I called up a friend of mine. She said, 'I can't talk now, I gotta get back to the TV,' and so I said, 'Why? What's happened?' And she said, 'A plane flew into the World Trade Center.' I quickly turn on the TV in our vault, and by now both towers are on fire ...

I used to live in NYC. I went to graduate school at NYU, and I used to work in the Village, and the minute I saw that it was a beautiful fall day ... It was the kind of day that you've just been through this horrendous summer – the heat and humidity – and you walk out of subways and you smell garbage and it's just gross ... And then fall comes, and you get these beautiful days, and you feel like a human being again. That was what New York City was like. I could tell right away that there was not a cloud in the sky, so this is not an accident. Even with one plane it's not an accident, but with two – of course we know it's not. Two minutes later, we get a report saying that the Pentagon has been hit ...

Ordinary Iraqis were watching too – student **Omar Mohammed** *was in Mosul ...*

I saw it on the TV. The crash of the airplanes with the buildings. We were watching the TV and we saw it in the news. They used the words 'Sheik Osama bin Laden', and also the word 'al-Qaeda' was there. It was the first time we'd heard the names. But what I can't understand is that there was some kind of happiness among people – in the school as well as in the mosque – where they said, 'America came on its knees. America is down. The heroes have taken down America.' To be honest, the way people looked at 9/11 was always connected to what happened in Iraq during the sanctions: that this is a punishment for what America did to the people of Iraq. Of course, I don't agree with this. Civilians shouldn't be punished for this. This is a terrorist act. But did the Iraqis feel sympathy? No.

... while **Waleed Nesyif** *was at school in Baghdad.*

When 9/11 happened, I didn't see it in the news. We were at school when that took place, and we were called into an emergency assembly, where the headmaster gave this speech. The gist of it was that our enemies have reaped what they've sown, in a sense. America has been attacked, we don't know who by, they didn't really declare who at that time. But Iraq is being blamed for this attack and, while we are, America is our enemy. I believe he said we had nothing to do with it. I'm struggling to remember his exact words, but the sentiment was that our enemy has been hit, it is a joyous moment for us. The same people that destroyed our country are now having the war basically happening in their country. And of course he invoked the name of the leader and stuff like that, so we were all clapping and chanting: 'With our bloods and our souls, we shall sacrifice for your sake, Saddam.' Yeah ... it was very conflicting feelings.

I'd be remiss if I did not mention that fact, having lived through the first Gulf War, and seeing what they have done to my country. It was a little bit of 'serves you right', you know. The way I understand life, if you have a cat and you keep flicking the cat, flicking the cat, flicking the cat, the cat is going to scratch you at some point. Right? And they've been doing that for a very long time, so it was to be expected, in a sense, that somebody is going to answer for their atrocities. Were we happy about innocent people being murdered? Definitely not. But, at the same time, in the grand scheme of things and especially because we had nothing to do with it – we, in Iraq, knew nothing, zero – we were, let's say, indifferent about it.

Colin Marks *was a major in the Royal Irish Regiment.*

I was on my first week at the Joint Services Command and Staff course. We had just started the course, I think it was day two or day three. We were all called into the central auditorium and we were shown the footage, and we were told that the Twin Towers had been destroyed. We thought this was the first planning exercise. This was going to set the tempo for the entire year: we were going to have these outrageous scenarios to look at and to think about and to contemplate and come up with answers to. And then we were told, 'No, this is real. This is actually happening.'

Marine Corps tank crewman **Nick Popaditch** *was in San Diego, working as a drill instructor at the recruit depot.*

I was at the end of my tour. It's a three-year tour, and you spend two years training recruits, doing the platoons and the real hard work of it. And then one year of it they put you on what's called Quota: you teach classes, stuff like that.

I used to listen to this morning show. It's a funny show, and I would listen to it in the morning when I was getting ready. When I turned it on, they were talking very serious and they never talked serious about anything. So I'm listening to it, and they're talking about how the first plane had already hit one of the towers, and nobody really knew for sure whether it was intentional or whether it was just an accident. And before I went out the door, the second plane had hit. Now they are saying this is definitely intentional. This is something.

When you are in the military, if you get hit, killed, whatever, you signed up for that. It should be hitting *us*. You know, it shouldn't be hitting people just going to work. The only thing I can really remember is being angry that people were just going to work. Because that's why you have a military: to go out and be that buffer between the people just doing their everyday thing and the bad things. You shouldn't have to deal with a foreign ideology, a foreign invader or anything like that. You know, that's just not how it's supposed to work. The military fights another military. Not civilians getting hit. It just seemed wrong. Just wrong on wrong. Terrible.

Rudy Reyes, *then a Marine sergeant in the 1st Reconnaissance Battalion, was onboard ship in the Pacific.*

Talk about surreal. Because when the sirens are going off on the ship and I'm watching the buildings being hit in New York, the first thing I thought, 'This must be Jerusalem or Tel Aviv,' even though it's obviously New York. My mind couldn't put it together. And they're recalling Recon Marines and SEALs to the berthing to get our orders, and to me it seemed like I was on the mess deck for 15 minutes hearing this – it was probably like two seconds or one second. And then a lot of the sailors are from New York, and they were screaming and yelling, and then they just sling-shotted into a whole other realm.

I wasn't even angry. I knew that I had a duty. I didn't even think about my wife, I didn't think about anything, except be excellent for my team, because they are counting on me and I don't want to be the guy that fucks up. I don't want to be that guy. As we say, the duty of the team superseded any personal feeling. Killing the enemy, I didn't even really think about that, that wasn't my issue. Killing the enemy is just part of the duty.

John Nixon
Then we hear that the State Department has been hit. That turned out to be a false report. Then my friend called me up and said, 'Are you watching this?' I said yes, and he said, 'Are you getting out of there?' I said, 'We haven't gotten orders to leave yet,' and he said, 'I wouldn't wait, I'd get the hell out of there now.' I hung up, and just then we got given the orders to get out, leave, to go home. Fortunately, because I had come in late, I got the last parking spot by the gate so I was able to get out immediately. For some it took hours to get out of the compound because it's just two lanes. Then I drove home. I could see the smoke – this big mushroom cloud coming out of the direction of the Pentagon.

I got home, and my sister called me and she said, 'Who did this?' I said, 'I think it's al-Qaeda,' and she said, 'Who?' I said, 'Well, it's Osama bin Laden ...'

I will say this. Immediately, when I first saw this, Saddam did come to my mind. Because I remembered, in the summer before 9/11, seeing reports of Iraqis training on aircraft. Storming aircraft and taking control. It was like a counter-terrorism exercise. That was the first thing that jogged my memory. Could Iraq have done this? And I talked to this woman who worked as an intelligence assistant at the Agency who had been there a long time, and she said, 'No, no, no, this is Bin Laden. I've been seeing reports about this for months.' And I said, 'OK, well, that makes sense.'

That was it. That was my day.

Critical Mass

John Nixon
The next day at the CIA was a very sombre day. The mood of the country was shock. Shock, sadness and anger. In the past, when somebody hijacked a plane, they flew it somewhere and landed it and made their demands known, and that was that. When I used to work in NYC, I used to look out the window and in my direct line of sight were the Twin Towers and I never thought, in a million years, that there would be a reason that they wouldn't be there any more.

Dexter Filkins
God, it all happened really fast. It was shocking, that first day. I managed to get to Ground Zero, I spent a few days down there, I just kept phoning in whatever I could find. It was weird, it was like being punched in the stomach really hard. The country was kind of in a panic.

And then I got on a plane and left. Whenever the planes started flying again, I went to JFK airport to get a plane to go to Tajikistan so that I could find my way to Afghanistan, and there wasn't anybody in the airport.

I certainly had a feeling – I think everybody did – that the war in Afghanistan was a just war. It was: 'OK, we got attacked, so we get to do this.' You know, we're entitled to take these guys out. I don't remember people screaming for revenge, but there was a sense of kind of righteous anger.

Colin Marks

It was going to bring America further onto the world stage in terms of facing asymmetric threats. America hadn't faced asymmetric threats in the same way as the British and some of the other imperial powers had. So that was going to pull the Americans onto that stage and, given America's superpower status and given how much they were hurting as a result of that attack, it was clear there was going to be a seismic shift in the strategic context because America was too big a player and that was too significant an attack for something not to happen.

Dexter Filkins

In a way, Afghanistan was sort of a trap, not merely for Afghanistan itself but for Iraq, because at the time it looked like it was a cakewalk. The Taliban collapsed in a couple of weeks and all the Afghans came out in the streets and cheered, and the Taliban ran for the hills, and it was amazing. You could drive anywhere you wanted in the country, all the Afghans were happy that the Americans were there because they had been through decades of misery, and they were just happy that the world was paying attention to them. And so it looked like we were the conquering army, and so who else are we gonna hit? I think that was kind of the feeling: 'We're not done yet.'

I didn't realise what was happening until I went to Washington in the summer of 2002 and everybody's attention had basically turned to Iraq. I remember walking around Washington and nobody wanted to hear about Afghanistan any more. Everybody's operative assumption was, 'We're going to war in Iraq, probably pretty soon.' I was stunned because I didn't know that there had been this conversation. And I'm not sure, of course, even today, how deep that conversation was, but it looked like the train was already leaving and everybody assumed that it was already leaving ... It felt like the whole country felt that way to the extent that there wasn't a lot of debate about whether this was a great idea.

There was a movement inside Washington – mostly Republican but not entirely – that believed, and had believed since the end of the first Gulf War in 1991, that the United States, when they liberated Kuwait, should have kept going to Baghdad and taken out the real problem in the region, which was Saddam Hussein. The main components of that were Paul Wolfowitz, who became the Deputy Secretary of Defense, Donald Rumsfeld, Doug Feith, Richard Pearl. Very, very smart, very aggressive people, who believed in very aggressive American foreign policy. They nurtured this idea that the problems of the Middle East could be utterly transformed if we just took out this cancer in Baghdad. It became this kind of article of faith.

They had a principal Iraqi ally in this, Ahmad Chalabi. He was [the] Iraqi faceman for this effort so they could just reach for Ahmad Chalabi and say, 'The Iraqis believe in this too, we are united together in this idea that we can transform the Middle East if we just take out Saddam Hussein.' America took a big hit on 9/11 … The hijackers were from Saudi Arabia, it was part of this larger problem which was the Middle East, and the Middle East could not change as long as Saddam Hussein was there. It's not a crazy argument. It's just, I don't think they really thought through what they were getting into.

John Nixon
It seems to me that there were many people who had been telling policymakers in DC, 'We've got to do something about Osama bin Laden. We've gotta get rid of this guy. This guy is going to attack us.' These people turned out to be right, and they weren't listened to. The Clinton administration had several opportunities where they could have moved, and every time somebody said, 'No, let's not do this now.' And then a new administration comes in, and Saddam was the person on George W. Bush's radar screen, not Osama bin Laden, and that's because it was personal to him. In George W. Bush's mind, Saddam had tried to kill his father. I think he believed that, and I think he still

believes it to this day. And the truth is that it probably never happened.

Then you've got the Cheney-Rumsfeld clique and the Neocons in the Pentagon. Their opinion is that the US has been far too lenient with terrorists, and has to start striking blows after 9/11. Terrorism is coming from the Middle East and we have to remake the region in our own image and we have to bring democracy there and we can't be allowing these tin-pot dictators to dictate things to us.

You get the mixture of those two things and they work in tandem. It becomes a really potent force. The day after 9/11, this is solidified and congealed in everybody's mind. And now it's like, 'We're going to get rid of this guy because he had a hand in this ...' and it's not 'Was he involved?' It's 'Go find a link.'

Before 9/11, the Bush administration felt it had to do something about Iraq. Saddam at that point in time seemed to be getting closer and closer to getting out from underneath sanctions. The sanctions regime against him, although effective, was starting to develop lots of holes. But after 9/11, on 9/12, that's the critical mass. That's when, all of a sudden, the issue gets super-charged for the Neocons. Now it's like, 'Ever since Beirut in 1983 or the taking of hostages in Tehran in 1979, the US has been kicked around, mistreated by these terrorists and we've never struck back at them. Now look what they've done, we have to strike back at them, and we're going to start with Saddam Hussein because he had a hand in this.'

The very next day, we were tasked by Paul Wolfowitz to examine Saddam's public speeches and find out how many times he had threatened the US. We came back and we told Paul Wolfowitz, 'He never threatened the US in his speeches.' After 9/11, taskings on Iraq coming from the White House or from the Pentagon went through the roof. Paul Wolfowitz was tasking the intelligence community on almost a daily basis. But the thing is, when we came back to tell the Bush White House that these linkages that you're talking about are not real – actually there are more things that divide them than link them – they wouldn't believe it. And that's when the Pentagon started to set up its own intelligence units. It started disseminating these really crazy reports linking Saddam to terrorism. And we would always say, 'We don't agree with this, we think that this report is nonsense.' It was a very, very difficult time.

I think the quality of analysis really starts to deteriorate around this time concerning Iraq, and there's no quality control, because the managers who are supposed to be overseeing this analysis are stretched thin themselves. The Director of Operations decided that they had had a lot of intelligence that had basically just languished on a shelf because it didn't meet the threshold for dissemination. The decision was made that we've got to disseminate this information simply because of the hunger for intelligence about Iraq and because we can't allow the administration to accuse us of holding on to information. So they disseminate this stuff, and it creates this perfect storm where you have newly minted analysts, who don't have much understanding of the region they're covering, lots and lots of garbage information starting to flow into the system, and pressure from policymakers on the seventh floor of the CIA to feed the beast.

Waleed Nesyif
Then I started hearing the rhetoric: Afghanistan, then Iraq, Syria ... you know, they started basically naming the countries. That's when we knew: 'We are getting blamed for this.' And there was a sense of relief, in a way. That we are going to get blamed for it, because that almost meant 100 per cent that America is going to come and take Saddam over. At the same time, Iraqis are no fools – with war comes great sacrifice for the nation that war is happening to. And I remember those conversations in my family where we were weighing the odds. Is it going to happen, is it not? We thought we were next, based on all of the reports that we were seeing, like the inspectors are now pissed off and they are going back and the US is threatening, threatening, threatening ... They had bombed us several times from after 1991. You have Desert Fox in '94, you have another bombing that happened in '98, you have another bombing that happened in 2000. And then you would

hear the planes basically flying over back and forth, pretty much from 1991 up until 2003. So war has never really stopped for us.

John Nixon
First it was, 'We've got to get rid of this guy because of WMD [weapons of mass destruction], we can't allow him to have WMD.' Then it was, 'This man is a menace to his own people and a menace to the people of the region.' Then we started getting the argument, 'This war is going to pay for itself, we'll be able to sell their oil and this won't cost us a dime.' Then Bush made a speech, saying that 'Facing clear evidence of peril, we cannot wait for the final proof – the smoking gun – that could come in the form of a mushroom cloud.' They all fanned out. I remember, I saw Rumsfeld say it, I saw Condoleezza Rice say it, and various other administration figures: 'We can't allow the smoking gun to turn into a mushroom cloud.' Well, when you're selling a product you need a good phrase.

And I have to be honest with you: at the time, I was a believer in WMD and I supported what George Bush was doing. I thought Saddam was looking to get weapons of mass destruction, and I thought this is a guy who has really run his country into the ground. Iraq should be a success story and yet he has sort of squandered all of the natural resources of the country and has isolated his country from the rest of the world, and maybe if we do remove him from power we can create a better situation for Iraqis and we can help them. And I look back on those ideas that I had and I think they were incredibly naive ...

Omar Mohammed
In my opinion, Iraq had nothing to do with 9/11. And it was weird that Iraq was accused of collaborating with the terrorists to attack the United States, but at the same time, you could feel ... there was a connection. Not because I have evidence, but you could feel that this was something related to Iraq. This was something about Iraq. It was something that logically could be done, with the collaboration of Iraq, or something coming through Iraq. But

Saddam working with al-Qaeda? No, the personality of Saddam, his policies, his character himself, will not allow him to do this.

Extremism wasn't a problem, because we didn't see it. It didn't exist. I mean why would we discuss something that doesn't exist? Why would I discuss security if I felt safe? Why should I discuss peace, if I already live in peace? What we had was the word Wahhabism, the campaign of Saddam against Wahhabism ... They weren't called extremist, they were called Wahhabist. It was about Wahhabism, the conflict between Sufism and Wahhabism.

After 9/11, religion was very present. I'm talking about extremism, 9/11 as a sign of the beginning of the global jihad against 'the enemy of Islam', not 'the enemy of Iraq'. This time it was referred to as the enemy of Islam being punished. And this became more obvious in the mosques. Most of what I have heard before was focusing on Iraq, but here you would hear the name of America, the word 'jihad', the name of the enemy of Islam ... There is a huge difference when you say 'the enemy of Iraq' and 'the enemy of Islam'. I was able to recognise this, and I was able to notice when it became different, when the cleric who was giving the Friday ceremony started using 'the enemies of Islam'. He didn't use it before. Because 9/11, which was done by Bin Laden, he did something Iraq couldn't do – punishing America ... What Bin Laden did is something they thought that Iraq should do, because Iraq was the country most affected by the United States. I don't justify this, I'm just trying to explain how I was exposed to this. The people thought it's a punishment, but I thought it was the beginning of how the United States prepared us to go to 2003.

After a failed assassination attempt, Saddam Hussein had attacked the village of Al Alam, 120 miles north of Baghdad. **Um Qusay** *was one of the survivors. Now she awaited news of the American invasion with both happiness and fear.*

We didn't know what was going to happen. We were scared, but also we were trying to convince ourselves that they would come, and maybe things would change for the better. We didn't really understand how things would turn out. Saddam said that he wouldn't surrender Iraq. He said, 'I will hand Iraq over as dust.' So we were scared that he was going to hit Iraq with chemical weapons in response to the American invasion.

Colin Marks
What does being British mean to me? I think it means playing fair, I think it means having core values which are consistent with fairness and tolerance. Being British to me means standing up to a bully when a bully needs to be stood up to. And Saddam Hussein was clearly a bully. He had brutalised the people in the south of his country, the Shia population, and that's where I operated, and it was very clear to me that that population had been brutalised by him and his regime, which manipulated power in order to maintain control over the people.

Um Qusay
Saddam was a good leader. What is it the Arabs say? He was a knight. But he didn't know how to act. He transgressed. He oppressed too much. He hurt Iraqis and they no longer wanted him. We didn't see rest. It was always war. Wars that were not even necessary. The Iran war, the Kuwait war, another war … We'd had enough of it. He really made the Iraqi people tired.

Saddam used to say, 'Starve your dog and it will follow you.' It's as if he was calling the people dogs. 'Starve your dog, it will follow you.' We didn't see him except on television. If he came to Al Alam, it was every two to three years, and he went to a specific place. We couldn't approach, we could just see him from far or on TV. He was elegant in terms of clothes but his eyes were very harsh and terrifying, not happy and calm. It was scary. When he came to Al Alam, the same as it would be for any president, everyone would clap for him and go around him and celebrate him. But later on people in Al Alam tried to assassinate him. And then he killed half the people responsible.

Issam Al Rawi *was in charge of border security on the Iraq-Jordanian border and remained a loyal follower of Saddam Hussein.*

He had a very powerful personality that influenced anyone that met him, may God have mercy on him. Even if his enemy met him, he would be influenced by him. He was handsome and well dressed, proficient. He was balanced, calm, kind. He would advise and direct. The opposite of what was said on the media about the martyr Saddam Hussein. We saw a comfortable personality, good-looking, elegant, eloquent. He spoke eloquently, with methodology. The specifications and the attributes that they used to describe Saddam Hussein, may God have mercy on him, whether it was the Western media outlets or what they call the opposition – and we don't call them the opposition because they are a group of thieves; they are outside of the law and are located in the West – they wanted to ruin Saddam Hussein. They describe him as a dictator. They wanted to make Saddam Hussein seem devilish in his life and his behaviour. But whoever knows Saddam Hussein and those in his close circle know that Saddam Hussein is the peak of humanitarianism.

Waleed Nesyif

I hadn't met that many Americans at that time. All I knew of America and Americans was basically their army and them destroying my country. That's it. That's all I knew of them. And then on the flip side, we loved everything that is American.

Growing up in Iraq, I was very prone to – you know, it was like what my father likes, what my mum likes, what your cousins, all the uncles and so on and so forth, and that happened to be Western music and films. So I grew up watching like *Superman*, *Spider-Man*, all of these things that pretty much every other kid probably in the West grew up watching, except ours was ten years behind ... I wanted everything that was Western. You know, it was like I wanted the blue jeans, I wanted the skateboards, I wanted the headphones. I wanted all of these things that I grew up watching and desiring. And I have got to say, if it had not been for this love of this culture that came through the small screen, I would not be here. Because that is what compelled me to actually learn English and that is how I learned English, from movies and songs. That is what compelled me to want to aspire beyond the life that I was in.

So when I hear statements like 'They hate our freedom and our democracy', it's like, no, we actually *love* it, we fucking love it, that is all we wanted. Like we never wanted anything else, like we wanted to be that, we wanted to be liberated, we wanted to do whatever the hell we wanted to do. You know, at least in the same way that we see it in films, yeah. Even growing up, I never really heard anything bad being said about America, to be honest with you.

So their administration's claim that we hate them because of their freedom and their values and stuff like that – no, no, no. That's the thing we *loved* about them. We wanted those things for ourselves as well. These are the things we appreciated about America. Like, I'm a heavy metal dude. I wouldn't have found that without basically England and America, you know. This is one of the greatest things that happened in my life. And I love it and will forever love it, you know. Music in general, film, all of these things. There are so many things about America that we appreciate, we like, we want. But then at what price, is the question. Every time I hear that statement – 'They hate our freedom' – and it was like, are you stupid? Like, how delusional must you be – and disconnected from the world you have – not to hear?

I was pro-war. Absolutely pro-war. And so were many, many, many, many Iraqis. I was pro-war not out of hate of my country, but because we were sick and tired of living under Saddam. It was short-sighted at my end, but at the same time we also had the political maturity of understanding there is no escaping it. The decision has been made. So we might be for it or against, but it doesn't really matter. Being against it, that means you gonna have to pick up a weapon and fight, and the question was then, 'Am I willing to do that?' And if I do so, then to what end? Say that the odds are stacked in our favour and we defeat America. That means

Saddam stays, and if Saddam stays, the situation stays, but now we're gonna be destroyed, down another few million people probably. So we were cautiously for it.

When we knew for sure that America was taking up arms against us and that we were next, after Afghanistan, and seeing what had happened in Afghanistan, we knew that the end was near. But at the same time we were scared that the same thing that had happened in 1991 would happen yet again – where they came in, Saddam was almost gone, and then they pulled out. And then he was left to reign supreme and literally just mowed down people. So we were scared, we were genuinely scared.

We were stockpiling food, water. Everybody was digging wells because of the experience we had in 1991, when we thought things were going to be similar to the Iran-Iraq War where you still had water and electricity. Soon after, we realised that's not the issue: people died from starvation and dehydration because there was no water. We dug a well at my grandparents' home, so that we could have access to water, and many others did the exact same thing all around Baghdad.

It was hard to ascertain news, because the only exposure to news we had was through one of two channels. In the '90s they opened a channel that belonged to Saddam's son Uday, and then you had the national channel which belonged to the Iraqi Broadcasting Corporation. And both of those were giving us the exact same news cycle: our leader is trying to negotiate, our ambassador is trying to negotiate. And then the radio, like Voice of America, was giving us as much propaganda as possible: this is what the American troops are doing, this is where they are right now, they're in Turkey, they're in Saudi, they're in Kuwait...

Pretty much from January to March 2003 – it's a countdown. Whether you're gonna live, whether you're gonna die, you don't know. So you live it up. But they were a lifetime. Literally, a lifetime. We were there with our families and loved ones and stuff like that. If you're here and you had an ounce of love for your family and your country and your people, it's death. Finally, there was an announcement, and George Bush had his famous speech: Iraq has one last chance. Saddam and his family have 48 hours to vacate Iraq, and if not we shall come in.

Dexter Filkins
The US government came up with this idea that they would take reporters into military units, a sort of 'embed' concept. Nobody knew how that was going to work out: are they just going to take all the reporters and put them in a warehouse somewhere, or are they going to put them in the back of the unit so they can't see anything and just feed them a bunch of propaganda? They didn't know. And so they thought, 'We're going to embed a bunch of reporters with all of these American units that are invading Iraq'.

I was in Istanbul. They called me and said, 'Look, we want you to kind of do what you did in Afghanistan which was just go there on your own, just drive around'. And I said OK. I had no plan. I found an Egyptian translator, there was a British photographer that I went with, we flew to Kuwait City. We went to Hertz rent-a-car, we rented an SUV. The guy said, 'You're not going to take this up in the ...?' And I said, 'No, no, no, we're just gonna go round the family a bit.' So, we didn't really have a plan, we just basically had a bag of money. There were three of us and we got in the SUV and we drove up to the Kuwait border, right before they'd sealed it off, and rented a farmhouse. I think we stayed there one night. We didn't know when the invasion was gonna go, I think finally it went on 19 March, and you could just hear the rumbling of the tanks. And then we just drove in. Yeah, it was nuts.

Operation Iraqi Freedom

John Nixon
President Bush decided to start the war when he did because the CIA believed it had real-time information about where Saddam was at that particular moment. They said that they had a source in Iraq who had eyes on the target and that Saddam is at a facility that is a command and control centre, and basically if we hit this place then we might be able to decapitate the regime and maybe not have to go to war after all because Saddam would be gone. And George Bush said, 'OK, let's go.' The problem is, Saddam was nowhere near this place. This was bad information, part of a cavalcade of bad information that we had been getting on Iraq from a variety of sources. At the time, Saddam was at the Central Bank of Iraq unloading pallets of money from the bank, putting them on flatbeds to take and put in strategic locations because he was getting ready to go on the run.

Issam Al Rawi
I will tell you something that nobody else knows about Saddam Hussein, God rest his soul and his family. During the war, he and his family held a meeting, and the women of the family requested permission to leave Iraq. He denied their request, and told them, 'You have lived in Iraq, and you will die in Iraq.'

That was Saddam Hussein, may God bless him. So how could we who worked with and served alongside Saddam leave? That was how we felt. Our spirit, our passion, our character, and our values were all dedicated to resisting the invading enemy. What would you do if someone tried to break into your house? Would you sit and watch, or would you fight? That's your house, never mind your country, its wealth, and its people. It is the instinct of every proud and patriotic Iraqi to resist all invaders.

Living with her family in Baghdad, **Sally Mars** *was just six years old when the invasion began.*

Before the war, the situation was stable. Every Thursday, my dad would take us for dinner, or we would stand on Al-Jadriyah bridge eating fish. Then, when the war began, I remember my dad came in, his face yellow and scared. He was saying, 'That's it, the war is going to start.' So the first thing we did was stock up on essentials. We bought a lot of petrol, and a lot of lanterns for light, because the electricity was completely cut off. My birthday's in March, and I think that's when the war started. Even the candles used for my cake were the ones we use for the house.

All that I remember is that we used to sit in the middle of the house. Properly in the middle. These were the instructions they always gave us: sit in the middle of the house, turn the lights off. We had a lantern and blankets in the middle, away from the windows. These bombings were daily. I don't remember for how long, but I remember they were the same instructions daily. From about an hour into sunset, we turn the lights off, light the lantern, and keep its light very low. My mum would pray and sometimes read a Qur'an. My dad would speak to us about his youth, about how he'd solve crimes, because he was an investigator. He tried to make us forget where we were.

I remember that there was a missile that hit very close to our house. The house was shaking. We thought that it came on us. I remember my mum threw herself over us, all of us, me and my siblings, to protect us, because she thought we were hit with a missile.

Waleed Nesyif
We didn't realise the extent of the damage and, like, insanity that was going to be exerted against us in such a short period of time.

When I say the bombing did not stop ... I cannot describe it to you ... You know the iconic images of Baghdad being bombed, it was like you were just seeing fire lighting up ... Yeah, that was continuous, that was just day and night. It was just bombs, bombs, you know, left, right and centre.

And that's when I finally started understanding why the parents and the adults in our family were clowning about. Because they needed to get our minds distracted. They needed to basically take our minds off of what's happening outside. And that this could potentially be the last minute we're alive and together. So, you know, I was tickling my brothers, we were joking around. Whenever there is a huge bomb that falls, we'd go and pretend that we're playing hide and seek. Everybody was there, we were playing cards, playing dominoes and all of that. I'd say we had a good time, because literally it could have been it. And then my uncle started freaking the hell out on me because media was calling me, like I had ABC call me, I had CNN call me, I had a few others calling me because landlines were still working at that time. And they were calling me and asking me to describe what's going on outside and I'm receiving all of these phone calls, and my uncles are just literally losing their mind. They were like, 'Everything is tapped, they are gonna come after us.' And I was like, 'It's the end, I mean, *so what?*'

We thought the start is going to be simple and easy, you know, just a couple of bombs here and there ... but no, they went at it ... When the first bomb hit, the ground itself shakes, everything around you starts rattling ... this sound ... it's just ... it's deafening, deafening. And then that coupled with kids and women crying, like literally wailing, you know. I'm trying to hug my brothers and again we started with the joking around and stuff like that. But you're so filled with adrenalin that you're almost numb ... It wasn't fear, it was literally you are as alert as it comes, ready for anything in a sense ... And then after the first few minutes of that continuous ... This is the scary part about humanity, you adapt. It kind of becomes like part of the background, you know ...

Palaces, official buildings, anything basically official – that was targeted. The Ministry of Defence, the Olympics building where they dropped a B-52 bomb, that's ... oh my, I mean that's a 4-tonne bomb. *Four tonnes*. I mean, the closest thing I can basically describe it to is an earthquake. And my grandparents' home wasn't very far, but it was far enough from it, you know, not like you're gonna get shrapnel and a blast, but just the sound and the ground shaking from it. And it was like, that was a big one. And then afterwards ... I mean, they call it friendly fire. You know, just houses. It was like, 'Oh, Saddam moved from this house into this house, so we're gonna bomb this house now.' And then it quietened down a little bit, and then it started again, and then it quietened down, and then it started again, and it just basically continued.

Dexter Filkins

I think we had the BBC World Service on, and we knew the invasion was going, so we jumped in the SUV and took off. We were about five miles from the border. And it was hard to get across, most of the roads were sealed off except for the military and they weren't letting us cross so we just went back and forth, back and forth, driving all along the Kuwaiti border just looking for one open road. A couple of hours later we found one. It was daylight and we went across, and because the sun was just coming up you could see, as far as you could see, rows and rows and rows and rows and rows of military equipment and trucks and tanks and ... just for miles.

This was just miles and miles and miles of trucks and tanks and soldiers and gas trucks and motorcycles and people and men, and it was just forever, an endless stream. And that's when I got really scared. I mean, that's when I realised how big the thing was. It wasn't like in Afghanistan where we just went in and whacked the government, and it fell over because it was a couple of houses full of guys. This was real, and that kind of freaked me out, I remember that.

I was pretty scared. As soon as I saw the magnitude of the armada that was going into Iraq, I got chills. I realised this is not going to be like the little tea party that Afghanistan was. And, I thought, 'God, maybe this is going to be like the real thing, what then?' And there's going to be a gigantic battle and the Iraqi army is on the other side, and *oh my god* ...

We weren't prepared for everything, but we were definitely prepared for chemical weapons. Everybody thought that that was a possibility. We had chemical weapons suits that cost many of thousands of dollars in our car, and I think we put them on once. There was a warning about halfway to Baghdad, there was a warning that we were under chemical attack, so everybody got in their suits. It was hot. It was really hot. Honestly it felt ridiculous, it felt ... 'This isn't going to save me.'

Nick Popaditch

Now I'm part of a battalion at this time, so we have 50-plus tanks as part of our battalion and we are one small cog in this whole big thing. Because not only do you have the Marine Corps tanks, you've got the army tanks. You've got a lot of tanks. I mean probably a thousand of them crossing into the country, and I don't know how you stop that if you're them.

We picked the least ideal time to fight. Because whatever is working against us is working against them too, and generally we are better trained, we have better technology. We can overcome it better than the enemy can overcome it. So generally when we fight, it's going to be at the least ideal time, because it may be hard on us, but it's going to be terrible on them. A lot of our night vision relies on passive infrared, in other words ambient light. If there is no ambient light, it's almost impossible to see. You can see through thermals, but you can't see very much through passive infrared. They don't have thermals, they can't see nothing. So it's a big advantage.

There was a big terrain feature there called Safwan Hill that we were going to cross right beneath. Safwan Hill was a big observation post for the Iraqi military. They used it to observe into Kuwait, and apparently it was pretty well defended. They said they were going to use the air to knock a few hundred feet off the top of Safwan Hill – guaranteed there will be nothing alive on top of Safwan Hill when we cross that border. So I was expecting a much bigger fireworks display on Safwan Hill than the one I actually saw. So that was a little bit underwhelming compared to the build-up of it, but we took no fire from Safwan Hill.

Dexter Filkins
The first town on the border is called Safwan, and Safwan is actually where the Iraqi army signed the surrender in the first Gulf War. We rolled into Safwan as the Americans were rolling out. The first thing which was so weird about it is that the town is in, like, chaos, and the Americans were leaving. They just rolled right through it. Came in, ripped down the Saddam posters, looked around a little and drove out. I remember rolling in, driving into Safwan, and I felt like we had pried the doors off a mental institution. In Afghanistan, when we rolled into these towns, people were just euphoric. You know, they were pulling their turbans off and people were dancing, and they were, like, hugging us. In Safwan, people were just in shock, the Iraqis, they were standing there, lined up in the streets, they were looking at us, open-mouthed, slack-jawed, stunned. Some people were crying, other people were laughing. It was like the whole range of human emotions but completely baffling.

As we came in, the Iraqis just descended on us. I think the first person who came to me was an Iraqi woman, and she was elderly, and she just said, 'My son, my son, I've been looking for my son for 14 years or 13 years, he was involved in the uprising against Saddam and he disappeared.' She just started telling me the story of her son. It was crazy. And it was one thing after another like this. And the Americans were already gone. So effectively there was no government in Safwan. The place was kind of in chaos, people had already begun to loot ... And then we left too.

Nick Popaditch
When we crossed into Iraq, the big unknown was the Iraqi civilians. You know, that was the big thing that General Mattis had

prepared us for: that we were the *no better friend, no worse enemy.* Share your courage with the Iraqi people. Show them if they befriend us they have no better friend. If they fight with you, make it so horrible they never want that to happen again.

Our first mission was to take an airfield, and then go towards Basra but don't actually go into Basra cos Basra is a pretty big city. There were bridges that came out of Basra to head into the oilfields, and we were to set up position watching over those bridges so nothing could come out of the city. At that part we met very few people. They were mostly farmers, and they were mostly just waving: 'Hi, how are you doing?' So when we were going through the countryside there, the first Iraqi I saw was a farmer. He was just out in his field, wasn't like working or nothing, you know – a whole parade of tanks coming by, so he's obviously not going to be going through his normal routine. But he looked and he waved. I waved back at him and said, 'Yeah, that's a good sign.' He didn't run into his house and get a rifle, that's a good sign.

I think the first military we saw was at an airfield, and they had a couple of tanks defending the airfield. We would get sporadic resistance here and there, but nowhere was there like a battalion organised together. They were still in uniforms, and most of them were surrendering. They had two choices: surrender or die. There was really no third option for them, so most of them chose to surrender. There were a few pockets here and there that fought, but not much. We dropped in leaflets and let them know – 'Just put your hands up, just to make sure you don't have a weapon.' They all seemed to kind of get that. They mostly put their hands up, or put them behind their head, and then would just walk towards us in a non-threatening manner. I think back then we just let them drop their stuff and go home.

A couple of places, I was amazed that it was really so lopsided, in the technology, the tactics, the equipment. My gunner on that one, this was his first combat, and by the time we get to our first defensive he's already got a few tank kills under his belt and a lot of infantry that he'd pulled the trigger on. And I remember asking him, 'Doesn't even seem fair, does it?' And he said, 'No, Staff Sergeant, it doesn't.' And I said, 'Well, you just keep pulling the trigger. You'll figure out how to deal with that later.' The initial invasion was very lopsided because we were crossing with a whole lot of force. Everywhere we went, everything was already broken. Anything that would have been active, 90 per cent of it was already hit by the air.

Dexter Filkins
Yeah, it's like there wasn't any resistance. There was none. The whole way up, there was almost no resistance. Here and there, there was some but as you drove down the road there was just uniforms everywhere. Guys were literally taking off their uniforms and throwing them in the streets. The Iraqi army had just disappeared. We saw guys in their underwear, and they were just taking their uniforms off and just throwing them, throwing their guns and just taking off. The Iraqi army just disintegrated. We were watching the American army and we kind of rolled in, shadowing them, expecting a fight. But there was no fight and there was no government, there was nothing. And so the American armies just rolled on through it just on to Baghdad.

The sort of cliché that they were all using was: 'We're going to cut off the head of the snake and then the body dies.' And so they just blew up to Baghdad and didn't occupy anything on the way, just go to Baghdad and knock off the government. And so we were just rolling through these towns and kind of going, 'Isn't there something you want to do here?' And of course, inevitably, stuff started happening in the rear, you'd hear stories. We were trying to follow the Marines, but you know those guys who had taken their uniforms off started staging attacks.

Nick Popaditch
The Iraqi civilians were surprisingly upbeat. Once the war started really moving, we covered a lot of ground quick. There were a lot of people just heading south just trying to get behind the line.

They were heading towards us to get behind us, which is logical because we are going to keep going north. They felt safe enough to at least know to get behind us. And the Iraqi people are really neat because they helped each other out a lot. They are very good people. People would set big pots out in their front yards with water, and then all the people heading south would just stop and rehydrate and stuff on their trip, and I was very amazed with that.

You know, I always had the appreciation for how does this look from their perspective. What they've got, see, is this is a foreign force coming through here with tanks. His life is getting ready to change pretty drastically and he doesn't know if this is for better or for worse. I don't know what life under Saddam was like, and you've got to think it wasn't that great. People would never see you as something they wanted in their country, and they were going to fight you or maybe just subversively resist you, but some people were going to say, 'He has got to be better than Saddam.' So we were prepared for both, and there was a lot of both. A lot of both. Very little active resistance from the civilians back then, though.

Um Qusay
We didn't know if it was bad or not bad. But any person, when a stranger comes to their area to occupy, they wouldn't like it. There is degradation, and it wasn't the Iraq we knew. It's an occupation, it's hard. It was very hard on us. At the beginning they called it liberation, because they came to free us. We were happy. We were very happy. Because they came to free us. But they stayed here too long and it became an occupation.

Rudy Reyes
We were all prepared to die in the first, I don't know, two days. We were prepared to die, and we knew more than likely that we *were* going to die. The Republican Guard was still there, the Iraqi army was still there, and also of course the NBC [nuclear, biological and chemical] – if we got hit by those weapons, we were too far ahead to be brought back to a clean area and deconned, so we would die.

That was the biggest threat because, if you recall history, Saddam Hussein had used nerve agents on the Kurds. He murdered 300,000 people up there and, of course, we know what he's done to his own people too. So we were prepared, I mean you have to prepare for that. I'm SERE-trained: Survival, Evasion, Resistance and Escape. I went to POW training and learned how to be tortured and keep it together, and learned how to resist being indoctrinated and learned how to escape. And also to understand the culture of Iraq and Saddam's culture about what would happen to me: my head would be cut off on TV or I'd be freaking brutally tortured in every way possible. These are the things that are in your head, yeah, these are the things going through your mind. So that's why your head is on a swivel. And that means you're going to make yourself as hard to kill as possible. Which means you're going to be as professional as possible.

Before we crossed over, we were already doing penetration patrols to disrupt the enemy's flow, their outer loop. We were training continuously, at night, during the day, in the sand. Or training with gas masks and MOPP [Mission Oriented Protective Posture] suit training all the time. Any time we had incoming orders and incoming artillery, we had to MOPP up. We got it down to about 30 seconds: don your gas mask, clear your gas mask, get the seal put on rubber gloves, put on rubber boots, and then be ready to fight. And not die.

It was the cover of darkness that we broke through and went across, artillery incoming and outgoing, small arms, the machine guns ... Imagine seeing their freaking Cobras crisscrossing above you. I'm driving the vehicle, I'm the assistant team leader, so I'm driving the vehicle. I got one night-vision [eye], and then this eye with human vision, because if all you are on is night vision, because of the cathodes and the green, if they break or they got torn off and you're right in the firefight, you're going to be blind. My night vision was on my left, so my right eye I could still acquire my sight. And then your brain puts the images together.

I was spearheading a division, 60 men. We were ahead of the tanks and light armoured vehicles. We could use close air support, but when we got into Nasiriyah, because of the weather and the small winds and sandstorms, it shut down all the air. Seeing chemlights on all the armour and tanks and the US Army and the Marine corps, it was really like a *Star Wars* movie on the ground: the walkers shooting, coming in; the people dug in, shooting back. It was immense, it was pandemonium in the ring. It was thrilling. It was gorgeous to look at, actually, seeing the impact of the artillery and the rock – it's exploding things around, and then the boom-boom-boom-boom, and then the rocket-assisted artillery, and then shoo-boom-boom-boom.

'Am I doing what I'm supposed to be doing?' 'What am I not doing that I'm supposed to be doing?' That's all I'm thinking. I'm looking at my team leader, Sean Patrick. I'm listening to the radio, and always checking in with my heavy gunner, always checking in with the team. I would recommend any of you ever go to war or any kind of fight, never overestimate yourself and never underestimate your opponent. So I was expecting the same amount of ferocity upon us as we were going to bring to them. Why wouldn't I? It wouldn't be prudent, it wouldn't be professional if it was any other way. And that's what saved the day for us as we went into Nasiriyah.

When we got into Nasiriyah, the winds were so bad, so rough for air power, and it looked like Vietnam. Right on the Euphrates river there are palm trees everywhere, and it's March, so all the elephant grass is high and it's swaying, there's palm trees everywhere, and we're in a city, built up everywhere. Shit's going off, blowing up everywhere, incoming and outgoing, and our first Marine division is held up there. Colonel Dowdy is taking casualties. I'm seeing blown-up American vehicles and blood everywhere. They are using Recon [Marines] as casualty evacuation to get these guys out, they are splitting up our teams right there.

Our SARCS [Special Amphibious Reconnaissance Corpsmen] – 18 Delta Green paramedics, on top of being Recon Marines, some of the best and brightest in the world – they are going to have to go in, in a few Humvees, completely open, and rescue these men, across a bridge, across a river into the city. And I'm embarrassed that my team leader's going to die a glorious death, a great death, because for sure he's going to die – we're probably going to die too, but for sure he's going to die. And I said, 'Pappy, this is fucking bullshit, I'm not letting you go by yourself, I'm going with you.' It was strange, I don't know how to explain it exactly to you all, but there was a shame I felt, that this better man than me was going to have to go in there and die, and then I'm not beside him, because the best thing I could ever be is half of this guy. And even though I know I'm never going to see my wife or my little brothers again, what was worse is that I feel like I would die worse, now that he's gone, because he's doing something braver than me. It's not because I was a glory hound. It was the opposite: it was because I was afraid. I was so afraid. So right there, Sean Patrick looks at me and goes, 'Shut the fuck up, Rudy, shut the fuck up.' The whole team was quiet, we can hear a pin drop, even though everything's blowing up around us. And he looked at me and he said, 'Are you a fucking professional?' Right there, I got it: never ever did I allow an emotion after that to get in the way of my duty and mission, my emotions were shut off. The professional supersedes anything personal.

Waleed Nesyif
One of the interesting things that happened that coincided with the war, as if war itself was not ominous enough – a sandstorm came about. Now for anyone that hasn't experienced a sandstorm, let me describe the scene. It's a bubble of sand that moves across the desert, literally like a giant behemoth, eating everything that comes across it. When you see it coming your way, especially if you are in an open field, literally it looks like a horizontal avalanche, you know, that is just moving. And once you are in it, everything turns red or yellow, depending on the time of day. At night, everything is red, the moon is red, everything is red. It looks like the sky is bleeding.

And daytime everything is in sepia tones. So it looks ... it's almost like you are watching your life flash back in front of you. It's such a weird feeling. And of course, you can't breathe, that's one thing. If you have asthma, you're just done, you know. You're locked inside the house and sand basically makes it in, and then the temperature drops. But the sheer feeling, the psychological feeling that you get from being in a sandstorm, like you feel your spirit is just being squished, you know, and it's quite scary again. So imagine this. Bombs falling, kids crying, people coughing, sneezing and all of that, all happening at the same time, and then you look outside, there is just literally nothing. You can't see like across from you because, especially when you're in the thick of it, it's like a very thick fog that you cannot see.

That happened during the actual campaign. We were looking, and I remember my mum joking, and she was like: 'So what else is going to happen?' It's kind of like the End of Days, you know, when you're looking at it. And everybody's praying, like, 'Oh my God, God is really, you know, is doing it to us this time, you know.' You've got everybody basically against you, you know, God, the elements, America ... Yeah. But we're still joking. We're still joking around, man.

Nick Popaditch
The sandstorms were almost biblical, I must say. They are bad. In one case, we had to actually stop and just wait for it to stop because we just couldn't move. I couldn't see ten feet in front of the tank. I couldn't see the end of my gun to shoot. They are just crazy on how much sand they are whopping around. I remember we were playing some silly game to pass the time. So we are just looking out our optics and playing this stupid word game just waiting for the sandstorm to pass. In tanks it's really not a big deal because the tank is not going to get blown anywhere. It's just going to stay right where it's at. It's not going to get buried. So really, it's just waiting it out. That one was a good 12-hour one.

Rudy Reyes
The first time we ran into Iraqis after the breach, they were just in awe. We had many surrendering to us. They were not targeting us, they were not enemies, so we were not shooting at them. They were in shock. This is a people that had been oppressed under a tyrant, and this is a region of the world in which strength and domination rules the day. So they weren't sure what to think, but they stayed as far away as they could, and in no way were threatening because they knew if they did that they would be killed. After Nasiriyah and the first big, massive battle, the Iraqi people were just trying to survive, they were hiding or fleeing, and I don't blame them.

After Nasiriyah, I believe, the storms came in, it was all overcast. That's why I said it looked like Vietnam. It was raining, it was overcast, it was wet. There was a lot of combat and a lot of stress. We hadn't slept, and we'd been fighting so hard. We had an officer who went away to make a head call, like 20 feet. And he was lost. We found him the next day. There was no visibility. We had to bury ourselves in biddy bags, and still the sand got through. The sandstorm was almost like a mud storm, because it was raining too. Mud over everything – optics, weapons, everything. Like Old Testament winds, rain, sand and mud. I think it took us all down for 24 hours. After a while, you couldn't even see this far ahead of you. You'd be a danger to your other men to start shooting.

Al Muwaffaqiyah came after the sandstorm. I remember seeing some women in the hijab fleeing, and I just had an idea that something bad was going to happen. And that's when we were massed into the city, and we got the order to clear the city. Not to skirt around it but to clear it, go right in the middle of it. Ballsy! A hell of a risk. Now we have MARSOC [Marine Special Operations Command]. That's all on our backs. Colonel Ferrando has a lot to do with that, showing our capability, what we can do, what we did do, what we will continue to do.

So the Iraqis were fleeing, were hiding, most of them can't read or write. We later killed some civilians because we put up signs in Arabic, to turn: 'This is a roadblock, turn around or else we will engage you.' We didn't know that they can't read, so they came pouring through in their vehicles and we killed every one of them. I feel sad for them. Actually, I don't feel too sad, because we killed them fast and they didn't suffer. But that's how professional we are. I mean, that is the profession: a threat or possible threat, you must neutralise. We are 60 men in open Humvees, leading the entire 1st Marine Division. Do I have a chance to interview every single person? No, I do not. Do I have a chance to set up some kind of little car park where they can bring them in? No, I do not. I don't have any time to do any of that stuff. We have a mission: get to Baghdad, cut off the head of the snake, kill the regime, and that's what we did. And we did it in a very professional way, and anybody and everybody we killed, we killed with good conscience. You find out if they're fucking fighters or if they're enemy afterwards, because you still gotta do a BDA, a Battle Damage Assessment, so we go searching and check 'em out and realised they were just you know, grandpa, mummy and the kids.

I only had a moment to think about it, less than a second. I had more stuff going on coming out of the radio, I had to keep going. You just don't have time to process. You can't process – you won't fight, you'll be freaking crying. So if you're a professional, you know that you must continue to fight because that's the only way you're going to get these men home alive. If you're stopping to grieve or you're stopping to think, the enemy now has five seconds to mask up. My people never tortured people, and we never raped women. That's the first invading force throughout history that has done that. We did not torture people and we did not rape women. That says it all.

Waleed Nesyif
After, I think, a couple of days or three days of being in Baghdad and the bombing just continued to intensify, the decision came to

be that we will be moving the family into another city, because it's becoming severely unsafe. Because we started seeing all of the reports of residential areas being bombed.

I was going out amidst all of that. I was looking for cigarettes. I'm a heavy smoker, and I heard that one of the shops is still open, and they're still selling cigarettes. So I took whatever money I have that is not for the family, and I wanted to go buy cigarettes. So I stole or took – borrowed – my cousin's small little bike, and here I am, cycling on this thing, and I got to the shop and then I had to fight with this other guy, basically over who is going to get all of the cigarettes. And the shopkeeper was like, 'Can you guys just sort it out, I need to shut down this store.'

As I was driving back, of course, you are seeing all of the houses that got bombed. Supposedly, America did not bomb any residential areas – that's bullshit. I'm on that small little bike, and I'm driving, and all of a sudden it got dark. Like just dark. And I look up and there is this black cloud that engulfed everything around me, that blocked the actual sun. I started pedalling faster and faster and faster ... And I was like, 'Shit, I need to get home. If it's chemical ...'

And then I discovered what it was. Here's what Saddam did, or the Iraqi army. They dug wells into random street areas, and they dumped crude oil in it, and they lit it on fire. So that they can create visual distractions for the American pilots. And I remember laughing so loud – they were thinking that these guys are using visuals to bomb, not satellite-guided missiles and stuff like that. They thought that, 'Oh, the plane is going to come, the pilot looks like this and he's like, oh yeah, there is a target over here, let's shoot right over there.' So then, all over Baghdad, all of a sudden you had all of these wells of oil burning up and the sky literally going dark. Black clouds looming over Baghdad.

Nick Popaditch

One time we were in this fight in Al Kut and, after the battle, my platoon got tasked with providing security while the rest of the battalion was refuelling. We call it consolidation and reorganisation, refuelling, rearming. It's doing the various things, getting ready for the next fight, and so it's a vulnerable time for the battalion. My platoon was tasked with providing security between the town and where this was happening – we have to stop anything from getting by; everybody is depending on us. So we are guarding the road, we are guarding the access to the battalion, which is one big main road. We've got four tanks set up in a line crossing it. And there's a large dump truck coming towards us and it's speeding down the road, it's barrelling towards us. If I remember rightly, they are flying some white stuff, white flags perhaps. They definitely look like they don't mean us any harm, other than the fact they are speeding towards us at about 50 miles an hour in a humungous dump truck.

I'm in the tank. Most of my crewmen are doing checks on the tanks. There's a couple of security guys up in the turrets watching the area. So he's coming toward us, we are trying to wave him tell him to stop, stop, they can't come this way. We are trying to wave them to stop, they are still just speeding towards us. I know they are not meaning to be hostile. I'm assuming they are not meaning to be hostile, but what they are doing is a very hostile act. They are speeding towards us in a dump truck, and yet the road is blocked by two tanks – there's nowhere for them to go other than drive right into the tank. The road is completely blocked, but they are still speeding towards us 50 miles an hour. So we have to stop them because the battalion is counting on us. I think this is just a case of being stupid. But there is that 1 per cent chance they are actually being hostile.

So I arm the machine gun, and we are waving at them to stop. My platoon commander fires a rifle round in front of him to get him to stop. They are still just speeding towards us. Now I'm thinking, 'OK, now we've actually shot at them and they are still not stopping. Now the odds of them being hostile is getting higher.' But there is still just the part in my mind thinking, 'I know they are just being stupid.' Now they are like 50 yards away and they are still speeding. So now I have to stop them, there is no other recourse whatsoever.

If I had to do it again today I'd still do the same thing. I fired a short burst of my calibre 50 machine gun right into the dump truck, and it stopped. It skidded to a stop and by then it is so close it's almost right at my gun tube. I could hear people screaming, and so I grab my rifle and my helmet and I climb up in the truck. I take the people out of the cab, and it's a driver, another guy and a lady. We pull them out.

The guy's got a bullet wound but not life threatening. He had a bullet embedded, you could see it right on the surface. It was above the rib and below the skin. I said, 'Go with the medivac. They will patch you up, they'll pull that bullet out, maybe even give you some money for your trouble,' because I heard we did that. This lady was translating for me, and he said something to her and she translated it back to me: 'Here in Iraq under Saddam,' he says, 'getting shot is not that uncommon. I'm just going to go and pluck it out with a knife.' He was talking to me like I was a sissy for wanting him to go and get it professionally done. Their people were always so tough like that. I always liked their people.

And then I climbed up in the dump truck and it's full of people and livestock, and they are screaming, there's blood everywhere. This was probably one of the scariest things I've ever seen, because I really thought there was a lot of innocent people had just been killed. I look for wounded people now. All the blood must have come from livestock – one of the animals must have got hit because there was a lot of it everywhere and it smelled. If you've ever been around somebody who's been shot bad, like where your guts are out, it had a very distinct odour and it really smells in the back of that odour. So I'm thinking there is something really bad here but I think it was just one of the livestock. Because the only guy who really had a bad wound, he was still there. And this guy was just patiently waiting for me to get to him. He didn't cry out. He didn't carry on. He did nothing. And when I got to him he was missing like a fist-sized chunk out of his upper thigh where one of these 50-calibre rounds had hit him.

And we got him out, rendered first aid to him. He was very calm through the whole thing. I had a phrasebook I carried with me if I ran across people who didn't speak English. I never told him, 'I'm the one that shot you,' but I'm feeling bad because I'm the guy who did it. And so I tell him, '*As-salamu alaykum*' ['Peace be upon you']. You know, I just want to give him a good wish. And he says it back to me: '*As-salamu alaykum*.' And then he kisses me on the cheek to thank me for doing the first aid on him.

The reason I remember it so vividly is that these are the people I'm there to help. These are just people who went into work that day and they got hit by something. You never want to see that. That's the sort of thing you fight to not have happen.

Dexter Filkins
Close to Baghdad, we came across a terrible scene. It was an Iraqi bus, and it had just been shot to pieces, and a whole Iraqi family had basically been wiped out. There were a couple of kids that were still alive, maybe one of the women, I think some of them were being treated. The Americans had just shot the thing to pieces, you know, and they were very upset, the Americans were. I went up to them and they were just 19, from Nowhereville, Kansas. I said, 'What happened?' And one of the kids said to me, 'We told them to stop, you know: *Stop!* It's, like, a universal word. Everybody knows the word stop. But they didn't stop. So we lit them up.' They didn't get the word. They obviously didn't know the word stop. One of the guys, I remember, was crying. One of the soldiers. He was sobbing. You know, it wasn't what he signed up for.

Nick Popaditch
After Al Kut, we turned right around and went to Baghdad and we crossed at the Diyala river. Once we crossed the Diyala river, it seemed like we were in Baghdad. And the Diyala river was a little bit of a fight. They resisted us at the Diyala river.

It wasn't a great resistance, it was just that they had a river that we couldn't cross because the bridge had been blown, so it took a while before we could get the assets across the river. So we are stuck on our side of the river, and they are shooting at us from their side of the river and we are shooting at them. We killed a lot of them on the other side of the river, and then eventually we got a pontoon bridge that all of us crossed. The infantry went across what was left of the actual bridge, and then we all reformed on the other side and continued into Baghdad.

Waleed Nesyif
Saddam is burning all of this crude oil, and the sky is dark.

I had taken my family closer to the Iranian border for safety, so we were able to receive Iranian TV. On Iranian TV you have this kind of wishy-washy information. Some of them are showing the Americans advancing, and then they would show a press conference with [Mohammed Saeed] Al-Sahhaf, our minister of information and media, saying, 'We're defeating Americans, we have destroyed them here, we have destroyed them here, we have destroyed them here ...' And it was like, 'I was just outside and houses are being bombed, what are you talking about?'

Such a compelling speaker. His English was perfect, and he was suddenly known for 'Those dogs, the American dogs have come here, thinking they can break Iraqis ... Look at what our army is doing, they have repelled them here, they have repelled them there, they have repelled them, and they went scurrying away, with their tails between their legs.' And then he would take the journalists to all of these places, showing the American atrocities, bombing homes, civilian houses. And then the Iranians [Iranian TV] would show the American side, how they were advancing. So we were confused.

It wasn't until the very, very end that Al-Sahhaf finally got faced with the fact that things really were going south, you know. 'They're not in Baghdad. They are not near us. They have not even entered the city.' And literally there was a tank driving over one of the bridges that connects to where he is. And then they bombed the hotel where he was. And he was like, 'They're not in Baghdad.' Sure, buddy, sure. It was good comical relief for us Iraqis.

Dexter Filkins
I was shadowing a unit of Marines, and we pulled up to a palm grove in the southern end of the city in the late afternoon of April 8th 2003, and the Colonel said, 'We're going in tomorrow, and maybe we get into a fight, maybe not, we'll see.' So we slept in the palm grove, got up really early, 4am. Even though the way up to Baghdad – 18 days, 600 miles, 800 miles, whatever it was – had been like a breeze, I was still really worried. I thought, 'If they're going to fight for anything, it's going to be this.' You know, it's like a quarter of the population and it's the regime, this is where they use chemical weapons, and everybody felt that way.

The Marines started to roll into the city at sunrise and – unbelievable – just one of the strangest days of my life. The Iraqi army just disappeared, disintegrated. Uniforms were all up and down the road. It was gone. Depending on where we were, there was a muted reaction from the Iraqis, it wasn't super enthusiastic but it wasn't angry. It felt like the conquering army has just marched 800 miles in 18 days and is now entering the capital.

Rudy Reyes
Yes, we got to Baghdad. There were some other units, some SEALs. I don't know if they were there first or we were there first. I just remember going into an area, and the cigarette factory and our snipers taking the fourth or fifth floor. We were talking through the hallway and setting up our fields of fire. There was a lot of officers talking to a lot of officers. We were trying to divvy up the pie of where to go, what to do from there. It was a little bit confusing.

Then we hunkered down in Baghdad for a little bit. Held tight in Baghdad and got ourselves together a little bit, worked out. I remember getting into a power plant factory, and our smart engineer types cranked open the fire hydrant and set up a pipe, broke out the windows of this factory that we were staying at, threw some chemlights in this room and put this pipe of water flowing out. So for the first time we could take a shower. Three weeks. I remember that. It was pretty wild, I hadn't fucking had a shower in a long time.

Then it was just such a blur, after all that heavy combat. I was just so stressed and probably so fatigued. We were all so fatigued. Everybody but me got dysentery, fever and diarrhoea and vomiting. Imagine fighting with your men who have vomiting and diarrhoea and 102-degree fever in the middle of a combat. I was the only out of the entire unit, I think, that did not get sick. My radio man almost died of fever in the middle of combat. Still monitoring the radios, shivering in a MOPP suit, soaking with sweat through this charcoal MOPP suit. Anytime incoming artillery or mortars, we had to put on gas masks, MOPP up completely, tighten the hood. Because we had to assume that it had nuclear, biological, chemical nerve agents.

Waleed Nesyif
There was one thing Al-Sahhaf said that was true. And that's when the Americans tried to take Baghdad airport, they couldn't the first time. They actually were repelled by Republican Guards. And they only did it after they used white phosphorus.

Now I know this because I had started a newspaper with some friends, and one of our correspondents was working at the Red Crescent [International Red Cross and Red Crescent Movement], and they were the only people allowed inside the airport to clean the dead bodies of Iraqi soldiers. He had taken some photos, and we published them. In the photos, basically, you see those soldiers lying on the ground, their clothes completely untouched, unharmed. Hair, totally fine; fingernails, eyelashes, anything that was dead in their bodies or on their bodies was OK, untouched. Their bodies, though, looked like they had been burnt from inside out. Some of them were turned orange. Some of them literally shrivelled up like a prune, but not outwardly burned. It was the weirdest scene that I have seen. After we started showing it to some experts, they explained that white phosphorus has the capacity to liquidate and attack all of the liquids inside of your cells, hence producing almost a look of internal combustion of individuals.

So Al-Sahhaf may have lied about everything, with the exception of that particular battle between the American troops and the Iraqi troops. The Iraqi troops actually won that very first battle, when it was fair and square. You know, it was only after they started carpet bombing and then they used whatever it is that they used against the Iraq army, that's when they took Baghdad airport. And that pretty much marked the whole fall of Baghdad.

The Statue Falls

Nick Popaditch

Once we got on the other side of the river we started going into Baghdad. And we got to low structures, I guess, like the suburbs. That's where we start seeing the people looting all the government buildings, and that's now our concern. They looked pretty celebratory, actually, they looked pretty happy. I remember asking my company commander, 'Should we do anything about this.' And he said, 'They are just stealing their own stuff back. Just stay out of it.'

If you went out in any city street in Iraq there was a mural of Saddam Hussein. Every town had a statue of him. Every room you went in had a picture of Saddam Hussein in there somewhere and these were reminders to the people: you don't speak out; bad things will happen if you speak out against this dictator. So I think there were a lot of people who saw this as, 'It's got to be better than this guy.'

A day or two after, when we start getting to where the big buildings were, the people were just gone. Just disappeared. It was kind of ... not scary, just odd, to see a huge city the size of San Diego, without a soul living; not a person on the road, not a person you could see walking around, nothing. Just buildings without a person you could see. So we just started taking ground. We were on these big boulevards, like three lanes on this side with a tree row in the middle, and three lanes on that side, and big buildings – 20-storey buildings on each side of the road. And not a soul. They all went into the buildings and they didn't come out on the street any more. Not until Saddam's statue fell. That's when they all came back out.

And we're just speeding down these boulevards, just taking ground, and we got to Firdos Square. That's where that big statue of Saddam was. You could see it from a distance because there was a boulevard leading right into it, and I remember seeing that statue and thinking, 'That's interesting looking.'

Waleed Nesyif
On April 9th, in the morning, I remember we were all up. My uncle worked the TV on the car battery and we started watching the Americans basically driving in the streets of Baghdad, which was very unreal. There was one of these bridges, it's called the Sinak bridge, and an American tank was driving on it. And I remember seeing the barrel of the tank turning around and pointing itself towards where Firdos Square was.

Nick Popaditch
And then we pulled into Firdos Square, which is a circle, and we pulled in around it and just set a defence. And that's when the people first approached us. It was just one person. One man walked up to our perimeter, and one of the guys on the ground just shook his hand, and met him as a friend. As an ally. And other people saw that and they started coming out. Before long, we had a couple hundred people down there in that square. They were in the grassy park in the middle, and they just started celebrating.

When they started celebrating, I told the guys on my tank, 'OK, you can get down and you can go talk to these people and go celebrate a little bit. And then come back. Because I want to do this too, so come back!' So they went down and they celebrated with the people a little bit, and then they came back and then I went down there.

The people all had these little flowers with them, and they're giving us these flowers. I remember talking to a guy who was about my age, and he was so happy. I was asking about his family and he said he had children. I told him I had children, and we were pulling out our pictures and we were showing each other pictures of our kids. And it was so neat. You could just see it in their faces, you could hear it in their voices, just the joy of what was happening that day. Just think about it. There's nothing, they're in a city with no power, no water, garbage piling up every day, but just this little celebration, that was a joyous event. That was life-changing for me. I mean, it didn't change the way I lived or anything like that, but for what I did for a living ... I felt good about it before, but boy did I feel good about it after that.

Waleed Nesyif
A couple of hours later, they're in Firdos Square. And it was such an unreal feeling. The weird part about it was somehow it was joyous. I was like, 'Finally, it's fricking over. We'll get to go home or proceed and see what this new era is going to be.'

There was this uncertainty as well. Like, is Saddam going to come back? Because he wasn't captured. The Iraqi army disbanded, but it's not that they disappeared. There's like a million-plus soldiers in Iraq, so we're really confused.

And then we were watching really clearly this footage of the statue being pulled down, and that was so unreal. Especially seeing the people, the hordes of people, running towards it. Those who were hitting the statue with their shoes. The other guy, the famous guy, the bodybuilder with his sledgehammer trying to destroy it as much as he can with this 10-pounder or 10-kilo sledgehammer. You know, you're looking at it and it was like, 'Where are these people coming from?' I remember that was the very first question I asked. 'Are people just in the streets in Baghdad right now? Because it's war still.' And you can hear the bombing still, it's like the Iraqi army are still resisting in small isolated pockets.

Dexter Filkins
You know, it was one of these moments where if you were there it wasn't a big deal, but I only learnt much later that it was like this iconic moment on television. I mean, it was like a joke. It was this crappy statue, for one thing. This kind of metal statue that

didn't look very nice, and it was certainly only one of many, and the Iraqis were kind of dancing on it and they were banging their shoes on it which is kind of insulting. And I think what struck me was that first of all the crowd wasn't very big, it was like a hundred Iraqis or so and some of them were just fathers with their kids like, 'Come watch these guys bang their shoes on and insult Saddam.' And it was not a big deal.

Then it became clear that some of the guys were going to try and pull it down but then they couldn't succeed, and so the American military shows up, and it's like, 'We'll tear it down for you.' They tie the rope around it and get the big troop carrier and they rip the statue down. And the crowd is just big enough that, if you keep the focus of your camera tight enough, it looks like kind of a big crowd. And to discover that that became the equivalent of like Prague in 1989, which I think was the way it was represented, it was a kind of popular uprising and the people kind of gathered around the great symbol of the great dictator and tore it down.

It just didn't happen that way. I went back to New York a couple months later, and everybody said, 'Did you see the statue come down?' And I was like, 'Yeah, yeah, I saw the statue come down,' but it was too late by that time!

Nick Popaditch

They first started trying to knock the statue down with a sledgehammer. This big hulking guy, he looked like a circus strongman, and he was beating on the pedestal. And I remember like kind of laughing, I think I was saying, 'That's going to take about a week ... it's huge.' And to beat through it with a sledgehammer, you'd go through probably a dozen sledgehammers before you ever made a dent in it.

I had to ask afterwards, because I don't really know how it happened, but some kid walked up to the M88 and asked the guy to help him tear it down. The M88 is like a tow truck for the tanks, it's got a big boom on the front, a 90-ton winch for pulling out tank engines, it's got a 1500hp engine for pulling stuck tanks out and stuff, it's really a pretty amazing vehicle. And it has tank mechanics, or the crew, on it plus a Corps man, and that's who went up there. And the cool thing about this is these guys do a pretty thankless job. The tank mechanics work hard, and they don't get the fun part of the tanking, they just have the dirty work part of keeping it running. And so it's cool to see these guys go out and have this moment. And they went out there and they put that boom out, guy's name was Eddie Chin, Corporal Eddie Chin, and he was a tank mechanic. I used to say, 'They're going to have action figures of these guys.' They were seen all around the world as a symbol of freedom, as a symbol of liberation, of victory. If I watch something about this war to this day, I'll see Corporal Eddie Chin up there with the Saddam statue, that's an iconic thing of the war.

And so, Eddie goes up there, he nooses up Saddam. He's got the rope out there, then Gunner Lambert's pulling the vehicle back and he's got all these people on top of that vehicle, all these civilians are climbed on top of that vehicle, and he's trying not to hurt any of them, so he's being real slow and real deliberate. Then the rope broke so they used the chain and they hooked the chain around, and Lieutenant McLaughlin's flag went up over Saddam's head. The people cheered, the people went nuts, and then the flag went down. And then they put an Iraqi flag over his head, and the people cheered that. I cheered that.

I think the reason they really cheered it was because the way he was noosed up with the chain, it was almost like a hangman. That's how I saw it. I saw it like a hangman's hood, and I think the Iraqi people probably saw it the same way. If we were going to raise a flag there, we'd have thrown it up on a flagpole, we wouldn't have draped it over Saddam's head! I don't think anybody saw it as like us planting a flag in Baghdad. And when it went down, they reacted the same way with the Iraqi flag went over his head. It was just a disrespectful thing to Saddam, and that made them happy.

The whole thing was a 'we' thing; it wasn't an 'us and them' thing, it was an 'us' thing. They pulled the statue down, and that's when they were disrespecting the statue. I loved it when I was looking at that video and you could see them like hitting it with the bottom of their shoe – all these things are culturally things that they would have been killed for before today. And there they were. You could just see the joy. The sheer joy.

Waleed Nesyif
But then the statue sure enough went down, and then it was dragged, and my uncle – who was a Republican Guard and he was retired at the time – looked at the news, and he was like, 'It's over. It's done.' And there was this moment of silence, and then there was this moment of joy. We were clapping, kissing each other almost like it was Eid coming, you know. Oh, finally! It was a congratulations almost, you know? We made it through this and now we enter this new chapter.

Sally Mars
I remember when the statue fell. The people were hitting it, and they were celebrating around the statue that had fallen. My mother said it was a shameful scene. Yesterday they were glorifying and praising Saddam and today they were hitting his statue with their shoes. She described this as savagery. They shouldn't do this because this was all broadcast by international media, so we didn't look good in front of the other nations. It was OK to remove the statue, take it away, or do what you want, but I didn't like this as a scene of celebration. I don't know, I didn't like the sight of it. I've got nothing to do with politics, but as a scene of celebration, it disturbed me.

Omar Mohammed
I came back from the school. It was midday. And when I went inside the house, I saw all my family watching the TV. So I saw the Americans enter. We were following the battle, like the rest of the country. And we would see American soldiers with their cars behind them, and a car is trying to take down the statues

of Saddam, with people having their shoes hitting the picture of Saddam.

But Mosul was still under their control. What's happening on the TV, in our city nothing is happening. It was still under the control of Saddam. The next day was Friday. The preacher said the same sentence, which was the last time in my whole life I heard it: 'May God protect the President and the region.' He said this. After a few minutes, a Humvee – with one soldier in the front, two soldiers in the other seats, and a tribal man in the front seat – stopped by the mosque. The preacher started shouting, 'Allahu Akbar, this is the freedom day!' And he started crying, many people were crying. I was shocked. What just happened? He was just saying the usual sentence. And the Ba'athists, who used to insult the people every day, started also shouting: 'Thanks to God, he freed us from the Ba'ath and Saddam ...'

These people changed from being supportive of Saddam, or working with him, to be with the Americans. In a moment. The preacher became a member of the delegation to receive the American commanders in Mosul airport. And they put his photo in the newspaper, with one of the Ba'athist officials and the American commander, and they put it on the mosque, on the wall!

And then the chaos came.

City on Fire

Dexter Filkins
And Saddam flees, and it was this sort of triumphant moment. And by 11am the looting had started, by noon the fires had started, and by 1pm the whole city was in chaos, the whole capital. You could just see the fires and the plumes from the smoke going up all across the city. I was so disturbed by it. I just felt like, 'What are you doing? You just marched 800 miles and did this extraordinary thing ... You're going to lose it all right now.' Like in every minute that this thing spins out of control, this is going to take another year to get back into the bottle because this is insane. You could feel all this momentum just turn around, I mean, it just did a 180, it was insane. Literally, the Iraqis came charging out and just started tearing everything to pieces, anything that had to do with the government or anything they could get a hold of and bring home and sell, really.

I remember pulling up to the Ministry of Culture or the Ministry of Sport, and the Iraqis were taking the furniture out, you know, just pulling it all out, and they'd smashed all the windows, but they were just ripping everything to pieces. It had this kind of surreal aspect to it. I pulled up to this government building that had a big banner across the top that said 'The Iraqi Olympic Committee'. The Iraqi Olympic Committee had been run by one of Saddam's sons, I think Uday, and it was his personal little fiefdom, and he could bring people there and do whatever he was going to do to them. But it was also a sporting thing, and there was an enormous horse stable. The Iraqis had gone inside, they had torn everything out, they were just marching out with the furniture and they were carrying computers out that, clearly, they didn't even know what they were going to do with, but they were just ripping everything out – and they were taking the horses. These beautiful, thoroughbred, Arabian racehorses, and they were walking them out, and the horses were getting hysterical and getting up on their hind legs and it looked like a Dalí painting. I mean, it was insane. And pretty soon, the buildings around us were on fire.

I remember watching this scene of total mayhem, and in the corner of my eye I see this American military unit, so I went over to the lieutenant, just this young guy, and I said, 'What are you doing?' And he said, 'I don't have any orders.' And so he did this completely bizarre thing, in keeping with this very surreal atmosphere. He had a company of about 40 guys, and they start marching in single file, in front of the building back and forth, almost like toy soldiers. As if the Iraqis were going to get really afraid and like go home. By that time it was too late, and they didn't even look up.

As night fell on the city, it was completely lit up. So a city of however big Baghdad is – six million people – on fire. Utterly on fire, completely on fire. It was so draining, emotionally. I mean, I had sort of gotten up at 4am that morning with the conquering army, and within 12 hours the whole thing was lost. It was all gone. The city was on fire.

Nick Popaditch

When I saw those people celebrate that statue going down and I watched what they did, the way they reacted to that, I knew at that point what I was looking at. I was looking at people being liberated. People who had grown up their whole lives under a dictator, and now they were just ... just getting their first taste of freedom. And I was seeing people celebrating liberty. And that was life-changing to me.

In the beginning, I wasn't quite getting it, but after a little bit, as it started getting near sunset, I started realising: this is oppressed people celebrating liberty, celebrating freedom. The next day we would deal with Iraqis out on the street and we're always trying to get them to help us do various things like get the power turned back on, get the water flowing again, all these various civic projects. We'd tell them, 'OK, come see us tomorrow at the waterworks building,' and they used to say, 'Perhaps you want a pass.' We'd say, 'No, you don't need a pass, just, just go there.' 'Perhaps you want a pass.' It was, to me, so eye-opening to see people that had been so regulated in their lives, so oppressed in their lives, that just the concept of being able to go where they wanted to go, they were scared to do it without permission.

Ahmad Al-Basheer *was 18 when the invasion began.*

The regime fell. We were in Albu Amer, and we came back to Baghdad, and then I saw the Americans. It was very new for me. And then people here started to criticise Saddam. At the beginning, I was happy. I don't know why, but I was happy. But, at the same time, I didn't say anything.

Even when I saw the statue of Saddam was falling, there were rumours in Baghdad that Saddam and his army were preparing a big ambush to the Americans. They will just go out from underground, where they have lots of tunnels. They will come out from the ground, and they will kill them all, and they will take back the country again. These were the rumours.

Waleed Nesyif

It was still a state of disbelief, because you didn't know whether ... OK, the Americans are in Baghdad, they pulled down this statue ... Is Saddam going to come back, because we knew he disappeared. Where was he, did he have another plan – do the Americans have another plan? We don't know ...

But then I decided it's time to go back to Baghdad, because the situation we were in was very dire: there were six families, each one has five members, and we were all stuck in two rooms, running out of food. Everybody's getting very anxious.

Yes, there was a celebratory feeling as we saw the statue being dragged down. There was cheer. This is for real this time ... There was a genuine sense of hope that people had, as well, particularly the first few days, you know, actual hope. Which was rare in Iraq at that time. Nevertheless, going back and seeing all of the Iraqi tanks, armoured cars, all of that, just destroyed on the street, and then the Americans – you know, it felt like you were in a movie, almost like an unreal situation. And I was excited, I was like, maybe again, this is the beginning of a good thing, you know, that was the hope.

Then I had to walk all the way to where I used to live, which is a five-hour walk, and I got to see almost everything in Baghdad – American tanks driving by, Iraqi tanks burned up. Katyusha rocket launchers left out in the streets, dead bodies, all of that ... Yet you see people standing outside, they were handing water and stuff like that to American soldiers. Some of them were inviting them into their houses. It was not choreographed at all, some of the images that the world may have seen, you know, of Iraqi children running towards Humvees, saluting and saying hello to American soldiers. We have this thing where if we throw water into the street, that means you are welcome. You know. People throwing water onto the streets again, offering American soldiers tea, which is an Iraqi way of saying you're welcome to my house.

So, yeah, that sense of joy, celebratory sentiment, was a definite truth as to what happened there. Now the question is, how long did it last? And that was not long.

Sally Mars
After the war began, the Americans came, and they weren't bombing, they were just roaming the streets. At the time, small kids would go around houses. They'd come and tell us, whispering, that the Americans are looking for guns – whoever has a gun should hide it. We had a machine gun, so my older brother covered it with cloth and hid it in an empty water tank above our house. He hid it from the Americans.

I was waiting, with anticipation, for the first Westerner. I hadn't seen Westerners, so I was excited: what would they look like? Were their accents like the movies? So I was waiting for them to come.

And then there was the first one, walking and entering our area. So I ran, screaming: 'Dad, Dad, the Americans are here!' So he said, 'OK, what is it to me? What do you want from me?' He was angry because he was a soldier before, and seeing the Americans enter was hard for him.

They were stood next to our school, and I went and stood beside them. Then a soldier came, telling me it's dangerous to stand beside them. The translator explained to me, 'He said you can't stand here.' But I was young, so I told him, 'But this is my school. You're standing here.' He told me, 'School is closed now, so don't come.' So I told him, 'Why?' He said, 'We are going to make it safe. Once it's safe, you can come.'

But I didn't understand them. I was curious. I wanted to know who these people were, so I stayed around them. I remember a soldier had his helmet and took it off to show me the inside. There was a photo of his daughter carrying a puppy. He said, 'This is my daughter and she's your age, so go, I don't want you to get hurt. I fear that someone comes or a fight breaks out, so don't stand here.' He calmly explained to me why I shouldn't stand there, and I understood. I got a flower from our garden and gave it to him. I don't know why I did that. I went home, and Mum had locked the door, out of fear.

Omar Mohammed
It's very hard to describe it, because I had mixed feelings … At one moment, I felt they were not humans, because I had never seen this before. I mean, I have seen such soldiers in the movies, but the most I saw was Rambo and Arnold Schwarzenegger. You barely see their face, because of this thing on their head, and they are full of weapons. The first time I had interaction with a US soldier was one in front of our house and blocking our doors, so I can't go out. So I pushed him. They wanted to arrest me. I started shouting at them: 'You are standing on my house. Go away! Isn't it enough for you to take over my country? You want to take my house!' Then my uncle became upset, angry at me, not the soldier that I pushed. The officer. And then they left me.

From that moment, I felt that this person is capable of doing anything, killing me or killing anyone. These American soldiers are capable of doing whatever they want. Because he has his hand on the weapon, on the trigger, he can just shoot at any moment ...

Sally Mars
When they first came, they were giving sweets to the children. Their Arabic was funny when they tried, we'd laugh at them. They tried to lighten the atmosphere. The only thing scary about them was when they'd carry their guns. It was the first time I had seen a weapon that big. But they tried to be friendly with us.

They weren't exactly what I imagined them to be – slighter, weirder. For a kid, they were very different. They were very tall. I don't know if it's because I was a kid, or if they really are tall. They were wide, and had their gear on their backs, and bags, so I saw them as very big. Once American soldiers passed us, and I asked them if they're Ninja Turtles with all those weapons on their backs.

Ahmad Al-Basheer
We never thought that Saddam would be removed, never. Until I saw American soldiers when we were headed to Baghdad to go back to our house. I saw two American soldiers standing in the street – I was like, '*Americans?*' I was very happy to see them at that time. Like, 'Hi! I can speak English!' My father was upset, like, 'Hmm ... Don't speak to them.' But no, I was very excited to see them. I wanted them to be my friends. And yeah, at that point, I realised that Saddam was falling.

I wasn't scared because – when I saw the army and the tanks, the Humvees everywhere and the soldiers – I thought they're here to change our situation to the better. It will be better than before. Everything that was forbidden for us will be now allowed. It's gonna be fine for everything, it's gonna be safe. It's gonna be new college for everyone, universities, there will be jobs for everyone, and everything we didn't have before, we'll have it now, starting from the Pepsi can to everything. So when I saw them, I felt hope that now we are mixed with these countries and there's people from the USA and from all over around the world, they will just take their experience to put it inside this country and it will be a new country. Very peaceful, very good, and we will see tourists from all over the world, and we will be able to interact with people. It's gonna be like, you know, the sunshine, the birds flying, and everything is good and the music everywhere. But after 2003 the first explosion happened. We know now that it's never gonna happen, it's never gonna be safe again.

Dexter Filkins
The American soldiers thought, 'We're gonna run up to Baghdad, take down Saddam and then we're going home.' You know: home by Christmas. When the Iraqi government fell on April 9th, within days the orders came down to prepare to go, and to draw down significantly by the end of summer. They had to tear all those plans up, but nobody planned to stay.

I was looking for the reaction of the Iraqis, and I didn't know what that was gonna be and I felt uncertain about that. Because in Afghanistan it was a no-brainer: across the board they were overjoyed to see the Americans and the British and all the other countries that came. *Overjoyed.* You could go to the poorest place in Afghanistan, and typically the Afghans are alive and really spirited and full of life.

I found something very different when I went to Iraq: it was much more guarded, much more sad. Just this feeling of a kind of overwhelming amount of sadness before we got there. And so it was just really weird ... There wasn't any one particular reaction to grab on to. Some Iraqis were really glad we were there. Others were not. Most of them were somewhere between that, but they were terrified. They thought that somehow this was going to come back to them – 'We're going to get into trouble for this. What the hell is going to happen when they're not here in the town? Something bad is going to happen.' Because that's the way it's always been. So there was this feeling of foreboding as well. Even though they were being told, 'This is your deliverance,' I don't think they really believed that. They had been through so much already that they just weren't going to believe it until they could feel it.

Waleed Nesyif
Remember the fear that I was telling you about? That Saddam could be coming back? We didn't know. People were still, like, 'Is it happening? Is it not happening? What do we do here? What do we *do*?' And, again, there were some Iraqis who actually loved Saddam. There were some Iraqis who rejected the American occupation, for it was unjust and will remain unjust. I represented a slice of society that, you know, apathetically accepted the fact as to what it is: this is a major power, but it is going to invade us, the invasion is happening; let's try to minimise the damage and the losses.

But then he was there, and people were all around him, you know, clapping and singing and doing the same thing. And then he went into another neighbourhood. He was standing up on a car, people were all around him. The interesting thing was that he didn't have enough aides, or enough bodyguards. Usually, he moved with a horde of them that surrounded him and didn't let anyone come near him. With this one, he was very close to the people, very close. He's standing there, laughing, smiling. 'Good for you, my sons, for standing against the aggressors.' He was talking to them, and they were like, 'Yes, sir. Yes, master. We shall defend Iraq, we shall defeat them.'

And then Saddam basically disappeared. He just fucking left … You know, it was such a deflating feeling. This man that once reigned with an iron fist, just – *poof!* – gone.

Now what happened at that time, was that the connections and the communication between the army ceased. It was cut. So the right hand did not know what the left hand was doing – or supposed to do. The centralisation of the command was gone. Now, they were supposed to be acting upon the orders that they received, but the army was largely made up of people that were sick and tired of war. And not many of them were willing to sacrifice themselves.

This is what my father told me. Once things got really serious in Mosul, my father and the commander of the unit at that time opened the safe, and they had petty cash. They gave the soldiers equal shares: 'Right, here is your money, wear civilian clothes, go home.' So the army defected. And that was maybe ten days into the war. The few fighting brigades that remained were the Republican Guard, Fedayeen Saddam, the guys with the black clothing. Some of them were in Basra. Basra resisted the most, they were the ones that lasted till the very end.

And Saddam had two recorded speeches that they showed on TV. He was saying, 'We are still standing' and all of that – you know, the same rhetoric that he would always. And then he disappeared. Nobody knew where he was. The 10th division of the Iraqi army was mowed down, because he left his son Qusay in command. From what I understood, he sent them to meet the Americans in the Western Desert. They didn't have air cover, planes were not flying from the Iraqi side. He sent this brigade of, I don't know, 10,000 soldiers or something like that, sent them out into the open, into the desert, and they just got ... mowed down. When we heard this on Iranian TV – and my uncle was explaining that this is probably the stupidest tactical move ever made in the history of war – slowly but surely, the belief started becoming more and more cemented that this is actually happening right now.

Dexter Filkins
I ran into this Marine general named John Kelly, who became the Chief of Staff for President Trump but he was a Marine general at the time. He said, 'We're gonna take Tikrit tomorrow, and that's Saddam's hometown. We're thinking maybe there's going to be a big fight. Do you want to come?' It's a couple of hours north of Baghdad. Pretty much the same situation, not much resistance, but we got into Saddam's palace right after they left. Saddam had seven palaces around the country, and they were just these utterly grandiose, preposterous, enormous palaces. They were huge castles. He denied himself nothing. I went into the bedrooms, and there

was underwear draped over the towel rack, there was toothpaste coming out of the tube, there was uneaten food on the kitchen counter, and it was like everybody had left in a real hurry. Amazing scene.

But I remember the Iraqis were just flowing into the palace and looting it, just taking everything out. The thing about the looting was it wasn't just the downtrodden of Iraq that were tearing these buildings apart, it was everyone. We were watching these middle-class, educated Iraqis go in and get whatever they could and walk out with it. And there was a woman that was coming out, very well dressed, clearly educated, carrying a huge stack of Wedgewood bone china, you know, top of the line. And I stopped her and said to her, 'What are you doing? You're looting, you're looting public property,' or something ridiculous like that. She looked at me and said in perfect English, 'Son, I've earned this.' And she just kept on walking with her stack of china.

Sally Mars
I started school, though I had stopped for a year because of the war. The first thing they did when schools opened was remove Saddam's photos, take them, throw them in the bins, burn them. This great feared leader, that comes on TV and no one can say anything about – they used to always tell us as kids, 'The walls have ears,' so we used to fear even speaking about him with ourselves – this great leader that everyone glorified is now suddenly hated, in an instant. But I don't know the reason.

I used to think that Saddam will come back any second, and he'll bring safety because, since he left, the situation deteriorated. Guns everywhere, people carrying weapons ... I connected the dots. Since he disappeared, the situation deteriorated, so if he comes back, things will get better. That's how I thought of it.

For a time, and in the period after the war when things calmed down and the Americans entered, life stopped, but it was a safe situation. Everything had stopped, the schools had stopped, all the government departments were stopped, but the situation was safe and secure and people were coming from and going to their places. We went back to living our normal life after the war. We weren't afraid. We weren't expecting that this deterioration in security would happen, or sectarianism and wars. We expected that a new government would be formed. Someone else would be there instead of Saddam. And we would go back, and the situation would go back to like it was before and maybe better. That's what we were expecting, but we weren't expecting that all these things would happen.

Ahmad Al-Basheer
I remember this time when I was with a taxi driver, and I was like, 'There's no Saddam any more, blah, blah, blah.' He said to me a sentence. He said, 'Starting from today, eight o'clock is better than nine o'clock.' It's very deep. Every day moves on, the next day will be worse than yesterday. Today is gonna be better than tomorrow. And after tomorrow it's gonna be better than the day after that. It's a very deep sentence.

I didn't listen to him. I thought it's gonna be a safe country, everything is gonna be OK, everything is gonna be good. We will have mobile phones, we will have satellite TV stations, we will have freedom, we will have everything. I didn't know why he was talking about this, why there will be death on the streets. Why there will be war. Later on I understood, and he was right about it.

Mission Accomplished

Dexter Filkins

There was an incident very early on, not long after the regime fell. It happened in Fallujah, 30 miles west of Baghdad. What happened was some American soldiers had commandeered a school, and a crowd of angry Iraqis had gathered round the school. They started to chant. It wasn't violent. And the Americans fired into the crowd and they killed a lot of Iraqis, 14 or 15. The word came back to Baghdad when that happened and I remember thinking, 'Oh god, how can they be so stupid?' And that, of course, became a regular thing: a bunch of Americans gets surrounded, they feel scared, they fire into the crowd. It just meant another thousand enemies.

That sent chills through everybody, because it just looked like we were doomed to repeat that again and again. It was a couple of days before the president landed on the aircraft carrier. Somebody said that Bush had landed on an aircraft carrier and declared that the war was over. And things were still pretty calm then, but it seemed a little premature at the time. I had this overwhelming sense that we just weren't that good at that sort of thing. It was a really depressing feeling. You'd hear this stuff coming out of the White House and it was, like, 'What are you talking about?' You know, the whole city – the whole *country* – has been stripped and looted, there is no government, there is nothing, and this is going to take years. It just made me sad, you know. I just thought, 'This is what we've come to, that it's just like a big PR job.' It was a problem to be finessed. It just needed a better slogan, and then everything would be fine.

Rudy Reyes

I never even saw that speech. I was still in in the country, and I was doing humanitarian work. After the first week or so of wanton violence outside, we got the order to go out and help with basic first aid, medical and water. And then we started interacting with the people. We didn't have television or anything like that then.

What I observed out there, after we sort of interacted with the people, is how poor, how uneducated they were. There was burning garbage and destruction and dead bodies and rot everywhere. There was no water, there was no public works – it was really like some kind of Hieronymus Bosch fricking hell out there. I didn't even consider winning the war, I didn't even consider it a war. I just considered it a mission. And I know we completed our mission. I did see all the suffering and the poverty, and I had very little hope that in any short amount of time the Iraqi civilisation and modern society and culture would rebound. I didn't really have any hopes in that. I didn't know what was gonna happen, but I knew that I did my job, I know that I completed my mission. And I was not being hubristic, I wasn't being arrogant. I knew it was just outside of my scope.

For instance, we went to a village to help with first aid and medical and shots and water. And most of the village had albinism. Some of them had mental retardation and tumours on their face. I mean these people were genetically damaged, I don't know from the first war or from inbreeding or, who knows, nerve agents from Saddam – all of it. But these beautiful people, they were sweet and they thought we were so good. They thought that we could heal them. They thought we could fix them. What could we do? Give 'em water, give 'em food. We gave 'em every bit of food we had.

Waleed Nesyif

I have it burnt in my head. It's one of the moments that I will never forget. The infamous speech that George Bush has given on one of the US plane carriers where he declared 'mission accomplished' in Iraq. America has won. Saddam is gone, and Iraq is secured. Sure. *Sure*.

I remember hearing the news and then being in the streets in Baghdad, and they were like, 'Yeah? Seriously?' I remember discussing with my friends: so what is the mission? Are they talking about the army invasion? Or are they talking about, you know, Iraq now is liberated and they're gonna put us on the right path? And there was this discussion amongst people that I knew at that time, and they were like, 'You know what, things are gonna get better. It cannot get worse than this ... we've already seen the worst, things are going to get better, let's have a positive attitude here.' And I really appreciated that sentiment, that glass half full kind of attitude. You know, it's like, 'Let's see ...'

Nick Popaditch

I think it's pretty cool that the president landed on that boat and said, 'Great job, guys. Mission accomplished.' But that's looking at it from now. Now if he meant it as a message to the nation ... Yeah, I don't know. I don't know what I would think about that. On the ground there in Iraq, where I think the insurgency really started more than anything, I don't think it was ideological in nature, I don't think it was political in nature, I think it was economic in nature. Because every day we were on the street in Baghdad, you saw the power out, you saw the garbage piling up ... no jobs, nothing happening. And you knew it just was a matter of time before people there started getting less and less happy about that.

So I think if there could have been some way to get that economy turning again, get people doing something productive, moving that country forward after that ... Now how you do that, I have no idea. Is that even possible, to take a falling government and turn it into a working economy in a short period of time? I don't know. But it sure would have solved a lot of military problems if that happened.

I used to think half the people shooting at me probably had absolutely no disagreement with me whatsoever. I figured they might have probably just been out-of-work people, starving people, that somebody was paying them to do what they were doing.

Waleed Nesyif
And again, that was a time when people started questioning. You know, it's OK saying this mission is accomplished and everything is good right now – when are we gonna get electricity? When are we gonna get water? When is security gonna be there? Because there is no security. Before the war had begun, Saddam released every single criminal in Iraq. Every single one of them was loose in the street, with the exception of political prisoners, who were executed. Now we're talking rapists, thieves, killers, you name it. Actual hardcore criminals. They were all released, right before the war. And I know this because one of my friends – or used to be a friend – had killed his grandma for her jewellery, back in 2001, and he was sentenced to be executed. And I remember seeing him in the street before the war started, and you're, like, 'Holy fucking shit. The guy killed his god damn grandma in cold blood, like choked her with a hose.'

Knowing that, we knew our homes are going to be under attack at this point, right? So the very first thing in my head was we need weapons, we need to go back home, we need to basically protect our houses. This is all we own. So I went. I hitched a ride to the gates of Baghdad, and then I walked. I was seeing the American troops lining up alongside all of the burnt-up Iraqi tanks, army personnel, dead bodies left right and centre. And the Americans standing there, wearing just their flat jackets with their tattooed arms and glasses and stuff like that. They were nice, and waving, and stuff like that. We were waving back at them. It's almost like a state of disbelief, or hysteria almost. In a sense you're happy, but you're happy about something you really shouldn't be.

As we got into residential areas outside of the highway, some people were taking trays of juice and tea to the American soldiers. Some of them were inviting them to their homes. Some American soldiers were giving candy and water to kids and stuff like that. So this is all real. This has all happened.

We started seeing some of the destruction that had happened in the war in this neighbourhood where my grandparents' house was. Civilian homes. I'm not a military expert to know this was targeted by the Iraqi army or by the Americans, but it was destruction nevertheless. We lived on the west side, my grandparents' home was on the east side, and it was about a five-hour walk in which I got to see some of the looting. Government buildings basically open, people just taking whatever they can. More and more tanks, more and more Americans just literally driving in the street. I saw a little group of Iraqi soldiers that were trying to change their clothes into civilian clothes. I pretended that I didn't see them and I just continued walking. Because you don't know what's going to happen at that point.

Colin Marks
When I went north to take the surrender of the Sixth Armoured Division, I was met on the road by lots and lots of people, and they were all crowding around me and they were all hugging me and they were all hugely happy to be liberated. One of those people told me he had been an army deserter, he hadn't wanted to be in the army and for his crime he had his eye gouged out, so he was minus one eye. They were quite wretched, the people, they had very little. It was clear that they were being subjugated, and they really had very little. When I look at the faces of the children, absolutely filthy, hair filthy, in rags, no idea where their next meal's going to come from, let alone what their physical security is going to be like – it's difficult to call it 'heady, new-found freedom'. I think it was just people trying to get on.

You saw children with shrapnel injuries. We treated one chap with burns injuries from an air strike. The normal medical attention that folk would need in that situation wasn't always possible, so for every person that was treated there's an awful lot of people who weren't treated. It's difficult with hindsight not to think things were going to get an awful lot worse, and there was false hope for them at that time that, as liberators, we were creating a much better scenario for them and a much better future.

Waleed Nesyif

We were having talks, my friends and I, that maybe we'll be like Saudi Arabia, or like the United Arab Emirates. Let those Americans take all of our oil, give us little bits and pieces, you know, the crumbs on the table, and then we'll live like kings and queens. Because that's how we viewed life in Saudi Arabia; I mean, they definitely live better than you and me, financially speaking, right? And Iraqis know Iraq is one of the richest countries in the world. Our land is super fertile. We have the majority of the world's old civilisations and stuff like that. If Egypt has Luxor and the pyramids, we have Ur, Nineveh, Babylon, Assur – it just goes on and on and on. If Iraq only opens up its tourist sites, we'll be frigging balling, right? We were even talking like, we should open up tourism to Israel and the Jewish people, because we have so many of their prophets over here; they can come do their pilgrimage and we can make shitloads of money out of these guys. Because we see our people going to Mecca and spending all of their money in Mecca over there. Why can't we do the same?

So we're talking about all of these possibilities. Maybe, maybe this is what's gonna happen. But, we were under no illusion that America came with the best of intentions. I need to stress this very clearly. We are not stupid people. We knew exactly what the purpose of this war was, and it is our oil and the geostrategic position of Iraq amidst all of these other nations. I mean, America tried to shut Iran up and then you have Turkey, and then you have Syria, and then you have Saudi Arabia. So, having Iraq was instrumental. You know, our heritage in understanding politics surpasses that of America by frigging thousands and thousands of times. Civilisations have come and gone on the exact same lands, you know. And you come and you wanna basically sell me this cheap-ass pitch, coming here to basically liberate us. Good for you, buddy. But they believed it, that's the scary part. That is the scary part.

John Nixon

One of the problems is we thought we knew what was happening in this country, we thought we had a clear understanding of his regime, and in hindsight we didn't have the foggiest notion of what was going on inside Iraq and what kind of country this was. Because of that, we were caught by surprise on so many occasions subsequently after his overthrow that we were always playing catch-up.

I feel like the country was let down by the Clinton administration, by the Bush administration. So much more could have been done. I had hoped that the US would decide we have to get smart about the Middle East. We have to learn more about this place. We have to have a better understanding about who we're dealing with over there. And yet what do we end up doing? We invade Afghanistan, that's understandable. We invade Iraq. And then we spend two or three trillion dollars there and get absolutely nothing out of it. Absolutely nothing. And the problems have not gone away. In fact, I think the problems are worse today than they were back then.

Chapter 2
How to Build an Insurgency

Timeline

9 May 2003 — Paul Bremer is appointed Presidential Envoy to Iraq by President Bush.

16 May 2003 — Paul Bremer issues Coalition Provisional Authority Order 1, beginning the process of 'de-Ba'athification' – the dismissal of all members of the Ba'ath party, who would also be banned from any future employment in Iraq's public sector.

23 May 2003 — Paul Bremer issues Coalition Provisional Authority Order 2, disbanding the Iraqi army and the country's entire security infrastructure.

15 June 2003 — US forces begin an operation to deliver humanitarian aid across Iraq while also finding and eliminating any resistance. Estimates of insurgent numbers in Iraq at this time vary from 40,000 to 200,000.

3 July 2003 — The Coalition Provisional Authority establishes an interim Iraqi Governing Council.

22 July 2003 — Saddam Hussein's sons Uday and Qusay are killed in Mosul.

7 August 2003	The first car bombing under the occupation is an attack on the Jordanian embassy in Baghdad.
19 August 2003	A suicide bomber attacks and demolishes the UN compound in Baghdad, killing 17 and injuring more than 100 people.
18 October 2003	The Al Jazeera TV station broadcasts a video message by Osama bin Laden, who calls on Muslims and Iraqis to deny support to US 'Crusaders', praising efforts at jihad, and predicting American economic ruin thanks to its invasion of Iraq.
27 October 2003	The 'Ramadan Offensive', a series of insurgent strikes against Coalition targets, begins with five near-simultaneous bomb attacks in Baghdad, killing 35 and wounding 244.
2 November 2003	Surface-to-air missiles are used against two US helicopters, killing 16 soldiers and wounding 20; it is the US forces' worst single loss to date.
27 November 2003	President Bush makes a Thanksgiving visit to Baghdad to boost troop morale.
13 December 2003	Saddam Hussein is captured in ad-Dawr near Tikrit.
28 January 2004	The head of the Iraq Survey Group confirms that no weapons of mass destruction have been found in Iraq.

2 March 2004   Coordinated car bomb and suicide attacks kill 178 Shia worshippers in Karbala and Baghdad.

8 March 2004   The Law of Administration for the State of Iraq for the Transitional Period, a temporary Iraqi constitution, is signed into law by the Iraqi Governing Council.

31 March 2004   Four Blackwater contractors are killed in Fallujah, their mutilated bodies hung from a bridge.

Introduction

By May 2003, just weeks after the invasion of Iraq, Saddam had been removed from power, and American troops were now crashing in his palaces, defacing his portraits and sliding down his ornate bannisters; but Saddam was not yet captured, and the situation in Iraq was chaotic.

For Waleed Nesyif and many other Iraqis like him, the most pressing need was for law and order to be restored, security established and basic essentials such as clean water and electricity provided. For many, it felt as if their needs were secondary to the commercial interests of the Americans and the British. They could not help but notice that while many buildings, including hospitals and museums, had been destroyed by fire or vandalised by looters in the chaos after the invasion, the one building the Americans had managed to protect completely was the headquarters of the Ministry of Oil. As the weeks turned into months and Iraqis still didn't see any improvements in the provision of essential amenities, any residual joy that they felt about the removal of Saddam was turning into anger and frustration. Some were even beginning to wish for his return.

How did the coalition lose the initiative that it had after the toppling of Saddam? Why did it fail to build on the fragile moment of hope that was tangible in those first few weeks after the invasion? The invasion of Iraq, as a military operation, had been successful. The mission now was to win the hearts and minds of the Iraqi people, a task that would prove to be far harder than anyone in the White House or Downing Street had imagined.

The year-long tour of Iraq of Colonel Nate Sassaman encapsulates, in microcosm, the story of how the battle of hearts and minds was lost. Through one man's experience, a picture of the next phase of the war emerges, as the mission to help reconstruct Iraq is replaced instead with fighting persistent pockets of armed resistance. Sassaman's actions, which were replicated by American and British soldiers across Iraq, fanned the flames of the resistance, growing it from its small Sunni beginnings into a horrifically violent, organised and well-funded insurgency, that would eventually engulf the entire country.

When four American contractors were lynched in Fallujah and their burnt bodies hung from a bridge over the Euphrates, crowds of Iraqis gathered around them in celebration. The images of the event that were beamed around the world sent a clear message: Iraq was out of control.

'Taste of Freedom'

Waleed Nesyif

Right after the war, you started seeing all these knock-off brands of restaurants. You know, it's not McDonalds its MaDonalds; it's not Burger King, it's Burger Queen. All of a sudden you had this massive surge of everything that is Western being served. The people flooded to all of these places because, you know, we can try these things now. Who cares if it is not McDonalds, it's MaDonalds? It has still got the golden arches, right? So there was this sense of positivity: some of the things we dreamt of are coming true. Maybe not in its true form, but still we are on the right path. Things are on the up – having the ability to have a burger. It's almost like a seal of approval. It's like, 'OK, first step done – this is your reward.' Burgers and fries. Taste of freedom, under the golden arches ...

Before the war, I started getting involved in media, because I knew that I could make money, fast. So I started making connections. They were paying me about fifty bucks a day for translation and guiding services and stuff like that. Fifty bucks a day – this is frigging awesome. Fifty bucks was my dad's salary for six months. I was making it in a day. Anyway, after the war I continued doing the same thing, because there were a few jobs that you can do in Iraq post-war, one of which was to work as a translator, and we kept filming on and off.

One of the jobs that I picked up was to go to the Convention Centre where I got to see a meeting where Jay Garner was delivering what the plan was. In my understanding, his original plan was that he is prepping the general council of Iraq to assume power; he wanted to give the power back to the government and council. They were part of the Iraqi opposition that helped consult on the efforts of the war. Ahmad Chalabi was one of the biggest architects that helped to draw the American plan as to how to attack Iraq and what to happen after. The governing council was set up, according to the Americans, to reflect the Iraqi ethnic distribution. Now Iraq is made out of 56 to 58 per cent Shia, and then you have Sunnis, Christians, Kurds, Yezidis and so forth. There are many other ethnicities that are marginalised, and they're very small. The government council was made up of 23 members, and they split them, the majority being Shia, some Sunnis, some Christian and Kurds, and then I think there was one Yezidi guy. But the majority of these individuals, if not all of them, were outside of Iraq. Jay Garner's idea was to basically pass the baton to these guys. At least this would have truly helped Iraqis focus their attention: 'Now the power is with these guys, so let's see what they're about, what they can do for real.' All we knew was that they were part of Saddam's opposition and that kind of automatically put them in a good light. But then Jay Garner's plan was not accepted by the American administration in the way that he wanted to stipulate. Soon after, he was just gone. And then we had Paul Bremer III.

A former diplomat in the US Foreign Service and chair of the National Commission on Terrorism, **Paul Bremer** *was by now chairman and CEO of Marsh Crisis Consulting, a risk and insurance services firm.*

About two weeks after the fall of Saddam, I got a call, essentially out of the blue, from Secretary Rumsfeld's office, asking me to come to a meeting with him the next day. I went in Thursday afternoon, and he basically said, 'We're trying to decide how the civilian side of the project is gonna go.' At that time, I don't think we had called it an occupation, I don't think the UN had passed the term. He asked me was I interested; I said, 'Yeah, it sounds like a challenge, to put it mildly.' And then his office called back, that evening at 7, 7.30pm, and said, 'You're going to see the president tomorrow at 10.' It moved rather quickly.

The first thing President Bush said to me was, 'Why would you want this impossible job?' Which showed that he had a better sense of how hard it was going to be than I did. And I basically said, 'Because I think it's the right thing to do, and I support what you've done.' We didn't talk very much about the job. As I recall the conversation, it wasn't very long – 10, 15 minutes maybe. One of the reasons I agreed to accept the job was because Bush described for me a vision for Iraq that resonated with me, which was to help them recover their country. To help them build a country where they had representative government and where they got control over their lives again.

Well, then I went through the intense – I guess it was two weeks – the classic drinking out of a fire hose, getting briefed by people at the Pentagon and Treasury and the CIA staff and State Department, all the people coming 18 hours a day, briefing, putting papers down, reading to me. One of the discussions in those days which was finally resolved was what is the job called and what are the authorities of the job. The UN passed a resolution formally designating the coalition as the occupying power; the occupying power has, it turns out, full legislative, executive, judicial authority over territory which it is occupying, which meant that I had those authorities, and this was made clear to me in a memo from Rumsfeld.

At the time we're talking about, there was a plan, but it was already beginning to be of questionable value. Why? Because the plan which had been developed by the State Department of 2002 called the 'Future of Iraq' study, a 2,000-page study, was actually not a plan; it was just a series of papers. And then the Pentagon had done some post-war planning, which involved setting up an organisation for humanitarian assistance. That plan had been based on assumptions that the situation after the 2003 war would be roughly the same as it had been after the Gulf War, meaning large-scale reconstruction of the oil facilities, huge refugee movements, humanitarian assistance. It gradually became apparent, certainly by the time I was in Iraq and maybe a bit before that, because those assumptions turned out to be wrong, that the plan was not gonna be adequate.

One of the briefings I had from the Joint Chiefs of Staff talked about their plan for the post-conflict, or phase 4 of the war. At that time, we had 180,000 American troops on the ground, and there were 20,000 British, so 200,000. As part of my briefings, an old foreign service colleague of mine brought me a study that showed – having looked at occupations from Germany, Japan, all the way through Haiti and Bosnia – that for a country of 27 million, which was Iraq's population, we would need 480,000 troops. So we had only half the number, 200,000, and the Joint Chiefs showed me how they were gonna draw down our 180,000 to 30,000 by 1 September 2003. I was ... shocked, flabbergasted. I didn't know whether the study was right, but it was an order of magnitude difference. They said you need 480,000, and we're talking about going down to 30,000 in four months. The study contrasted with what I was hearing from the American military in such a dramatic way that I thought I'd make it available to Secretary Rumsfeld, so I sent him the executive summary and highlighted the numbers, and I said something seems wrong to me. I did not hear back from him.

If we were gonna be the government of Iraq, which under occupying power laws we were, the first job of any government is security, and this just didn't look right. The president had invited me to a one-on-one lunch at the White House, and I told him about the study. I said, 'It looks to me as if we're on a track where we're not gonna have even close to the number of people we need for security.' He said, 'I understand. I want to reassure you, Colin Powell is now trying to recruit more countries,' and that was the end of that particular part of the conversation with the president. His answer was at least satisfactory to me: Colin Powell is trying to recruit more countries. That was a logical answer.

I also brought up the timescale, because I figured this was going to take a long time. We're talking a country which is, really, a young country – it's less than 100 years old as Iraq, old culture but a young country – and we've got to try and turn it into something very different. And it's going to take time. I said to him, 'This is gonna be more like a marathon than a 100-yard dash; this is gonna take years,' and he said, 'We'll take whatever time it's gonna take.' Bush repeated this point directly in a full National Security Council meeting three days later, just before I left for Iraq, and Secretary Rumsfeld had circulated papers about how we had to take our time to get this right, we mustn't rush elections; that would take time.

It's been written by some of the participants that before the war there was a disagreement between two executive bodies about what would happen after the war. One group, which is characterised as the Pentagon, wanted to get in and out quickly. The State Department and the CIA allegedly said, 'No, this is gonna take more time than you think.' Therefore the pre-war planning was bifurcated also, with some of the people saying this is gonna take longer. I certainly felt that the military part was on a track that didn't make any sense.

Just before I left for Iraq, the general who had been running the reconstruction operation, Jay Garner, announced he was going to appoint an interim Iraqi administration in a week, which was completely inconsistent with the guidance I was hearing from President Bush, the Vice President, the Secretary of Defense and the Secretary of State. And this struck me as an indication that things were not being coordinated smoothly.

Under American law, the presidential ambassador has authority over all civilians and no authority over any military who are serving under a commander. In other words, my authority over Americans in Iraq was civilians, no military serving in the military forces. I had a letter from the Secretary of Defense after we were identified as the occupying powers that I had full legislative executive and judicial authority of Iraq. The Iraqis understood that. It became a sort of a game where they said, 'You'll threaten to veto something we do,' and I said, 'I don't ever intend to use my veto.' And I never did use my veto. The laws that got passed were passed with the Iraqis; I had to sign them to make them law, but I never once vetoed anything they proposed.

The decision was made that the new organisation would be called the Coalition Provisional Authority – all words important.

Coalition because it wasn't just America. It was provisional, our job was to put ourselves out of a job. And authority basically meant we had the legislative, executive and judicial authority. And I was the administrator. The most important contingents were the Americans and the British. Both of those groups had very senior Arabic-speaking professional diplomats. My colleague at the beginning was Sir John Sawyers, who at that time was serving as the British Ambassador to Egypt – a fluent Arabic speaker. He was replaced by Sir Jeremy Greenstock and David Richmond. So, we had a group of very senior people. We had a lot of younger but also capable people, and then you had a lot of younger people who just volunteered and came.

Waleed Nesyif
After the invasion, one of the things that I used to do was basically drive around the city, you know I would hire a cab, take a journalist with me, and we would just drive around, see what the city looks like. And it was such an odd feeling because not two months ago I was driving in the exact same street and it was a completely different city, shops are open, people are walking, buying, selling, eating, drinking and dancing. And now it's a ghost town. That is destroyed either by bombs, or looting, or just abandoned. I drive by the Iraqi National Library and you look at it and it's burnt. Destroyed. The Iraqi Central Bank, gates are open and it's burnt. The telecommunications tower, burnt. I said, 'OK, these are the major areas. Let's start getting into like side streets and some residential areas.' And it was the same. People were just hiding, not knowing what is going to come next.

Each neighbourhood formed a taskforce where the boys or the men in the neighbourhood made blockades and took turns in guarding the neighbourhood. Everybody had a gun. There was an altercation in my neighbourhood between some American soldiers and some of these guys who were guarding, and the guy is telling them, 'When there are thieves in the neighbourhood I need to stand over there,' but he is speaking to them in Iraqi, and the Americans didn't have a translator. I was trying to explain to this American guy, and he was like, 'My orders are to disarm.' So I asked him, 'Are *you* going to protect us? Are you going to stand here and protect us?' And that is when he pushed me with the barrel of his gun, and he was like, 'Get back home before you get hurt.'

There were lots of roadblocks. And then something else started happening. We started noticing many, many traffic jams in the street. We didn't know what was going on in the beginning, and it turns out that the Americans had blocked any road that leads into any strategic place where they are located right now. This includes the Iraqi Republican palace, which is near one of the major bridges in Baghdad that basically connects east to west. Without it, you have to drive all the way around the city and basically use a different bridge, which created a huge congestion in traffic. It was a different city. It was one of those things where you close your eyes and you open them and you are in a different place. Except you know it definitely wasn't an Alice in Wonderland kind of experience. Probably it was in her nightmare land.

The immense poverty that people suffered during the sanctions had changed morality at large. Things that were prohibited became OK. One of the examples of that is looting. Sadr City was one of the places where they were literally in squalor: no food, no jobs, didn't even have prospects during Saddam's time, let alone now with the country being destroyed. And all of a sudden you have no law and order. The Iraqi Central Bank is open, all of Saddam's palaces are open, everything government-wise is open, and no supervision. So, I ask myself, if my son is starving, nobody is helping me out or giving me a helping hand, what would I do? I would loot. I was one of the fortunate ones who had a skill that translated into money and was able to work almost immediately after the war. I was making enough to fend for my family, but I was one in a million. Everyone else didn't have money to begin with.

And now you don't know what is going to happen and somebody just opened the bank for you. And by somebody I mean the

American army because they literally opened the bank doors, and Saddam's palaces. So you started seeing people running away with sofas, chandeliers, beds. They even frigging looted the insane asylum, man. Obviously, one of the first targets for those professionals that really wanted to smuggle artefacts from Iraq, they went to the Iraqi museum, and that is basically where all the statues and everything started getting smuggled. Rare books that are found in the general library in Baghdad – some skilled people went there and picked up all of the good ones.

And this is the insane part: they would loot, take everything, and then they would burn the place afterwards. All of a sudden you started seeing fires here, fire there, all of that, but there are no bombs. What's going on? All the ministries with the exception of the Ministry of Oil. That was the one ministry that immediately got protection by the American army. Everything else got looted and burnt. I walked into the National Theatre – it was all just caved in. I found a bunch of artists that had graduated from the art institute trying to salvage some of the artwork that they worked on, trying to find any of the film cameras still working, some film stock.

Probably one of the most frustrating things was that it felt calculated, but you can't put your finger on *who* is doing that. You are seeing regular Iraqi people looting, but it felt organised. It felt like it was an unspoken thing. Then I actually started noticing that most of those places the American army would go, open it up, 'liberate' it, and then the people would go in. The American army is the most formal authority you have in the country right now, and they are opening the door to you. Walking away after the door is open. Standing idly by.

There are no words that can describe the damage, the destruction that happened to my country. There is one guy that I interviewed who said something so profound: 'We are selfish, and we think all of this belongs to us Iraqis. But this is not only the heritage of Iraq, this is the heritage of the world.' I think that is the saddest thing, that everybody stood by, yours truly included. Because I didn't want to get killed.

All of our homes are made out of bricks, and bricks retain heat. The war ended in April, right? So that's the beginning of the summer. Our spring starts at 35°C. That's spring. As you head towards May, June, July, temperatures start rising, where they settle around 50, 52°C. Now there is no water, there is no electricity, and you're supposed to somehow survive. When you enter a house, the house is hotter than the outside because the whole day the sun has been beating on this house. Literally heating it up like an oven. And you go inside and you're supposed to somehow sleep, function as a human being.

One positive thing that came out of the looting, I would say – some people sold government generators. They started selling electricity lines to people. If you're lucky and fortunate enough to have some money, like my family, you would buy ten in pairs or something like that to turn on an air cooler, a fridge and a TV. But for the majority of people, there were no jobs, the army got disbanded, you can't do anything. There was no work. So picture yourself in this impossible situation. You have just got out of a war, you don't know what's going to happen next, the elements and invading force and your current so-called government are all pretty much working and conspiring against you as a citizen in that country, and you're meant to continue functioning as a sane human being. Not go crazy, not be radicalised, not, not, not, not. My question is if you were put through 10 per cent of that hardship, what would you do?

There was a genuine lack of services and amenities in Iraq. The majority of the infrastructure got destroyed during the war, and even before the war it was being maintained and held by a thread by the government. Nevertheless, it was functioning during Saddam's time. We had electricity. We had scheduled blackouts, but at least you can prep yourself for it. Telephones were working. But then they destroyed everything.

And Iraqis were under this impression: 'OK, this is the greatest power in the world. They're going to come and rebuild everything in, like, months. Pactal, KBR, Halliburton ... all of these companies are coming with the Americans to actually do reconstruction.' We started hearing about all of the deals that were made even before the war started, and I was, like, great. They've already allocated the oil; this much is going to go for construction, this much is going to go to them, this much is going to go to Iraq. So we were hopeful that things are going to come about.

Month one passed. There's still no electricity. There's still no water. No telephones. Roads are pretty much blocked. Anything that leads into an American camp, Saddam palace or anything like that now is blocked and blocked and blocked and blocked. And you started getting the murmur of people: 'So why aren't they fixing the electricity? Why isn't there water still? What's going on?' See, the problem is Iraqis had a benchmark, it's very important for us to remember that. The benchmark was this: when America came in 1991 and did the exact same thing to Iraq, destroying the infrastructure, Saddam had foresight, even under sanctions – he rebuilt everything. And when I say everything, I mean *everything*, within six months. Roads were reconstructed. Bridges were rehabilitated. He built a brand new bridge to ease the inflation of the traffic. He dug two new rivers. Everything was functioning within six months. So Iraqis had this thought: 'OK, Saddam, under sanctions, managed to do all of this within six months. You mean to tell me that America, the greatest country in the world, is unable to bring one of those massive generators and give us electricity so that we can alleviate ourselves from the heat of the summer?'

People started taking matters into their own hands. In terms of sanitation, people at the beginning were paying attention: 'Let's gather all of the garbage, put it in one location. Once things start getting more controlled and then we have those service come about, at least it will be located in one place.' But that was short-lived. All of a sudden, Baghdad became a city of garbage. Just garbage everywhere. *Everywhere*. Sometimes you can't tell the stench of a rotten body from a two-week-old food bag. Even during Saddam's time, Baghdad was clean. There was sanitation, there was cleaning. And, of course, a sense of apathy sets in amongst the people themselves. If you had the attitude of throwing a can in a garbage bin before, now you're seeing somebody getting literally shot in front of you and it's like, 'OK, so I'll drop the can on the ground.'

So the jig was up, and people started understanding slowly that this was all purposeful. It is not a delay caused by logistical problems. It is actually something that was planned in a sense.

Paul Bremer

We landed at Baghdad airport May 10th or 11th. As we were approaching, you could see from 10,000 feet fires burning all over the city, buildings on fire. We got on the ground and got hit by this blaze of heat. The temperature was well over 100°F, it was like a blast furnace. What struck me most of all was the chaos in Baghdad and the fact there was no law and order. As we drove into town, there were no policemen to be seen and you could see the burning buildings on the right and on the left. And on the sidewalks outside the buildings you would see little knots of Iraqi men, and they were looting. They were going into the buildings and had little wheelbarrows with television sets and desks and going up and down the street at will, with nobody stopping them. The coalition had 40,000 troops in Baghdad at that time, but they were obviously not stopping the looting. So this was a quick introduction to the security problems, one being not enough troops, the second one being very restrictive rules of engagement, as the military call them. They were not under orders to stop the looting.

My view was that if we were serious as the government, and if the government's job was security, we needed to do everything we could, including if necessary ordering our military to shoot the looters. I was reminded by one of my colleagues that we did this in Haiti. We sent Marines into Haiti and there was a lot of looting going on. They shot four or five looters, not a huge number, and the looting stopped. The message I thought we were conveying by not dealing with this security problem was we – the government – were not serious about the job we had. We were saying to our friends, 'Don't count on us,' and we were saying to the people who eventually became our enemies, 'We're not prepared to do what is necessary to take care of you guys.' I made the mistake of mentioning this idea of shooting looters in my staff meeting, and of course read about it on the front page of the *New York Times* the next day. Which was the end of that discussion. I don't frivolously order people to be killed, and I wasn't even saying they had to be killed. I was just saying shoot them in the knees if you have to, make it clear we are prepared to carry out our job as the government.

The looting had, I think, three effects. One was it suggested we weren't ready to perform the security obligations of the government. Secondly, it had an extremely high cost: we didn't know immediately, but by August the team had calculated the cost was 12 billion dollars. Just to put that into perspective, we estimated the GDP of Iraq at 20 billion, so the cost of the looting was 60 per cent of GDP. The third problem was most of the looting was directed at government ministries – Ministry of Finance, Ministry of Transportation, Ministry of the Interior – and those buildings were damaged. The Ministry of Finance was so damaged that for the entire 14 months we were there they could never bring the full staff in at the same time; they had to work in shifts because there was so much damage to the buildings.

Nate Sassaman *was a Combined Arms Infantry Battalion Commander, who took command of the 4th Infantry Division's 1–8 battalion in June 2003.*

Saddam's birthday is the same day as mine, 28 April, so I share that in common with him. And everybody's excited, you know, they're shooting their weapons, because he wasn't in power any more and had started to go into hiding. There was … the word's not *hope*. You just felt really good for the Shias, because for 35 years they were not able to openly express their religious freedom. For them it was sheer joy. I can't tell you how many of those folks told us, 'For the first time in 35 years, we're able to celebrate this holiday and this religious event and this religious event.' It wasn't hope, because the Sunnis were the losers, and the Shias were the winners now, and the Kurds were just saying: 'Please, can you just leave us alone and let us live our life up here in northern Iraq.'

In the early days, there was this feeling that we're doing what's right here, we're liberating the Shias; on the other side, you had this sense that the Sunnis were losing out. It probably took me about 30 days before I knew – this is really gonna take a long time. Because these people hate these people, and these people hate these people, and this has been going on for centuries. And now this Western country is going to drop in 100,000 guys and we're going to fix this? I felt like I was Tom Cruise and had just been dropped into a movie. Except that people were dying for real.

In May I was still en route. So I landed, like, the 31st [of May] to the 1st of June, but as soon as I got there ... you know, if the war's over, why am I going? Why aren't we pulling folks back? I was rolling north, trying to find my unit, and these Aussies were like, 'G'day mate, you know the war's over? Good luck cleaning it up!' Bush wants to say, 'Success! It's done, we're good.' And he says that, what, because Saddam's in hiding? Labor Day weekend, I'm on the tarmac with [US journalist] Dan Rather, and he's going, 'Hey, the war's over.' And I'm going, 'I wish someone would let me know because we're getting ready to go capture Saddam Hussein. I'm ready, I'll come home.' Because we haven't captured him; we don't get him till December. And from May until that time, we do a lot of operations. The vast majority are focused on either those top 55 that were the card deck, or Saddam. And you can't start reconstruction until after that's taken care of. But we make some calamitous mistakes that set us up for a long, protracted occupation. Every day we're there, we are not the liberators that the Shias see us as when we come in and we become more and more the occupiers.

Maybe there was a lull where we'd gotten forces into the country, which I still think was what all the planning was about – how are we going to get everybody in. But then, once everybody's in, it was like, 'Now what?' There was about a 100-day window there where we could have reconstructed the country, if we could have had some kind of Marshall Plan coming in, if we were serious about rebuilding Iraq.

I got a bunch of guys who want to be home by August. We're not going anywhere. For a long time. This is way more complex and we're here now, and this is going to take a long time. All my unit could talk about was being home by August. I took over in mid-June. So in my initial talks with the soldiers, I said, 'Forget the August thing. Just purge it from your brain. We're going to be here until they tell us to go home. But I'm going to tell you, it's not August. And it's probably not Christmas. So we need to lock in.' No, the guys wanted to go home in August. That's what they'd been told. They said this thing was going to be an easy, quick win, and we're out. And I couldn't have guys thinking like that when we were still conducting combat operations.

Where I took command was Samarra East Airbase, right there in the heart of the Sunni triangle, on 17 June 2003, and I remember General Odierno telling me at my brief, 'You're going across the Tigris river, you're going to be on the other side, and you're going to be in the fight in three weeks.' I changed just about everything in those three weeks. We went right back to the basics of cleaning and firing and re-zeroing our weapons. I was really adamant at trying to give the guys some downtime and a break, because everyone looked exhausted. Everyone got one litre of water a day, and it was hot, it was hot, it was hot. You know, it's 100, 110, 120°F there, and you have one litre. I felt guilty drinking my one litre of water as the commander. I knew that these guys, we were asking them to do a lot, and all we had was one litre, so I was really just trying to get ice and get some basic things organised, and then I was focused on morale.

My area of operation was focused around Balad proper and then the 800 square kilometres around that up to Ishaqi and out to Abu Hishma. I think each area has different demographics, and it's probably a different kind of a fight. I just know that we were able to rapidly understand our environment, understand our strengths and weaknesses. The first 100 days we took it in the teeth a little bit from the enemy, until we could figure out how to, instead of react, start being way more proactive on both fronts.

Paul Bremer
The Ba'ath Party came into being in the Second World War in both Iraq and Syria, initially as a nationalist opposition to Western imperialism. It took on the tone as it developed of being inspired by the Nazi party, intentionally. For example, I visited the Iraqi Ministry of Foreign Affairs the first week I was there and over in the corner of the library the minister pointed to a stack of 80 copies of *Mein Kampf* in Arabic. It was required reading for Iraqi diplomats and also for the Mukhabarat, the intelligence services. I tell the story because it is very hard to conceive what it was like to live under this kind of regime, where you intentionally say, 'Our model is the Nazis.' That was the Ba'ath Party – it was Saddam's instrument of control over the Iraqi people. Like the SS in Germany, the Mukhabarat hired children to spy on their parents. There were neighbourhood watches for both the party and the Mukhabarat.

Torture was legal under Saddam's rule. It was an almost unspeakably brutal regime, and the Ba'ath Party was central to it. So, before the war, the State Department said there can be no place for the Ba'ath Party in post-Saddam Iraq. Coalition Provisional Authority Order 1 was drafted in Washington and agreed to by the US government before I was even called back into service. I was presented with a draft of it the day before I left for Iraq.

The Ba'ath Party was essentially an instrument of dictatorship because it had only 2 million members of a country of 27 million – so less than 10 per cent of the Iraqi people were even members. The de-Ba'athification idea came from the de-Nazification that took place after the Second World War, but it differed from the de-Nazification in two important ways. First, the decree said only that the top 1 per cent of the party would be affected by the decree; in Germany it was much deeper. And the decree said of those 1 per cent, they can continue to work, they can set up a company, they can become farmers, they can set up a newspaper . . .

They're free to do all that, but they can no longer be members of the government.

Furthermore, the decree said in its last paragraph that, as the administrator, I had the authority to not let it take effect on people if I was advised that they were essential. It said I had full discretion to issue waivers, and I issued scores and scores of waivers. A ministry would come to me and say, 'Listen, this guy was in the Ba'ath Party but he is the only one who knows what the pay roll is at the Ministry of Finance; we've got to have him at least for the time being while we run the ministry.' Or someone would say, 'He is the key engineer in the South Oil Company – we've got to keep him.' So, I approved all of those. So it was a very narrowly drawn decree. The CIA told me that they thought that it would affect 20,000 people, so you're talking about less than 1 per cent of the Iraqi peoples.

Jay Garner's team were concerned that this decree would collapse the capacity of some of the ministries. In fact, one of the prevailing myths about de-Ba'athification is that it did that, that it collapsed the government, which is nonsense. I can understand – these were people in Garner's team that had been working like hell for the last 60 to 70 days in very difficult conditions; they had formed some kind of relationships with whoever was left at the ministry. I understood that, but it was also important for me to emphasise to them that this was President Bush's policy, this was the clear stated policy of the United States government before, during and after the war, and I also agreed with it. The more I learnt about the Ba'ath Party, the more I agreed that there was no place for these Ba'athists in post-Saddam Iraq, and we just had to get on with it. And we did.

When I signed the decree, I said publicly that it was our intention to turn over the implementation to the Iraqis because our intelligence was so poor that there was no way we could tell if Abdul became a Ba'ath Party guy because he believed in the Ba'ath Party ideology or because it was the only way he was going to get a job as a teacher. The initial implementation, we were doing in early November. Six months later, I turned it over to the interim Iraqi government that we had appointed. They in turn turned it over to strongly anti-Ba'athist politicians. So politicians wound up implementing what was a narrowly drawn decree much more broadly than we had intended. It took another four months after that for me to get that mistake corrected. What I should have done was found a panel of Iraqi judges. The Iraqis had a long history of serious legal work introduced by the British in the 1920s. They had good lawyers and good judges, and I could have found – and should have found – a panel of five judges and said, 'OK, you Iraqis can figure out whether Abdul should really lose his job or not – we can't do it.'

De-Ba'athification, which has been criticised a lot, turned out to be the single most popular thing the CPA did the entire time we were there. We began opinion polling in September: de-Ba'athification never polled less than 95 per cent approval, which means that there were plenty of Sunnis approving it and plenty of Ba'athists approving it. It did go off the rails when I turned it over to the Iraqi politicians. They then started laying off teachers – 11,000 teachers were laid off, and the minister of education came to me and said, 'I can't run the educational system if they are just going to throw these guys out of work.' So we had to put them back to work. It was bumpy, but it was the right thing.

If we talk about disbanding the army, again it's important to take the context. What was this army? Saddam's army was the military and security arm of his dictatorship. This was an army which in the 1980s had run a genocide campaign against the Kurds, killed nobody knows how many hundreds of thousands of them. They also put down the Shia uprising after the Kuwait war and again killed hundreds of thousands of Shia. I went to visit a town about 40 miles south of Baghdad where our marines had just uncovered the first of the mass graves from the Shia uprising. I went to a field that was twice the size of a football pitch where there were, by our counts, something like 30,000 bodies. They had been effectively underground for 12 or 13 years, so there was almost nothing left but bones and some scraps of clothing. During the next 14 months, we found over 100 mass graves. So when you come to the question of what to do with Saddam's army, you can't ignore this comprehensive programme of killing his own civilians over a period of 20 years. This was a monster. The lowest estimate I ever have seen was that during those 20 years he killed 75,000 Iraqis, and of course many, many more died in the Iran-Iraq war.

About this same time, an Iraqi said, 'I have to tell you, Mr Ambassador, for my wife and me it was a good day when the Mukhabarat took our neighbour's daughter and not ours.' That explained another related thing – the fact that we hadn't captured Saddam Hussein bore on the minds of every single Iraqi, because they said, 'He will come back.' He had come back before, he would come back again.

When I announced the decree, I also said that we respected the Iraqi army in history had played an important role in its country, and we said we were going to build a new army and enlisted men up to the grade of colonel were welcome to apply for a position in this new army. Now I made a mistake of not announcing at the same time that we were going to pay pensions to all of the NCOs and officers. There's a reason why that happened, but it still was a mistake. The reason was because we had no order of battle of the Iraqi army till the middle of June – the grade of the officers, and how many people were there. Only with that could we know how much we would have to pay them and how much it was going to cost us. We had no revenue at this time with the Iraqi government, and I had already decided that our top priority was to pay the two or three million Iraqis who were civil servants who hadn't been paid for three months. The monthly payroll was $250 million, so we're talking big numbers. I said to my colleagues, 'Look, I really need to know what that big total number is down there if we're going to pay these handsome pensions.' We probably should have found some words to fudge the number to just say that we plan to pay pensions. The immediate reaction to the announcement was we started having demonstrations by former army officers, or people who were said to be former army officers or NCOs. As soon as I announced the pensions, all of the disturbances stopped and we immediately put the first battalion into training.

I've heard the argument that disbanding the army created the resistance or whatever – I don't buy it. I don't exclude that some of these demobilised soldiers went and resorted to violence. It is true that unemployment in May was 50 per cent, but a year later unemployment was down to 10 per cent, so the argument that there were no jobs simply doesn't hold. Furthermore, these people were getting a pension calculated to be two to three times what they would have gotten under Saddam, so they conceivably had some capital if they wanted to buy a farm, if they wanted to set up a retail outfit to sell television sets and buy goods which were moving off the shelves so fast you couldn't keep them full. They had an opportunity to participate in the Iraqi economy and if they didn't choose it and chose to be in the opposition, well, that was their choice but it was largely because they didn't accept that there would be a democratically elected government some time in Iraq. They did not accept that vision.

Waleed Nesyif
Society got split. You have the extreme poor. You have the fortunate people like myself, who was able to do one of the very few jobs that were available. Right after the war, in my calculation, outside of owning your own business there were four jobs that you could do. Four. One is to do what I do, which required language skills and having a good network of people – working as a translator for the Americans. Two, working for any of the multinational divisions. But both of those put you in a very precarious situation: (a) they don't pay that well; (b) this is gonna paint you into a target for any of the sleeper cells of the Ba'athists or any other groups that will be going against the Americans, because you'll be considered a traitor. Three, you work as a taxi driver, and that in itself is, again, a very dangerous job. Or, four, you join either the Iraqi army or the Iraqi police. That's it, for jobs.

And then Paul Bremer disbanded the army. Now you have a million-plus individuals – who are trained, skilled, they have been in the army for a long time – jobless, with no prospects, no salary whatsoever, and they are in the city. And weapons were readily available. Everywhere. And our borders were open. I used to go to the Jordanian border and you could just drive through. I used to go to the Kuwaiti borders, and you could just drive through. No security, zero. People got killed, you know. The people did whatever they could in order to protect their neighbourhoods. It became kind of like the Wild, Wild West.

The whole government was disbanded. No police any more, no fire fighters, no army whatsoever. As ordered by the Americans. Because the Iraqi army was all Ba'athist, and how can we allow people like that to govern themselves, right? And there was this ridiculous notion ... I remember talking to one American, a captain or something like that. He was, like, 'We can't trust the Iraq army, they're all Ba'athist.' And I was like, 'I was a Ba'athist.' And I was. Everyone in Iraq was Ba'athist. You cannot *not* be a Ba'athist. It's basically saying no to Saddam, and who dares to say no to Saddam? No one. Those who do, they pay the price. So for the Americans to come and do this whole sham of the de-Ba'athification ... Months and months and months after, they realised, 'Uh-oh. We really screwed up over here.' And that's when the resistance started actually picking up.

When that CPA order came, there were hundreds of thousands of people depending on the army – this was their salary, this was their job, this was the only thing that they knew. The army was disbanded, and you have people like my father, who spent all of his life serving in the army. And anyone that had served in the army, they understand: an army person is a completely different type of person. You can't re-engage them in society just like that, you know, especially having seen as much action as Iraqi soldiers. All they did is just war. Paul Bremer and the CPA disbanded the army – now all of a sudden you have hundreds of thousands of individuals with actual skills, and abundance of weapons, abundance. Lack of security, absolutely no amenities, no sign that America is even interested in restoring any of these amenities that people needed in order just to get by. No work, no salaries, and people are meant to survive. So what do you expect? Once that happened, we kind of knew that resistance was going to start almost immediately.

The Village People Operation

Sally Mars

At any moment someone could be walking in the street, everything looks normal, seeing a car passing by or parked – a car passing by someone then exploding. It was very important to be cautious. A car kills a larger number of people because its blast will be bigger, its shrapnel has a longer range. It can make the cars nearby explode as well, so it will be a catastrophe, an entire street would burn. A whole street would be destroyed. So everyone was very afraid of the car bomb situation.

Fear was everywhere. There are mothers who lost their children. Families lost their fathers, who'd be the family's only breadwinner. It was scary, being in a situation where someone can lose a brother, a father, because they're not allied with a certain sect, or go out to get something for the house and doesn't return, or a student going to college and gets killed on the way for no reason. There were people carrying guns with silencers, and just kill at random – just like that. Young people, seniors, or children – didn't matter.

Nate Sassaman

I'm in Iraq for maybe a week or two when I roll into Al Duloiya, which is this peninsula part right off the Tigris river. It was just lined with unemployed young men. Lined. And there was no love lost. I mean, we were in a Sunni deal, man. I'm trying to follow all my training, I'm setting up my retrans – which is a communication section – so we can have clear communications across a large space. And I put the young lieutenant and his section on the top of the police station, thinking that, you know, we're with the police on this, trying to restore order and stability and security operations.

Frank, the lieutenant, calls me: 'Sir, I'm getting kinda nervous here, there are like hundreds of guys that are surrounding the police station right now ...' And it's 9 or 10 o'clock at night, it's dark. And I just made the call: 'Frank, I'm coming down, we're pulling you out.' And I did. We rolled in, man, and it's pitch black, it's dark, and there's a bunch of guys. And we're not even across the Tigris river. And I go, 'This is hostile, and it's just a matter of time before it's going to get worse.' There's a lot of young, bearded robed folks that were not happy. No, they hated us, man. 'The infidels are in our country, and we got to get them the hell out.'

I never thought the war was won, bro. I just had all these conflicting emotions when I saw those guys on the side of the street. One was, we need to get ready for the fight of our lives. Two, this is pretty sad, because we promised these folks that if they don't fight us we're going to take care of them, and it's getting pretty clear we're not. Because I don't even know what I'm supposed to do with 'em ... We'd promised them, I think, a lot. I think we over-promised and under-delivered big time, on the reconstruction piece. Everything is moving way too fast in March, April, May, June of 03, and it's setting the seeds for when the fight starts, which is right around July 4th. The 100-day window is gone. I mean, we're using most of that just to get our forces into the country. We asked them to not fight us, so other than the initial actions around Baghdad they're not fighting us now. But we're not reconstructing anything and they've lost their jobs and there's no money coming in, to support themselves and their families.

It was soon after the disbanding of the Iraqi army, which I think had about two million soldiers in it. This is a large force. Saddam paid and fed a huge middle bureaucracy to kinda keep the country to a certain level of violence, and those two million men were part of that. We had secured the weapons, we had 'em. But the order was to continue advancing, and once we left those, we didn't have enough forces because Rumsfeld didn't follow General Shinseki's recommendations of 500,000 or 600,000 – it's going to take a lot of guys if we're going to do this right. Rumsfeld wants the sexy solution, you know, and it doesn't work. So now the weapons are all over the place. You couldn't throw a dead cat in Iraq without finding a weapon in a house.

Um Qusay

Someone went and told them that in our house we have weapons that are not normal. So they came to us at night. To be honest, they destroyed my house, and until now I'm waiting for them to compensate me. They broke all my things, they destroyed the house, they got me scared. They made us go outside. On that night I was so hurt, I can't describe it.

We had one gun. It was old and rusty. And it only had one bullet in it. So we told them we just have one and it only has one bullet and you can take it if you want. After they broke all the things and messed up the whole house, they saw that there was one gun. It hadn't been used in about ten years. And it had one bullet. And after they destroyed our life, they said, 'I'm sorry.' You're sorry after you destroyed my house? What will it do? What is the use of 'I'm sorry' after it destroyed my life?

If I'm honest, if I had had a gun, or a bomb, I would have killed them all. No one could stand by silently watching someone destroy their home, especially if they were poor, and they have nothing to their name. To watch someone come in and destroy their home, for no reason, it's not a small thing to go through. I didn't eat or drink for three days, all I could do was cry. I was angry. But we didn't have any weapons. They had tanks. So we had to supress the pain and the bitterness. By the strength and the will of God, all we could do at the time was watch. If I had had a weapon, I would have killed them all. Put yourself in my shoes: I just come and take over your house, how would you feel? I had nothing against them. I had never hurt them. I had never treated them in a horrible manner. I didn't even know them. They came and attacked my house out of nowhere. They threw the food on the floor, the rice, the tea. They destroyed all our belongings, ransacked the place, with such hatred! The children were terrified. It wasn't a small thing to go through.

We internalised all of this pain. We suppressed it. There was nothing we could do. They came, they wrecked the place, and then they left. They didn't find a single thing.

Nate Sassaman
So there's weapons everywhere. And then you overlay that with we're going to target two million folks who have been getting a pay cheque from the government for their profession, for their career and they're going to basically become unemployed. Fighters, killers, man. And they're from a long lineage of warriors who have fought for centuries to protect their homeland there. Dude, that country's not 200 years old. I mean, these tribes have been around for a long time. And they're not older generation people, they're in their 20s; these are the most physically able men in Iraq. So now we have plentiful weapons all over the place and we've got unemployed men who don't have a working wage any more to provide for their families. It's a recipe for disaster.

That's why the whole rush thing, it bothers me a little, why we couldn't have taken some more time. OK, this Saddam guy's a bad guy, there's a large majority in Iraq who would prefer not to have Saddam as their leader, so let's work with the military and work with some of these agencies to find this guy, get him out of power and set up the opportunity for you guys. I just think a lot more good might have come out of this if we'd come alongside them and been able to work together on this deal. Because we said we're gonna disband and we're going to take care of you, and it only took 100 days to see that nobody was coming in, there was no Marshall Plan. And that goes to the second critical mistake – de-Ba'athification. Because that's brain dead.

They disbanded the army and then they did this whole de-Ba'athification. Basically, if you're an Iraqi, now you're being told that you cannot work in your profession because you have a Ba'athist card. Brain dead. Not only does the whole country come to a standstill for a week or two, because the teachers can't teach, the hospitals are shutting down ... I mean, we're not letting anybody do their job because they have a Ba'athist card, and then we have to backtrack and there's different levels, but the message it sent was: I don't think the aid's ever going to come, I don't think there's a plan. Who's going to reconstruct the country? Me and my soldiers, are we going to? We're going to be the guys to restore power and teach the kids and set up the police stations? We're not staying there for the rest of our lives, so it has to be the guys who have the Ba'athist cards.

That just showed, I think, a level of misunderstanding at a brutal level. And it really was kind of marked, now [it] was game on. Because I think, whatever hope they had of seeing things improve, they weren't seeing it. For economic reasons and religious reasons we started seeing a lot of different insurgency cells pop up, attacking us with the weapons that we had secured months earlier on the drive north into Iraq.

It would have helped if we could have had enough forces to blow through these bases that had these large weapons caches. And that's the killer, man. You know, I don't know how to explain it. Because if you haven't seen Americans just torn up by IEDs or RPGs or AK-47s, or just seen the death and the destruction that comes with war ... and we had it, we had it. We had those ammo, those large bases secured and we gave it away and it just led to all kinds of issues later. It basically sets the stage for 15 years or longer of being in Iraq. Oh, and it might sow the seeds for ISIS. It just might ... I don't know, maybe I'm way off. But the disbanding of the army never made sense to me. It only made sense if we had the Marshall Plan right behind it, and we were able to start showing the good will and reconstruction effort immediately.

Sally Mars

The first bomb site I ever saw was when I was around 8. I saw people being picked up from the street and lifted on to pickup trucks, and the pickups would be dripping blood, because they were covered in blood. The way they lifted the bodies is like it's just some meat or furniture. Lifting like so, then putting them down in a violent way, and so the body would move like so, making the blood splash. The slam of the body was frightening, with the shaking and blood dripping.

It was a very slow scene, I was sitting in the car with my family. We were all in the car, the whole family. I sat in the back; because I was the youngest, I'd often sit there and see the whole street. It was in slow motion, driving by this pickup truck stacking bodies from the street.

Nate Sassaman
We were not welcome. Even when we were with the police and the government officials, we were not welcome. Early on, we were trying to do some reconstruction, and we would bring in a lot of medical supplies for the local clinics. I can remember the first one I went to in that area. I'm telling you, the woman running it had to have been 50 or 60 – she was as hard as woodpecker lips. And she basically said, 'I don't want any of your stuff, I don't want you here, I want you to go back to the US, I never want to see you again.' That's my first personal effort to reconstruct the area, and we had a lot of medical equipment to help them out with. She didn't want to touch any of it. And of course there's a lot of reasons for that: she might have got targeted if she took resources from the Americans; it might have been she wanted 'em but if she did take it, she's in collusion with the Americans and now she's a target for the Saddam Fedayeen or whoever. So my take was she didn't want us anywhere near her. No, this particular group didn't welcome us as the heroes.

I used to do something called the Village People operation. It took a lot of the soldiers that worked in and around the operations centre to get them out. The whole idea of the village people patrols was to gauge the whackability, the American factor. Some of the places they went, they got rocks thrown at us. Some of the places, they got shot at. Some of the places, it was like, 'Hey, come in and have tea with us.' So we would label all of these different areas around our area of operation with the American whackability factor. Abu Hishma was at the bottom of the barrel. They sucked. Hardcore Sunni, dudes want to fight all the time. It's a little sleepy kind of village, right on the banks of the Tigris, 12 to 15 kilometres east of Balad proper where our base was at. And that's where our first attack is at, on our Bravo company, early July. It's where we have our first soldiers wounded, and, tragically, there is a young Iraqi pregnant woman, who was killed in the crossfire. And that's where we got into ID cards. Things got real draconian after that. That was, like, right off the bat, establish our forces as the legitimate authority in the area of operation, and that included absolutely no open defiance to American forces. So I wanted to address everything.

Once the fight started, I think we started averaging seven or eight attacks a day on our forces. It took us a while to get that down to about seven or eight a month by the time we left. I was adamant that if anybody shot at one of our soldiers, I was going to do absolutely everything in my power to make sure that whatever insurgent, terrorist, you know, Saddam Fedayeen group, that that was going to be their last day on the face of the Earth. And I went to extraordinary lengths to make sure that happened. The philosophy when it came to the engagement part, with the violence, was akin to killing an ant with a sledgehammer. They were going to disappear. We want to put more forms of contact on the enemy than they put on us. Mortars, artillery, air, engineer obstacles, direct fire – I was bringing it, OK. I didn't care what time of day it was, I didn't care where we were at, I didn't care if the air force was having steak dinner. If we needed 2,000lb bombs, I was expecting the Brits or the Americans and the F15s and F16s to bring it. Yeah. We were going to finish it off.

It became readily apparent that people in this kind of part of the world, they only understand a couple of things and that's raw power, fear, violence. Whoever's got the most guns wins. Who's the most violent. We kinda got to the point where we had to be ruthless in our attacks because I needed the people to respect us in our area of operation. There was just going to be absolutely no allowing of Iraqi people to humiliate or embarrass the Americans. I was not going to allow any form of resistance against us, or lack of respect. And so if there's a bunch of kids and they threw rocks at us, we threw rocks right back at them, and if there were cells that want to engage us with mortars or IEDs or direct fire, then it was going to be their last day on the face of the Earth. It's a warring area, they don't understand appeasement, they don't understand rolling up your sleeves and soft caps and hey, we're here to bring you democracy. No, they would sneer and laugh at that. But if you brought it and you eliminated some of the insurgents and the cells that were operating in their area that were terrorising some of those communities, they totally respected that.

Um Qusay
My cousin was coming back from the shops, in Tikrit. He was leaving the market in his car. He was an old man, not young at all. They saw him and shot at him straight way. He didn't even see it coming. He was just carrying supplies, getting ready for Ramadan. Then they inspected the car and found no weapons. They apologised. They said sorry. What if you had killed me? What would I do with 'sorry' after that? What use is your apology to me at this point?

Nate Sassaman
In my mind no real progress could be made until the community realised that, you know, we were the legitimate force here to bring around security, stability and then follow-on reconstruction efforts and all of that was being hampered when we were having threats against us from all the different cell-like groups. They definitely understood fear and intimidation and violence. The more we were able to be aggressive, and use those tools of power, we started gaining respect and then folks were willing to talk to us. There are different ways to tackle this problem. Some folks were clearly in it to win the hearts and the minds through some softer tactics,

economic measures that, I think, most of the folks just sneered at and laughed at and took advantage. And some of those units got hurt bad. I think, at least in our division, we're rolling heavy and when we're attacked, we're eliminating those threats. And I think that was totally in line with being able to set the conditions for the reconstruction. So once everyone's kind of been stamped out, now we can go about the business of like figuring out how do we want this to look.

The problem is, it's like Whack-a-Mole: the enemy always follows the path of least resistance, and so if we don't have consistent tactics and strategies across the breadth of Iraq then it was just the enemy moving from one place to the next, finding the units that were not taking the aggressive stance and wreaking havoc there. Then, I think, there's no chance for reconstruction. You can't even get security and stability. There's no predictability.

The Rules of Engagement were such that you know, you're out after 10 o'clock on a motorcycle or bongo truck – ROEs are you can smoke 'em. You can take 'em out. So I mean, the predictability got real, it got real consistent, and the feedback I got was that this is cool, man: the kids go to school in the morning, the boys in the morning, the girls in the afternoon and everybody home at 10pm, and there's nothing going on after that. And if there was, it was activities against us – you know, ways to attack the Americans. I said, 'We're going to use force that's commensurate to the force they're using. So if they throw rocks, we're going to throw rocks back. We're not going to allow anti-American graffiti be anywhere in the area of operation.' I made the police, within 24 hours, clean it up. So any time we saw anything – whether it was graffiti, somebody flipping you off, throwing rocks at you – we were coming, we were coming right back and addressing that defiance. And I actually got a lot of great feedback from the community.

We had that 2200 curfew – anybody outside after that curfew, man, it was open game. It's a little draconian, I get it, but stores were open, folks had jobs, there was some commerce, we were making some political reform and we weren't tolerating dudes being defiant to us. But that was step number one, just to be clear that *we* were the legitimate authority for the area of operation, not *them*, or anyone else. We were trying to push the reset button here, and eliminate all these different threats, so that we could set the conditions for reconstruction.

We were trying to do these things simultaneously – take out the insurgent cells and reconstruct at the same time. One in the daytime, the other at night-time. Forming a city council, setting up the elections, helping re-establish the police station, trying to work with these institutions of education and social welfare and political reform and economic growth – these huge democratic institutions that we have. And so we're trying to push the reset button here and help them on that way, while at night taking out known targets.

While I was working on the city council elections, I had CPA officials come up from Baghdad and basically tell me: 'You cannot run elections, we're going to have national elections first then regional then the city and local elections. We're going to do this in order.' And I said, 'When's that going to happen? Because we got to go.' And he said, 'We don't know.' And I go, 'Well, one year, two years, three years?' He goes, 'We don't know.' And so I was really discouraged by CPA and some senior legal officers out of Baghdad who are like, 'You're not authorised to run elections.' I go, 'This is why we're here. And there's no sense in waiting ... We may never have national elections, so let's just start.'

So we picked a date, they decided how many council slots they wanted to have for this city of 100,000 people, and we did the whole roles thing between men and women, ages of 18 and over, I think, that were voting, and they kinda got into it. The whole city got into it. The police did a real good job of securing each of the polling sites because there was a real fear that one of them was gonna be attacked, so we had a partnership thing with the police and my units to set that up, and then we monitored it, and then they wanted all the votes counted that night. And we had all these council members that were voted in, and the names were read off;

they went up, pictures were taken, and I remember it being, like, 'Man, if there's one thing I can hang my hat on, we did *something* to give them a chance. This was the one thing.'

It was very well received. I think we had, out of 50,000 people who could vote, we had like 40,000 vote. It was ridiculous. You don't see this anywhere. I mean everybody wanted to vote. People were walking for miles to cast their ballot for their city council person for their area. It was very well publicised and we had several meetings where candidates could get out; the whole area was divided up into maybe seven or eight regions, so we had five councilmen per region and people ran against each other, and they had their meetings and candidates. My main concern was security on the day of the event. I didn't want any of the polling sites to get hit, because this was going to be a major step forward – this is a win, man, and we need to celebrate the wins.

Things started to get really serious in September. We'd had the attacks in July and some in August, but the attacks had stepped up, and Ramadan was in the October, November time period. I was very wary going into Ramadan, because higher headquarters had signed some deal that we're going to stay out of the villages and the cities, we're not going to patrol there any more. And, you know, I'm all about keeping the pressure on. It was really working – things were settling down, because the attacks spiked in July, August. So I had all the sheiks come in, and we had a signing deal, saying, 'You guys are taking responsibility for your areas and if Americans get attacked in your area, I'm holding you responsible.' Well, nobody wanted to sign that; partially, I think, they couldn't enforce it.

So we're in Ramadan and we go into this ridiculous tactic of rotating observation posts in just key areas across the region. That was a brigade initiative. It's as dumb as rocks. Guerrilla forces are trying to break up the good order and discipline of military units, and any time we have predictable patterns, we're setting ourselves up. That's why I was really focused on changing our patterns every day with our logistic re-supply packages. With this Ramadan thing, we take the foot off the gas pedal. We're out, we're not patrolling. And 17 November is a marker change for me. That's when Staff Sergeant Dale Panchot is killed in what's pretty much the most sophisticated attack I think we saw, which was launched with a volley of RPGs, eight or nine, from across a canal about 4,500 metres away. One of the RPGs penetrates the two armours of Bradley steel and hits him with a direct shot, in his chest, and he's killed instantly. Some other folks are wounded. Our philosophy was always to cut off the egress routes of the enemy and, as we were setting that in and more reinforcements were coming, now they start mortaring us. And that's when I'm going, 'Hmm, OK, they got this thing figured out.' Because they had egressed out already and now they're hitting us with mortars.

The attack was around 06:00, but the whole thing rolled into around 11 or noon. During this craziness of the mortars coming in, and we got Apaches on site, and we got reinforcements moving in, I'm just watching this Iraqi woman come out of where she lives, and she walks like the 50 or 75 metres to the water well. She gets her water, and she walks back, like it doesn't matter what's going on. 'In my world, it's time to get the water, for me to get the cooking started for my family.' She just didn't care what was going on. And I was like, 'Oh my god, please, I hope nothing happens to her.' One of the oddest sights I ever saw in Iraq. She doesn't care if all hell's breaking loose right there around her, she's got to get her water to start the day.

Part of me died over there that day. If there had been any kind of fun, or light-heartedness, you know, in this combat environment, that day wiped it out. I think that was the turning point for me: it was going from this optimistic guy who was trying to do what's right with the security, stability and reconstruct the country, to where I'm kinda pissed right now.

Once Dale is killed, it escalates up. The Ramadan thing was over. The 'stay out of the villages and cities and don't patrol' – that ended that day. I was done with the observation post programme we were doing and we went right back to patrolling. We also detained about 20, 30, 40 sheiks in the area that potentially could have been connected to the attacks and Dale's death, and we put them through probably a week or two of interrogations and questioning. We barbed-wired the entire village. Triple concertina wire, laid on top of each other. Probably about six, eight feet tall. We just wired the city in. Surrounded it. Took a while. It was a huge effort. Huge effort to get that done. There was just too much evidence that a large proportion of attacks was emanating out of this area. So we wired 'em in, and they had to have an ID card to leave and come back in. And that went on for probably a month or so. And guess what? The attacks went down. Probably because they left. Probably because the active members in that group that were attacking us decided, 'OK, we're out.' And they moved somewhere else. Except for the ones that we were able to take care of. And there were quite a few. It didn't improve relations at all. It actually probably made 'em worse. It was more just punishment and retribution for the attacks that they had been committing on American forces. It's a hard take, but in my estimation, whoever from that area that was doing the attacks, they were long gone, and so we're punishing the people that are just living there. So things started badly, and went way worse.

Sally Mars
A car exploded opposite our front door. Our neighbour's father was a police officer. He probably had enemies. They placed a bomb in his police car. There was a big window above the sink. I was reaching forward to get a glass of water to drink. At that moment, the front door flew off. A big metal door. It flew and hit the big window in front of the sink, and the whole window fell on me, but I wasn't hurt. I saw our house's metal front door in front of me – the window had disappeared, and a door was in its place!

I had my mouth open from the pressure of the blast, because I got pressure in my ears. I opened my mouth involuntarily to lessen the pressure. I began to walk slowly, because there was dirt and I couldn't see anything. I was trying to get to my family, and see if anyone got out, because my mom was taking my little brother to school. I thought my mom had gone out, and so I was scared, thinking my mom had died in the blast.

My dad was panic-stricken, didn't know what to do, just shouting: *'Where's your mother? Where's your mother?'* He thought she'd gone out, and so he was running between the rooms in a hysterical way, looking for her. He found her then grabbed her, saying, *'Where's your mother?'* She was saying, *'This is her! This is her! It's me!'* He calmed down, shaking as he realised she was facing him, alive and nothing wrong. All of us, no one was hurt.

After the shock wore off, was the first time I ever saw my father cry. That was the first time in my life I saw my father's tears. They were tears of terror. First time I saw them.

We went out to the garage. That was the most horrifying thing I ever saw in my life. Our neighbour who was a police officer, his leg was severed. The only thing still linking it was a small thread of flesh. He was trying to pick it up, to place it on the other side. The link was a single strip of meat. There was a cat on our wall that got torn apart so I didn't know if this flesh on our doorstep was the cat's or the man's. I think his hand was also wounded, but his face and all was bleeding. As soon as the dust settled, I saw him lying in the street and trying to drag his leg. As soon as I saw this image, I spun around and found my mom sobbing hard with her eyes shut, as if she's the one who was injured. My big sister came and held her, trying to calm her down, telling her it's OK, but then my sister became like her. I fought myself, not to get like them in this moment – we didn't all have to start crying and not know what to do. I took them and pushed them into the living room and shut the door.

They carried him away. His eldest son came out to the guy and they took him in the first car that stopped. As soon as it passed, the driver quickly stopped, opened the door and said, 'Get him in.' They took him to hospital. The council came and cleaned the place, of course. We got a blacksmith, he rebuilt the door and made a second one. We built a new kitchen window. We cleaned the kitchen, because everything was broken, it had dirt and broken dishes.

We all remained repulsed and silent for the entire day. It happened in the morning, and no one spoke until nightfall. No one ate. No one did anything. We were silent.

I remember the smell. I never smelled anything like that before in my life. It's a smell of death! Precisely the smell of death. I used to hear people saying 'the smell of death'. But this smell – the smell of blood and the sight of flesh – I truly sensed that's the smell of death. That's what it is. I'll never forget this smell.

The Spider Hole

John Nixon
I was a leadership analyst at CIA, I knew a lot about key regime figures, and I volunteered. I was told, 'We're going to have you at the airport, and you're going to be working on captured documentation pertaining to weapons of mass destruction.' I thought, 'This is insane, why are you having me doing this? There are lots of other things I could be doing.' I thought it was a little bit beneath me, and also I hadn't worked extensively on weapons of mass destruction, so I called up the person who made these lists and said, 'Is there some mistake?' She said, 'No, we've gone over this very carefully and we think you'll be very good there.' And I said, 'OK, great.' And then one day the head of my office came over to me and said, 'The HVT1 analyst in station has to come home in early November because he's getting married. We really need somebody to replace him. We can't just have that position to sit idle or vacant.' And I jumped at it. HVT1 is High Value Target number 1, and it was the designation that Saddam was given in the hunt for him; once he was captured it became HVD1, which is High Value Detainee. I jumped at the opportunity. In typical CIA fashion, she said, 'Oh, thank god, because we've asked everybody and no one can go!' I'm like, 'Aren't you supposed to tell me that I was the first that you thought of?' Either way, I was just really happy to be doing that.

I left on October 22nd. We got picked up at the airport in Baghdad and taken to the villa where we were housed. I remember driving, and there were these children playing by the side of the road. The person in the front seat said something to me like, 'Well,

'We thought we knew what was happening in this country; in hindsight, we didn't have the foggiest notion.' – **John Nixon**

'The insurgency against the Americans didn't come as a surprise. The growth of extremism didn't come first.'
– **Omar Mohammed**

'The way I understand life, if you have a cat and you keep flicking the cat, flicking the cat, flicking the cat, the cat is going to scratch you at some point.'
– **Waleed Nesyif**

'We were the no better friend, no worse enemy. Show them if they befriend us they have no better friend. If they fight with you, make it so horrible they never want that to happen again.' – **Nick Popaditch**

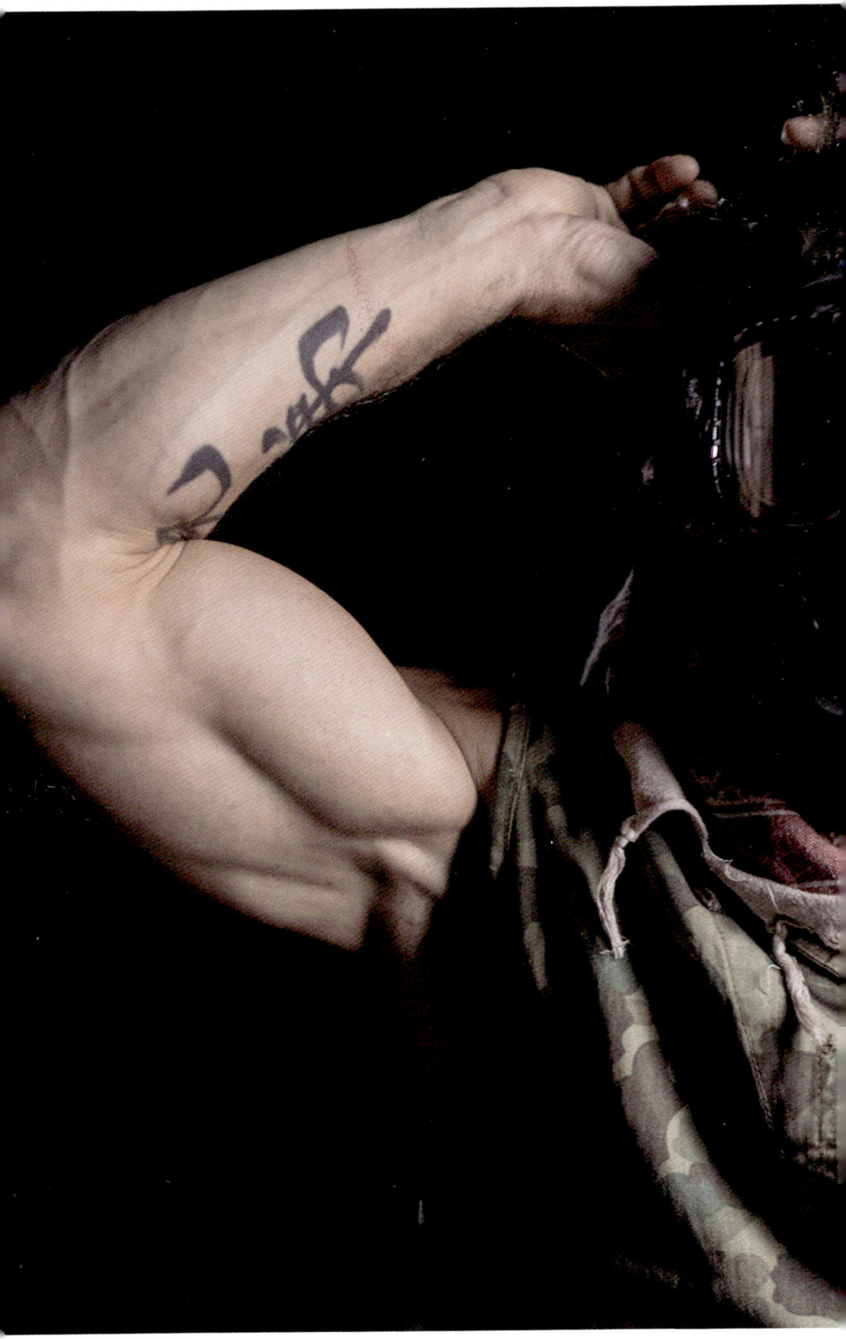

'There was burning garbage and destruction and dead bodies and rot everywhere. It was like some kind of Hieronymus Bosch fricking hell out there. I didn't even consider winning the war, I didn't even consider it a war. I just considered it a mission.' – **Rudy Reyes**

'We expected that someone else would be there instead of Saddam. The situation would go back to like it was before and maybe better. We weren't expecting that all these things would happen.' – **Sally Mars**

'In my mind no real progress could be made until the community realised that we were the legitimate force here to bring around security, stability and then follow-on reconstruction.' – **Nate Sassaman**

'The next thing I know is Mustafa is next to me with his guts in the dirt … An American missile had landed next to us. There was no al-Qaeda. Just families.' – **Nidhal Mustafa**

'It looked like Star Wars. You saw the city get lit up for hours by tracer rounds, aircraft and small-arms fire.'
– **Christian Dominguez**

'I remember thinking, "This is not Iraq any more. This is not the Iraqis' country any more." The rise of the private contractors felt particularly damaging.'
– **Ashley Gilbertson**

'Am I glad Billy's dead? Absolutely not. Do I wish somebody else would have died instead of Billy? No, I don't. And Billy wouldn't have wanted somebody to die instead of him. He always wanted to be first.' – **Susie Miller**

'I just remember a big tall black guy with white gloves, holding my hand, telling me that Billy had been killed. The only thing I could think of was 'What can I tell my mum?' – **Sabrina Miller**

'In the middle of Saddam's prayer they pulled the switch. Everybody in that crowd started cheering and going crazy.' – **Brandon Barfield**

that's why we're here – to help them.' Nothing could have been further from the truth, but that image kind of stuck in my mind.

I still had hope we could turn this thing around, and catching Saddam was a very important part of that hope. Once I got my feet on the ground and started working with my colleagues at the Agency and the Special Forces and the military, I came upon this very disturbing trend, which is this belief, similar to what President Bush had: we've got to cut the head of the snake off from its body. We've got to cut the head off and everything will be fine. If we find Saddam, we'll end his regime once and for all, and we'll shut down this insurgency that seems to be gaining speed and more lethality, and everything will be great. Us at the Agency believed that this was a completely erroneous assumption, that there are issues here in this society that run far deeper than just the fact that Saddam is on the run and was once the president of Iraq and we want to capture him. Also there was this great belief, especially amongst the military, that Saddam was directing the insurgency, and we saw nothing to suggest that – in fact, the insurgency was basically running itself.

The thing is, this sucked up a lot of man hours, having to argue about this and having to debunk a lot of false reporting that we were seeing, particularly regarding Saddam's direction of the insurgency, because that fed into the military's narrative and we would have to sort of pour cold water on that. It creates institutional frictions that can be very, very harmful for getting things done: 'Why are you not cooperating with us?'

Waleed Nesyif
There were all these rumours coming in: 'They have found Saddam.' Iraqis were still scared that he might come back. We never knew. Everybody wanted it to happen but nobody thought it could happen – him being gone – because he almost became like a deity. You know, Saddam is unstoppable, untouchable, a person that is not going to be removed, an ethereal being ... So rumours would come about and the journalists were like, 'They said he is

in A.' So we would go to A and interview people. Meanwhile, I was being asked, 'Do you think it's true?' and I was like, 'No. I don't think Saddam is in Iraq, I don't think he will ever be in Iraq. Probably he has gone, a long time ago.' Many Iraqis believed Saddam was not in Iraq, because there were all of these stories about all of his doubles, and nobody thought this man, who was feared so much, could be captured or be stupid enough to stay in the country.

It was the biggest manhunt I think in the world at that time. You have got a whole army coming running after him, and there was a reward as well. It was like $1.5 million dollars or something like that, some stupid number that we haven't even dreamed of seeing, so Iraqis were looking as well. Iraqis were looking, Americans were looking, everybody was looking for Saddam, you know – we are running around like frigging headless chickens. It was so comical at the same time.

Some people were like, 'If we find him, we will hide him,' because at that time some of the truth of the invasion started coming out. Seeing that, I guess the people had this kind of shadow thought in their heads: 'What if he comes back? What if they just pull off right now and then he emerges and then all of those who supported America, now they are screwed.' So people were really cautious. I was cautiously optimistic, but there was this lingering fear.

It was the word on the street, you know. You go to cafés, you speak with your friends, family members, taxi drivers as you get into a cab, and that was the thing: 'Where do you think he is?' Somebody says in Australia, somebody says in America, someone says in Jordan, someone says in Syria, and lots of people said in Israel. England was another country that we thought Saddam to be in, because we never separated England from what had happened to us. England was always part and parcel of every American decision that led to the destruction of Iraq. People are like, 'They all want the same thing, and he helped them achieve it so obviously they are going to pay him off, right? They are not going to let a guy that works so hard for them just go like this.' Because that was the mentality, that Iraq was an agent of the West.

John Nixon
We were getting a lot of pressure from Washington to find Saddam Hussein. The Chief of Station took me aside once: the Agency had developed a source who claimed to know where Saddam was, and I didn't believe him. I thought this guy was just stringing us along. I don't think this guy had any notion of where Saddam was, but we were paying him. I kept on telling the COS that these reports that we're getting from this asset were nonsense. It was part of a pattern of reporting that we just kept getting from all over. I mean, we're in Baghdad now, the Iraqis know that the CIA is in Baghdad, and they also know that they're paying money for information so there's a lot of reporting coming in, and most of it is garbage.

One of the other things I had to deal with right in the beginning was we had gotten reporting that said Saddam had sent hit squads to the United States to kill Bush's daughters in revenge for the murder of Uday and Qusay, his sons. Right off the start we just looked at this and said, 'This is absolutely ridiculous. Saddam cannot do this. He cannot be sending hit squads to the United States, he has never sent hit squads to the United States, and it is doubtful that he has the capacity to do this.' Even at the height of his power he might not have had the capacity to do this. And yet the more you said that the more people believed it to be true. It was a pattern of crazy, crazy stories that we would have to chase and basically debunk for policymakers back home who had a tendency to believe everything, especially if it was negative.

We interrogated Saddam's driver. It was one of the first interrogations that I did when I was in Baghdad. He had taken Saddam out of Baghdad. I learned from him that Saddam got through three army checkpoints. I don't know how he did it but he did it, and he went to a few places. The first night of being on the run, the driver told me, he went up to the door of this house and knocked on the door. A woman answered, and he said, 'I have an important person in my car, and he would like to stay here for the night.' She started yelling at him, like, 'Do you know what time it is? What makes you think you can come here and knock on my door and that I'm gonna just throw open my house? Get out of here! Get out of here!' Samad, the driver, went back to Saddam and told him what happened and Saddam started laughing, and they just went up the road and went to another house.

As the Americans are coming into Baghdad, Saddam is exiting the city. I once said to him, 'When you fled Baghdad—' and he just was like, 'Stop right there. I did not *flee* Baghdad. I left in order to oppose the occupation.' It's an important moment. We in the intelligence community had been waiting for this day forever, for years, and now it was here, and there were a lot of people who had these ideas about Saddam Hussein and what would happen on the day that his regime crumbled and what would he do and where would he go. We used to hear all sorts of stuff: he has these underground roadways that will take him out to the airport; there is a plane that is loaded with gold bullion and Saddam will get on that; this plane is kept in perfect condition and is maintained to be able to fly at a moment's notice; it's always fuelled up ... The reality couldn't have been more opposite. Really what it came down to was that, when the United States came into the city, the genius of Saddam Hussein was that the plan he had was he had no plan. They just met up at rally points, they got into cars and they left. There was no real plan to do anything other than to get in cars and to leave. In a sense it's brilliant. If you have a plan then there are people who might know about that plan and they might sell that information to your enemy. But if you don't have a plan, those people can't dime you out and therefore you can just go.

He kind of disappears, and he only appears again in a couple of videotape recordings to play on television. I think they get sent to Al Jazeera, and that's it. I don't know if he used disguises, but they left and then at some point they split up. In his party it was himself, his sons, one or two bodyguards, and the presidential secretary, Abid Hamid Mahmud, a Tikriti. At that point, Uday and Qusay and Abid split up this way, and the driver and Saddam and maybe a bodyguard or two go this way. The plan is to get Uday and Qusay out of the country, and Abid went into Syria to negotiate that. On the way back to Iraq, Abid gets picked up by coalition forces and jailed, and suddenly Uday and Qusay are in Mosul and they're staying at a distant relative's house, a sheik. And they make a crucial mistake, and this is something that Saddam would never have done. During the first Gulf War, Saddam always managed to avoid anybody finding him because he always stayed in a different house every night. He would be in a car and he would tell his driver, 'Stop there. We'll go in there.' He decided where it was, and he didn't tell anybody until he picked it out. Uday and Qusay stayed in this place for a couple of weeks, maybe even a couple of months – and they overstayed their welcome.

Eventually, the sheik decides he's kind of getting nervous because there's a lot of US military activity in Mosul and he can tell they're looking for them, and he asks them to leave. Qusay very rudely tells him to go to hell and we'll leave when we want to leave and you've been paid so just leave us alone. And then they went back to playing video games. At that point, the sheik says, 'Well OK,' puts on his hat and coat and walks outside. He walks down the road and goes down to a military division at the end of the road and says, 'Listen, I know you're looking for these guys. Are you still looking for them? OK, they're in my home, and I'm trying to get them to leave but they won't.' And that's all he has to say. The military drives up, they surround the place, and in the process they basically destroyed the home but they also destroyed Uday, Qusay and also Qusay's son.

Every day we used to get 'Elvis sightings.' Each one was more far-fetched than the last one. The one that I always thought was the funniest was that he was dressed as a woman and hiding at a Baghdad bus station. Unfortunately, oftentimes we would have to actually run these things down for fear that if it was ever found out that Saddam actually was hiding as a woman in a Baghdad bus station and we didn't believe it to be true, then that would end up on the front page of the *Washington Post*, and the CIA would take another black eye.

Nate Sassaman
We were definitely serious about capturing Saddam, and I think it's real important they wanted Saddam alive. So we spent an inordinate amount of resources across the theatre to capture this guy. It felt like the noose was tightening, but I didn't really have a feel for where he was at. Or even what he might look like when we captured him. But he was remarkably close to our area of operation. We were searching about 12 miles away the night he was found and captured. I'm almost positive this guy drove his beat-up bongo truck or beat-up white and orange Toyota through our area of operation, maybe more than once.

I talked to a fella in Samarra once. He was on the side of the road, and we stopped and we were talking about something. He'd lost his arm. We saw a lot of guys without their arms and legs, and I assumed it was from the Iraq-Iran war, but I'd always go, 'How'd you lose your arm?' And he goes, 'Well, I hated Saddam, and Saddam's convoy procession was coming through our city and everybody was waving but I didn't wave.' And so the convoy stopped and out jumped a couple of Saddam's men, and they put his arm on the trunk of one of the black cars and they just chopped it off. Because he didn't wave. He kinda talked about it as a badge of honour.

Saddam was this mythical figure that was out there somewhere, and I guess for us Elvis was a pretty popular guy in his day, and Saddam was a pretty popular guy for us in Iraq. So that was kinda code: 'We've got an Elvis sighting.' And then we would just launch forces immediately to that location. We had the regular security operations going and reconstructions, but if there was an Elvis sighting everything just dissipated immediately and it was: Go. Now.

HOW TO BUILD AN INSURGENCY

Steve Russell *had commanded the 1st Battalion, 22nd Infantry 'Regulars' in since the spring of 2003, and was part of the hunt for Saddam.*

What we know now from the FBI interviews with Saddam, and what we suspected even then, is that Saddam knew he couldn't keep the United States Army out of Iraq, but he decided to set up an apparatus where he would have loyal foot soldiers with his Fedayeen. He would have his closest families and associates that would protect him. He would go into hiding. They would develop this insurgency and they would begin to attack our soldiers where it would have great public fanfare, and that would cause politicians in the United States to lose heart, and then America would lose interest. In his mind, we would go home, like Somalia, and then he could be restored to power. It wasn't an implausible strategy, but again Saddam was a master of miscalculation.

We knew when we occupied Tikrit that, it being Saddam's hometown, we might have some association with the hunt for him, but it was never imagined that this would ultimately be the centre of where the hunt was occurring and ultimately the area where he would be caught. But it's not surprising in retrospect. When we first got to Tikrit, we had lists called black lists, and these were people that were associated with Saddam. In May, after Saddam's army disintegrated, there were three or four days of fighting when we got to the Tikrit north military complex. At that point, it was kind of a few wake-up calls. I could sense it. I could see it. I could feel it. And I knew it was just a matter of time before these bad actors, these nasty looks, turned into action. And the initial actions against our soldiers demonstrated some skill and organisation. They showed the ability to use small rifle tactics, combined weapons. To use manoeuvres. This was important to note, because somebody had to be behind that organisation. These had to have been people that worked together before. So was it military or was it something else? And the roads quickly led to it being the Fedayeen, and we would see symbols of this. They would put their little 'God, country, leader' emblems up, you know, marking their territory.

So that was a start, but these were the foot soldiers. Who was behind it? That was the key. We developed a three-tier strategy. You had the guys that were fighting us. You had Saddam at the top and his henchmen. Who was in between? That would be the key group to go after. If you could go after that middle tier, then not only could you disrupt the command and control of the foot soldiers but you could also get on the trail that would lead you to the man himself. That was the theory. And you know my unit certainly got on to some of these leads early on.

The idea of Saddam defying the world's most powerful nation and the allies that were involved in the effort – Saddam had kind of pulled these tricks before, when he was a young 18-year-old and tried to kill the Iraqi prime minister. He had escaped this once before. He had fled, he had come back, he had risen to power, and he had become The Man. He had always defied the odds, he had always had a second or third life. As long as he was at large, in Iraqi minds they would never completely relax and look towards a future. There would always be the dark shadow of Saddam and his sons, who were just horrific, and this dark cloud that would hang over Iraq. They were in the grip of it and, it's also important to note, not only were they in the grip of Saddam's shadow but they were in the grip of a Ba'athist, Saddam-loyal, Sunni-led governance and administration. And as long as Saddam held that grip on the educated class, on the administrators, on those that might be looking forward to working towards a new Iraq, you weren't going to get anywhere. They had skill, but they were Sunni Arabs and they were associated with the Ba'athist party. So this idea of Saddam had to die. It had to be brought to a conclusion. So it was great urgency that we should find him.

In the May and early June timeframe, we were trying to chase down leads of where he might be. There were reports that he had gone to the Haditha area. There were reports that he had gone to the town of Hit. There were rumours that he had fled to Syria. That his wife had gone to Jordan; that proved to be true. Rumours were flying everywhere but you had to go off of something concrete, and you couldn't go off of anything concrete until you got on to those that would be associated with him. That was something that would develop rapidly, but it was something that was not crystal clear in the May timeframe.

We would get reports from everyone early on. That cultural strength of the Iraqis in wanting to dream big – they would come with information. 'We have some information and we need to tell you.' At first, we lapped this up. You try to run it down, and it was a rumour of a rumour of a rumour and nothing to substantiate it. It was usually something that was in the past and so it caused us to be a little jaded and we would get reports you know Saddam was seen you know as a goat farmer. He was pumping gas at a gas station. He was out on the streets fighting with an RPG, and he was seen and he came by and kissed kids and babies and shook hands or who knows what. It's just amazing the reports that we would hear about Saddam. But then he was a larger-than-life figure in so many people's minds for so long. And in Tikrit he's their hometown boy, they are rooting for him. So trying to sort through what could have a basis of fact and what didn't was not an easy task. We called all these supposed sightings of Saddam 'Elvis sightings.' I don't know who came up with it, but it stuck.

Paul Bremer

It was very important to us to find Saddam because, as the months went on, the rumours were all over the place: he was seen driving a taxi; he was seen in a teahouse. The Iraqi people were not persuaded that this would last. It is important to remember that Saddam had been thrown in jail before, had been thrown out of power before, and had come back. And when he came back he was more vicious than when he had been thrown in jail. So quite understandably this was in the minds of a lot of Iraqis, and they raised it with us: 'Where is Saddam? Why can't you find him?' It was certainly in the background of all of our thinking, particularly at the time when we found the two sons. It raised the question again of 'Why can't you find Saddam?' and the fear of many Iraqis that he would come back. We didn't know who was where at that point. He seemed one step ahead of everyone for quite some time. It was dubbed 'Elvis sightings'. One of the more amusing ones was that he was riding in the back seat of a Baghdad taxicab in a Santa outfit! But these kinds of rumours came in, and it was basically the intelligence guys and the military who had to sort through them all.

It was a late Saturday night, but the time I got the call it was Sunday morning Baghdad time. December 13th. I got a call from my staff saying that General Abizaid, the commander of all the military forces, wanted to talk to me on a secure phone. He said to me, 'We think we have got Saddam.' We had a bunch of special forces guys who got a tip, went to a farm in a little town out of Tikrit. They found him in ... I think Abizaid used the term 'a spider hole', and told me the story about how they found him.

Steve Russell
Our first big breakthrough came when I was checking an outpost, and these two Iraqi businessmen came up to the gate. One of my sergeants came up and he said, 'Sir, there's these two guys out here they've got some information. They say they won't give the information to anyone but you. They specifically asked for you.' This was one of those moments that something in my gut just ... I had no expectations but I called them in. For the next two and a half hours they laid out Saddam's security apparatus on sheets of butcher paper. It was staggering. I thought this is the most organised lie I've ever seen or there has got to be some truth to it. They talked about how Saddam had associated himself with about half a dozen controlling families, much like a mafia don, and that these families were related by blood, they were related by marriage, they were related by long association with him. Families with names like Hussein and Majid. And you had the Musslit family.

Taking that information, we quickly began to look at who are these families, is this the middle tier, are these the enablers? As we began to unravel what Colonel Hickey, my commander, called a big ball of yarn, it was something that had immediate pay-off. Immediate. We got tips, and we even got a tip about Saddam's actual location at a fish farm located in a tiny little village. We went out there, and we almost got Saddam in that raid. How do we know that we almost got him? Because we got things that you would not have found except, you know, had he been present. For example, we got Saddam's personal family photo albums. I mean the stuff that you would grab out of your home after it were on fire. That type of stuff. Pictures of little Uday and Qusay's birthday parties. Saddam at the beach in a speedo. We captured $2 million worth of jewellery, $8.5 million dollars of cash.

Saddam's most trusted bodyguard, a guy named Adnan Abid Al-Musslit – we captured him. The fact that he was recalled to serve Saddam and was showing up in Tikrit, that was big news. We got a tip on it. Immediately after dawn we got him. We found that Saddam had this special trust in the Musslit family, and so we began to peel that back. We began to piece together a picture of the Musslit family along with the Husseins and Mijids and all of them who were related by blood.

The Musslit family was intriguing. It had ten brothers. The granddaddy of all of them was Omar Al-Musslit. The last public appearance of Saddam, April 2003, Saddam shows up in the town square, everybody is cheering, he gets on top of a car, I think it was a white Mercedes. And the guy that was driving him gets on top of the car with him, wearing a green shirt with white horizontal stripes on it, and he has a pistol in his hand to protect the man. That was Mohammed Al-Musslit. He was a lieutenant colonel in the army. His posts were interesting. He became the key guy. What we know now is that he was related to Saddam's wife, Sajida. I try to describe the hunt like this: that we were driving on the freeway at a high speed. You are getting some geographical sign posts as you drive by. You are not catching every detail and every little town, but you know you are heading in the right direction. And that was really what it was like. You know as you go back, it makes perfect sense. We had a sense of it. Most of the search had revolved around the Musslit family. They became very key to find.

We at first thought that the Fedayeen elements, the insurgent elements and Saddam's entire security operations were being done by Rudman Al-Musslit, one of Omar's ten sons. Rudman had the background for it. He was very mercurial. He had had time in the military forces. He became a focus of the search throughout the summer. By October, he had fled out of our area, out towards Haditha, and they managed to do a raid out there and they got him. Unfortunately he died of a coronary, the stress. I mean, these guys were haggard. They were on the run. They didn't have a good diet. Believe me, none of us wanted him dead; we wanted the information he had, but he literally just distressed, ticker went. Whatever information he had, we never got. We had captured a couple of the Musslit brothers prior to this time and other units had got a couple more, so we were thinning the ranks of them, but it became very clear after Rudman's death that it was Mohammed Al-Musslit that was doing most of the organising and most of the protection. The one that was standing on the car. Mohammed Al-Musslit clearly had to know where Saddam was.

As we began to really thin out a lot of these families, we began to get more and more tips and information, a lot of things really began to flow. One of the things that I never divulged at the time – and again it goes back to these relationships that we built – we showed an act of kindness to a policeman by helping his dad. He'd had diabetes and it was just awful, so we got him some help clandestinely, got some Iraqi doctors to give him aid and antibiotics. They amputated his toes and he perked back. This was a very elderly man but he came back to health, which was great. We were over at his home in the middle of the night, very private meeting, and the son says, 'I wanna show you something.' And he goes down into his basement and he comes out with these big ledgers, and he opens one and he points to an 18-year-old Saddam Hussein. It was his military photo and his registry and entry when he entered military service. These are the registry books of everyone from Tikrit and

Ṣalāḥ ad-Dīn province and the area that has been in the service. I said, 'For what years?' He said, 'All of them.' 'What do you mean, all of them?' 'As long as we've been keeping books.' I said, 'How many of these do you have?' He says, 'All of them.' My mind's just racing. I'm like, 'We've got the goods, we've got everything. We've got people's families, associations, locations ...' His dad was the registrar, so not only did they have these military books, they had all of the registration books for births and marriages in that area, we were able to confirm or deny associations on a grand scale. It was an incredible find. All because of an act of kindness.

One of the problems you had with all of these marriages in a single family, it was like playing Whack-a-Mole – you know, you hit one and it pops up somewhere else. So if you hit a home and they weren't there, then you weren't gonna get the other eight. It became important through these associations and networks to try to find out what are the six likely homes we could hit simultaneously, so we got a chance of catching these guys. We did one on December 4th, it netted some important people; we followed up with another one a couple of days later, and it put us clearly on the trail of Mohammad Al-Musslit.

Then a teenage boy walked up to a checkpoint, talked to some of the soldiers there and said, 'I know where some important people are hiding.' We decided to believe him, so Colonel Hickey ordered me to take a force out to a farm west of Tikrit, just to see what we could go find. It amazingly not only turned up people of part of this family network, but it turned up people that were a part of the very family that had harboured Saddam in 1959 when he tried to kill the Iraqi prime minister. They hid him on a farm. When the Iraqi authorities tried to surround that, he jumped into the Tigris, swam across it, got on a white charger – supposedly – and rode off into the sunset to become the tyrant that he became. Little did we know that that very same family and that very same farm would come into play in a matter of about a week.

Things really began to snowball after that. There were a series of raids, trying to go after Musslit specifically. We hit two targets in

Tikrit, and other teams went after them in Samarra and Baghdad. It was a simultaneous raid, three different cities. I got a call from Colonel Hickey early morning December 13th, and he said, 'Did you get the latest reports? They got the Fat Man last night – Mohammad Al-Musslit! Get all your forces ready, I want everything available because we don't know how quickly this is gonna unravel.' The initial information was that Saddam was somewhere in the area of Tikrit. Musslit had fingered an orchard area which had two farmhouses, and there was another farm that was associated south of it, not too distant, so really there were three target objectives that were going to have to be hit simultaneously and maybe even a fourth. The two that became the focus were in the orchard on the Tigris river, and if you were to stand on that bank and look straight west you would have seen Hadoshi farm where we nearly got Saddam that summer.

We started to get very excited because we knew we had about a 24-hour window before someone would discover that Musslit was not around. So Colonel Hickey and the team get around a table and pull off a sheet of butcher paper – the raid that ultimately would catch Saddam was so sophisticated that it was planned with magic markers on a sheet of butcher paper. It was a good force going into it, about a thousand all told. You had the Special Operations Forces and their teams: you had the Task Force 160 element and the aviation support for them; you had the quarter cav gunships, one for aviation with Apaches on station; you had one-tenth cav with their reconnaissance scout helicopters; you had an MH53, which would have a Special Operations Surgeon with a fuelled hospital capacity that would be hovering above. My force was to set a blocking position on the west side of the farm. You had two 99th engineers that also would set slightly to the south west; you had the field artillery battalion that would set to the south of that near the city of ad-Dawr; you had the 1–10 cav, and then you had the Brigade Reconnaissance Troop.

The plan was the Special Ops team would come in and hit the multiple farms simultaneously. The Brigade Reconnaissance Troop would be the ground element that would immediately link up as the little birds came in with the Special Operations Forces. But before they could hit the farms, all of us had to be set in cordoning the area and to surround it, and Colonel Hickey had even given instruction that we might be out there for days looking at every single inch of ground. We knew the odds were extraordinarily high he was there, and so we were prepared for this to be a multi-day operation where nobody could get in or out. We were just gonna squeeze it down until we had something.

And with that the raid went off at 20:00 hours, on plan. Two men tried to flee immediately from the south end of the orchard in the southern farm. We think they had hidden Saddam in his hiding place and they ran to try to divert the soldiers away from it. They were able to capture the two guys. Later we learned it was Saddam's cook and his brother; the cook's name I think was Kais. Twenty, twenty-five minutes passed, everybody focused, everybody looking intently for any movement. The Special Operations Forces are scouring the orchard. Kais and his brother were brought back to the farm from which they had fled. They had tried to get some information out of them – they weren't cooperating. Nothing was working to get these guys to talk, but Mohammad Al-Musslit had been brought along for the raid. He wasn't too happy about it. He's brought into the location. It wasn't very big, it was a patio, maybe a 10 by 12-foot patio, something like that, and there was a foot mat near the patio, looked perfectly normal. Now at this juncture, it's 8.25pm, 8.26pm, there were only a handful of soldiers there. Musslit didn't wanna say anything but, when he saw Kais and his brother, it was obviously game's up. He motioned with his foot towards the foot mat and he said in a very low voice, 'He's here.' So they got Musslit and the other two guys off the area and they pulled back the foot mat and they began to brush away the dirt and bits of rope and the ropes turned into handles.

The ropes were attached to a top, a Styrofoam big square – like 18 inch, 2 foot square top – and there was brickwork around it.

The Special Operations guys had their weapons ready, they had a flash-bang grenade ready to throw down in the hole. They pulled the top and at this point, shining the lights down in there, they saw a guy down on all fours. Couldn't visibly see a weapon; he did have a pistol at the back of the hole, a Glock 18C which is now in the Bush Presidential Library. But at this moment they began to shout, 'Who are you? Come out, put your hands up,' you know the sort of thing, and the translator, Samir, began to shout the things that the soldiers were saying. Samir worked with the Special Operations Forces. He was Shi'ite. He had survived a lot of hardship after the first Gulf War. He managed to gain refugee status, made it out of Iraq and then he eventually made it to the United States. After 9/11, a lot of these guys answered the call, American citizens, and Samir was one of those.

And from the bottom of the hole you heard a voice: 'I'm Saddam Hussein, the duly elected President of Iraq, and I'm willing to negotiate.' So one of the guys says, 'Well, President Bush sends his regards.' Then one hand came up, and then another, and when they saw he didn't have a weapon they grabbed him by the scruff of the neck, the beard, the hair, whatever, pulled him out of the hole, got him out of there. Saddam had a sunburst tattoo on the back of his right hand, a three-dot tattoo on the crook between the left thumb and four finger. Those were visible marks that were in all of our brains, that if you ever had somebody that you thought was Saddam or looked like Saddam, he should have those tattoos. He had them. Jackpot.

One thing that you could say about Saddam, he was not a cowardly man. He was scared when he was captured, but then after he realised he was captured he became defiant. He comes out of the hole and when they tried to check him for these physical marks, these tattoos, he became a little uppity and he tried to fight back with one of the Special Ops soldiers. That was a stupid thing to do, so they straightened him out. That's how he got the cut on his eye and his mouth. After that, Saddam became more cooperative.

HOW TO BUILD AN INSURGENCY

A refugee from the aftermath of the first Gulf War, **Samir Al-Jassim** *returned to Iraq in 2003 as a civilian translator for the military, and was eventually sent to work with the special forces hunting for Saddam.*

We brought Mohammed inside the farm. I was like, 'Mohammed, now is the time for you to tell us what's going on. You said there is a bunker. Where's the bunker?' He was like, 'Right there where you guys are standing. You guys are standing on the bunker.' He just starts walking a little bit slowly and looking around, and he starts tapping with his feet. He's like, 'You got a shovel? Bring the shovel and dig in here.'

There was a piece of rag buried under the dirt. When they moved that piece of rag, something's in there with handles. It looks like a sewer. I was like, no way, Saddam Hussein? In here? It can't be true, no way, he's lying, there's no way Saddam Hussein – the person we see on TV – has been in that hole? How?

They pulled the lid, and we saw the hole. I was like, 'This is the bunker, he's in here, he's said he's in there inside that hole.' I guess they decided to just shoot with those sound bullets, fire a couple of them in there and see what happens. There's just sound, no bullet, but it's so loud. Imagine yourself inside that bunker with those two or three shots in there. It would scare you, it really would scare you. That's when we heard somebody inside the bunker talking and yelling and screaming. And they said, 'Samir, come and talk to him.'

I was like, 'OK, I'm coming, but I don't think it's Mr Saddam.' I tried to talk to him: 'Come out, come out, put your hands up.' I hear somebody saying, 'Don't kill me, don't shoot, don't kill me.' It keeps repeating the same thing: 'Don't shoot, don't kill me, please don't shoot, don't kill ...' I was like, 'Come out. Come out. If you stay you get killed. For your safety, please show me your hand.'

I saw a hand coming out of that hole, just one hand. I was like, 'Let me see your other hand. Both hands up, both hands up, put both your hands up.' When he put his two hands up, I reached deep in the hole, and I grabbed his hands and I started screaming:

'I got him I got him I got him I got him!' Once I got him, everybody's right there, they pulled him out, we all pulled him out.

And it's an old man. He did not look like him at all. I mean, his beard, a lot of grey hair, it looked very tired, an old-man skin wrinkles – like, this is not Saddam who we see. Until he starts saying something, and then I was like, 'It's him.' From his voice, because that's all we hear and see on TV in Iraq – his voice. Saddam, Saddam, Saddam. He said, 'America, why? America, why?'

From his voice, I can tell it is him, and I start saying, 'This is Saddam Hussein, this is Saddam Hussein!' They didn't believe me. I start screaming and yelling, saying, 'This is Saddam!' Nobody believed me. They said, 'No, no, no, ask him, ask him what's his name?'

I was like, 'What's your name?' He was like, 'I'm Saddam.' I was like, 'See? He said Saddam.' It was like, 'Oh, ask him again. Did he say Saddam Hussein or just Saddam? He has to say his full name.' I was like, 'Are you serious? You're kidding me, I mean, it's him, I can tell it's him.' But he has to say his name, and that's what he said: 'I'm Saddam Hussein.' It was a great moment.

As soon as they know it's him, it's like everybody on top of him, start taking his clothes off after we find a pistol in his belt. We cut all the clothes off. He was butt naked, completely butt naked on the floor. I tried to hurt him so bad. Every time I tried to grab something from him I get pushed away by some guy. I tried to reach anywhere I can. Finally, I stood on his legs, tried to break his legs, walk on his back, anything that can hurt him, and start kicking him and kicking him and kicking him.

Then we put him in handcuffs. He was in handcuffs on the floor, and I was like, 'I want to talk to this motherfucker. Right now, face to face.' I told him about who I am, told him: 'I was part of the uprising against you, your government. You destroyed the country, you hurt my family, you killed a lot of Iraqi people, you destroyed the country. I haven't seen my family for 14 years because of you.' I start cussing him: 'You motherfucker, asshole, I'm going to kill you today, I'm going to fucking kill you, motherfucker.

I'm going to rape you today, you're going to be my bitch today.' He did not like that at all. I don't think anybody told him that in his life. I did say all kinds of stuff to him: 'You coward, you are nothing, you're a pussy. You promised the Iraqi people that you're going to fight against the Americans, and look what you did. You came out, you had a weapon, you didn't even fight, you're scared, you lied to me, motherfucker.' And he starts calling me names, telling me I'm a spy: 'Don't talk to me, you're a spy, you're an American, you're nothing, you're a traitor, don't talk to me, you're a traitor, not even Iraqi any more, you're a traitor, you came with the Americans, you spite your own country ...'

I was like, 'I'm here to help my own country, I'm here to free my country from you.' He kept telling me I'm a traitor, I'm a spy, and I'm like, all right, there's something else I can do here to make me feel a bit better. So I grab his beard, shake him like crazy, hard as I could, spit in his face. I just want to piss him off so bad. I start kicking him, kicking and kicking and kicking and kicking – like, let me take my chance, let me take my revenge, you know. And then finally, my boss goes, 'Enough. You can't do this any more.' I was like, 'Please, please, let me take a picture with Saddam. Please.' And he said, 'No, Samir, you can't do that.' I was like, 'Boss, look at me, I'm a victim of this man. This man destroyed my country, destroyed my family, my father was tortured, I was away from my own family for 13 years because of him. I want to prove it to the whole world. I want to talk about it so people can believe what happened. Please let me take a picture.' He said, 'Do you have a camera?' I pulled my camera. I gave it to this German guy – 'Take my picture, please.' And I hold his head up, took that picture. And I'm glad I did, otherwise nobody would believe me. I have that picture.

And then one of the Special Forces came. 'Samir, tell him the reason we're here is because President Bush sent us to get your ass, you motherfucker.' And I translated in Arabic to him, exactly what he said. 'The reason they're here is because they want to get you, motherfucker.'

Saddam's response was 'Lick my shoes.' In Arabic, anything to do with shoes is a bad thing. Telling you you're not worth my shoes is a big insult. Anything to do with the shoes and respect to Saddam is saying like my shoes better than you are and your country and your president. If I translated this to the German, it has no meaning. I translated it in a different way and made the German really upset, and he started kicking Saddam in the chest. He kicked Saddam in his chest so hard I felt the impact. Everybody was cheering. I kicked him in the face while he's lying on the floor. Hit him so hard in the face, I saw blood coming from the thing. He was hurt, yeah. And then we walked him out of the farm, helicopter came and ready to pick up Saddam and take him back to our place.

I got in the front, looking at Saddam, just looking at him. He was looking up, and I don't know what he was looking at. I was like, 'Guess what, this is the time you're going to see a star. You're done. You're going to jail and you're going to be executed soon. This is your last moment.'

He's like, 'I'm not looking to the stars. I'm looking to Allah. To God.' I was like, 'You're looking to God? You think God likes you? For what you did?' And he was like, 'Oh, God loves me. God loves me. And the people of Iraq love me.' Crazy man, crazy man.

Paul Bremer
I spoke with President Bush a couple of hours later, and I told him that when we made the announcement I was going to try and set the stage: that this was a time for reconciliation among Iraqis. This pulls down the curtain on the Saddam era and it is time now to try and see if everyone can work a little bit together. The president said, 'You go ahead and do that, that's fine. I am going to focus on congratulating the military for the great job they did.'

The word had gotten out, as I knew it would, which is why all I had to say was 'We got him.' I didn't have to say who. I didn't have to say, 'We got Saddam.' All I had to say was, 'We got him.' They knew who we were talking about. It was a great victory. Finally, we had this guy. In this press conference, they put up the picture of Saddam, who was bearded and almost unrecognisable, and everyone cheered again because then they saw it. Then they knew it was him. Yeah, it was quite a scene.

It really, we hoped, marked a turning point in Iraqi history. Finally, after all these years – really starting in 1958 with the Ba'athists coming into power, the Ba'athists leaving, Saddam coming into power, Saddam leaving, Saddam coming back – it was time for the Iraqi people now to try to work together. It was a message for aspiration for reconciliation among the Iraqis. It was a moment of hope and expectation. High expectations that we could move along.

Waleed Nesyif
I was like, 'That is unreal, quite literally unreal.' I still maintain that this was a set-up. Him being found in his childhood home, in this hole – it doesn't make sense. It doesn't add up. I know Saddam was captured, but I think the theatre needed to commence, and that was like a great big point in the story that came to be the liberation of Iraq and the success of America in this campaign. I think Saddam's news of being captured came right after the reports where it showed that there is no WMD in Iraq. They are like, 'Well, we failed at this thing but ... we got him, ladies and gentlemen!' So the fact that Saddam would be hiding in a hole in his hometown – the first place that they would look for him if they had any brains, and they do – does not add up. I think he was captured long before that, and they were just saving him up for the right moment.

Saddam is not an idiot. When you study his character, there are books written about him and books written by him, you understand three things very clearly and very fast: delusion of grandeur was one of the things that he suffered from greatly, wanting to be great is the other thing that he always sought, and number three he never thought he was wrong. And the guy is not stupid. Here is what I think happened with Saddam. Here you are revered by the

Arab world, as the defender of the Eastern front of the Arab homeland. For eight years you fought Iran. You stood against America and you bombed Israel, which gained him shit loads more popularity in the Middle East, even though 39 of the 40 rockets that he launched just fell into the sea. For him, to admit the fact that he was complicit, or that he got caught somewhere else, maybe in one of his palaces, will hurt the character that he worked on constructing all of his life. For a man of that intelligence, he knew what his end would be, so his priorities changed. It's not about saving his life or gaining a trial, it's about continuing the legacy he had worked on weaving in Iraq: he is the true Iraqi, he is Iraq and the one that is standing against the invader till his very last minute. And he managed to sell it.

The Road to Fallujah

Nate Sassaman
And then I got orders to take the battalion to Samarra. Samarra's completely out of control. The unit up there was not proactive, and it was the Wild, Wild West, and they openly defied American authority. So we got orders to go up there and I'm pissed. Big time. Because we'd done some great work, in our area, both politically and economically, even in some social reform and education, and we'd really taken the attacks from seven or eight a day to seven or eight a month. So we were kind of in a good place. And now I was going to have to pick up the battalion and go up to this godforsaken place and have to deal with it all over again, because the unit up there couldn't get it done. Send in Sassaman. Send the 1–8 Infantry. Send the Fighting Eagles. Yeah. Send Sassaman. And I probably wasn't in a great frame of mind – from Dale's death on.

But we got orders: we're moving the first weekend of December, up to Samarra. There's the golden dome mosque, at least it was there until it got bombed; I don't know if they rebuilt it or not. About 500 metres to the west was the Arnold Schwarzenegger gym. There were no gyms in the cities I'd been to, until I get to Samarra, and it's like a gym with weights. And the guys we had dealt with were kind of smaller in stature; you got to Samarra, the dudes were thugs, man. Thick necks, big dudes, guys lifting weights, and they're ready to fight. Now.

It's a very dreary place, and it's not 120 degrees any more, it's cold and it's rainy and it's messy. Christmas in Samarra was not where I'd thought we'd spend Christmas. The guys had to leave where they'd been based, and we had to go to these makeshift warehouses, kind of a barracks-style cots, so I know folks were already disappointed. I was disappointed. But I played the Christmas music, the holiday music.

Christmas Eve was kind of harking back to my days growing up. In the church, there was always a Christmas candlelight service, and so I told the chaplain, 'You're going to go ahead and organise a Christmas candlelight service, and we're going to do a Christmas Eve,' and I told the cooks I wanted to have coffee and cake or brownies. It wasn't mandatory, a total optional deal, but we had everybody in there, and it was just something. All these soldiers lighting candles, singing Christmas carols, and the chaplain delivering a Christmas Eve message.

On Christmas Day, I had the sergeant major and a lot of the soldiers decorate this makeshift cafeteria as best we could. We patrolled, but we were trying to get everybody in so they could get a good Christmas meal. I had the officers serve it. It was one of the best meals of the year. It was hot food: turkey, mashed potatoes, stuffing, cranberry sauce, bread rolls, and a bunch of pies. It was great, compared to what we'd been eating and how we'd been living. I tried to make it the best I could for them. I shook every soldier's hand who came in. I think I even had the officers sing Christmas carols, and I had my HCC commander, Kevin Drew, put on a Santa Claus suit. And so, in this really dreary, godforsaken place, where the mission sucked and the people hated us, we just kind of hunkered down in this warehouse and tried to make the best of what was really a rotten place to be for Christmas.

I have great memories of this band of brothers, this togetherness. Yeah. And some good food. Christmas may be my last best memory of that time there.

Paul Bremer
In the immediate aftermath of Saddam's capture, there were both political and military indications that maybe we really had turned the corner on moving towards reconciliation. Very soon after we got Saddam, the CPA got a feeler directly from a leading

Sunni tribesman saying that he was in touch with the resistance in Samarra, where there were constant battles going on, and the Sunni leaders of that group were willing to start trying to figure out some disengagement. We went back and said, 'OK, we will give it a try. We need to know that you are really talking to the people there ... and the test is you need to get them to have a ceasefire. No attacks on other Iraqis or on our forces for 48 hours.' The first 24 hours went fine, and then all hell broke loose again.

Within a few days of Saddam's capture, I was told by somebody in Washington that the UN had also had a similar kind of feeler from some reputable Sunnis. If you look at that conflict, there was a dramatic drop-off in attacks on coalition forces in December, January and February. So there was some indication that Saddam's capture might have been the turning point on both the political side and on the military side. It turned out more on the political side than on the military side.

I think the Shias felt that it was possible to imagine now an Iraq not under Sunni domination. The Sunnis had effectively dominated Mesopotamia for a thousand years. No Shia had ever said this to me, but my gut feelings told me that what we had done in getting rid of Saddam was also challenging the political order as it had been under the Ottomans, under the British, under the Hashemites ... It was a real shift. The Shia, when we talked to them, said, 'We are the majority in this country; if we're going to have representative government, we need to have a voice as the majority.' I understood and agreed, but said another thing about representative government, which is minority rights. Democracy is not majoritarianism. You can still have an effective role in a country if you're a minority as long as minority rights are observed. These were difficult concepts, I think, for both the Shia and the Sunni to grasp.

Waleed Nesyif
At this time, Iraq was in absolute chaos. Freedom was understood in a very backward way where people were doing whatever they

wanted. Within the governing bodies that were trying to kind of erect some semblance of a policy and structure, there was an attempt to actually establish a structure. I've seen that first hand: meetings in the convention centre where they were talking of policies. But it all just felt unreal. Whether that was going to take Iraq to where it needs to be, for the people, for Iraqis, or not ... that was still a big question. The insurgency, or resistance, to the American invasion at that time was brewing, but I would say lots of Iraqis were still like, 'Let's give it a little bit more time.'

Paul Bremer
I don't know when I first heard of Muqtada al-Sadr, probably some time in June or July. An Iraqi magistrate came to our people in the Ministry of Justice, saying that he had prepared a case that Muqtada al-Sadr had arranged for the killing of another Ayatollah who had been, in Saddam's time, in exile in Britain, and was assassinated the day after he arrived in Iraq, the day after the statue went down. At almost the same time, Muqtada al-Sadr began publishing a newspaper. Something like 100 newspapers started to be published right after liberation, which of course was an example of how much freedom they got, but his newspaper attacked the coalition and particularly named a number of Iraqis that were working as translators for the British and American forces, and effectively called for them to be killed. Two of them were subsequently killed within a couple of days.

Muqtada took steps in the fall of 2003 to actually have his people start killing Americans. They attacked and killed American soldiers in Karbala, another town in the south. We started to get rumours in December, and then confirmation in January, that his people were running kangaroo courts and torture chambers, very much like Saddam. We had a policeman who had been captured by them, who had been tortured. He couldn't walk because they had done so much damage to him. Then in February or March, Muqtada's newspaper began to 'praise God for the 9/11 attacks on America'. That would be incitement in our country. So we closed down his newspaper. His reaction was to attack the CPA offices in several provinces – in Najaf, in Kut and in Diwaniyah.

At exactly the same time, we had several American Blackwater contractors killed outside Fallujah and then their bodies desecrated, hung from a bridge.

Waleed Nesyif
At the time, four civilian contractors were captured by the Fallujah people: killed, dragged, burnt and they made effigies of them. Civilian contractors are anything but civilian or contractors. As Norman Schwarzkopf described them in one of his speeches, they do the role or the job that any Marine dreams of doing. They don't fall under martial law. Nor do they fall under civilian law. And the Americans used them very heavily to do the dirty work that the army couldn't really do, simply because there would be an international tribune, putting the Americans on the spot as to allegations and violation of human rights. There are all of these videos that you can find of how the civilian contractors used to have fun: as they were driving in the streets, they would be just randomly shooting at cars, killing people, left, right and centre. So the four people who died were not innocent people. They were not civilian NGO workers that were there to help the Fallujah people. They were armed men belonging to a group of assassins, mercenaries that were hired to do a dirty job by an army.

I'm not for killing. I detest that fact, but there was this sense of helplessness and it was like, 'Well, this is what you signed up for.' I know how much they get paid: some of them were getting paid a thousand dollars tax-free a day. So the risk that they signed up for is exactly what they've gotten. Nevertheless, I don't claim to know why the people of Fallujah actually killed those four particular individuals. Perhaps because they were a symbol that represented others that have harmed the people of Fallujah.

When the American assault started, I remember trying to go [to] Fallujah, but it was just impossible. The Americans had blockaded everything. They wouldn't let journalists into the city, no

NGO workers, no Red Cross, no Red Crescent, and they were just bombing the living hell out of the city. Claiming that all civilians were informed and therefore they should have vacated the city. Yeah, they did. They announced it on TV. But the reality was not everybody can afford to leave the city.

And you wonder, is this the action of a nation that has any good intention? Sure, they killed four people of your civilian contractors. Let's say they were innocent, couldn't there been a better way to investigate this? To try and get the actual guilty parties? As opposed to condemning a whole city of 350,000 people to death, destruction and despair. The people of Fallujah ... I mean to say, 'on edge' is an understatement, you know. To say they were distrusting that was also an understatement. And they had every right to be.

Paul Bremer
By the beginning of April, Muqtada al-Sadr's army was basically occupying two provincial capitals, and Fallujah was in uproar because of the problems of Blackwater. The question was: what were we going to do about Fallujah. And eventually President Bush ordered our army to go in and get control of Fallujah. We had to react, we had to figure out what to do, and it felt a bit overwhelming frankly because – quite apart from the problem of security – we also had the problem of trying to keep the political crisis on track. We were supposed to leave at the end of June and turn over to some new Iraqi government. We were also working with the Iraqis, helping them draft a constitution; we had just finally finished the constitution in early March. So, while that looked like it was going forward, all of a sudden this stuff hit us and it kind of raised questions of whether the political process could itself survive this double crisis.

Waleed Nesyif
I think Paul Bremer single-handedly started the path of Iraq's destruction with the policies and the demeanour he imbued on

Iraq and the CPA at the time. Whether he was acting as the main adviser, giving his reports to the Americans, and then they were saying, 'OK, go ahead and do that,' or he was acting upon orders that he was receiving, I don't know. But I know for a fact that he's the one who disbanded the army. I know he's the one that actually, you know, established this law that prevented street vendors from functioning, which is one of the only jobs that people could pick up. Once he declared this new law that these guys are outlawed, it's like the one hope people had to make some money has been taken away from them.

I was going to work at that time, and the cab stopped on the side of the street. Right across from me, there was a kid, couldn't be more than 10, 11 years old. He was selling gasoline. An American patrol passed by. And then they stopped. There were two Humvees and an armoured carrier. One of the soldiers came back, hopped off the Humvee and went back. He took one of the canisters and ripped it with his knife, and started pouring it down the street. Now the kid was screaming, 'My dad is going to kill me!' and trying to stop the soldier from pouring it. The soldier poured it all down. And as the kid is trying to fight back, the soldier slapped the kid so hard that the kid literally flew a couple of metres back and fainted. And the soldier turned around and waited for his friends to take a photo of him. This was broad daylight, we're talking 10am, Iraqis were passing by ... I cannot describe the rage. I can't. I went to the kid and was helping him up, and he was crying, and the only thing he was thinking about is, 'My dad is going to beat me because I lost all of this petrol.' That they probably waited for two, three days to get. Because the CPA have declared street vendors to be a lawless thing.

I think it participated heavily in creating the resistance. All we wanted to do was just survive. And had America done something very simple, like brought us power, water, some semblance of security, things wouldn't have to have taken that turn. But they weren't interested in that, were they? Because they had multiple chances of doing this. Instead, you started having reports of so-and-so who was a high-ranking member in the army that we need to go and take and put them in jail. So they started breaking into people's homes, right? In the middle of the night. Getting information from informants that were completely unfounded.

New Year's Eve, my friend's family were sitting down having dinner. All of a sudden, 20 American soldiers broke into their home. They don't speak a word of English, my friend's family. My friend's brother made a wrong move, so they shot him, point blank, in front of his parents. Dragged him by the hair outside and then put a torchlight on his face. And the informant was like, 'Oh, not the right guy.' So they told my friend's family that they are not to speak of this, otherwise there will be consequences.

Things basically were brewing now. I don't think there was any interest from America to establish any form of stability in Iraq because it did not serve their purpose. Logically, had there been security and stability in Iraq, and the government is functioning, everything is there – there would not be any need for an army presence there, would there?

They had the sham of the WMD which they have wrapped this whole campaign around, and which are nowhere to be found. And they tried to attach al-Qaeda to Iraq as well, with 9/11. If you know anything about Saddam, you would know he hated religious groups. He destroyed them. Saddam literally just wiped them out. So none of their arguments actually held any water. What America wanted from Iraq was, obviously, the oil. For 13 years we were not allowed to export our oil in the way that we should have been, right? So you have a huge amount of reserves. Second, they needed the geostrategic position of Iraq. You had Iran on this side, you had Turkey up north, you have Saudi Arabia and you have Syria. By being in Iraq, you have a window across all of these other countries that could have been problematic for you, and being stationed in Iraq is pretty much the best position to be in if you are trying to dominate the Middle East, which they did. They needed to make sure that their presence there is guaranteed.

History is going to reveal itself, just like it did many times before. And, unfortunately for you, your fantasy will be no more that you have represented a country that is supposed to carry out a mission to help others. You did not help us. You destroyed our country. I don't blame you as individuals, because you were sold a story that, yes, perhaps you are going to help another nation in dire need. But your naivety and lack of willingness to learn from your own history is what will continue putting you in this position.

I did a big series going around the city seeing where people are living. One particular one was the Iraqi Aviation Club. It was an architectural marvel at that time, really beautiful, really nice, a three-storey building. Driving by it, we weren't allowed in because my dad is not an aviator, but I remember it looked so nice. So that placed got bombed, and now homeless families that had lost their homes had been forced to relocate over there. Walking in, you're seeing the kids playing soccer in the front yard, there's rubble, pieces of metal and stuff like that, and of course most of them were barefoot. They took us to the second storey and, as we started climbing up, there was this smell. This invasive, strong, godawful smell. It wasn't the smell of death, but it was equally rancid. Walking up, the smell's getting stronger and stronger and stronger, and then we got into the second floor, and it felt like I got hit by a brick wall, you know, how strong the smell was.

Families had made makeshift shelters, making a wall with a piece of cloth, a sheet of metal, stuff like that, just basically trying to keep decent in this new dwelling that they made up in this impossible situation. The smell was just destroying me. I wanted to vomit at how strong it was. But I'm looking at the faces of the people around, and they're unfazed by it. A lady came out with a plate of sweets, and she's welcoming in the famous Iraqi way where people compete over how generous they can be. As an Iraqi mother would do, she took a piece and she shoved it in my mouth. I'm now chewing this thing, and finally I discover what the source was. I was led to the source by a stream of flies that was just circling it. I tried to swallow this thing and not vomit so that I don't insult them, and I started walking towards that source.

It was a fountain in the second storey, that now families are using to dump all of their excrement. For months and months and months. And it was overflowing and the outside was crusted, it looked like a melted candle of shit. And then there was this swarm of flies, you know, the colourful flies, the flies of death, that basically was just going around it. Around and around and around. Here is the messed-up part for me. As I came close to the source, I realised that I'm smelling it no more. It was OK at that point.

Chapter 3
The Killing Machine

Timeline

4 April 2004	The First Battle of Fallujah begins, in response to the Blackwater deaths.
28 April 2004	Photographs are published showing US personnel abusing and torturing Iraqi prisoners at the Abu Ghraib prison.
1 May 2004	US forces are withdrawn from Fallujah.
28 June 2004	Formal sovereignty is handed to an interim Iraqi government.
5 August 2004	The Battle of Najaf begins.
7 September 2004	US military casualties in Iraq pass 1,000.
1 October 2004	The Battle of Samarra begins.
3 October 2004	US and Iraqi forces win the Battle of Samarra, retaking the city from insurgents.
7 November 2004	The Second Battle of Fallujah begins to retake control of the city from insurgent forces.
8 November 2004	The Battle of Mosul begins.

Introduction

It had now been more than a year since George Bush declared the mission in Iraq to be accomplished. The battle to win the hearts and minds of the Iraqi people had been lost, and American and British troops found themselves entrenched in fighting an insurgency that was increasingly violent and destructive. Reports of abuse in American-run jails, and the humiliating, degrading photographs of Iraqi detainees that emerged from the Abu Ghraib prison, further fuelled the ferocity of the insurgency. In the West, the publication of these images galvanised a growing anti-war movement. The significance of these photographs was certainly not missed on the civilian population of Iraq either. Even a young girl like Sally Mars, who was still only eight years old at this time, felt completely disempowered by events. For Waleed Nesyif, it was with anger and regret that he remembered his original enthusiasm for the invasion. Even this pro-Western teenager now felt compelled to sympathise with the insurgents. And there were even darker elements entering Iraq.

Since the start of the war Islamic extremists had begun to enter the country, attracted by the presence of the Americans and the obvious power vacuum that the removal of Saddam Hussein had created. Saddam himself had never tolerated Islamic extremists. In his Iraq, he was the ultimate power, and any threat to that hierarchy would be destroyed. Now, without Saddam to stop them, the extremists came. Eliminating Islamic extremism from Iraq was one of the justifications given by the Bush administration for the initial invasion. It is one of the dreadful ironies of the war, therefore, that it was the invasion itself that would help to establish Islamic extremism in Iraq.

Under the command of Abu Musab al-Zarqawi, a Jordanian criminal, a more violent offshoot of the original al-Qaeda was formed: al-Qaeda in Iraq. They were better funded, better armed and tactically superior to the home-grown insurgency. The result was the emergence of an extremely effective killing machine, that set in motion an unprecedented wave of violence across the country, targeting both the Coalition troops and the Iraqi Shia population. It was through al-Qaeda that the car bomb made its first, barbaric appearance in Iraq. Unsurprisingly, the death toll rose dramatically. It wasn't long before the terrorists had taken over huge swathes of northern Iraq and established a headquarters in the city of Fallujah, just 30 miles outside Baghdad. For the Americans, having an al-Qaeda base so near the capital was unacceptable. They were forced to react. The resultant Battle of Fallujah would be the biggest and deadliest battle the US Marines had fought since the Vietnam War.

Christian Dominguez and Billy Miller were Marines in 1/8th Bravo Company, which, along with a number of other companies, led the American attack on Fallujah. Journalist Dexter Filkins and photographer Ashley Gilbertson were embedded with the same squadron and experienced the full horror of the battle. Nidhal Mustafa, along with her two-year-old son, was a resident of Fallujah who did not have the means or the funds to leave before the fight began. She and her family were forced to stay in the city as the battle raged around them.

What happened in Fallujah in November 2004 would change all these people. For many, their lives continue to be defined by being either before or after Fallujah. The city itself was the setting of some of the most intense fighting of the entire war, and would go on, in the following years, to host even more violence. In 2014, ISIS seized control of Fallujah, starting yet another dark chapter in the city's recent history. For those who tell their stories here however, the physical and emotional scars of that first battle are still very present to this day.

'We Have to Respond'

Abu Mustafa's *home was Fallujah, where he lived with his wife Nidhal and their two-year-old son, Mustafa.*

Fallujah was a lovely city, it was a special city, it was beautiful and it was a nice city full of nature. I was working with sheep, buying and selling sheep. I was living my daily life: married, I go and come from work, there's no problem. The world in Fallujah was normal, everyone was working. Normal jobs and living normal lives. There were no problems. Mustafa was born in 2002. Mustafa is my first child. We were living in my uncle's house, but it was just us three. So we would organise our expenses, and we lived by our means and had a limited budget.

But in 2003, after the fall, everything in it changed. There was law and government; the fall happened, and there was chaos. The Americans entered Fallujah. After they came, they stayed a while. People didn't like them. They said, 'They're occupiers, coming here and occupying Iraq.' They stayed a while and then they retreated and handed Fallujah over to the security forces.

The Americans returned to Fallujah in 2004, and there were armed people and they refused to let the Americans enter Fallujah. The American army surrounded Fallujah. The Americans were attacking the armed people, and the armed people were attacking the Americans. So when this happened, we said we had to leave. Because we were scared of the bombs. We left for the outskirts of Fallujah, where Mustafa's grandparents' house is, in an area called Al Azraqiya.

And that is where the saddest story happened in my history, and I still remember what happened on that day.

Nick Popaditch
I'd see stuff on the news. I knew that insurgency was starting there, there was more disorder there than I thought would be happening at this point. I didn't know anything about Fallujah one way or the other, then we started getting classes on it, when we knew that's where we're going. We were doing the security and stabilisation operations, we were standing up a new Iraqi army, a new Iraqi police force, new Iraqi government, so we had to get very schooled-up on Iraqi culture. We had to get very schooled-up on operating very close with the civilians, because this one was going to be not fighting the military but fighting bad guys in amongst the civilian population. So we trained to do a lot of different things, which was a fun time in my Marine Corps life. It was fun training for these things, I was in a unit that was full of volunteers, and I was going back to do what the Marine Corps was out doing. So I was very happy about it. Very happy.

My company commander explained that there is a group of people in amongst the civilian population – they estimate their strength at about 10,000 – and they're trying to sow disorder and those sorts of things, and trying to undermine this new democracy, this new police force, this new military we're standing up. The way he presented it to me – and this made perfect sense to me – was that terrorism doesn't grow in free nations. Free people do not become terrorists. Free people repel terrorists. They would become an ally. Plus he also showed us the map a lot, where the nation of Iraq was, where the nation of Afghanistan was, and, with respect to Iran, that it had geographic significance. So I felt the mission was very solid. I was proud to be part of it.

We got back, we landed in Kuwait, we went in. We went out there in Humvees. We did get our tanks in Kuwait, and we put them on trucks and used Humvees to guard the convoy. My platoon, we were the security for the entire battalion. Because by now they're starting to use IEDs, we had to check every overpass, and there's a lot of overpasses in that 500 miles to Fallujah. I got in good shape running up and down overpasses.

Waleed Nesyif
Fallujah is as Sunni as they come. It's actually a part of the Sunni triangle, which is Ramadi, Tikrit and Samarra, three provinces north and west of Baghdad. Fallujah had a long history in Iraq. They were one of the first cities that actually started resisting the Brits, back in the occupation at the beginning of the twentieth century. They are proud people. Independent, proud people, very tribal. We're talking tribes that are prominent, that go back thousands of years – some of these tribes, they are ancient. They have their own history and culture and all of that. It's a traditional place that had some structural power in place, independent of governments, which is the tribal leadership. They didn't really jump the gun and immediately start resisting or fighting against the Americans. They actually gave America the benefit of the doubt. The people of Fallujah didn't fight them when they came in, you know; they could have, but they didn't. They weren't conglomerating in a way that produced a massive threat. I would argue that it wasn't any more or less than anywhere else in Iraq. So what happened to them was just uncalled for. Somebody had extended you an olive branch, and you just broke it and shoved it down his eyes. That's what America did.

These contractors are four people, and we had you bomb us for more than two decades. Destroyed everything we love, everything we stand for. As a human being I feel for them, but in the larger context of what it is, why they were there from the first place – they weren't there to kiss cheeks and hug children. That's not why civilian contractors are in Iraq. Civilian contractors are in Iraq to kill and do the things that the army cannot. As we have seen from the filth that came out of them years and years after.

Photographer **Ashley Gilbertson** *had been embedded, alongside Dexter Filkins, with US forces in Iraq since the start of the invasion.*

It certainly felt like it had changed from being the Iraqis' country to being the Americans' country. On a particular day in Baghdad, we were driving through a traffic circle near our bureau, we were caught in a traffic jam. From out of nowhere this massive SUV just bristling with guns – out of every window, and the top and the back – came pushing through and rammed all of the cars out of the way. I looked up at one point and there was a rifle stuck in my face. I'm just sitting in the car. And it was the Blackwater guys. Going through the traffic circle, not waiting, just ramming through people's cars. Total impunity. I remember distinctly at that moment thinking, 'This is not Iraq any more. This is not the Iraqis' country any more.'

I think the rise of the private contractors over there felt particularly damaging for what the Americans were trying to do, claimed to be trying to do. You would see that behaviour constantly. The military hated the contractors, and the more educated guys in the military hated them specifically because they felt like the contractors were undoing any work that the military were doing that might create some sort of good will. Blackwater would be in your town, they would like kill a bunch of people and leave, and then who pays the price? The army. And how does the army respond? And it feeds itself.

The contractors were America's second army in Iraq. They were everywhere. Triple Canopy, Blackwater, all those guys. All those guys acting out there as though it was the Wild West, they could do anything they wanted. How much money must have been made off those contracts, with those contractors? You would go out with the generals, you would go out with the CPA, like Bremer – none of those guys would use military. Generals wouldn't use their own military. They were using Blackwater. You use Blackwater, and it is not to protect you. What is done – to get traffic out of your way, to clear a line so you can drive to wherever you are going faster – doesn't get traced back. It's not in some report, it's not on public record. It's hidden behind the contractor wall. There were some bad guys.

Dexter Filkins

No journalist likes to embed with the military; it's too confining. I'm a journalist – I want to know what's going on inside people's heads, in their hearts. Imagine you're walking through an Iraqi village, and you're standing with a group of 19-year-old Americans with giant guns, and you ask an Iraqi guy, 'Hey, how's it going?' You're not going to get a real answer. So most journalists didn't like to embed. But it became essentially impossible to work in a growing number of areas around Iraq unless you embedded with the military, for the simple reason that you would get killed. We all had so many close calls: kidnappings, shootings, bombs … By the time I got to Fallujah, I thought I'd seen it all. I thought I'd survived it all. But no. God, no. No. That was a whole different level of violence. And it was just a whole different experience.

One of the bogus justifications for the war was that Saddam and al-Qaeda were kind of breaking bread together, and it was nonsense, basically. But after the war started al-Qaeda had very fertile grounds. It was an opportunity. The leader of al-Qaeda in Iraq, Abu Musab al-Zarqawi, was Jordanian. He had grown up in Jordan as a petty criminal, spent time in prison, had transformed himself in prison. He'd gone in as a secular street thug and he came out as a tattooed radical Islamist. And he wanted to fight. He went to Afghanistan, and when the American invasion of Iraq started he saw his opportunity. He was a lunatic. He was a bloodthirsty, murderous psychopath by any reasonable standard. But, man, the guy must have been really smart, because the operation that he set up in Iraq was basically this kind of un-killable killing machine. They couldn't stop it. They could not stop it. They cut off a piece of it and the rest of it would just keep going. It was incredible.

Sally Mars

When al-Qaeda first appeared, people saw them as saviours. They were the owners of the real jihad. They would free us from the Americans and get the Americans out of the country. But then al-Qaeda's attention became not just towards the Americans. They would bomb anything. They changed from people defending their country, who wanted to get the Americans out of the country, into terrorists. They recruited teenagers and young people. They only wanted power, power and weapons.

Dexter Filkins

Fallujah was bad from the beginning. It just wasn't a nice place to go if you were American, but I used to go there a lot because it was a hotbed, from the very beginning of the war, of anti-American activity. It was being run by the Mujahideen Shura Council. It was essentially like the caliphate. Enemy territory, owned and occupied. One of the focal points of the insurgency, so I used to go a lot. I'd go in, I'd do my work, and I would get out. I would try to find Iraqis who would talk and who were friendly, and I would try to get the hell out of there as fast as I could.

There was a restaurant there, one of the best kebab restaurants in Iraq. It was called Hadji Hussein's. Big place, fantastic kebabs. Early 2004, I walked into Hadji Hussein's, it was probably two o'clock in the afternoon, and it was filled. There were 200 men eating. It was loud – you know, everybody's talking. And as soon as I walked in the door, everybody stopped talking, the whole place. Just like in the movies. It got worse and worse, and a couple times we had to leave in a hurry and then we stopped going altogether. Then, summer 2004, right before the invasion of Fallujah, the Americans just flattened the place. Just wiped it out. The Americans said Hadji Hussein's Kebab House was a way-station for insurgent activity. Frankly, I found that a little hard to believe: I think the owners were Kurdish, it just didn't make sense to me. But they just dropped a giant bomb on it and destroyed it.

The story of Fallujah begins basically with a bunch of Blackwater guys and a bunch of contractors. I think I saw it on television, the contractors hanging from the bridge. It was another occasion where the Americans did, like, everything wrong. Everything. The Blackwater guys, they're civilians technically but they have guns and nearly all of them were former military or former CIA. They were incredibly aggressive, and they basically weren't accountable to anyone. They were trying to protect themselves as well, but they had a terrible reputation amongst the Iraqis and I think it was well deserved in many cases. The Iraqis hated them. I remember myself just driving through traffic in Baghdad, and if the Blackwater guys were coming through, they would just be hanging out the windows. They would stick their guns right into your windows and just look at you like, 'I can kill you any time I feel like it so don't even think about it. Maybe I'll kill you anyway.' So they were hated.

There was a group of four Blackwater contractors who were driving around Fallujah, and they got ambushed by some insurgents, pretty much in the middle of town. It evolved into this crazy scene where they fire an RPG at the SUV, it blows up, the thing catches fire, the Iraqis gather round – this is how much they hate the Americans in Fallujah, and how much in particular they hate Blackwater – they start gathering round and having a party, watching these four guys burn to death. One thing leads to another, and they picked up what was left of their bodies, which was basically some charcoal, just these black shreds of nothing, and the Iraqis are hitting them with shoes, you know, which is a very insulting gesture, and then they take them up to the bridge on the Euphrates and string them up. That was the end. What a frigging nightmare. It was a message: 'We hate America, go to hell. And we're having a party over their dead bodies.' Pretty ugly message.

The Americans did a lot of dumb things in Iraq, but this has got to be among the absolute stupidest things that they did: they said, basically, 'Teach the Iraqis a lesson.' Like, what the hell does that mean? Well, in this case it meant send the Marines into Fallujah and occupy Fallujah, because four contractors got killed. *Four contractors*. But it was on television, beamed around the world, and the Iraqis are partying and they love it and they're making fools out of the Americans, and they're hitting them with their shoes, so 'We Have To Respond.' It just made no sense, as any military person would tell you – what the hell are we going to do? But they told them to do it anyway. And the decision to do that came from the White House. 'Teach them a lesson.' 'Gotta look strong.' 'We're the authority here.'

Nick Popaditch
The murder of the contractors changed it from security and stabilisation operations into offensive operations against insurgents. Changed it back into more traditional fighting, as opposed to trying to positively influence community things going on. I think we'd been out there three days, when that had just hit the news: four American contractors had been murdered, and their bodies were being desecrated. Hung up, burned, dragged through the street. I remember being pretty mad about that. Word came down to, you know, mount up, we're going right back out. So we just went right back to the tanks.

The first thing we did was what they would call shaping operations, where we surround the city and then we start getting ready for the battle. The Iraqi army was going to come in and they were going to relieve us – manning the perimeter, making sure nobody got out – and then we would go in. When it came time for them to do that, hardly any of them showed up – like 20 of their guys showed up. So we ended up doing both parts of the operation. People would always say, you know, they're not standing up and all that. And I think, just having seen it on the ground, even if it's 20 guys that are fighting, I think that's worth fighting beside. I never got mad about not enough of them. It made me fonder of the ones who were standing up.

Fallujah resident **Abu Mohamed** *joined the local resistance against the Americans with his father and brother, wanting to defend their country and resist the occupation.*

Fallujah is the city of mosques. It has many mosques. There is no pressure to pray there. If you want to pray, you can pray – and if you don't, it's your problem. Allah will judge you, not the mosque. Fallujah is a nice town. It is peaceful and wants the best for others.

And its people are similar to Baghdad. Its people are kind and like living. Living in Fallujah was good. You would come to Fallujah and live there, you would find wealth. Fallujah is the mother of goodness and is the heart of Iraq. If Fallujah stops, the whole of Iraq will stop. If the heart works, the person lives. When it stops, you die. So Fallujah is the heart of Iraq. In its people, its goodness and its beauty.

Then the occupation came, and they ruined everything. The factions came along and started making trouble. This person kills that one and that one kills this one – there started to be sects. This discrimination started – this one is Shia, and this one is Sunni and this one is Kurdish and this one is Christian ... They and al-Qaeda were the same. None of them were serving the country, they were serving themselves.

When the Arab Fedayeen came, they came to fight. They called it Fedayeen Saddam. But the Fedayeen were fighting for Iraq. There was a resistance, it happened in all areas, from the north to the south. All these people didn't resist because of a president or because of a sect; they were fighting for Iraq. Everyone defends their country.

The Americans couldn't enter Fallujah. They entered by mediation. There was a mediation between the Americans and Fallujah so they can enter. So the mediations happened with the elders of the tribes and they allowed the Americans to enter Fallujah. They entered Fallujah and then they retreated from it.

Abu Mustafa

Fallujah had a strong resistance, so it looks like the Americans wanted to enter Fallujah in any way they had to get in. So the bombs and things like that happened. If al-Qaeda wasn't there in Fallujah, the Americans wouldn't have hit it like that. So I blame them, at the end of the day. The ones who lost are the people. The citizen loses in any war. He is the one who pays the price of the war.

The 4,000-Mile Screwdriver

Rudy Reyes
I didn't think I was going back. I thought I was gonna be an instructor for four years and work on my marriage with my wife and have some time out. I didn't even know the city Fallujah. I knew about the Sunni triangle but I got the brief about Fallujah about seven weeks before men were hanging from that bridge. The brief was that the army is not holding Iraq and insurgency has taken hold, and that we're gonna go train with the British Royal Marine Commandos in Kuwait for a few weeks to learn how they could identify and then defeat the IRA at their zenith of guerrilla warfare. How did they fight? How did they survive insurgency? This was all new territory.

We're very trainable attack dogs. We train so we can do it, and so we were trained by the Brits, the Royal Marine Commandos, tough guys, strong guys, much respect to them. They're still English, they've still got a fucking stick up their arse, but not arrogant at all, very matter of fact, and everything they taught us they were exactly right. And some of our commandos were not happy with this training they were getting, because the Brit commanders were saying, 'If there is no clear-cut mission, you do not send your men out. There is no purpose because every moment they're outside the wire, they're in ten times more danger. They're already in danger because they're in the country. Take down all of your flags, take down all the indicators of where your command post is, take down everything that's gonna draw attention. Because you will have spies in your hard bases and they're gonna collect. And you're gonna get mortars or you're gonna get homemade rockets shot into your position.'

And, sure enough, that happened. I'd been in Fallujah for two weeks. Some homemade rockets hit the BAS Battalion 8 Station, next to our command post. Hit a gas main, blew up this fricking hospital, killed a surgeon that was getting ready to go home. And I was putting out a fire and I was rescuing people. We ran in there, and we were so switched on by then, so experienced. Boom, immediately ran in, pulling bodies out, saving lives. And everything the Brits had taught us was all true.

We were seeing the signs and the placards and messages everywhere when we got in there. 'Americans go home.' We're going to kill you every way we can and we're gonna do horrible things to your body, and you care much more about life than we do. So do yourself a favour: pack up your kit and get the fuck out.

They had these massive ammo dumps all over Iraq, and the soldiers were not guarding them, so the insurgents were taking those ammunitions and making roadside bombs. Failure of leadership and maybe failure of their training: they were not aggressive enough and they were not personal enough. Their policy was to do the minimal amount of work possible and, whenever outside the wire, drive as fast as you possibly can going to where you're going. Completely passive and reactive. That's what I inherited. They had built up these 'Fobs' – fort operating bases. Massive bases, they had showers, they had dining facilities, they had ice cream. They were overweight, they smoked cigarettes all the time. Compared to the military discipline I was used to, they were just embarrassing.

Those contractors were hubristic as well; thought they were too cool for school and the basics of patrolling and of war fighting didn't apply to them. Soldier convoys running out into town to get liquor. Contractor convoys coming out without machine guns and close air support to get chickens and pitta bread. That's all weakness. That's what those contractors were out doing. They were driving to get chickens and meat because they didn't wanna eat rations. They have no machine guns, they only have assault rifles.

They did not coordinate with people and so they got engaged, they got defeated and then they got killed and were strung up. The message was: 'Americans, you don't have the stomach for war. It's obvious, so get the fuck out.'

Nick Popaditch

Once we went into the city, it turned into pretty much a constant fight, all the way around the clock. You got a little respite here and there, but it was pretty much a constant fight. They're not really good at operating at night, so at night we could hit times where we would shut down and leave like two guys awake up in the turret, the other two of us would sleep and then we flipped. An hour, you know, but that's enough. Honestly, when you're really tired, an hour goes a long way.

I had a platoon of infantry that I'd been operating with. We'd been going up and down in the Jolan district. We would take a lot of ground then we'd give a little bit of it back, and we'd take a lot of it and give a little of it back. Not everybody was as far in the city at that point; we could only go so far, and then we'd have to pull back, just so we wouldn't get over-extended. Really, we had just been killing a lot of bad guys, and not really so much concerned about taking ground – more concerned with taking down the enemy.

We were sat in this street, not very far from where those contractors' bodies were hung from that train trestle, probably like a block or two from there. One of our infantry up in a building next to me said they had a squad-size group of enemy insurgents assembling round the corner, like two blocks away from where I was at. And so I radioed up to the company commander and said, 'I can go get 'em right now.' He said, 'Go get 'em.' So we hit them up. They were assembling outside of a mosque. What they did in Fallujah was they used the mosques to stockpile weapons. They would move around as civilians and then, when they got ready to fight, they would go in and get all their weapons and assemble. So there was about a dozen of them. We took about half of them down right there outside the mosque, and the other half went around a corner so I pursued them.

It was a very narrow street, but it would be a narrow target for them to get away as well, so I kept pursuing them down the street. We're chewing them up with machine guns as we're going down and we're getting some, but they're still getting further and further. I was heading into a narrow intersection – the cross street's about eight feet wide, it's a very narrow street. That's a good place to get hit from the side, so I took my loader and I put it down below the armour line. I hunkered down and I went into the intersection and I scanned to my right, and there's an insurgent up on a rooftop and he's real close, about 50 feet out, and he's got a rocket on his shoulder and he's looking right at the side of the tank.

This is not a bad thing because the tank can eat these things up, the tank can take the RPG shots. I stop the tank, so that I can get a shot at him before he gets away. His rocket hits the side of my turret, doesn't penetrate, it's not a big deal. And when I'm swinging my machine gun over to get him, there was another one I never saw and he was a little bit to my right rear, and he put a rocket right in my hatch and blew my helmet apart. It blew this eye out of my head, and it blew my left eye, knocked this part of my skull out, knocked my eye down into my sinus cavity.

I didn't really know any of this had happened. All I know is I heard the hiss. The RPG makes like a snake, *ssss*, as it cuts through the air. I heard the hiss and then, you know, I felt that I'd got hit in the head with a sledgehammer, and I saw a bright flash of light, and then nothing, just blackness, just darkness. I was still conscious. It knocked me down, and I got back up, and I felt my head and it was all wet so I knew I was bleeding pretty badly. And I remember knowing what it was, knowing I got hit by an RPG, and knowing I'd stopped the tank.

If you get hit, what do you do? Move. I used to drill that into my guys, I'd make them just repeat it over and over. Move. Because if you get hit once, they're going to hit you again if you just stay there. I remember knowing that I needed to move that tank or they were just going to keep pouring fire on until they lit it on fire. I remember talking to my gunner, his name was Chambers, and saying, 'Chambers! You got to get the tank moving.' And when I was looking for him, he wasn't there, I couldn't find him. What he had done – you know, I was bleeding on the turret floor, and he saw that and he took command of the tank to get the tank moving again. The other guy, Hernandez, my loader, he got up and got back on my machine gun and he'd been wounded himself. And the driver, Lance Corporal Freres, 19 years old, the year before he's at his high school senior prom, he said, 'I know the way,' and they pressed through and they got me to a medevac site or I'm going to bleed to death real quick.

And that's what saved my life, was those three guys got me to that medevac site. And getting expert medical attention that stopped the bleeding out of these holes in my head.

I never for a second thought I was going to die. I think I may have, perhaps, been closer to that than I thought or realised. Probably the biggest danger was bleeding to death. The only thing I remember was, once that tank got moving again, feeling really happy, like everything's OK, and then I remember feeling really sleepy. Just the strongest instinct in me was saying, 'Just lay down in the turret floor and go to sleep.' And I knew, OK, don't do that. Because that's how you die. When you're bleeding real bad, don't go to sleep, you won't wake up, you'll die. So I remember thinking, 'Don't do that. Just stay awake, just focus on staying awake.' The whole thing was pretty painless, really. I didn't feel much pain. I didn't remember being very scared, or scared at all for that matter. I was probably pretty loopy, you know. I was concussed pretty hard, so my logical thought processes probably weren't that great. But I was relatively conscious through it, I remember most of it.

I remember being actually somewhat calm when the Corpsmen were working on me. I remember being nauseous, like sick to my stomach, like going to throw up. And the Corpsman was working on me, he's like, 'Hey, Gunny, where are you from, you got kids?' I mean, I know what he's doing, he's trying to keep me from going into shock because we've all been trained to do the same things. So I remember telling him, 'Look man, I know what you're doing, I'm OK, I'm not going to go into shock, the only hurt right now is talking to you because I'm sick to my stomach.' And he said, 'It's cool, it's cool.' And I ended up throwing up all over these guys, him and the other Corpsmen. And then they took off their own body armour and piled it on me, to protect me from mortar rounds that were landing at the medevac site. So do I remember being scared? No. Do I remember being in pain? No. The only thing I remember were those two Corpsmen that I have no idea who they were – they weren't from my unit, they were just two people I never met – taking off their own body armour and piling it on me to protect me. That's what I remember about it.

They took me to the place we called the animal hospital. I don't know where it got that name from, but they took me to the animal hospital, and that's where they started working on me to pull the shrapnel out, stabilise me and all that. It was all pretty painless going in. Coming out is a whole lot different because now they're digging in this remaining eye with scalpels and everything else. And trying to get it back up in the eye socket and do the various things they have to do. Now it's starting to get painful. I started fighting with them, and I remember the doctor talking into my ear and saying, 'You know, Gunny, you got to help me out here. You have to work with me a little bit here.' I remember just trying really hard to cooperate while he's digging in my eye with a scalpel. And he was keeping me awake – they weren't anaesthetising or knocking me out, they were keeping me awake because they're trying to save this eye and they had to ask me questions. Apparently throughout this, they had to ask me questions and I had to respond to them. Had he not done that, I'd be sitting here totally blind for the rest of my life.

When the rocket hit, it destroyed one eye, but it did what's called an orbital blow-out on the other eye: it blew the very bottom of the eye socket out, and knocked my eyeball down into my sinus cavity. I had a piece of shrapnel go through my right temple, went all the way through my head, and ended up on my left eye on the optic nerve, so I was blinded in both eyes. Well, one eye was gone, but the remaining eye was blind. They did a surgery where they drill a hole through the bottom, went up in there with a little camera, grabbed that piece of shrapnel, pulled it out, and filled the whole thing in and restored sight to my remaining eye. It's not perfect sight – I lost 92 per cent of my field of view – but when you went from total darkness to 8 per cent vision, 8 per cent vision feels like a million.

Dexter Filkins
The Marines are ordered to move into the city, kill every insurgent they find, occupy the city and establish authority – essentially, it's like, punish them. Send the Marines into Fallujah and ... do what? Kill who? Because the insurgents are not the whole population. They're *in* the population, but you don't know who they are so what are you gonna do? So they moved in, and it was bloody, it was bad, it was ugly and it was *really* bad on television. American gunships are over the city, they're firing rockets at buildings that look [like] they're filled with civilians. They're killing civilians. No doubt they're killing insurgents, but it's hideous. And so American Marines moved into the middle of the city. They were literally a couple of hours from being in the centre of the city, and they were ordered to stop and pull back.

I was talking to this Marine colonel that was involved in the offensive and he was enraged, he was just beside himself. He said, 'First they tell us to go in, and then they change their minds. The first order was stupid, and the second order was stupid. My god, if you want us to move in we can move in, but don't change your mind.' And I said, 'Who? Who are you talking about? Who gave the order?' And he said, 'Son, that's the 4,000-mile screwdriver.' Which is, like, 4,000 miles – all the way back to the White House.

Rudy Reyes
My mission was to go there to secure and stabilise that area. And nobody's gonna stop me and my people. We did everything and

anything. Undercover operations. Direct action, covert action. I did so many sniper missions I can't even remember how many missions I did. We shut down the IED threat by killing anybody digging holes, anybody. Man, woman or child, I'm gonna kill you if you're digging a hole. If you're a little kid digging a hole and you're paid five American dollars to go dig a hole, we drop you. Pretty soon nobody's fricking digging holes. You can't put an IED if there's no hole to put it in. And at night if we saw three vehicles together at night, we smoke 'em all. At night, if you see five males, smoke 'em all. I didn't even need to see weapons or explosives. Smart, because people get together, they spread ideas and they're working together, that's a threat.

We'd set up snap vehicle checkpoints. My team would melt off of the vehicles and then run as fast as we can, armed to the teeth and skirt the dogs. We'd lived in zone so long and we didn't smoke cigarettes – we didn't smell of tobacco, we smelt like the shit and piss of Iraq – so the dogs would not be alerted. When we got information from the people we would kill, we would use signals intelligence and our other government agency assets to find out who they're talking to and at 4am in the morning fucking blow open the door of those houses, go and arrest or kill everybody in there and then take them to Abu Ghraib. I took so many people to Abu Ghraib. But you know what, in two months there's no IEDs. I would call that mission successful.

I'm a scout sniper, so every man, woman or child I had behind my crosshairs, I had their life. They're already mine. I only pulled that trigger on that rifle when I absolutely checked off every bit of criteria and with no doubt in my mind, I had to pull that trigger. That's called professional killing. But then when you're in firefights and battles, it's much easier and much, much faster, much tighter. In real gunfighting, first and foremost is fire superiority. Pouring fire in and the fire manoeuvre. So, every time you're firing, you're also moving closer to them. You're destroying their will to fight and you're dividing them, routing them. There's even an elation because you're alive and, you know, you're joyous. You're alive, they're dead, and you're still moving on. And you and your team talk about it just like a football game. You talk about whooping that arse. And then you talk about how to keep that winning streak going. So your whole reason for existence when you're in that kind of environment is really making yourself more lethal to kill the enemy. Looking back, I guess that changes you.

Same area which Blackwater contractors were hung up, we were doing sniper missions and blocking positions, and shit was just crazy. We killed 35 enemy and they were dressed as Americans, so they got the drop on my brother platoon for a moment, killed one, wounded quite a few. We killed every one of those motherfuckers, let them know this is who you are fucking with now, you're not fucking with the army, you're not fucking with the Airborne, you're fucking with the Marine Corps, you're fucking with Recon. You're fucking with the wrong dudes. We killed those 35 men, those men were strung up on the vehicles, like meat, like deer, and drove like a promenade through the centre of Fallujah, to let 'em know that there's a new sheriff in town.

And they bucked up again, they tried harder. But they were no match for us. Because our whole mission, our whole existence was war. They were also fathers, sons, business guys, whatever. We were only there for one thing, war, and we were there to win it. I mean, how can you beat that? The only thing is, we didn't stay long enough. If they left us there for three years straight, then we would never have had ISIS. Three years straight. The world would be very different.

Dexter Filkins
So they kill a lot of civilians, and the shots are beamed around the world for everyone to see. And then they change their mind and it falls into the hands of the insurgents. Fallujah falls under the control of really the darkest, craziest, meanest insurgents, which was al-Qaeda in Iraq, led by Abu Musab al-Zarqawi. That was their safe area. Essentially it became a giant car bomb factory. They were just making car bombs and shipping them to Baghdad

every day. And the city stayed under their control from April until November of 2004, and it became the big safe haven in Iraq for insurgents. I mean, it was just one catastrophe after another, and it was emblematic of pretty much the whole enterprise at the time. The Americans weren't wanted there. They were trying to make it work, and everything they tried went to hell.

Abu Ghraib

Waleed Nesyif
Abu Ghraib is a notorious prison. During Saddam's time, everybody knows what Abu Ghraib is: you go there, you're fucked. But then I went, and they were doing rehabilitation to the prison and reconstruction. We walked in, and the walls were painted, there was a cafeteria area that they made for them. There is a shower area, there is a toilet, there is this, there is that. The Americans were showing us that, you know, as we were filming. And that section of the jail that they took us through, it was empty, right, because they are doing all of this reconstruction. And then I asked the guy, 'Do you mean to tell me that you are going to put Iraqi prisoners in those clean cells?' And he was like, 'Yeah.' 'And you are telling me that you are going to give them toothbrushes and soap and stuff like that?' And he was like, 'Yeah, let me take you.' So he took me to this storage area that had like hundreds and hundreds of mattresses, it had toothpaste and toothbrushes and brand new soap bars and all of that. And I was like, 'You mean, you're going to treat these guys with dignity?' And he was like, 'Well this is as mandated by our constitution.' Blah-la-la-la, you know, giving me this American spiel.

And then they took us to the other side where the prisoners were being held. I'm looking at the prisoners, there must have been, like, 50, 60 guys in a cell that is four by three. You know, just literally standing like this, and they were screaming. I was asking, 'What is your charge? What is your charge? What is your charge?' 'Oh, you know, it's been reported that he's a Baathist and he got thrown in jail.' Let's give the Americans the benefit of the doubt – *some* of them were criminals.

It wasn't very long after when the scandal came about. Of the notorious treatment, of what they were doing to those prisoners. Truth is, it wasn't very shocking. You know the stories and what people had experienced during Saddam's time – it wasn't that much different, to be honest with you. The difference is, it was done by Iraqis. This time, it is done by Americans.

Sally Mars
I remember the pictures and the reports about it. Once I took my brother's phone and tried to get on the internet and see the real pictures which weren't censored or the videos they didn't show on TV. At the time I was shocked – what *was* this? Bodies without clothes, and dogs biting them, and they were laughing. What's enjoyable about forcing a person to be naked and making a dog bite him? Or having yourself standing over him? Or putting a naked person over another naked person? It means you're a psycho, a person who isn't normal, a person with something in their head. You see this as something enjoyable which you laugh at.

I imagined at the time, when I saw this scene that Iraqis would stand up against this thing, and that demonstrations would happen. All the Arab and Iraqi advocates and lawyers would go to fight for the rights of these prisoners and get their dignity back. But what actually happened? Maybe all the Americans who were responsible for that prison are now living life normally. They're still there now and maybe they've started families and are living their lives normally. But all those who were subjected to rape and extortion and all these kinds of torture, most of them committed suicide. Most of them killed themselves, because they couldn't cope with these memories. They couldn't handle the thing that happened to them. Those who lived, lived with mental illness. I thought that we would get justice but the people didn't make a stand, or no one heard us. At this time I felt that we were in the weakest country. We didn't have a voice.

I felt I had a big responsibility at the time, because they would always tell us, 'When you grow up, you will have a duty to the nation.' I felt that this was a responsibility for when I grow up: how can I help those people? How can I get justice for them? I wish I could get justice for any person who was humiliated at the time, because I didn't go through this. My life was much nicer than many Iraqi people's lives. I was almost – relatively – living a normal life, but it wasn't normal in the way that people around the world live.

So I remember these pictures.

Waleed Nesyif
Anyone could go to jail, and this could happen to anyone. There were no Iraqi courts and stuff like that, that will process you properly, you know. They were judge, jury and executioner. So that could happen to anyone. And the sheer reality is that this is the new face of Iraq. And now it's out, it's public. Look at it. It's indescribable. And that wasn't the only jail. Abu Ghraib is a prison, that's what the structure is meant to function as. Imagine all of the other makeshift jails that they put through. The ones that we don't know anything about. What happened there?

'They Were Ghosts'

Nidhal Mustafa
Fallujah was beautiful. Its mosques, schools, hospitals, people, streets, electricity, water, security were beautiful, but they all got messed up. When the war started on it, it fell apart. It was attacked. It was attacked from all sides. All its beauty was gone. When they hit Fallujah, Fallujah was destroyed. The mosques were targeted, every mosque was hit. The schools, the hospitals, the homes were hit by the planes.

Fallujah was destroyed.

*In April 2004, in Pearland, St Louis, **Susie Miller**, her husband Lewis and their daughter Sabrina were waiting for news of son and brother Billy's latest posting with the Marines.*

You know, when an eight-year-old kid tells you that they want to join the army when they grow up, it's sort of like 'I'm going to be a cowboy' – you figure that it's just a phase they're going through. But Billy never wavered. He always wanted to be in the military, from the time he was about eight. And it was always the army, until he decided he wanted to be a Marine in his sophomore year in high school.

When he was in junior high school, he still wanted to be in the army, and he wanted to talk to people about being an army ranger. His freshman year, a friend of Lewis's who was a police officer, his son was an army ranger, and he came over to talk to Billy. Told him the different things you have to do, the different training that you had to do, and Billy was all for that. And then he just decided he needed to be a Marine, because, you know, they looked sharper than the army. I'm just saying – they do look sharper than the army!

Lewis Miller

I was very proud, very proud. The difference between the army and a Marine: every Marine is a rifleman, every one of them carries a rifle. In the army, you take ten soldiers, they're all different, they're trained in different fields. Out of ten, maybe three are trained to carry a rifle. The others cook the meals, drive the trucks, do this, do that ... but if you have ten soldiers, maybe three are carrying a rifle, so that makes a big difference between the Marines and the soldiers.

Susie Miller

I don't know if my brother Billy being a Marine had anything to do with my son Billy deciding he wanted to be a Marine, or if it was truly like he told me, just that he wanted people to go, 'Wow, he's a Marine.' But he did love being a Marine. He did early enlistment, so he was sworn in before he went to his senior year, so he was in the Marines for a year before he actually left for boot camp. When he graduated from high school, two weeks later is when he left for boot camp and we both went to watch him be sworn in.

The bus picks them up and takes them to wherever they're going, and we were there. My baby was leaving, you know, we're not going to see him for 13 weeks. It was hard. Then, of course, you're told that you can't send them anything, you can't write to them or anything for a week and a half. We didn't hear anything for about two weeks, and then we got the usual form letter from whoever was in charge of the San Diego Marine Corps Recruit Depot, and the letter, you know, goes, 'Your son –' because it's only boys out there – 'arrived safe and sound.' Like they would know, please. About a week after we got that letter, we got our first letter from Billy telling us, 'This is my address, and you can send this to me, you can't send any packages, you can only send letters, don't send anything else.' And he implied in the letter that he would get in trouble if we screwed up, so I didn't do anything but send him letters, but I wrote him, probably at least two, three times a week. I didn't want him to be inundated and be the laughing stock of the barracks or anything like that, you know.

After boot camp, you go to your advanced infantry training, and that's at Camp Pendleton. That's another three or four weeks. Then you go to your MOS, and I can't remember what it stands for, but that's their 'job' that they're going to do, so he went to the Dismal Swamp in Virginia. All the turmoil was really new at that point in time, because it had only been just over a week after 9/11 when he graduated from boot camp. I felt a lot better when I found out that he was supposed to be going to Rota, Spain, after his MOS. I thought, 'Well, he's going to be overseas for two years, you know, he's never going to have to go to Iraq or Afghanistan.'

He was supposed to come back in March of 2004, from Spain. December, like the 17th or something, Lewis and I went out for lunch. We got home and Joey, my grandson, who was like five years old, was in the house with Sabrina and there was this big box in the den. All wrapped up in Christmas paper. And she said, 'Mum, this is a Christmas present from me and Billy.' And I said, 'Is Billy in that box?' And she said, 'No, Mother.' I says, 'Did y'all buy me a dog or some animal because I don't want any animals.' 'No, Mother, we didn't buy you any animals. But you need to open it up now.' So I unwrapped it and underneath all this packing stuff and pillows, up pops Billy. I was so excited, and I started screaming, they taped me. I didn't know they were taping me.

I was really, really happy because he got home like three-and-a-half months earlier than he was supposed to be coming home. I said, 'So do you have to go back to Spain?' He said, 'No, they released me after 21 months instead of 24 months. In January I'm going to Camp Lejeune.' I said, 'OK, where are you going from there?' He goes, 'I have no clue.' So that was Christmas of 2003, and we had a great Christmas because Billy was not supposed to be home that Christmas. He went to Camp Lejeune in the middle of January, and they didn't know what unit he was going to be with for two weeks. He was in this limbo land. Some time in April, he said he was going to be going to Iraq, going to be deployed in June of 2004.

He called us a few times. He emailed a lot, when he could. I learned a lot of chatting things on the net because of Billy. Me and him would instant message back and forth when he was in Iraq. Not near as much as we did in Spain, because he could do it in his barracks in Spain; he didn't really have barracks in Iraq. I don't know exactly where they all were in Iraq, most of the places he couldn't tell me where he was, but when he got a chance he called us. I made sure he had a phone card that had lots of minutes on it, and I could load more minutes on it from the States so he could call me from Iraq. Didn't take many minutes to use up a whole chunk of change from Iraq to the United States, but he had to call us. Sometimes he would only be able to be on the phone for two or three minutes, but he waited in line for an hour to get to the phone for that two or three minutes. One of the calls that he made, he told me, 'I just wish all the times I was home on leave, I'd spent more time with you and Daddy. Because I needed to be with people I love, and I can't wait to come home and be with people I love again.' It was tough for him over there.

We knew he was going someplace. He told me on the last phone call that he was going someplace in a couple of days and we wouldn't be hearing from him for a while. I knew at least a week before they went in that they were going someplace, maybe it was two weeks, I'm not really sure. I can't remember the date that he called me, but it wasn't until after they started the push that it was on the news that they had invaded Fallujah.

Dexter Filkins

Another order came down which was move into Fallujah and occupy it and destroy the insurgency and destroy the safe haven, and that's what took place in November of 2004. We all knew the moment was going to come. The generals were pretty clear about it: we're not gonna let this safe haven exist for much longer, we're going to obliterate it. They telegraphed it so many times that the civilians – not all of them but most of them – utterly the overwhelming majority of civilians left Fallujah. Ninety-eight per cent of the population just emptied out. The Americans had surrounded Fallujah, but they would let people leave. So when the American attack began, there weren't a lot of civilians around to get killed. That was a good thing. But the bad thing was the insurgents were ready, because they knew it was coming too. Because Fallujah was a magnet for insurgents – I mean, there were thousands of them in there – and because the civilians had left, the battle had a kind of purity to it. It was like a conventional military battle, the type of which you just didn't get a lot of in Iraq. Iraq was this war in the shadows, the insurgency and roadside bombs and snipers; this was like something out of the Second World War or Vietnam. A full-on military attack.

Christian Dominguez *was a Lance Corporal Marine in Bravo unit, fighting alongside Billy Miller in Fallujah.*

My family knew that I wasn't academically inclined. My goal was to be in the Marine Corps, and I knew that in the 11th grade. So for my family it was like, 'Just pass, Christian. Just get through this and you can start your new adventures.' So that's what it was for me. It was concentrating on passing summer school again and just checking that box so I can move on into what I wanted to make my career. I made it.

Right before you graduated, we had a wall in my high school, and on the wall was everyone's stars, and in their stars they wrote what school they were going to go to. At the top was these great schools – Yale, Princeton, Cornell. I always felt special because mine said US Marine Corps. That for me at 18 years old was already my biggest accomplishment. To put my name on the star on this board to say, 'I am marking my name in history and something I am going to make myself in my future.'

November 14th 2003 was when I graduated. You get about ten days off and now you are going to report back to North Carolina, to the School of Infantry for three months, and it is the fear of the unknown. I said goodbye to my parents and I went to North Carolina, and that was that. It's a training event centred around training infantry. They are training you to be a fighter at that point, and you do that for about three or four months, and you get assigned your unit. At this point of my Marine Corps career I didn't know anything about Iraq or the Middle East, but as soon as I got to the School of Infantry, the first time I heard anything and it is when they captured Saddam Hussein, and that's the only news I really even understood, right? Summer-school student, you know. I am not paying attention to world affairs. I didn't really know what was going on, and to me when I hear that I am thinking, 'Did we win? It sounds like we won.' You know?

So at that point we were getting divvied up into our units and I had to go to mine on February 14th 2004, and that is when we start to learn that we are going to Iraq. The very generic mission statement is 'We need to go to Iraq to win the hearts and minds of the Iraqi Coalition and the civilian population,' because there was an insurgency going on and the only way that we were going to win the insurgency was to cooperate with the local Iraqi national guard and try to influence what was going on with the civilian population. That's the big picture, but the small picture of Lance Corporal Christian Dominguez was: 'Right now it is my job to get on the bus and then maybe eat tomorrow and do exactly what my team leader tells me to.' The big picture was somewhere always in the background.

It's the only way that you can be successful in combat. A superior tells you to do something and you act, that's it. There is never thinking about it, there is no questions asked, because you lay this foundation in your Stateside training when you get to your unit. It is important, especially in Fallujah. I believe that there is a garrison leadership style versus a combat leadership style. In combat you need to be able to give a confident order to go and make entry in a house, knowing that it is possible the person standing in there is going to get shot. That's a difficult decision, and you need to be confident about it. You need to lead from the front. Feeling my team leader behind me, knocking on me, saying, 'Let's go,' and they put their gun next to you and you are clearing this together – that's a leader. Stateside leadership is different. We have to focus Stateside about career development and making sure that your dress uniform is a certain way. There is a lot of different things that you need to make sure are up to standards. Combat is about killing, saving lives, and our team leaders, our squad leaders – they excelled in it.

Yeah, so the day of the deployment it is just a logistical nightmare. Everyone has two huge green bags, and your big backpack, and it is all lined up in a row. The low-ranking people like myself, we had to load everyone's bags onto these huge vehicles, and you take a bus to a different part of North Carolina where you are going to fly out of. And I remember thinking I was glad that my family wasn't there because you have to put this shell of a person around you for your peers. So I separated those two lives for myself. I remember looking outside the window and listening to a CD player and was trying to tune out everyone else's tears because I saw a lot of wives, girlfriends, children crying and I couldn't handle that. So I put my CD player on and I would focus on the seat in front of me.

We left North Carolina, and our plane landed in Ireland and then into Kuwait, and then we got on the bus bussing us to Al Asad, Iraq, a huge base in Al Anbar province. It was dusty, it was hot, but it mimicked an environment that we had in California. It was our training environment before we went overseas. When I first got off the bus, I thought I was standing in the exhaust of the bus. This is how hot it was. I thought the wind that was blowing had to have been from the bus and it wasn't. That was just what the air felt like at 11 at night. So I knew it was a hot place.

We stayed in Al Asad for about two weeks before we made our way to various parts of Iraq, and during that time we really just were getting used to the climate up there, and making sure our bodies were adjusting properly. They gave you briefs of what was going on in Iraq at that point. They made sure you have got your first combat load: 7 magazines of 30 rounds; 210 rounds for a rifleman. We were issued illumination pop-ups, and you quickly learned what a combat load was. You were given breaching tools to get into houses and the amount of batteries you have to carry for radios. Your backpack was almost not manageable. You learnt pretty quickly that your gear probably isn't the best gear to carry this, especially your backpack. We had a saying: 'How much can you fit in your backpack? One more thing.'

While we were there, we worked a lot with Iraqis. There were two in particular that we had a contract with that they would go and collect rebar from these blown-out shelters. Nafa and Jaba, they would come with ten workers. We would provide security and make sure they weren't taking ammunitions and making sure no one hurt them, and we would work with them. Sometimes they would invite us to dinner. We would go to their house and sit around in a circle and eat rice and lamb.

We were manning checkpoints with the Iraqi National Guard and we would be on a checkpoint with a four-man team. We would man these checkpoints, and the Iraqi National Guard men would hang out on the first level and the Marines would hang out on the second level and they would come and bring us some ice or some watermelon or whatever. We kind of needed it. We had a great relationship with them, but we found out after we left those posts that those posts were overrun and most of them were killed.

A lot of them were part of Saddam's army beforehand that didn't necessarily believe in his views. A lot of them, when I looked at them I could tell they had been through a lot. They were a lot older and you could see it in their eyes that they have seen a lot of death through the years. Especially their recent years. They weren't the most tactical fighters that we had, but they were a valuable resource because they were also our liaison to the local populace. Sometimes we would have to stop vehicles. One time we stopped a vehicle running down this one highway, and we ordered this guy to get out of this vehicle and he refused. He did not want to get out of the vehicle, and when we took him out of the vehicle there was a box in his trunk. We told him to open the box, and he didn't want to, and it turned out that it was the funeral of his brother. It was his brother in the box. We needed the Iraqi National Guard there to help soothe issues and say, 'Listen, we apologise for this, this was never our intention. If there is anything we can do for you and your town please let us know and we will help remedy any issues we can.'

We always judged the atmosphere off the children. The children will tell you everything. If they are taught to run from you, you understand the town is not supportive of the military coalition. Kids aren't born with this; they are just a product of what they are being taught. I loved when the children ran to us, and 90 per cent of the towns they did. They would run to us and we would give them candy or water bottles, or whatever we had. But there were definitely times that they wouldn't run to us, and it is unfortunate. At that time, we believed in the hearts and minds mission winning over the local populace.

We conducted two other major operations before Fallujah, and we might have only got shot at one time. So we were in the country for five months without a real firefight. You kind of thought Fallujah was going to be big, but I didn't think it was going to be more than a day or two, maybe three. I started taking things out of my pack because I had to fit other things. So I didn't pack another pair of socks or any other creature comforts that I would have wanted. You are sitting there three weeks later with the same socks on, the same shirt on. I wasn't really mentally prepared for something that severe. I didn't know. It was tough for me to imagine Fallujah was going to be anything different than what we just did, but there were indicators that it was bigger.

We took over an area called Camp Fallujah, which was probably three miles outside the city, and is where we staged all of our gear to go into combat. There was a lot of old buildings there that we practised clearing houses, and we really refined our skills for calling casualty evacuations. How do you properly set a defensive position? How are you realistically going to carry someone out of combat? You start refining and developing your new operating procedures for how you are going to get your casualties out of there. It becomes real at that moment.

November 5th, Ashley Gilbertson and Dexter Filkins reported to my platoon and I was thinking why was the *New York Times* here? It was an indicator of something big happening. You are trained to not like reporters because you just have an assumption that something bad is going to come of this. They are there to tell a story that we might not like. They are there to tell a story of things that are happening on the battlefield that we deem is necessary and it is difficult to be put in a position that you are being watched, right? So we were told to stay away. They are there, they are doing a job, and we are doing a job and that was it. They had phones that we couldn't use. So off that we didn't like them, you know? They had phones, internet and computer and we were like, 'Fuck these guys with that shit.'

November 6th, we got a huge speech about how much money in destruction was authorised for this thing and what our Rules of Engagement were. The Rules of Engagement were a little different: you are able to engage anybody within the city because we have instructed civilians to get out of the city. As long as you felt like there was a threat you could engage. Previously you couldn't.

Nidhal Mustafa
The morning came and we saw the streets full of paper. The leaflets thrown down on us were thrown down by the Americans. They'd thrown them in the night. We read what they've written, in Arabic. They've written saying, 'If you can get out, get out.' That's it. They would throw these leaflets daily. They kept throwing papers on us but we're surrounded. Where do we get out from? We can't get out because of al-Qaeda and the Americans. We're surrounded from both sides. They put up checkpoints. We couldn't go out, unless the US army would come and take us out themselves. The roads we would go to, they would have them closed. If you move, there would be a sniper pointed at you.

Dexter Filkins

The Marines and the army never bring you in to the briefing on Rules of Engagement – in other words, when they're allowed to shoot – because those rules change depending on the situation. Usually it's something like you can shoot if you're shot at, or if someone is raising a gun – not carrying a gun but raising a gun and pointing it at you – you can shoot them. It's something pretty logical. But we got brought into the Rules of Engagement briefing, and the rules were dialled really far back, like, really loose. Guy picks up a cell phone? You can kill him. Guy's carrying a gun? Kill him. If an ambulance is coming at you, one warning shot; if they don't stop, you can light it up. The expectation was, and I think it was correct, that pretty much anyone we see is gonna be an enemy. It's not gonna be a civilian because the civilians are gone. If you are in this city, we are going to presume that you are a bad guy.

Ashley Gilbertson

When they were reading the Rules of Engagement, in the room with the Marines were Blackwater contractors, working side-by-side in offensive operations with American soldiers. That's this country's foreign policy and you've got private security guards doing it, who are not answerable to the authorities in the same way that the military are to the public? That's not right.

That was definitely a wake-up call, what these guys were expecting. We looked at the plan of attack that they had. All of these different units that were coming in at different sides of the city. They talked about the roads that we would be going down and, like, this railroad berm is here and you were going to cross that and go down this main road, but we're going to fire this charge, which is like plastic explosive on this 400-yard rope – we're going to fire that down the road, explode the whole thing to clear the road of IEDs, because apparently there were booby traps and roadside bombs all through the city because the insurgents knew they were coming so they had planned. So I was, like, 'It will be fine, it will

be a couple of hours and then the clean-up house-to-house ...'
And then we went out.

Christian Dominguez
On November 7th, we did a dry run. We essentially loaded up our vehicles and we pushed toward Fallujah. I remember loading up our assault vehicle and driving towards the city, and we practised lowering the hatch and getting out. That was the last rehearse before the assault. So that night we pulled in to the outskirts of Fallujah, outside the train tracks, and we dismounted, and we were essentially in fighting positions just looking at Fallujah. Observing it. That's when your stomach starts to tighten, and that's when I knew things were about to get hot. That moment was when I realised – 'Oh shit.'

And the thing about Fallujah is they were all warned beforehand. The assault had happened previously more than once beforehand. They knew exactly how they wanted to fight. They were dug in. They knew how they can earn the advantage in some aspects and the night time was one of them. It was very scary. It was how they moved from house to house, oftentimes even after we had cleared a house.

Dexter Filkins
Fallujah's really weird, it's like a movie set. There's an edge of town, then there's a street, and then the buildings start. It's not like a suburb, one building, two buildings; it's like a border. We rolled up in the troop carriers right up to the edge of town, and everybody piled out. It's night, it's pitch black, it's horrifying. As we were assembling, the voices came over from the mosques: 'Come to fight. Come, and defend the city. Defend your city.' There were so many mosques and so many loudspeakers, and they were screaming into the loudspeakers: 'God is great, God is great. Come to the fight, come to the fight. They are here. The Americans are here.' They were firing rocket-propelled grenades out at us and they looked like fireworks from the Fourth of July. They were exploding,

everybody got on the ground, there was gunfire everywhere. It was incredibly loud. The voices were screaming from the mosques, and I just wanted to go home.

The commander was standing straight, and he was talking on the radio with a calmness that was kind of eerie, it was like he was bored. It had this amazing effect, which was, 'This can't be that bad if he's talking in such a laconic voice and so slowly.' It does have that effect: you look at the guy who's in charge and you think, 'Oh well, he's not afraid, can't be that bad.' And so we all got up, with all the craziness going on, and we just started marching in.

Christian Dominguez
It looked like *Star Wars*. You saw the city get lit up for hours by tracer rounds, aircraft and small-arms fire. Shortly after that, we mounted our vehicles and we got taken to where we were going to make entry. They had a breach, a hole into the city, and we were basically filing in. We were 1st Platoon, first fire team, first squad. I was the point man for that team. I was one of the first people into the city. My squad leader told me to take a light and put it in my helmet. It was green, and they did it so that everyone could know where front was.

Dexter Filkins
I'm not sure I saw a person firing at us the whole time I was there. It was just gunfire coming from *somewhere* – a lot of it, tons of it, but you just couldn't see anything. It was pitch black for one thing, but even during the day it was really hard. There was a moment very early on where we were walking down the street, it was two o'clock in the morning, it was pitch black, you couldn't see anything. The Marines had night-vision goggles on. We didn't have those. We were walking down the street and we came under fire from the street ahead. Some snipers were shooting, and we tried to back up, and some guys behind us started shooting, so we couldn't move. We were trapped. And then they started firing mortars. They were getting closer and closer, and the mortar shells were just terrify-

ing, they were gigantic. We all scrambled for a wall, and we were kind of clinging to the wall because we couldn't go forward and we couldn't go back and we couldn't see anything. Everybody was ready to die. I remember my legs were shaking. I could barely stand up, because I thought we were going to die.

These four, really strange-looking guys showed up, with hoods and flight suits and tennis shoes. I remember they had night-vision goggles on, and their faces glowed kind of green. I found out later it was a group of Navy SEALs, and they had formed an anti-sniper team. With the hoods, they looked like executioners, and they were absolutely calm. I saw them talking to the captain, and they said, 'Tell us where they are,' and then they just peeled off. Within a couple of minutes, everything stopped.

Ashley Gilbertson
I'm with 200 men in United States Marine Corps uniforms, with M16s, M4s, with this Abrams tank, and then from out of nowhere we hear these pops above our head and you look up and it's these shells that have exploded. It's like this octopus and these tentacles coming down from the sky, and it's white phosphorus. White phosphorus is something that burns so hot, it will burn through your clothes, through your skin, through your bone and come out of the other side still on fire. So I see everybody starts taking cover, but they're taking cover looking up. Normally when a big bomb comes in, an artillery shell or a mortar, you eat dirt. In this case, you're looking up and rolling out of the way of these things as they fall down around you. It's like small bricks falling around you. Dexter took cover eating dirt, and one of the pellets of white phosphorus burnt through his sleeping bag, so he had this Swiss cheese sleeping bag for the rest of the trip.

Dexter Filkins
When you were in the middle of a fight like that, you had no idea what was happening. It was pitch black, it was 4 o'clock in the morning. This thing comes sailing in, this kind of bright light, this

bright white light, with a trail on it like a comet. It comes sailing in, and then it explodes right above us. These flaming chunks of rock were coming off, and people were just scrambling and trying not to get hit. Some Marine threw me into a bush and got me out of the way and then … then we all just took off running.

At the time I thought, 'This is a flare, and someone's trying to light up the sky so that they can shoot at us.' But it was white phosphorous and those were American rounds. They were fired by American guys – for what or at whom, I have no idea, zero. It's a terrible weapon: it just burns and it burns. It burns through water, it just keeps going. It burns through your skin, right through your bones. They would drop a phosphorous shell on a group of insurgents, and the term was always 'Shake and Bake,' meaning the people that were getting hit with the stuff.

Ashley Gilbertson

They told me it was white phosphorous which was accidentally fired by the Marines onto us. The sister union of Bravo Company is Charlie Company, just a couple of hundred metres away. They somehow mistook Bravo Company as being insurgent. Insurgent to the American uniform, to the American weapons and an M1 Abrams is next to them. And they called a fucking white phosphorous track on our position. They called a blue on blue, but it doesn't nearly capture the drama of how stupid that is. Nobody was hurt, amazingly.

Christian Dominguez

Throughout that night we systematically cleared houses throughout Fallujah, making sure we stay in line with our brothers to our left and to our right. That night was scary. It was the scariest part of Fallujah. Although you have the tactical advantage of having night-vision goggles and infrared sensors on your weapons that you can use for better capability, it's scary. You are in someone else's house, someone else's town and they know the lay of the land and you don't.

Ashley Gilbertson
It was violence like you've never seen. Violence that is difficult to describe without having been there. We're right on the edge of the city, and it's a big city. Two hundred metres in, they get to this big east-west road that crossed Fallujah, six lanes and a raised bit in the middle. Just to get to that road, it took them all morning, hours and hours of fighting, like, every step of the way they had to fight. At one point they came under machine-gun fire, and so you're running down the street and you can hear the bullets ricocheting around you, like bouncing off the street, coming off the concrete. And then it stops and you get up to this area that the fire was coming from, and there's a Marine scout team up there and three dead insurgents on the right. I've got a picture of one guy with his head blown open like someone dropped a watermelon ... He has a machine gun next to him, the other two insurgents are there. He was wearing a vest that I guess had spare ammunition clips in it but they wouldn't touch the body or clean up the bodies or anything because they were worried that they were strapped with suicide vests.

We got into this house on a corner. We had to cross this road to get to what everyone was calling the cultural centre – this big five-storey building on the other side of the street. One of the lieutenants stands at the gate and says, 'All right, go, 1st Platoon go,' and these 40 guys stream out and run across this street. And then it begins. From everywhere, it's like the whole city lit up. Just gunfire coming from all angles, and the Marines are in this house on the roof firing back, firing back, I don't even know at what.

This is the thing: I saw so many bodies, and I saw so many Marines go down, but I never saw an insurgent *alive* with a gun. They were ghosts. The way they would fight was, like, ducking out of the alleyways, shooting for a while, ducking back in, and then finding another position, I guess. But they blended in with this environment so perfectly, you would just never see them. I guess it was their city – you know, they know the terrain. I watched 1st

Platoon go out; all of this gunfire starts; a guy falls on the street; 2nd Platoon goes out; some guys drag this guy out of the street, and another guy gets dropped. I'm with this last platoon sitting in this house, and I remember saying to Dexter, 'I don't know if I can do this.'

I don't remember what he said, but I remember them just shouting, '3rd Platoon, go go go!' So I watched everybody go out, and I just ran. You could see the tracer rounds kicking up under your feet while you are running and you can see the blood trail on the road. You can see the sergeant bleeding out on the ground. I remember running, and I remember time slowing down. They say time slows down, but it really, really does. You can feel every step that you're taking, you can see everything taking place in slow motion around you. The guys falling, the guys dragging the other Marine, the bullets coming in … You're wondering where the fuck it's all coming from and what the hell is going on. I remember crossing, and I remember lane by lane. I made one lane, I made two lanes, I made three lanes. I remember the little raised area in the middle of the road, jumping up on that and then crossing the other lanes. I remember there was a high gutter in front of the cultural centre that didn't provide any cover. I remember the entrance to the cultural centre was filled, because there was two Marines, one of whom ended up dying there. I remember jumping up on this kerb, at the same time as putting my hand down and taking pictures of the sergeant being carried off the road by the Marines, and I remember tumbling into this wall and trying to make myself as small as possible.

Once we got inside this cultural centre, there was this round atrium area, where you've got balconies and you can overlook the centre of the building. I went onto the second or third floor of that and just collapsed against a wall. All the Marines were also collapsed against the wall, and we were all just like staring off into nothing. And one Marine turned to me and said, 'This is as bad as it gets, right?' I said, 'I've never seen anything like this – sorry.' I wish I could have lied to him that this is nothing, don't worry about it, but I couldn't. This was obviously going to be an insane fight that they had gotten into. This is the first two hours.

Christian Dominguez
Iraqi houses didn't really have bathrooms inside. They had outhouses, which were outside, and it was a logistical nightmare to go to those. So oftentimes we would take an empty box and we would find any chair in the house and we would take our bayonet and cut a hole in the chair. We would put the box underneath it and you just try to use a box. Keep at it all combined, condensed. And then pack it up nicely and put it in the corner because you don't want to be disrespectful while we are in Fallujah. We especially did that inside the mosques. You know, we did have Iraqi soldiers with us that were upset. They weren't even wearing boots in there, let alone killing in there, or shitting or peeing! So we tried to remain cordial and we shit in boxes and seal it up. Hopefully someone got rid of it one day! I don't know where the reporters shit.

Ashley Gilbertson
Weird things do happen, that are sort of funny, in these really dramatic situations as well. I'm photographing all of this stuff, dead and wounded Marines and dead insurgents, and it's like end-of-the-world stuff. It's really violent. And then I go to photograph the sergeant. He's just sitting down in a room, with the captain, chatting. Talking about what is going on and where they're going to be going next. And he's like, 'No, no, no. No pictures!' I'm like, 'What's the problem?' and he's like, 'My wife knows that I'm here and everything is fine, but she doesn't know that I smoke.'

And then, from the same room, I was looking out the window, and I see Dexter exit the cultural centre, the safety of the brick walls of the cultural centre, and run out into the middle of the street to a burnt-out car. He opens the bottom of the car and starts to pull out the battery because he needs the battery for his computer so he can file his story. This dude is insane. That is crazy. So many guys have just been shot on this exact corner. The insurgents are everywhere, and they're good shots. This isn't like spray-and-pray insurgents, these guys are real fighters. And Dexter is out there trying to pull a car battery out of a burnt-out car. Of course, the battery doesn't work. Cause it's a fucking bombed, burnt-out car. But it was classic Dexter. He will file no matter what.

The Marines, of course, had to use the toilets throughout the week. It's just a hole in the ground in a brick box. They were very precise with their rifles. They were not very precise with a hole in the floor in the toilet. So there was just stuff everywhere. Like, everywhere. Every night, I had to file pictures: eight to ten pictures back to the *New York Times*. The computer screen has a glow, and if you have any lights on then you will attract sniper fire. So I would say, 'Captain, where can I file my pictures?' He's like, 'You know where you have to go. The only room in the house with no window is the toilet.' So I would go in there, I would sit on the ground, amongst all of the shit and then put a sleeping bag over the top of me to make like a nice sauna of shit. The satellite downloaded my pictures, I'd edit, caption, and then file them back to New York as fast as I could, because I didn't have many batteries and I was in the grossest toilet in the world. I like to think that the Marines that were there got some enjoyment out of that.

Christian Dominguez
November 10th, the sun started to come up and you started to see Marines' heads pop out of the rooftops. You never really knew where people were, especially someone at my level on the totem pole. November 10th is the Marine Corps birthday; the Marine Corps takes it very seriously. The sun started to come up, and one of the team leaders from my platoon screamed out 'Happy birthday, Marines!' and the city erupted: 'Hooray!' You know we had been there for two nights already. We hadn't taken any casualties, but you were tired and you didn't know what was going on and just hearing that and knowing that it was the Marine Corps birthday and Marines all over the globe are celebrating this thing by getting

drunk and eating cake, and we were fighting the Marines' fight. It was cool.

Ashley Gilbertson
I made this picture. It's called 'Danger Close.' When they drop a bomb from an aircraft, you have to be a couple of hundred yards away to be safe – the percussion can blow out your hearing, or the shrapnel can kill you. The force of the explosion can topple the building you're in, so 'danger close' means that they're going be dropping a bomb within that couple-of-hundred-yard radius. They could also miss and accidentally hit your building. So everybody prepares: usually, you open your mouth so that the pressure can come out of your mouth rather than exploding your eardrums.

They had an AC-130 Spectre above us. An AC-130 is a really heavy plane. A big heavy plane. It's outfitted with Gatling guns and artillery, and it can fire its artillery down. When the Gatling gun opens up, it sounds like a really loud, disgusting burp. You hear it, and then the bullet just rips anything that it comes to into shreds. They're 40mm bullets, and it fires thousands of them in a second.

One night, three or four nights in, everybody was in this house, on the roof, and they were looking at this mosque across the street, and they knew that the insurgents were in the mosque. I was up there with the captain, looking at him peaking over the edge down on this mosque. And over the radio, they said, 'We can see 40 insurgents in a house right by you.' He's like, 'Where?' Everybody is taking cover. 'Right near you. You're going to be attacked.' So people are getting ready for an attack, but nobody can see them, can't hear them. So they say, 'D'you want us to bomb the insurgents?' The captain was like, 'Yeah. Yes, please.'

So we're waiting. Two minutes out. A minute out. Thirty seconds out. And the captain is like, 'Fuck. It's us. They can see us on the rooftop.' All I remember is everybody getting up and running as fast as they possibly could out of the house while they're trying to cancel this strike on the house that was us. '*We see 40*

guys with guns ... d'you want us to shoot them?' 'Yes.' 'Oops, it's us.'
We ran out of the house as fast as we possibly could. We called off the air strike, somehow.

Right across the street there's another house, and the Marines are stacked up and ready to go in, so I run over. They bust in the front gate, and they go inside. You would find these weird little sorts of oasis in some of the houses in Iraq, and so they kicked in these gates and it opens up and I remember all of this ... it looked like a textured grass area, like really manicured grass. Obviously, I'm not going in first because I'm a photographer. These guys are going first, they're looking for the insurgents. So I stood over on the grass, feeling soft under my feet. And I watched them kicking the front door of this house and they all streamed in, and then there was all this gunfire and then I heard a huge explosion and there was just screaming and screaming. And a really fucking awful screaming, like ... I don't know how to describe it. Like a wounded animal. It didn't sound human any more. A Marine had been hit with a grenade, and it blew out his entire jaw. The screaming was just like ... what was left of his face.

Christian Dominguez

It came up to about the 11th or the 12th. We were clearing a street, and 3rd Squad was ambushed in an alleyway. Carlos Dominus took a shot to his trap, Russell was shot in the shin, and it was tough. That was our first casualties for 1st Platoon, and we were trying to act on it. My squad leader ordered us to go and flank the enemy that we thought were in this alleyway, and we were moving up to the rooftop when we got the clue over the radio that there was 1KA – one killed in action. You just lost one of your brothers and you didn't know who it was. We didn't use names over the radio. Before we went to Fallujah they issued us with something called kill numbers. Inside your flap you had a number, and your number was alphabetical order and it was a way that we would be able to talk over the radio without affecting the fight. 'One killed in action, number three.' You knew it was someone with an 'A,' and you are trying to do the maths all the while clearing a house.

Suddenly you realise that it was Nathan Anderson, a popular Marine in our platoon. He was a bulldog, he was a team leader for 3rd Squad. He realised he was too heavy to go sprint down the alleyway with all of his gear on. So he took all of his gear off and sprinted down the alleyway and got all of them out of there. Anderson didn't make it; he was killed. He was one of my squad leader's best friends, and at that point we realised that the best action was to consolidate for the night, maybe get a little bit of rest, get some food in us and continue the mission tomorrow. So we went to take over a house, and the squad leader was intense at this point. He just lost one of his best friends. He ordered me to kick in the door, but I noticed that this house had a wire hanging down from the front door and it looked like a booby trap. I remember telling him: 'I think this house is booby-trapped.' He said, 'Go, kick in the door, go.' I said, 'Something is going on with this.' He pushed me out of the way, and about six Marines went in and I was the seventh Marine. Within seconds the house was pitch black. I saw sparks – you know, the kind that looked like sparklers from Christmas – and two loud bangs went off. There was two insurgents upstairs that lobbed grenades down to the first level. The squad leader was the first one up the staircase, and the grenade landed basically right in front of his face. He has had countless surgeries to this day trying to reconstruct his face.

We decided to pull out of that house, take our casualties out and blow the house up with tanks. It was the easiest way to eliminate the threat without taking any more casualties. We moved all the Marines to the house next door. At this point I didn't have a team leader or a squad leader. So just initiative. I went into a closet and there was a window and I had rear security. Some Marines had front security, some Marines were looking to the left or to their right. They told us all to get down because there was going to be an explosion, and when I jumped down I fell. I hit my head on the table and passed out.

I wake up 30 minutes later, and no one is in the house. What happened was the house where the insurgents were caught [was] on fire, and it was affecting our night-vision goggles, so our platoon decided to leave the house and go to a house further down the road to sleep there for the night. I didn't have a team leader, I didn't have a squad leader, so no one is thinking, 'Where is Dominguez?' I remember waking up, asking quietly, 'Are there any friendlies out there?' and no one answered, and I knew immediately that I was in trouble. I didn't have a radio. My night-vision goggles had taken shrapnel from the previous house and I realised that if Marines saw me in this house they would shoot me, and if insurgents saw me in this house they would shoot me.

For the next 45 minutes, I gathered my belongings and crept down the first level of the stairs, and I was trying not to make a sound. I got to the middle of the street in the courtyard and I saw a tank in the middle of the road about a block away. I told myself, 'I am just going to run to this tank. It's my only option.' I ran to the tank and I jumped on the front. I was trying to bang on it and then I realised there is a radio in the back. I learned that just a week ago in the training operation right before Fallujah. I go to pick up this radio and it falls off the cord, like some kind of horrible movie. As I do that, I see someone light a cigarette, maybe about four houses away. And I said, 'There is no way an insurgent would smoke a cigarette here. We own the skies, we have drones, it wouldn't happen.' So I ran to the cigarette, and I was screaming: 'There's a friendly outside.' 'Dominguez what are you doing here? Where were you?' And of course I start screaming. I was like, 'You guys left me.' To their credit they thought I was hit in the first house. Why wouldn't I be? My whole team was hit. And I go in first.

Ashley Gilbertson
One night, a different night – it all blends in at some point – I remember just waiting to be shot at again. I remember squatting and resting this heavy backpack. We were all wearing heavy backpacks; mine, I think, was 80 pounds or 50 kilos, whereas most of

them had much heavier packs on. I rested it against a wall. And there was a car on fire down the street. A sergeant came and squatted next to me. He didn't say a word, because everyone was moving as quietly as they possibly could down the street, waiting to be attacked, like every other day, every other moment. And I remember listening to the sound of this car burning, just the crackling, crackling of the vinyl inside the car, the plastic, all of it, crackling as it burned. That sound, it's usually reassuring. A reassuring, beautiful sound, like a campfire. But there it is, in the middle of this messed-up city. It's just violence and death. Since then, I can't listen ... I mean, of course I still love a campfire and everything, but the sound of a crackling fire is the sound of a burning car in downtown Fallujah for me. I can't break those sounds apart. Or those moments apart.

The Minaret

Christian Dominguez
One mosque that we entered, about November 11th, we had Iraqi soldiers with us that were a little bit upset that we didn't take our boots off. There was glass everywhere, we are definitely not taking our boots off. Our Rules of Engagement said that we had to get the clear to enter mosques in Fallujah – we had to call up and get permission from our higher echelons. Often it took a great deal of time, and it was a really good tactic by insurgents there because they knew that we couldn't just enter any mosque. And we saw on November 17th that they were using it as a position of cover, and they knew it would cause outrage to the Arab world. It was dual-purpose. They can use it, you know, and likely not draw fire; and they can use it and draw fire and use it as propaganda.

We had pushed to the edge of Fallujah. We thought we were done. I remember seeing no more houses; there was only desert. I turned to my then squad leader, I said, 'Are we done? We have been doing this for 11 days already. We got to be done.' He said, 'You know, I am not sure but just keep driving on.' At that time we got word that there was a dead sniper in a minaret, and Ashley Gilbertson wants to go take a picture of it and send it back to the US.

Ashley Gilbertson
According to the Geneva Convention, religious sites are sanctuaries: military cannot enter, unless they are being used as staging grounds for an attack. Fallujah is called the City of Mosques.

The insurgents knew that Americans couldn't go into the mosques, so they would use them to stage and attack Marines, because they knew they had more safety there than they did in a regular place.

The Marines over the week pushed from the northern tip of Fallujah all the way to the southern edge of Fallujah. This mosque, just short of the southern edge of Fallujah, they had been taking fire. They returned fire and then a tank fired a shell through the minaret. The minaret is like the church tower where the imam would go to call to prayer. And they apparently killed the insurgent who was inside. I said, 'I have got to go and see that,' because I knew at this point all of my images were being stolen by the Arabic news networks to show that the Marines were breaking the Rules of Engagement and they were going into mosques. I needed a photograph as evidence to show that these mosques were being used as staging grounds. A picture of a dead insurgent inside a minaret showed that, without question, these spaces were being violated and were therefore no longer being protected by the Geneva Convention.

We went to the captain and said, 'Can you please radio everybody and tell them that we are gonna be running up the street to this mosque a stone's throw, a few hundred yards away, and just tell everyone not to shoot us.' And he said, 'No, you got to go with a squad.' It was too dangerous out there because the city was crawling with insurgents and there was hand-to-hand fighting. I said, 'No, I have this non-intervention policy where stuff shouldn't happen on account of me.' So the captain said, 'Well, you can't go.' I said, 'Well, I need the picture.' Dexter and I agreed that we would go with the squad, so we linked up with the guys and started running up the street. As soon as we went out, all the guys ... like, you can almost see how the bodies change. As soon as they go out, it's like they are on high alert. Looking everywhere around them, rifles are raised, and I was like, 'Shit, we shouldn't have done this. This is a mistake, this is dangerous.'

Marine Sergeant **Sam Williams** *was part of the squad detailed to accompany Dexter and Ashley to the minaret.*

We got word that there was a dead sniper in a minaret, and Ashely wanted to go take a picture of it. So I was chosen to lead a patrol, along with my lieutenant, out down to this minaret that was 400 metres away, maybe. I was angry. I did not want to do it in the first place, because we were pretty much done with the city, so for me it was like that 'one last patrol' thing. It was like, 'I don't want to do this, just so he could take a picture.' And all right, if that's the job and that's the mission then that's what I'll do. I don't agree with this at all but, you know, I'm going to do it. So I assemble what's left of 1st Platoon, and we head out.

We get down to the minaret. If you could picture, you enter a compound and the main mosque is to your direct front and left, the minaret is to your direct front and right, and there's two groups of auxiliary buildings, one is on your immediate left before the mosque and the other is on our far right past the minaret. No one in the mosque, no one in the auxiliary buildings, and the last building left is the minaret, so we're going to clear the minaret, see if we can get up and find this dead sniper. Billy Miller was on point. I think Goggin was right behind him. I think Dominguez was behind Goggin on the first run-up of those steps. I was down with the platoon commander, holding the perimeter.

Christian Dominguez

So they brought this squad together and it was a mixture of us. We had taken so many casualties already. It wasn't the original 1st Squad. It was kind of a hodgepodge of Marines that we all knew but we were never in the same fire team or squad together. Sergeant Sam Williams led us to the minaret, and when we got to the base of the minaret Lance Corporal Billy Miller was stacked at the door. He said, 'Dominguez, come and stack on me.' Stack means 'get behind me and we go up there together.' So I went there.

Ashley Gilbertson was there, and with his Australian voice he was trying to tell us, 'Hey, you stay back, I am just going to go run up there and take a quick picture.' At this point we still didn't like him because he was in the way. We didn't have a real relationship with him – 'Just get out of the way and let us do our job.' So Billy Miller starts going up, and I am behind him walking up the minaret. It never crossed my mind that we were doing this for a photograph. I didn't put any weight to it. I just knew that someone told me to do this, and this is what we are going to do.

Ashley Gilbertson

We got to the mosque. I remember them stacking up, as they always do before they go through gates. I remember they kicked through the gate and they went and cleared the mosque. I ran over to the minaret, which is just on the right-hand side and I went to go upstairs, and before I could go up a Marine stopped me and said, 'I will go up and clear it.' 'No, no, no, I got to go up, just stay here and I will go up really quick, we will be out of here in a minute.' He was like, 'No, this is what I have got to do.' That was Lance Corporal William Miller. He went up first. He was followed by Christian Dominguez, then me, then Dexter was apparently behind me.

So we start going up this minaret, and it's dark. It's a tower with slits in the windows, and we are climbing, and it is just the sound of rubble and crunching concrete under our feet when we are climbing. And just as you start to get a little bit of light through a hole in the wall, where the tank shell went through and killed this insurgent, and I am thinking, 'This is almost over, get my picture and get out …' Then there was a gunshot, maybe multiple gunshots, and I felt water all over me. I thought immediately, 'Shit, somebody released their rifle by accident and shot these camel bags they all wear.' Little backpacks filled with water – they must've accidently shot their backpack and I just got hit with water.

Christian Dominguez

So we start going up there and there was a whole bunch of rubble on these stairs and it was such a confined area, and Billy Miller was almost a full step ahead of me. We kept tripping, and he almost said something. He almost said, 'Shit.' And all of a sudden shots rang out, and I remember feeling wet. We basically walked into this guy's gun. He shot Miller in the face, and then Miller's body kind of turned, and then he shot and it hit him in the plate but it exploded his Camelback where his water source was and we got soaking wet. At this point Miller kind of fell down, and I was standing just below Miller and the shots ... This guy was lighting up the wall, shooting relentlessly, and the rocks were exploding in my face, and it was so loud because of how confined the area was, and at this point I couldn't reach Billy Miller any more.

Ashley Gilbertson
Then I heard Dominguez screaming, and he was screaming, 'Run, run, run.' I just remember all of us starting to run down these stairs. And I remember falling and just rolling, rolling in circles like head over heels, and I remember my helmet falling off, and I remember somehow grabbing it and pulling it back on to my head. I have never really worked out why I remember that so vividly, the helmet bit. It doesn't matter. It doesn't mean anything. But I think, I think that that's the only piece of evidence that I can remember that I wanted to continue living after I found out what happened. Because we got out, we rolled out of this minaret, and I looked down at my camera and my hands, and it wasn't water. It was blood and brain, and it was Billy, like, just all over me.

I sat on the ground on the little raised gutter in front of the minaret. Dexter says that I sat there and I rocked back and forth and said, 'It is my fault, it is my fault.' Which it is.

Then they started fighting to go up and save Billy. And they went up and down those stairs while the insurgent fought them from the top, and Billy's body was up there, and more guys got injured, not severely but more guys got injured, and they tried to throw grenades through the hole and shrapnel came back. And I think it ripped a hole in somebody's ear. And all the while I am sitting on the ground watching this.

Christian Dominguez
I was sitting there trying to engage, but there was nothing I could do. It was a curved entryway; my bullets wouldn't have done anything. At that point I realised I am not equipped to win this fight and I went down to the bottom and I explained what happened and I remember I couldn't breathe. Sam Williams was down there and he said, 'Dominguez, what happened?' I remember hearing my voice was weird and saying, 'Miller is dead,' and the look of confusion in his face, like 'What? How would that be? You were just in this minaret.'

Sam Williams
I heard two shots. Everybody came running out of the building. Except Billy.

'OK, what's going on, what's going on?'

'Miller's down, Miller's down.'

'OK, well, we got to go get him.'

There's no question as to whether we're going to leave him behind or not, obviously we're going to get him. They were saying that Billy had gotten hit, but you never really know, there's always assumptions and speculations and things like that, but something that severe you have to be absolutely sure. So we organised a team to go back inside.

It was Corporal Mulack who was going to lead the charge back inside. They'd tried to get up those steps again and they all came running back out. So I realised – all right, we're not going to just be able to climb these steps and get to Billy, we're going to have to do something. So I set up everybody in sort of a half-moon around the minaret in defensive positions, and I said, 'Look, when I say so, I want all of you to rip this minaret to shreds. I want two or three rounds up there, I want machine-gun fire up there, I want to rattle this guy's cage. I don't want him just to be sitting there waiting for the next Marine to poke his head around the corner. OK? I mean, if I could get him bleeding out of his ears before we get up there, that's what I want.'

I had my support team light up that building. Couple of seconds later, DeMarcus Brown comes running round the corner. He actually took some shrapnel, it went through his lip and knocked out one of his teeth. So he had this really huge like swollen lip. So we put him on the ambulance to get him out of there.

As I'm coming around the corner, I see Corporal O'Brien grab his neck, spin and fall down, so I run over to O'Brien, and he's holding his neck and I'm like, 'Let me see it, are you good?' And he's got a little bit of blood coming out, right between his fingers, and he's like, 'Yeah, I think I'm good, I think I'm good.' And I'm like, 'Well, you're getting on the Medevac, you're getting out of here.' He did not want to, but I was like, 'You get your butt on there, we're going to fight.'

My point man was Goggin. I was right behind Goggin and I told him, 'Every time I tap your shoulder, let go of some rounds.' He had a saw gun, and I knew that as we were going up those ones were going to bounce and skip off the wall, inside that minaret – it's super tight, if you've ever been inside of one, there's a centre column and then the steps are in a really tight wrapping pattern. So, I knew that if I shot rounds, they would bounce along that wall.

So I've got everybody lighting it up out there, we make entry, I shut off the outside fire, and I pick up the fire inside with Goggin, tapping him on the shoulder, and he's letting go of some rounds every time. As we're going up, this starts pushing debris down on top of us. We had thought that the sniper was dead. The sniper had killed one of our guys and was now pushing debris on top of us. The only thing I could think of is, 'If this guy's got a grenade, we're all dead.' So everybody came flying back out.

I was like, 'It's not going down like this, we gotta go again.' So we get back in there, we get up there. Couple of times I tap Goggin and he lets a few rounds go. We get up close to Billy and I can see his weapon, I can see his flashlight. I was in the process of tapping Goggin on his shoulder again for like the fourth time, and Goggin just reaches up and grabs Billy and we all just fall, tumbling back down those steps. We get Billy outside, and Billy has this huge V-shaped canyon in his head.

This sniper is still alive up there. I told everybody who was in that supporting fire position to start tearing up that tower again because I wasn't going to have the sniper poking out and shooting any of us as we're waiting and taking care of Billy. So they all pick up their fire.

I tell the lieutenant, 'OK, we're getting out of here. I don't care about that picture or anything at this point, we gotta get Billy out of here. We've gotta get out wounded out of here. The mission's over, we're going home.'

I've Billy's weapon in my hand and my weapon is slung. I had stashed Dexter and Ashley in the mosque because it was the most secure building. The walls were like a foot and a half thick. I come around the corner into the mosque, and all hell is breaking loose outside. As I get inside the mosque, I'm telling them, 'OK, guys, when we count to three you're going to run.' They couldn't hear me because it was so loud that they just couldn't comprehend what I was saying. I took Billy's weapon that has blood all over it, and I hand it to Dexter, and I remember when I handed it to Dexter he just had this horrified look on his face and he just let the weapon drop. And I was like, 'You're going to take this and hold it. You don't have to fire, but you're going to hold it. And when I count to three, you and you are going to run out this door and stay right behind me.' They both nod, so I count down from three, we go outside, we get out to the street. I kind of push them to the right, which is where our friendly lines were.

I run out to the street, and you've got Lance Corporal Hughes out there, a guy who had three Marines tucked under, where a house had blown up. He had been wounded in that house, but he refused to leave. He's out there, he's got a light machine gun and he's just kind of one-arming this thing, and just blowing the crap out of the minaret. I can see the tailgate on the ambulance coming up, and Corporal O'Brien jumps off the tailgate with his hand on his neck and a bandage, goes trotting past me – he's like, 'Fuck that, I'm not going back.'

They start getting machine-gun fire, from these two-storey buildings across the street. I was shooting, and we're turning fire up on these buildings, and I kept feeling stuff hitting my legs and I thought I was getting shot because it hurt. But what went through my mind was, 'If you're getting shot, if you're *really* getting shot, it's going to be tearing the meat off your bones. If you can still stand they are not bullets, because the meat's still there. But you've gotta cover these guys.' So I would shoot this direction, dump a whole magazine, flick out the magazine, shoot this direction, dump a whole magazine, shoot this direction, dump a whole magazine, until everybody was outta there. And then I realised, 'OK, if you're going to keep standing there, you're going to die,' so then I took off.

Ashley Gilbertson

They dragged Billy out. A casualty evacuation vehicle turned up. They put him onto a stretcher. I remember seeing the vehicle turn up and remember seeing them get the stretcher. And I remember thinking, 'Don't look, because what you see will ... what you see, you did ... and what you see will ... You can't look.' So I turned around and looked, and it was Billy on a stretcher. He'd been shot point-blank in the face.

He was still alive. They put him onto the casevac. They drove off, and then Sam got the unit together and said, 'We have to get back.' Sam was holding Billy's gun, and he went to throw it to me so I could carry for him. And I don't know how he read my eyes. Another guy who saved my life that day. Because I know if he had thrown me the gun, I would've ended it, because I didn't know how I could live with the death of another man. How I could live with the death of another man that I caused.

Somehow, Sam recognised that, threw the gun to Dexter, and we ran down this street back to the firm base. The second we started running, a machine gun opened fire from insurgents behind us and I remember thinking, 'If there is a God then I will die now because I don't want to make it back to that base. But I am also not gonna be responsible for standing here and trying to get shot, with another Marine trying to help me and get shot as well.' So I ran.

Sam Williams
As I took off down the road, the assault section fired a couple of rockets to cover me, and I remember those rockets going over my head and hitting that minaret. It was another two or three minutes and they called in a 500-pound bomb and dropped it on that minaret, right at the base. It didn't topple the minaret, but the beauty of a 500-pound bomb is that you don't have to blow the building up, the shock wave will turn human flesh to jello. So if that guy was in the minaret and the bomb hit at the bottom, he was done, even if the minaret was still standing. He was done, there was no way that he survived it.

So we got Billy Miller out of there. That's how we lost Billy. And how we regained Billy, so he could come home with us. That's important.

Ashley Gilbertson
I ran with these guys. We made it back to the base. Nobody else was shot. We got in. Sam told us that this is what happens in war. That it wasn't our fault. We went to the lieutenant. I said, 'I'm sorry.' The lieutenant said, 'Yeah, yeah, it is your fault.'

I don't take a breath, I don't live a day not acknowledging the fact that Billy died in a place where I should've been. Billy died doing something that ... Billy died protecting me. I wish that it could've been me and not him, and I am also so thankful that he took his job seriously. And saved me. When I photograph, when I spend time with my family – I know every day that is with thanks to Billy. I know all the therapy: 'It is not your fault. You didn't do it. You didn't pull the trigger.'

When these things happen, this is not the place for rational thought.

Christian Dominguez
I would never in a million years blame Ashley for the death of Billy Miller. That doesn't even come into my mind. Billy was killed by an insurgent who was taking advantage of our Rules of Engagement in a mosque. That's it. My heart goes out to Ashley that he feels that way, but in no way does the 1st Battalion Marines blame Ashley for what happened to Billy Miller. It is a horrible situation, but it is what happens in combat.

Sam Williams
I was ranting and raving about it, smoked two cigarettes back-to-back, and I never smoked but at that time I was so amped up. I told Gunnery Sergeant Brown – and I think I even grabbed his shoulder – and I was like, 'The next time they wanna play chicken with my Marines' lives over a stupid picture, tell 'em to find somebody else, I'm not dealing with it.' He had this certain way about him, where he was very calm and very wise about the way he would respond, and he said, 'Hold on, this was important.' He just left it at that, knowing that I would chew on it, until I figured out what he meant.

Ashley needed to get a picture because Ashley's job was to tell the story. And I knew that, I was just in a heightened emotional state, so I didn't want to admit it at the time. But again when Gunny said this was important, knowing I would chew on it, he knew I'd get to that and circle that until finally I figured it out. So I never blamed Ashley or Dexter or anything like that because I knew that it was extremely important that that picture made it [to] the *New York Times*, and if we were doing it in service to that, then so be it. There's just a higher sense of duty and purpose, that's not about the politics of it, it's not about an agenda, it's not about any of that crap. People need to know. This is who these people are: they'll use a holy place for a firing platform and then blame us for destroying the firing platform. I want that on that *New York Times* front cover, big bold print and it's worth a life to get it there, yes.

For the record, Ashley should know not to blame himself. He had a job to do just like we do. He shouldn't blame himself any more than I blame myself for ordering Miller to go up that tower. It's Miller's job, it's Ashley's job, it's my job. War sucks. That's it.

Sabrina Miller
We found out that they had actually come to my parents' house at one in the morning, and they came back the next day with more people to see if they could figure out where they were. My mum's neighbour actually saw them get out the van and at first he's like, 'Oh, Billy's home.' Then he realised none of them were Billy.

I worked at a day-care and I was at work, and my boss had just come out and said, 'Someone just called to see if you still work here, and they hung up.' I said, 'That's weird.' I automatically assumed that it was my oldest daughter's biological father, even though he had given his rights away and hadn't seen her, but then a few minutes later my mum's neighbour from across the street came in, and he's like, 'Hey, can I talk to you for a minute?' I went to the office and he just kept walking out of the building. I'm like, 'Where is he going?' So I followed him out of the building, and he didn't say anything and he looked over, and I looked over, and a van of Marines got out. And I just knew.

I don't even remember what he said his name was or what he looked like, I just remember a big tall black guy with white gloves, holding my hand, telling me that Billy had been killed, and they were trying to get a hold of my parents, and if I knew how to get hold of them. The only thing I could think of was 'What can I tell my mum, to get her to come home without telling her that my brother died?' I mean, I thought, 'Do I tell her the house burned down?'

They were in their house in Conroe, which is about an hour and a half north of Houston. So I called Mum and she answered the phone.

Lewis Miller

She answered the phone, and I knew something was bad ... and what I do, and I've done this before, I have to shift into a control mode, a controlled atmosphere. Somebody's gotta be in control, somebody's gotta be in charge. When the world is falling apart around you, somebody's gotta be in control ... And that's what I tried to do. I tried to get control. It's my police nature ... I've been on scenes out there, people be laying in the grass, fighting and screaming and hollering and doing everything and what, and I'm standing there just as cool as I can be. Somebody's gotta be in control. And this is what I had to do. I felt like, 'OK, it's all right for her to scream and holler, and Sabrina to scream and holler, and everybody else to scream and holler, but somebody's gotta be in control, and this is what I do.' I can't explain it any other way. Somebody's got to have control. If everybody loses control, nobody's in charge.

Susie Miller

I didn't think I was screaming, but later she said, and several other people said, that I was screaming. 'Is Billy dead?' Well, you don't send Marines to a Marine's family without it being a bad thing. So we went back home, took my mother with us because I wasn't gonna leave her by herself, and they were waiting at the bus barn parking lot until we came into the house and then they came to the house and informed us that he was dead, and he was killed in Fallujah.

We found out how he was killed from the *New York Times* – Dexter Filkins wrote an article about his death. And if it wasn't for what he wrote, I don't think we would have known the actual circumstances of his death, because the Marines didn't tell us. They just said he was shot, and I'm not even sure they told us it was a minaret ... I think we got that from the article too. If it wasn't for that article, I don't know how much we would have known. We were grateful for the fact that they really printed what happened. And what he wrote in the papers was what the Marines told us happened. I got some more details from some of the Marines that wasn't in the paper, but close enough.

Sabrina Miller
We were at the funeral home. Mum and I wanted to see him, we wanted to make sure – 'Are you sure you got the right guy?' They said that his head was wrapped so we wouldn't be able to identify him. We had one of my dad's police friends there with us, and Mum described my brother's scrawny legs, white legs, and said he's got some scars on his left knee from when he was at camp and he crashed and got rocks and stuff in his knees. He was like, 'Yeah, his knees are just like that.' He said, 'But I think ya'll would be OK looking at him,' because he was in his dressed blues, but his face was just wrapped.

So Mum and I went and looked at him. And we actually took pictures, mainly if Dad ever wanted to see. It made me feel better to know that, you know, he was really in that casket, it wasn't really empty or ... That sounds weird but, you know, you want to make sure that they are really in there. Even though his head was wrapped, you could tell by his profile, you know, his nose and his mouth and stuff, we could tell that ... I mean, I felt like you could tell that was him.

We had his funeral on his birthday. After the funeral, the church had prepared food and stuff for everybody to go eat. When we went in there, Mum wanted to sing happy birthday to him, so we did. He hated being the centre of attention like that, but he liked to be the goofball. And he definitely would've been the one, you know, partying and having a good time, and so we tried to. Even though it was a funeral, we still tried to make it as happy as we could because that was what he would've wanted.

Sam Williams
I got moved to 1st Platoon from Headquarters Platoon just before we deployed, and Billy Miller was also one of the new guys in 1st Platoon. So he and I were not only in the same company but we

were in the same platoon. Billy was a good-hearted, pretty fun-loving kind of guy. He was more serious than his peers but I don't say that to mean he was eyes forward, chin down all the time. When you meet Billy, you feel very good energy on him, you know. He pays attention, he's articulate, more articulate than most. Very bright, very observant. Knew his knowledge and his techniques and tactics very well. You can just kind of tell when you meet a Marine – 'I'm going to have to work on this guy' or 'Oh, I'm going to have to watch this guy.' Billy wasn't one of the ones you had to go behind with a pooper-scooper and scoop up his messes, you know. He knew his stuff. He knew how to handle himself. Yeah, he was fun to know.

Susie Miller
We sent him a box every week while he was deployed in Iraq. Things like ... Billy loved peanut butter so I'd get him little plastic jars of peanut butter and get him snack stuff. He would share it with some of the other guys. A lot of the guys didn't ever get anything. So he always shared stuff that he got with other guys that was in his group. They held up those boxes. We didn't know it. I didn't know that they weren't getting to him. Our mail lady returned seven boxes to us. And every day she brought a box back, I cried.

Ashley's told me a number of times he doesn't understand why we don't hate him. And I've told Ashley over and over, I said, 'Ashley, you were doing your job, Billy was doing his job.' Am I glad Billy's dead? Absolutely not. Do I wish somebody else would have died instead of Billy? No, I don't. And Billy wouldn't have wanted somebody to die instead of him. It's ... He always wanted to be first. That's what got him killed. He was first going up them stairs to the minaret. I know that Ashley had huge problems after he got back, huge guilt. But neither one of us, and Sabrina, none of us were ever angry with Ashley or Dexter.

So many of these parents have no closure. We have closure, we know what happened, we know exactly where it happened, we know exactly how it happened. We have closure. Some of these people have no closure and they're just hanging in limbo. And we know that the person who killed our son was killed. He's dead. And I'm good with that. I don't care how it sounds, I'm good with that fact. I'm not good with him being dead, that's not it, but I feel like I do know that there was closure there. And it took three bombs to take down the minaret, but the insurgents were dead. So, I'm good with that. They're not gonna kill anybody else. Makes me sound like a cold-hearted bitch, doesn't it?

Ashley Gilbertson
So 2004 became one of the deadliest – if not the deadliest – years for the American military since Vietnam. One thing that had really set it off was when the Coalition shut down Muqtada al-Sadr's newspaper. He was a Shia cleric, and his newspaper was critical of the coalition, so this idea of the free press and free speech apparently doesn't extend beyond our borders here at home. So they shut down the newspaper, which started a massive insurgency, not just from the Sunnis that was already taking place, due to the Ba'athist party and the army being dissolved, but now from the Shia down south, who up until that point could have been an ally. So then the Americans were being attacked from pretty much all angles. Iraq was 360 degrees, 24 hours a day.

Some of the decisions Bremer made and enacted without even passing those things by Washington. So this guy, who thought he was a fucking viceroy of Iraq, made these unilateral decisions that in my opinion led to the deaths of thousands of people, Iraqi and American and English. Thank you, Paul. There was no plan after the invasion, I know. That's Washington, that's the Pentagon. But then post-invasion Iraq being managed by Bremer, to me was a total and utter disaster that could have been avoided. And he is almost singlehandedly responsible for that. How he lives with himself ... I can barely live with myself, and I feel responsible for the death of one person. He's responsible for the deaths of thousands ...

Christian Dominguez

Fallujah was a battle that everyone thought they wanted. It was a conventionally fought battle with insurgents in an urban environment. I think the main reason why we have to almost dehumanise them is because it is easier to look at someone that's dead wearing a different uniform, than someone that's dead wearing your uniform – when you see that it is just horrible. It is tough seeing your friends die and being shot, and not seeing that you have the advantage and you are winning. So when you would clear a house and there would be a dead insurgent in there, you wanted to make sure that you knew one for one. We lost one; we wanted to make sure that we were getting one as well. You would see them lying in streets and lying in homes, and oftentimes the rigor mortis set in and they were swollen and it wasn't a pretty sight, but it brought you to a reality that this is what war looks like. It would give you peace of mind: 'Our shots are hitting something.' It is what winning looks like. It is what doing your job looks like, and you want to see the results. We are losing Marines, but we are accomplishing our mission at the same time. Looking at them, we didn't really give them any kind of person or background. It was just a body. At the time, they weren't people. They were something in our way and we were doing what we had to do.

Dexter Filkins

The Marines are different than the army. The US army is this gigantic bureaucracy, and they have cooks and car mechanics and pilots and clerks and dish-washers. The Marines are a much smaller force, and every Marine is trained to shoot. Their job is assault, that is what they do. They go to the gunfire, they run right into it, and they are incredibly aggressive. When you have 8,000 moving into a town like that with all that firepower, it's a terrifying force. I mean, 590 Marines is a terrifying force; 8,000 is a massive killing machine.

What they got was this kind of urban street fight: who's your enemy, where are they? It's definitely not playing to their strengths;

their strength is to attack, manoeuvre and destroy. The insurgents were playing cat and mouse. They would fire some shots and then run to the next floor of the building and fire some more and so on. And the Marines would just destroy the building. There might be one guy in that building – building gone. They just ploughed through the city. You could see a couple of blocks down there was another company of Marines, and a couple of blocks down that way was also another company, blasting everything, moving through together. We went from the top of the city all the way to the bottom, one end to the other, and that took about a week. And we blasted everything along the way, and I thought, 'There's no one alive here. We killed everything.' It was total destruction.

'The Rest is Up to Allah'

Nidhal Mustafa
They bombed us from the air, then the army attacked. Mustafa was sick with a fever. He kept crying, saying, 'Mama, Mama, I'm hot.' There was nothing the matter, just a fever. In the morning, his father took him to hospital. The doctor prescribed a shot, but there were no doctors because of the bombing. Some staff were at the hospital, some others couldn't make it. He couldn't find a nurse to give him the shot, so he brought him home. I was out working at the time. I came back. His father had bought clothes for him. I bought him sweets. Things were good.

Abu Mustafa
On 3 November 2004, during the time of Ramadan, Mustafa was ill, and his mother told me I needed to take him to the doctor, so I took Mustafa to the Fallujah general hospital. The doctor gave me medicine and needles and said we had to give him the injections. The hospital was across the river from Fallujah, you had to cross a bridge, so I picked Mustafa up. I carried him, and we went to the shop in the city. I bought him shoes. I really love Mustafa.

I took him back home, to his grandparents' house, where we were staying. I told his mum, 'This is the medicine and these are the needles. We need to give him half a shot a day.' She said, 'I'm going to the neighbour's house, and I will give him the injection there.' It was around six in the evening, so it was Maghrib prayer time. I usually go to the mosque to pray and then come and break our fast.

Nidhal Mustafa

After I'd given him the shot, I was carrying him home. The next thing I know, Mustafa is next to me with his guts in the dirt. My sleeve is torn and I couldn't feel my side, and my arm was torn open. Mustafa was on the ground, his guts hanging out, and shouting, 'Mama!' There was no one around. I was alone in the street. I had no idea what was happening. I didn't even see Mustafa's leg, just his intestines hanging out.

An American missile had landed next to us. There was no al-Qaeda. Just families.

Abu Mustafa

When I was at the mosque, I heard a big explosion. The windows and doors were shaking very hard. When we went outside and saw smoke and the explosion and saw people running and heard screaming, we knew something had happened. I started running because the explosion was near Nidhal's parents' house.

It was an American bombing. They used artillery on the area we were living in. They bombed it because there were always armed groups who resisted there, so they hit it. I rushed to Mustafa's grandparents' house, and I saw a boy with his shirt off and he was holding a baby. From far off, I knew it was my son Mustafa, because he was wearing a red shirt. Mustafa's legs were detached, and his intestines were coming out. His body parts were ripped apart.

Nidhal Mustafa

My senses started to come back to me. My injuries weren't hurting me then. All I could feel was my clothes torn and my side. All the flesh was in ribbons. I didn't care about myself, all I cared about was Mustafa, lying there with his guts in the dirt. I went over to Mustafa and scooped him up in this hand, and crawled away. I couldn't stand up.

I saw a relative of ours shouting out to me. They couldn't tell I was hit. I was around the corner and poked my head out. I tried to gesture to him, but I couldn't. Then he saw me, and saw that I was hit. My brother came and threw his dress over me. He told me that Mustafa was dead.

Abu Mustafa
They were carrying his mum in a blanket, four people. They told me, 'She's hurt and we have to take them to hospital. We have to hurry.' In the hospital, we went to the emergency. They saw Mustafa and his mum. They said, 'We need to take them into operations immediately because their injuries are dangerous.' After they took them into operations, we waited around four hours.

A doctor came out to us. He said, 'You saw Mustafa's condition, and he is under two years. His legs were torn and his intestines were coming out. We did the operation, but I can't tell you. I can't guarantee if Mustafa will live or die. We did what we can and the rest is up to Allah. But his mum is a bit better. She is injured on her hand and she is wounded on her side.'

Nidhal Mustafa
I didn't even know that Mustafa lost his leg. I kept asking them, 'Have you sewn his guts back in?' That's all I knew about, his intestines. They would say yes. Then they told me it wasn't just his guts, it's his leg, his testicles, his rear. Mustafa had tubes in his nose and throat. Tubes all over. He couldn't breathe.

Abu Mustafa
We stayed about four days in the hospital, and they were treating them. The American army started advancing to Fallujah. There were bombs, and fighting in the city. The American army came to the hospital, and the Iraqi army was with them. We were inside the hospital and they entered. There was fighting in the hospital and gunshots. They made a group of people leave the hospital and they told us to stay. Mustafa was being transfused blood and nutrients, and his condition was very poor, so they told us to stay and not to come out.

On the next day, there was an Iraqi general and we spoke to him. We told him we couldn't stay there, there is a war and the hospital might be hit. So we wanted them to let us leave to Ramadi or Baghdad, because this place would now be a military target and a fight would happen in it. He said, 'Until we get orders from the American forces, we can't let you go.' But the next day they gave us permission to go to Baghdad.

Nidhal Mustafa

The Americans came. The hospital doors were shut. They were throwing grenades at us. They were trying to blast the doors down with grenades and storm in. Them and the National Guard. Both the Iraqi Army and the Americans. For three days, we were besieged. There were no doctors or treatment. My side was infected, rotting because there was no medication.

They got everyone out, the Americans. But for three days, the Americans were bombing right on top of us. We were moving from room to room. The doors and ceilings were collapsing on top of us. They let us out after three days. Mustafa and I were in an ambulance. They were taking us to Baghdad, but the Americans had blocked the road and turned us back. They wouldn't let us through. We couldn't go back to the hospital either.

Mustafa was in a serious condition. There were no doctors or medicine or anything. We took him home with pipes in his nose and throat and all over him. His whole body was a mess.

The next day the doctors went with us, and this time the Americans let us through. We got to Baghdad. Mustafa's condition got worse. Much worse. They treated Mustafa and me. We were in hospital there for three months. Mustafa – what was left of him? His kidney was gone, his hip, his leg – he can't even go to the toilet like normal people. That was the state he was in. I don't need anything for myself or my family – just for Mustafa.

Tell them.

Chapter 4
A False Dawn

Timeline

12 January 2005	The search for weapons of mass destruction in Iraq is officially abandoned.
30 January 2005	Iraq holds its first free parliamentary elections in 50 years.
28 February 2005	A suicide bomber attacks army and police recruits in Hilla, killing 122 and injuring 170.
16 March 2005	The opening of the temporary Iraqi National Assembly elected in January.
2 April 2005	The Battle of Abu Ghraib begins.
4 August 2005	The Battle of Haditha begins.
15 October 2005	Iraqis vote in a referendum to accept the new Constitution.
19 October 2005	The trial of Saddam Hussein begins.
26 October 2005	US military casualties in Iraq pass 2,000.
19 November 2005	US Marines intentionally shoot and kill 24 Iraqi civilians – 11 of them women and children – in retaliation for a roadside bombing that killed one of their soldiers.

15 December 2005	Elections to a new Iraqi parliament are held.
22 February 2006	The golden dome at the Askariya shrine in Samarra, one of Iraq's most revered Shi'ite shrines, is bombed and badly damaged, swiftly provoking a series of reprisal attacks in which 1,300 Iraqis are killed.
22 April 2006	Nouri al-Maliki is chosen by Shi'ite leaders as their nominee for prime minister; he becomes the leader of Iraq's first full-term government since the fall of Saddam Hussein.
20 May 2006	The Iraqi Transitional Government is replaced by the new government elected in December 2005.
7 June 2006	Al-Qaeda insurgency leader Abu Musab al-Zarqawi is killed in an airstrike in Baghdad.
17 June 2006	The Battle of Ramadi begins.
16 September 2006	Blackwater contractors open fire on civilians in Baghdad, killing 17.
5 November 2006	Saddam Hussein is sentenced to death by hanging.
30 December 2006	Saddam Hussein is hanged in a dawn execution held during the morning call to prayer.
31 December 2006	US military casualties in Iraq pass 3,000.

Introduction

By December 2003, the war had been going on for nearly nine months. The small insurgency which had started in the Sunni heartlands had now spread across the country. Al-Qaeda had firmly established themselves in Iraq, deploying horrific terrorist tactics and promoting a radicalised Islamic ideology. Car bombs, never before seen in Iraq, became a daily occurrence, frequently killing hundreds of innocent civilians. With each passing day, the number of US soldiers killed in action also increased. Meanwhile, the man they had come to kill, the man who many believed was orchestrating this escalating, violent insurgency, was still at large. Saddam Hussein had last been seen leaving Baghdad in a white car, just as American troops entered the city. The optimum time to capture him was in those first few hours. Instead, the American army had occupied itself by pulling down his statue. Since then, CIA officers had worked tirelessly to find Saddam.

The CIA team charged with tracking the dictator down included John Nixon, a man widely regarded as the US expert on the Iraqi president. John had been working the Iraq desk at the CIA for a number of years when he got the call to leave Langley and travel to Baghdad, for what would prove to be the biggest assignment of his life. John's obsession with the Iraqi president, and the insight he had developed over the years of studying him, were essential in formulating a plan to track and capture Saddam.

Others also joined the search. Back in 2003, when the war started, Samir Al-Jassim was working in the second-hand car lot that he owns in St Louis, Missouri. Originally from Iraq, he had come to the United States as a refugee, escaping the vicious reprisals for his part in an uprising against Saddam in 1991, after the first Gulf War. This uprising had been encouraged by the then US president, George Bush senior. When Samir heard about plans for another invasion, this time conducted by Bush's son, George W. Bush, Samir volunteered to return to Iraq and was assigned to aid forces tasked with hunting Saddam.

Much to Washington's disappointment, the capture of Saddam did nothing to quell the rising violence that had spread across the country. In fact, the violence worsened. As Saddam faced the long-fought-for justice that many Iraqis wanted, the country disintegrated into a sectarian civil war.

By the time Saddam was sentenced to death, the civil war was rapidly destroying Iraqi society. The different tribal and religious factions were ripping themselves to shreds. Bodies were appearing daily, dumped on the city streets, marked with obvious signs of torture. Al-Qaeda, who had had very little presence while Saddam ruled Iraq, were now an extremely dominant force. When Saddam was executed, on 30 December 2006, reprisals began immediately. Anyone hoping that the solution to Iraq's problems lay in the death of its once all-powerful president was mistaken: his execution sparked one of the most violent days of the war to date. The anger expressed by some after Saddam's death acted as an ominous prelude to the violence to come.

'We Called Him Saddam'

John Nixon
It was about 4 o'clock on the 13th of December (2004), and I was talking to my friend Mike, and he said, 'Special Forces think they know where he is. They're gonna go out tonight and try to pick him up. They feel that they're very close to this.' I said, 'Wow, OK,' thinking, 'Is this another wasted effort?' Some time between 7 and 8 the atmosphere became almost electric. Word started to spread that the US military's picked up someone, they think it's him, they're not sure. Suddenly there's a lot of activity, and people are kind of running around answering questions and sending off emails back to headquarters, and it's at this point in time when I get asked to come down to the Chief of Station's office. The Deputy Chief of Station is running things and Buzzy Krongard, who was the executive director of the CIA, just happens to be in the country and he's there, and that's when I heard that the military's picked up someone, they're not sure who it is – 'How would you identify him if you were asked to?' I said, 'I think there are certain markings. Saddam has tribal tattoos on his wrist and on his hand. He also has a bad back; that might be something we can find out about.' And then I mentioned the bullet wound on his leg and also, from watching pictures of Saddam Hussein, he has sort of this droopy lip and it just sort of hangs there – I spoke with the doctors and came to the conclusion that this is probably from a lifetime of smoking cigars. So I said, 'I think that's the best way we can probably identify him without doing blood examination or DNA tests.'

Shortly after I got out of the CoS's office, this guy Steve, who was the head of the Detainee Exploitation cell in Baghdad station, took me to one side and said they were going to ask me to go out and identify if this was really in fact Saddam Hussein that had been picked up. He said, 'Work up some questions that you think only Saddam Hussein could answer.' A jolt went through my body because all of a sudden everything had changed. This was no longer intelligence work in the sense of trying to help find him. Now I was really a part of things. The adrenalin that I felt at that moment was something that powered me on for at least the next 14 hours. I didn't actually go to bed. The morning of the 13th, I got up at around 9 or 9.30, and I didn't go back to sleep until 11.30 or noon the next day. And, to be honest with you, I never felt tired throughout that entire time.

Samir Al-Jassim

When we got back, he was already sitting in the interrogation room, sitting with all the folks. I opened the door, I walked in. He was talking, there's another guy translating for him. As I walked in the room, he saw me. He stopped talking. It was like, 'Oh my god, he's back again.' I think that's what he thought. He's telling the translator to say, 'I want *him* to be out.'

I was like, 'Who you talking to? Me? Out?' I'm like, 'Shut the fuck up. You? You're not president, you're a prisoner. You have no power, you've got nothing. You're done. You're done, I'm not going to go. You want to kick me out?' He's like, 'Yeah, because you're a traitor.' I was like, 'Look, your sons went to hell, they got killed, and you're next, you're going to hell.' And again, of course, he tried to call me all these names: 'Traitor, traitor, traitor.'

I got pissed off again, ran to him to kick him out, to kick him. Got stopped by these guys. They said, 'Samir, enough is enough. Leave the room. That's it. What you did on the farm, you can't do it again. It's done.'

John Nixon

We drive out there in the middle of the night, and the drivers have night-vision goggles on, and they're not driving with any headlights and we're doing about 100 miles an hour. It was a little tense. We get out there and first the military wouldn't let us in, then all of a sudden they lifted the gate. After about two hours, someone from the military pokes his head in and says, 'All right, guys, it's your turn, you're up.' Show time. I walk with my colleagues down this long hallway and it was sort of like being backstage at a rock concert, but instead of there being groupies and roadies and stuff it's just all guys in fatigues. We get to a door and the door opens, and there he is. He's sitting in a folding metal chair, and he's looking up, listening to something and then listening to a translation, and he's saying something ... and the minute I saw him I couldn't believe it. 'Holy shit, it's Saddam! It's actually him!' The minute I laid eyes on him there was no need for the questions that I had, there was no need to look for the tribal tattoos, it was him and I knew it. I was 100 per cent certain it was him.

I started off by telling him, 'We're here to ask you some questions and we want you to answer these truthfully. Do you understand what I'm saying to you?' He listened to the translation and he just shook his head and he sort of gave me this look. I used to have this book on my desk called *Republic of Fear*, and it was the same look that he's giving the photographer that's taking the picture of him on the cover, and it kind of sent a chill down my spine.

I launched into my questions. I thought the first one I would just shake him up a little and see how he reacted to it, so I said, 'When was the last time you saw your sons alive?' He listened and then he just leaned forward and he had this mean laugh: 'Let me ask you something. Who are you guys? What are your names? Where do you come from? What are your organisations? Are you Mukhabarat? Istihbarat? Identify yourselves to me.' It was a taste of Saddam that we would get to know very well. He's our prisoner now, and yet he's acting like we are his guests, this is still his country. He had this demeanour that said, 'Well, I come here every Saturday night and I always greet my guests this way.' Steve, the head of our group, said, 'We're not here to answer your questions. You're here to answer our questions.' So I moved on to the next one.

We called him Saddam. We weren't going to call him 'Mr President,' we weren't going to acknowledge his title. We would just call him Saddam, and that's it. At this point, we're beginning a process. We want him to accept the fact that he is not the president any more and accept the fact that he is now a prisoner. It was important, especially in the beginning, to establish this precedent and also to get at the truth. Usually when somebody gets captured and is brought in for questioning immediately, that is probably the most vulnerable time in the life of a prisoner because their life has been turned upside down and they're very unsure of themselves, and now they're isolated and they have all these strangers around them asking them questions. Normally, it's a time of great confusion for a prisoner and they're trying to figure out, 'Should I be truthful? Should I lie?' And that's probably the time when you're most likely to be able to get at the truth. With Saddam, that didn't necessarily apply. One of the things that I found with Saddam was that he was almost unflappable; he's been through this before and he knows how to handle himself. That's not to say that during the course of our subsequent debriefing there weren't times when he would slip up – he did exactly that – but at this point he was very calm, very collected.

He had a couple of moments in this initial encounter that were almost funny. At one point, we asked him about weapons of mass destruction. He said, 'You found a traitor to turn in Saddam Hussein, why don't you go and find another traitor to turn in these WMD?' Then he launched into this whole thing about how he didn't have WMD, and he said, 'You're being misled by your leaders. Your leaders are terrible. They are people who don't know what they're doing and they don't know the trouble that they're causing and they don't know the problems that they are creating for themselves. Your leaders are terrible!' And then he looked around at us and said, 'But you guys seem all right. I'm not mad at you.' OK, Saddam, thanks.

One of the dynamics I thought was the most interesting part of the evening was there were two interpreters in the room and they were CIA and uniform military in the room asking questions. At one point the CIA interpreter interpreted what Saddam had said, and the military interpreter took great issue with how he had interpreted Saddam's statement. He just sort of cut him off and said, 'No, he didn't say that! You're conjugating the verb wrong, he said *x* not *y* like you're saying it.' The next question gets asked and the interpreter does this again: 'No, no, I'm sorry, but that's not what he's saying.' This goes on for about five or ten minutes where their interpreter starts correcting our interpreter and the room is starting to feel a little tense, and I remember watching Saddam during this. He's just sitting back in his chair, watching this going back and forth. It's almost like he's watching a tennis match. And then he got this smile on his face. The next time the question gets asked, Saddam answers, our interpreter interprets, their interpreter interrupts, and then Saddam just rolls his eyes, like, 'Please save me from these fools.' Saddam sees that there are people in uniform and there are people in civilian clothes, and he begins to notice differences in what we're asking, and he now sees that there is a conflict between two people who really should be on the same side, and he starts trying to drive a wedge into that. And he is able to do that, because I remember when we walked outside the head of my team was furious and saying how he was going to complain to the military the next day. And the thing is, this was all caused by Saddam. In a sense this was a metaphor for how he used to run his country: he would have to deal with certain factions and ethnicities who really had the same goal of removing him from power, and he would always find ways of exacerbating their differences so that they ended up focusing their anger towards each other rather than towards him. It was very successful. That's how he ruled Iraq from 1968 to 2003.

'Only for Presidents'

John Nixon

Saddam basically sits in his cell for a week and no one comes to speak to him, and he's genuinely curious to know why this is happening. He even asks one of the interpreters, 'Why is nobody coming to speak to me?' This happens largely because Washington is completely taken by surprise that he has been captured, despite the fact that this had been our goal all along. There had been a steady stream of reporting saying that Saddam Hussein would die rather than be captured, that he would kill himself before he would fall into the hands of the Americans, that he had suicide belts and, basically, he would go down in a blaze of glory. The CIA had said, 'This is nonsense, Saddam does not fit the profile of a martyr, he does not fit the psychological profile of someone who is going to harm himself and destroy himself,' and yet the more we tried to give people that information and our interpretation and analysis of that, the more people believed he was going to, because it was an easy way of thinking and it fit a layman's idea of what would you do if you were about to be captured. Ironically, he's the last person on the planet who's gonna kill himself. When I got to know him I began to see the narcissism and the love of self – this is a guy who's never going to harm himself. Having said that, Washington is caught by surprise: they have a live Saddam Hussein on their hands – what are we going to do with him?

It takes a couple of days and eventually we find out that we're going to be the ones in charge of debriefing him. One day we go out to inspect the site where he was held, and the head of my team calls back to the Station and learns that they want us to get started right then and there. So that's how we begin debriefing Saddam Hussein. Not a great deal of preparation put into it. Surprisingly, we got very little guidance from Washington. The Agency had a few questions, the White House of course wanted to know about weapons of mass destruction – that's number one and that's really all they wanna know. One of the few bits of guidance that we got was, 'Just try to get him to engage with you and keep him talking until the FBI shows up.' Once we started debriefing Saddam, we never were certain how long we had. We kept on hearing that the FBI will be out any day now, and so every time I saw him I always thought this might be our last session. It impacted the way we presented ourselves and the way we dived into topics, when a lot of times I think I would have preferred to take a more leisurely way into talking about certain things. I think sometimes when we did introduce topics to discuss, we did it very abruptly.

In debriefing Saddam Hussein, both sides – the CIA and Saddam – had certain things they wanted to accomplish. Naturally, we wanted information from Saddam about certain issues like weapons of mass destruction and support for the insurgency; Saddam had certain things that he wanted that compelled him to participate in this. It was always open to him to say, 'No, I don't want to do this,' but Saddam, being who he was, I think actually he looked forward to this process because it filled up his days. Saddam was a real people person, and he liked the give and take. He also wanted to get a better understanding of what it was we were interested in. He could try out his answers, see if they were accepted, or he'd at least know, 'This is the stuff that they keep asking me about, and this is something, if there's a trial, that I'm gonna get asked about and I need to build my defence up on this issue.' When we told him that we wanted to ask him questions, we also said to him that his answers would be read at the highest levels of the US government. Meaning the President of the US. And they were. And that appealed to him a great deal because that is something that he had wanted for a very long time. He wanted a dialogue, and Washington was never really interested in that. That was also a key element in his cooperating in this debriefing effort.

We brought up the topic of 9/11, and I said to him point blank, 'What was your reaction? When you learned about what happened on 9/11, what was your reaction?' I wasn't sure what I thought he would say – something like, 'The United States got what it deserved' or 'This is what happens when you're an arrogant country and people dislike you.' Instead he just said, 'My reaction was relief.' 'Why relief?' He said: 'I thought that the United States would see once and for all that Iraq was not a threat to it. And that Iraq harboured no ill will towards the United States and that the people that flew these planes into the buildings in Washington and New York were the same people who are the enemies of Saddam Hussein. And that this would force Washington to reconsider its policies towards Iraq and see that Iraq could be a friend and a helpful ally in this fight against extremism.' I was blown away by this, because what he was saying made total sense.

I said, 'What was the biggest threat to your regime?' I expected him to say either the United States or Iran, and he didn't. He said, 'Islamic extremism.' He said it was the ideology of Wahhabism that was emanating out of Saudi Arabia and was beginning to sweep into Iraq and infecting his Sunni community, and he could not allow any Sunni Islamic extremism to take root because he knew that, if that happened, that would rot his regime from within. Despite the fact that in his later years he became rather aloof from governing the country, he never took his eyes off of the challenges to his security, and that he judged to be a very big challenge. Why would he cooperate with al-Qaeda if he feels that this community is something that could eventually unseat him from power? Nobody wanted to hear that, and nobody cared. The history of the Bush administration with Saddam Hussein is, 'Give us the dirt. We're only going to listen to the bad stuff, and everything else is just blather.'

Military Policeman **Brandon Barfield** *was deployed to Iraq in 2006, where he became part of the platoon assigned to guard Saddam.*

The highest person I have ever guarded was Saddam Hussein. Everybody who was on trial, we guarded them too – I mean, I fed them, I took them to the showers, I took them to see their lawyers, everything – but our main goal was to watch over Saddam, and basically we were babysitters.

I was in my room. I had just come back from the gym and I was getting my clothes on to go and have a shower, and Sergeant Coleman knocked on the door. He was like, 'We have got a formation right now. We have got a new mission: we are going to be guarding Saddam.' I'd picked up a DVD called *Uncle Saddam*, and it basically talked about how he came to power and shows some live footage and stuff and basically all the bad stuff he has done. They talked about how the first time he ever killed somebody was his schoolteacher at age 11 for giving him a bad grade; his uncle gave him a pistol and told him to go back to school and shoot her. I was just like, 'Man, I can't believe I'm going to be guarding this dude.' You know, he was killing people, you know what I'm saying?

John Nixon
One day he had a bit of a cold, and Bruce brought him a cup of tea. Saddam said, '*Shokran*,' and he was just sipping from it and he said, 'Oh, it's very good tea.' Bruce said, 'You know, Saddam, that looks like a really great cup of tea, I wouldn't mind sharing that with you,' and Saddam just sort of looked at him and said, 'Only for presidents.' We all cracked up.

Another time, I was trying to get him to discuss issues pertaining to his intelligence service. That was a no-no because we had established the ground rules in the beginning: Saddam had basically said, 'I am willing to talk to you about history and the history of my regime, but I won't submit to interrogation.' Of course, we're trying to talk about everything with him and so, in trying to get him to talk about his intelligence service, I made up this story about this bet that I had with somebody at headquarters about who would be his next intelligence director. He just looked at me and said, 'You know, you're not very smart, are you? Your intelligence is very low. Why would I put this man that you thought would be my intelligence director, why would I put him in that job?' Bruce said, 'Oh, not smart? Low intelligence? Sort of like sending your planes to Iran?' During the first Gulf War, Saddam had sent his air force to Iranian airfields; they landed there and of course the regime kept them and never gave them back. Saddam just looked and for a second he couldn't believe that someone had said this to him, and then all of a sudden he laughed and his shoulders were shaking and he held up his finger and said, 'Touché.'

It was fascinating. He would tell these stories that he thought were funny, but they all had a similar theme and that is of there being a chaotic situation and Saddam basically takes control of the situation and in the process someone has physical harm done to them. He talked about how one day he went up north and he didn't have his regular security detail. Everybody started coming around and clapping and trying to shake his hand, and the bodyguards couldn't keep things under control. If you've ever seen Saddam when he does these sort of trips, the bodyguards can be pretty rough, they're pushing people out of the way. There was this young boy who was standing there, and one of the bodyguards pushed him down. The boy got angry and he picked up a stick, and Saddam saw him do this. He winked at him and then motioned to the bodyguard, like, 'Come here, I want to talk to you.' And when the bodyguard turned his head the boy took the stick and whacked him in the head. Saddam broke out laughing, thought this was the funniest story but really what is at play here is that Saddam basically made it possible so the boy could inflict some physical harm on him. I think Saddam would have liked silent movies where people slip on banana peels. That was his sense of humour. *The Simpsons* with guns.

Brandon Barfield
He would tell me jokes sometimes. I can't remember the jokes now, but he would make the weirdest laugh. He would crack himself up. I would be thinking, 'That is not even funny, it is not even close to being funny, and you are laughing your butt off. That's stupid.' I didn't say that to him, but I sat there thinking that. I tried to get along with everybody and respect him. I called him 'sir' and everything, and he respected us.

John Nixon
He always answered questions with questions of his own; almost everything that I asked him, he would have a question first. When he was answering questions, if he didn't know why you were asking, he would be wondering about where you're going with your line of question. He wouldn't start out directly; he would start out on the side and then move, and he would just sort of look at you, and then he would pick at his fingernails. Then all of a sudden it would dawn on him what exactly it is that I'm getting at and he'd have this smirk on his face. And then, if I asked something that he really didn't want to talk about, then he'd pick at his fingernails to show me that this dirt that he picked out from underneath his nails was more important than my questions. If I really pressed the point, he'd extend his arms fully and pick harder, looking at me and looking back at his fingernails, and it was done to humiliate me. I thought it was hysterical at the time, but I just let him do what he wanted. While he was just picking his nails he would have this puzzled look on his face, and he'd look at you kinda like 'Where are you going with this, why are you asking me these kinds of questions?' And then it would change, all of a sudden he'd figure it out and get a look on his face, like 'Now I'm really bored with your questioning, I'm not going to answer that.'

A lot of the time we would end our session on a softer note. We'd give him a softball question, especially if we had been arguing. His favourite book? *The Old Man and the Sea* by Ernest Hemingway. My father loved Hemingway, but my father could explain to you why Hemingway was great. Whereas from Saddam's standpoint, his way of looking at it was: a man, a boat, a fish and some fishing line – these are the elements of a great story. To him, that's what was so great, the simplicity of it, I guess. But he loved it. He had a CliffsNotes version in Arabic of *Crime and Punishment*. Saddam was not an intellectual. He fancied himself an intellectual, but he wasn't. He always wanted reading material. It was carefully controlled, until one night he had asked one of the guards for something to read and they looked and they saw a whole stack of books in Arabic and so they just gave it to him, brought it to his cell and gave it to him. And they were all books of his speeches. All week long we had been addressing him as Saddam, making sure that he knew that he wasn't the president of Iraq any more, making him accept his new status. In that one act of giving him these books, the next day all of a sudden he was back to president of Iraq again and wanted to read from his speeches to explain things to us ignorant Americans.

Even when he was telling the truth, you thought he was lying. Saddam Hussein was the most suspicious man I've ever met in my life. That comes through in the man and it comes through in the regime. Everything was scrutinised and every question was met with a question. It didn't inspire confidence in the people in the West who were prone to believe the worst things about him, and also didn't believe that he was telling the truth and felt that all he was trying to do was obstruct the process. He's already kicked weapons inspectors out, and you conclude he's hiding something.

He didn't wanna talk about issues in relation to his own security, intelligence work and sensitive government issues, and there were certain topics that he wouldn't want to talk about, probably just out of cultural reasons. He didn't want to talk about his wives or his children or his daughters. He got very sensitive about human rights abuses, whenever we asked questions about that, because I think from his standpoint he was, like, 'Who are you to be asking me these questions? Who are you to be asking me to justify what it is I have to do to maintain myself in power and keep my country under control? Also who are you to be here in the first place and ask me anything?' Also, when it came to human rights abuses, I think he thought the West had a very hypocritical stance on that. But one day I was trying to get at the question of Halabja, and he just kept on saying, 'I'm not talking about it and I've told you this.' I, as the debriefer, have to be very careful because you can't let him shut down on you. So I took a very circuitous route, talking about how he governed Iraq and his use of the Revolutionary Command Council to govern Iraq because that was where the power really flowed from. I got him to say a lot of things about the Revolutionary Command Council. Chiefly among them that he was in charge and that when the council made a decision and he was the chairman that decision was implemented, and then I asked him about Halabja. Then it dawned on him that I had tricked him. He didn't see where I was going with this and all of sudden he's realised that he has now painted himself into a corner, and I put him in that corner. He got very, very angry at me. It was a chilling moment, it was scary. He started breathing through his nose and clenching his teeth like a wild animal, and he's like, 'I am not afraid of you, and I want you to listen to me. I am not afraid of you, I am not afraid of your president. If Saddam Hussein wants to make a decision to protect his people then Saddam Hussein will make that decision. I don't care about the US, I don't care about the international community. I don't care about the West, I will make that decision. But I did not make that decision.' I felt like I was looking at a wild animal.

The only other time we came close to this level of anger was, I was talking about the first president of Iraq after 1968, which was Ahmed Hassan al-Bakr. I said to Saddam, 'There are people in the West who believe you had him killed.' He just looked at me like, 'What?' The next day, I started off by saying something and he said, 'I have something that I want to say. I want to talk to you about saying hurtful things. Yesterday you said that I had Ahmed Hassan al-Bakr killed. Do you understand that I loved this man? Do you understand that he was a relative of mine? Do you understand that he was the most wonderful leader that we've had in Iraq? Do you understand that he came to me and told me one day, "I can't lead Iraq any more, and Saddam you're the only person who could do this." Do you understand all these things? Because if you do understand them then you would not be asking me all those questions.' His anger is rising this entire explanation. And then he began saying things like, 'I know I have certain rights here. Where is the International Committee for the Red Cross? I know I can get to see them. I know that I can get a Qur'an. I'm allowed to read the Qur'an. Where is my Qur'an? Where is my Geneva Convention?' He wanted a copy of the Geneva Convention even though he had never asked for these before. And we're getting a little nervous because he's getting angrier and angrier. It was sort of like dealing with an angry 15-year-old.

Brandon Barfield

The only thing he mainly talked about was his first wife. I can't remember exactly how many wives he had but, man, he loved his first wife. That scarf that he wears all the time, even the one that he got hung with, he refused to take it off because that was his way of his wife being with him, and he would always talk about his first wife. How much he loved her and how, out of all his wives, she was the best one, she was the most loyal. She would do this stuff for him, it wasn't a forced marriage – all the rest of them were basically forced – and he just liked her more. I guess it was his first love or something like that. When we first got there, she would send him stuff but he just quit getting stuff. He got the scarf, but after the scarf I don't remember him getting no nothing. I don't know why they stopped that, because he got everything he wanted.

John Nixon

Periodically we lose electricity and the room goes dark. The lights go out, and we're all going, 'What happened? What's going on?' Saddam never flinched. He was the calmest person I've ever met. It didn't faze him one bit. When we'd be talking, you could hear explosions in the background going off. Sometimes they're controlled detonations that the military does, other times they're not. Either way, Saddam hears this stuff and he's fully aware that things aren't going well. He makes this really famous comment that has always stuck in my head. He said: 'You're going to find that it's not so easy to govern this place. You have to understand Iraqis, they're always plotting, and the Shia are the worst. The Shia are always plotting against you, and you have to keep your eyes on them 24 hours a day.'

Another thing he said: 'You people don't understand what you've done. Because of what you've done – you removed Saddam Hussein from power – Iraq is going to become the playing field for international terrorism. And if you think that it's not going to extend outside Iraq, guess again. It will. You've created conditions for more terrorism, not less.' He understood his country far better and far deeper than we did. He also had a much more granular understanding of Islamic extremism because he had, in a sense, studied it: he was always watching it, and he knew their techniques, and he knew how they met, and he knew which parts of which tribes could be counted on to be loyal, which ones could be disloyal, and that you had to put your people in place so that you could keep your eyes on them. Saddam would have called it good government.

I debriefed Saddam Hussein from December 13th through January 12th, that's about four or five weeks, and I think I had about 15 or 17 sessions with him. Going to meet Saddam Hussein as many times as I did, the more you got to know him, the less you liked him. He could be a really nasty individual. At times near the end I would wake up and say, 'Oh god, I can't believe I gotta go talk to this guy.' Just because every day was turning into a nasty experience. He was on his guard with me because, after our chat about Halabja, he kinda didn't trust me any more, and he would try to do things to blunt my questions. But on the very last day, I decided to go see him. I talked with the rest of the team right beforehand, and we had agreed that I would go in there, tell Saddam that I'm leaving, introduce him to my replacement. And then I thought to myself, 'What I'll also do is, I'm going to say something nice to him so that we can have a smooth transition.'

So I went in there and we talked to him for about a half hour. We asked him a few questions, then we cut the meeting short and I told him: 'Saddam, I have some news for you. I'm going back to the US, there are things that I have to take care of back home, and I want to thank you for this discussion about history with us. Based on our discussions, I feel I know you better and I feel I know your country better than I did before and I want to thank you for your answers and your honesty.'

Saddam seemed a little annoyed. He cut me off and said, 'What, you mean I'm going to have to answer these questions all over again?' I said, 'No, no, no, Saddam, I have briefed my successor here and told him about everything you've said and he's read all of the reports. You won't have to answer these questions again.'

We both stood up and, for the first time in all of our meetings, instead of waiting for him to put his hand out, I put my hand out first. I offered it and he grabbed it and he went to shake my hand. What I didn't know, though, is that he had me in a death grip now because he grabbed my hand and then put the other hand on my arm, and then he had me. I don't know if you've ever experienced this, where someone is holding on to your hand and it's starting to get uncomfortable because they won't let go. He said words to the effect of: 'You and I have disagreed on many things, but I think the reason we have disagreed is because you are in your position and I am here, a prisoner. But I want you to remember one thing when you go back to the US and you do your very important work for your country, I want you to remember one thing. The best qualities, the highest qualities a human can ever have is to be just and fair. Those are the best qualities. Look, I am Saddam Hussein, I am not a politician. I don't say these things because I want to say them. I say them because I believe them to be true. To be just and fair is the best thing that any human can offer.' And at that point he finally released me.

'The way he was executed demeaned the significance of the law. It is against the rule of law. Barbaric.'
– **Judge Raouf Rahman**

'I have dreams, thoughts, and, despite the person in front of me being armed and foreign, I didn't consider him my enemy. But he considers me his enemy.' – **Tahany Seleh**

'On any given morning in Baghdad I would wake up to the sound of multiple car bombs echoing through the city.' – **Mark Kukis**

'I felt hope that it will be a new country. Very peaceful, very good, and we will see tourists from all over the world. It's gonna be the sunshine, the birds flying, and everything is good and the music everywhere. We know now that it's never gonna happen, it's never gonna be safe again.' – **Ahmed Al-Basheer**

'I'm not sure I saw a person firing at us the whole time I was there. It was just gunfire coming from somewhere.' – **Dexter Filkins**

'When I look at the faces of the children, absolutely filthy, in rags, no idea where their next meal's going to come from – it's difficult to call it 'heady, new-found freedom'. – **Colin Marks**

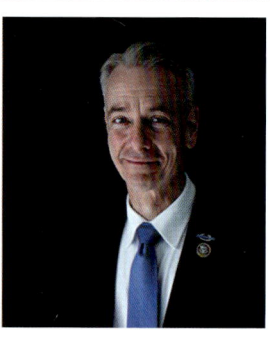

'How could we who worked with and served alongside Saddam leave? That was how we felt.' – **Issam Al Rawi**

'In his mind, we would go home, and then he could be restored to power. Saddam was a master of miscalculation.' – **Steve Russell**

'He was captured as a coward. He was afraid to fight. He wants to be alive. That tells you right there he is a coward – he is scared to die.' – **Samir Al-Jassim**

'At the beginning they called it liberation, because they came to free us. We were very happy. Because they came to free us. But they stayed here too long and it became an occupation.' – **Um Qusay**

'The first thing President Bush said to me was, "Why would you want this impossible job?" Which showed that he had a better sense of how hard it was going to be than I did.'
– Paul Bremer

'Then the occupation came, and they ruined everything. The factions came along and started making trouble. They and al-Qaeda were the same. None of them were serving the country, they were serving themselves.' – **Abu Mohamed**

'There's just a higher sense of duty and purpose. People need to know. This is who these people are: they'll use a holy place for a firing platform and then blame us for destroying the firing platform.' – **Sam Williams**

'We should never, ever forget Saddam Hussein and his two sons and what they have done in Iraq. If you forget Saddam Hussein, what will happen? We will grow another Saddam Hussein. It's a cycle, it's a vicious circle.' – **Mowaffak al-Rubaie**

I was in his grasp for about five minutes. I didn't know what to do. I didn't think I was ever getting out. I said, 'Thank you for those kind words Saddam.' And then he was led out. The head of my team came in, and he said, 'What the fuck was that all about?' and I said 'I think he was just saying goodbye, that's all.' And that was it, that was my final day with Saddam Hussein.

Brandon Barfield

The main place we kept him was in a blown-up palace. If you looked at it from the outside, it looked like a blown-up building, but that is where he was, he was actually inside. Part of his rec area was literally where it had caved in. When we first took over in 2003, we dropped a huge bomb and it didn't explode – it went through the middle of this big old palace and it just tore the building up. So they decided that would be one of the best places to hide the man, because that would be one of the last places they would think.

We walked in, he was in his rec area outside smoking a cigar, listening to his radio, and we all went in there and introduced ourselves. He was walking around, shaking everybody's hand, and he got to me, looked me right in my eye and just kind of skipped over me. I just met the dude, I ain't done nothing wrong, so he can't just not like me. But he heard me speaking and he didn't like my accent. So he said that he didn't want me around him at first because he thought that I was what he called 'a country person', and he thought I was Jewish. He didn't like neither one, so he wanted me to stay away from him. He heard me say 'Y'all ain't been around' and he told me that was it. So I had to wait a few days before I could even start watching him.

Whatever he wanted, he got. I mean, any time, it could be 12 o'clock in the morning and if he wanted something, if he told you to call a colonel and wake him up, you called a colonel and the colonel came out and would smoke a cigar with him. He wanted

Cuban cigars; in the United States, if you get caught with these you go to jail, but the government is buying him these and, man, we have stockpiles of them.

He wanted to go outside for his rec one day, and it was raining outside so he had to stay indoors, which was a smaller room right next to his where we kept him in the cell. He was sitting there reading a newspaper, and I was so bored, and we had a plastic table set up. He couldn't see my feet or nothing, but he saw me lean back in the chair and I brought my feet up on that metal part underneath there. He was sitting there reading his paper and did not even make a noise. He just folded it up and rolled it up, like he was about to kill a fly, smacked me on the leg and told me, 'You are to get your feet down.' It was disrespectful to show the bottom of my feet. I remember telling him, 'Don't you ever touch me no more, don't you ever put your hands on me. You are a prisoner and I will respect you just as long as I can but don't you ever put your hands on me. Back in the States, if you had of done that, you would be in the hold or you would get your tail whacked and then go in the hold.'

So I was sitting there, and he flat asked me: 'How come you don't like me?' I told him, 'You killed the soccer team, you invaded Kuwait, and if you had us right now you would be torturing us to get information.' He held his hand up and goes, 'That's war, that's what you do in war.' I said, 'Yeah, but we don't do that. We follow the rules of the Geneva Convention.' He looked me right in my eyes, and he said, 'That is called the United States, it's stupid.' He said, 'You ain't going to get no information if you are nice to people, that is why we torture. By me torturing those people, I got the information to save my soldiers.'

'That makes a good point,' I said, 'but I don't know how you can torture somebody like that. You know, you are doing World War 2 stuff like shoving stuff underneath their fingernails and cutting the tips of their fingers off. It takes a crazy person to do some stuff like that.' And he said, 'That is war, that is what you do if you want information.'

I said, 'I don't hate you, I really don't know you. I hate the stuff that you have done, you are a murderer, and it isn't like you did it once or twice. You know for a fact, right now, if you weren't in this cell, you would be out shooting someone if you wanted to because that's how it is.' I brought up the newspaper guy who had wrote a bad article about him and he had him killed for writing a bad article. I told him, 'You are just a big baby. If you don't get your way, you go out and murder somebody, and I think that is horrible.'

'You know what?' he says. And he told me that he would be proud to have me as one of his soldiers because, even though I didn't like him, I didn't mistreat him. I followed the rules of what I was told to do. I would do it because that is what I was ordered to do. He told me I was just like a robot soldier. And I was like, 'No, I'm a robot soldier, but I've got my own opinions.'

It was weird, because after that he wanted me to come in, he wanted to play chess with me. I played chess with the guy, and he beat me both times and he laughed at me. And he had a weird laugh, man. He beat me in three moves, and I said, 'You ain't going to beat me again.' I will be darned if he didn't beat me in five. I don't know how he can do that, to this day. He told me I needed to practise some more. I was so mad when he said that. But me and him ended up, I wouldn't say we were best friends but, you know, I treated him like any other prisoner. I'm respectful towards you. I don't care if you are the president or if you are somebody that just deals drugs, I'm going to treat you exactly the same because you are already in prison, you can't go nowhere. I will treat him with respect but he knows I'm still in charge. I will take you your toilet paper, I will get you whatever you need, and I will bring you extra milk sometimes or whatever, but I'm not mean to him like the other units were. I even told some of the guards, 'You know, I'm firm with him but I don't have to be mean to him, and I guarantee you if he was to try and escape right now he would probably kill all of you to get out, but he would give me a choice. Say he got hold of a gun, I would say he would probably point the gun at me and say, "You need to stay out or I'm going to shoot you," but I'm saying he would think twice about shooting me.

He would get up every morning after he ate breakfast, and they would check his pulse and stuff, and he would get on his bicycle and he had to exercise a certain amount of time every day. He would always joke, tell them that he was on his bicycle running away from us and we were chasing him trying to capturing him and stuff. Until the day he died, even when we had him walking up to the noose, he would always look around, because he thought his people were going to get him.

We treated him like a regular person. There was no need to treat him bad, because he didn't do anything bad to us. When he did act up, we took his rec time away, because the only thing really he could have was rec time. Or if he wanted a certain meal, we were like, 'No, you didn't do what we asked you so you are not getting your meal, you will get a regular meal.' So when he acted up he got punished a little bit, but he didn't act up all the time, he just mainly did what he was told. But I think he knew he was dying anyway.

He just acted like an old man. He could hardly walk. From what I was told he had prostate cancer, and that is one of the reasons why they were trying to hurry the trial – they didn't want him to die while we had him. Because we had technically told everybody that the United States had handed him over. That is why, every time we took him to court, you never saw us and even when they said it was live there was always a ten-second delay. I found that out because one of the army soldiers was hiding in the courtroom and he stuck his foot out too far and the camera caught it. We had to stop it and delete that footage and then keep re-rolling it.

The Defendant

*Also known as Dr Mow, **Mowaffak al-Rubaie** returned to Iraq from exile in 2003 and joined the Iraqi Governing Council before becoming National Security Adviser, which put him in charge of dealing with the captured Saddam.*

I don't think The Hague would have been a good idea, or any international tribunal or court, for that matter. Number one, The Hague would probably take [a] much longer time: we're talking about The Hague with the different language, with the different delaying tactics, with no evidence in foreign languages, and it would take ages. And number two, even if they found him guilty, there is no death sentence in Europe, in the European Union. Probably, he will die in prison, because the man was approaching 70, remember. After ten years in prison, he probably would have died in prison.

We wanted Saddam Hussein to be tried in Iraq, with international monitoring and with a full defence team, because this was a healing process for the Iraqis. If he has killed my mother and my sister, he has also killed hundreds of thousands of Iraqis. I wanted to see him tried in front of people and I wanted to give him the right he denied me and he denied hundreds of thousands of Iraqis before they were executed – I wanted to give him that right of defending himself live on television in front of millions of Iraqis.

The overwhelming majority of people in Iraq wanted him to be tried. Most Iraqis were watching the trial every day. They wanted to see. Those who were pro-Saddam wanted to see how brave he was in his defence, and the majority of people who have lost their loved ones were waiting for him to be humiliated, or get cornered by the Prosecutor General and the judge. So they enjoyed it. I honestly believe it was part of the healing process. Iraqis wanted to try this dictator. It has nothing to do with Shia and Sunnis; Saddam Hussein was not a Sunni leader, Saddam Hussein does not represent the Sunnis, he killed Sunnis as he has killed a lot of Shias and Kurds. But unfortunately the al-Qaeda terrorists, former regime elements and some of the regional countries depicted this as the Sunni leader being tried by a Shia-dominated government, which was not true.

Samir Al-Jassim
I watched most of it. It was on the local channels, while I was working in the Green Zone. Personally, I did not agree because I think Saddam had more opportunity to be on TV and send messages through the court. I mean, he was captured as a coward. He was afraid to fight. He wants to be alive. That tells you right there he is a coward – he is scared to die. But you see him at the court, he was screaming at the judge, yelling, and he is acting still like a president. I was like, 'This is not right, you know.' Pissed me off big time. At least the judge should not let him talk the way he is.

At first, Saddam was in control in the court, and I'm glad the first judge is not there any more. The first judge, he looks young, I don't think he has a lot of experience about him and basically he did not stand up for himself as a judge. The last judge was pretty fair. I liked him the most because he does give Saddam a chance to talk but at the same time he stopped him and his brother from giving all these speeches and messages in politics.

Mowaffak al-Rubaie
Saddam Hussein's number one tactic against the trial was delaying tactics: 'I want Arab lawyers to represent me, Iraqi and Arab and international lawyers.' Second was trying to discredit the court itself, by saying that this was an American court – 'You were brought by the American occupiers; had it not been for the

Americans occupying Iraq, you wouldn't have been here to try me.' Discrediting the credibility of the court and then the legitimacy of the court. Also trying to ridicule the Prosecutor General and make him be seen by the public as small, and saying he has a history of being Ba'athist as well. Nobody can deny that the man had a charisma, there is no doubt. But it was an evil charisma.

I think the first judge was overwhelmed by the presence of Saddam Hussein. He couldn't believe, probably subconsciously, that he was trying Saddam Hussein. Saddam controlled him. He overpowered him, psychologically. And he probably outwitted him, to the extent that the judge said, 'Yes sir, Mr President.' That was a huge setback for the trial. I mean, if he's Mr President, why are we trying him, then? If he's innocent, why are we trying him? If he's just, what is the point of *you*, judge? You are not going to judge him, obviously, and you will not have guts to sentence him. That went really badly, and he was fired.

The replacement chief judge on the Supreme Iraqi Criminal Tribunal was **Raouf Rahman**.

We went to Baghdad, and we watched Saddam being trialled by other judges. We followed the trial closely, every hearing and session: evidence for and against, lines of questioning, the character of the accused, the character of the witnesses. I studied all of this closely before I ever set foot in the courtroom of that trial.

The point of view of the judge is different to the point of view of the people watching the trial. The judge is the one who oversees the court and directs the questioning and proceedings. A judge should be aware of the traits and personality of the accused, and be prepared to deal with them. Judge Rizgar Amin had his way of doing so, but the public were restless. They were expecting the old ways of the courts in Iraq when public opinion would be the judge. Rizgar stepped down. The trial was broadcast on live TV to the public. People would gather daily to watch the trial. I suppose Rizgar was vexed by all of this, and he said to them, 'I'm no longer anonymous,' then he left the court. Rizgar carried out his duty in a proper way, but his manner is different to mine, and mine is different to others'. When Rizgar withdrew from the committee, there was an emergency meeting held by the court, and they decided to move me from the second division to the first, and to carry on the trial.

Before I was a judge in the Baghdad criminal court, I was a judge in Kurdistan, in Sulaymaniyah and in Erbil. I was Vice President of the Court of Appeal, so I was the top judge. I was a criminal judge and a civil judge and a commercial judge, all areas. When the decision was made to establish the Iraqi High Tribunal, they took judges from Kurdistan, from Duhok, Erbil and Sulaymaniyah, and a few of the top judges and lawyers from Mosul. They formed two chambers, the first criminal chamber and the second, and each chamber was made up of a chief judge, four judges, three lay members and two lawyers – assistants, really – to explain the law in ordinary terms. Later, I became chief judge of the first Trial Chamber. I was the president of the first chamber, and the issue fell under the jurisdiction of this chamber.

A judge is committed to the rules governing his role. The Iraqi High Tribunal was linked to the old law, to international criminal law. It wasn't a new thing for us. Our studies were all based on the old laws, on the previous legal system, which was based on Nuremberg. We studied these laws in Italy and in Britain. We were trained in the area of international criminal law and in the ways of the international criminal tribunals of the International Criminal Court. This was the fundamental basis of the law of the Iraqi High Tribunal.

We did think of it as an extraordinary court, one that differed from the Iraqi criminal courts, and we counted on the fact that these trials would be studied, that we were judging people accused of international crimes on the legal basis of laws that were not the laws of Iraq. It was going to live on for years, the whole world would be talking about it, it was going to be studied in the same way Nuremberg has been studied. When we were judging, we would do so on the basis of international criminal laws, and we would use Iraqi criminal law for guidance and follow the procedures of Iraqi criminal law. So it was a mixture between international law and Iraqi criminal law.

The accused were not ordinary. They were accused of crimes of a different category. Saddam Hussein was a prominent individual, a head of state, and a figure of leadership for a number of Arab countries, on account of his stature, his reputation, and so on. The judges understood this well.

A judge is supposed to fairly and honestly apply the law. Any judge, even in a regular court, often angers some party in the trial. A judge is meant to put these implications aside. Fear is part of everyone's life, but we weren't afraid to the extent that we would refuse to work on the case. Incidents occurred where people fell victims, but this is normal, especially considering the parties of the case. But, even so, this also occurs in civil cases. A judge is threatened with murder, violence – this is the cost of justice. A judge practises law to deliver justice. This comes at a price. A consequence. Especially in a susceptible society. At the time, the heads of the court warned the judges and the lawyers, they even warned witnesses, that for that period of time they shouldn't leave the Green Zone and go to the streets. But there were people who did not care, who would come from the outside to the Green Zone, hence the incidents. But this happens even with normal trials. It's dangerous being a judge in Iraq, regardless of whether it's Saddam Hussein's trial or another.

One of the things we learned in our judiciary studies is that some accused seek to influence the mind of the judge. Saddam Hussein was this sort of person. He was, in truth, an intelligent man. He had the ability to read the personality of anyone before him. He would always study the personality of whoever he met, whether they were a judge, an ordinary citizen or even a friend. He would study someone's personality before dealing with them. He studied the personalities of the judges before me, he studied mine, and probably the other judges, too. Anything a judge might do or say, he had a response prepared. As judges, we had studied this sort of thing, and we had seen that he had a habit of doing this.

The trial of Saddam was different to the trial of any other of the accused, such as Taha Yassin Ramadan or Tariq Aziz. Those others may have been disruptive or difficult, but Saddam was different: he wanted to have an effect on the judge. If the judge wasn't careful, Saddam would succeed in doing so. Before the trials, I used to see him daily on TV, speaking, sometimes being provocative. He is an eloquent speaker.

Samir Al-Jassim
I mean, Saddam was a guilty man. When he was in that hole, he looked older. He had a long beard and he looked like he had been sitting there for a while not taking care of himself at all. I mean, I don't know if he ever took a shower. He looked disastrous, really, he looked very old. When we pulled him out and I was looking at him, he did not look like the President of Iraq – 'Saddam? That is not Saddam' – and the only way I recognised him was when he started talking. From his voice, that was him.

At the trial, it's more like he's taken care of himself a little bit. I think he was under US custody at the time and he was probably taken care of – they fed him pretty well and he had a place to stay, sleep and shower and shave. That is why he looks a little different because he didn't have a beard at the time. Even with his beard you can see it's trim and he looks a lot better.

Mowaffak al-Rubaie
Saddam was given a lot of chances, more than he deserved, to defend himself. And it was show business. He was given a platform, an unnecessary platform, to promote his justification and his reign. He was given more time than he deserved and, with hindsight, I wish that he was stopped and shut up. As soon as he started this media campaign, it was like a press conference. He was addressing the press, and he should have been stopped by the judge. Defend yourself on the material evidence these witnesses and the court has

produced in front of you, and stick to that. He started to lecture – lecture the court, lecture the audience – because he knew the outside world was listening, and all the Arab world is listening.

With hindsight, I wished as well that he was tried for the other crimes that he had committed. There were huge crimes that he had committed in the uprising, huge crimes in Halabja, in Anfal against the Kurds, against the Shia. Even against the Sunnis. We could've produced more material evidence to prove he was criminal.

Waleed Nesyif
I did not watch it. Partly because I knew the theatrics that is going to unfold during those trials. You see, the two sides were not interested in what actually happened. They were both putting on a show and they played it really well. The new Iraqi government demonstrating that we are the hand of the just, we are going to give Iraqis what they are owed by trying this dictator. There was no way Saddam was going to speak of his prior affiliation with the West because it was going to damage whatever image he's building over the past 30-odd years, so he gave them the patriotic figure. He was speaking to the populace outside of Iraq; they were speaking to the populace inside Iraq. Very smart game on both of their parts. So when I saw the first part of it and the way he started orating ... He was not speaking normally, he was an orator. He used classic Arabic tongue, which is very interesting. I knew that this was a matter of time until they conclude everything. And surely enough, they tried him and executed him on his smallest crimes, really. It wasn't the big ones that they killed him for.

Judge Raouf Rahman
When he was in power, no one could breathe or dare say no or look left or right. His way, during parliamentary or council sessions or the revolutionary council meetings, was like that. I remember once, one of the members had an emergency situation and had to leave the room. Saddam told him to stay. The guy had an urgent

matter, so he left anyway. This guy was fired, and then prosecuted and sentenced to 11 years. Just because he disobeyed Saddam Hussein and left a room.

There were two sides to Saddam's personality, two personalities that were very different. One personality was normal – whenever he was away from the cameras, a loveable personality. He would make jokes and laugh with others; he would shake hands with others and greet everyone. This was his main personality. His second personality – whenever he would be in front of the TV cameras, the foreign broadcasters, in front of the people – his personality would change into a very confrontational one. Even during the time when he was in jail, he was sitting in jail and he was writing poems. When you read these poems, when you see these writings, you would think that this man is very calm and serene, not the character of a dictator. But when he came before the cameras, and saw foreign broadcasters, he realised other people would see him, he would immediately change.

Saddam wasn't sectarian. He championed Arab nationalism, on the one hand. On the other hand, when he was President of Iraq he wanted to bring all the Iraqis together under his leadership. This caused friction between him and other leaders in the Ba'ath Party. He killed leaders of groups from within the Ba'ath Party and denounced them as sectarian. Sectarianism was there, but you couldn't say it was just Saddam – it was all of them. Most of the Ba'ath leaders were sectarian, but Saddam, when he was in office, wanted to rule over all of the Iraqi people. For him, he was the first and the last person who could rule over Iraq. Whoever opposed him would be eliminated. That was his style of leadership.

The first time he entered the court and I saw him, he gave me a look, a fierce look. I smiled. The other members asked what was going on. I said, 'He gave me a look, so I smiled back.' Later on, when we spoke, I asked him why he gave me that first stare. He said, 'Did it scare you?' I said, 'I fear no one but God.' He said, and I remember his words, 'Bless you.' I said, 'No, I don't want your blessing, you can have it.' I was there at the first hearing, behind the glass with the journalists, and he gave me the same look, but I didn't know if he could see me. When he looked at us, honestly, I felt goose bumps all over. I was scared. It was my first time seeing Saddam. He had a fierce look, strong, and could affect anyone around him. His look and the way he moved his hands had an influence. His look was known to mean doom, if given to anyone in his government, and truly his stare was scary and intimidating. Sometimes he would smile, but this smile wasn't friendly. A 'bitter smile,' as they would say in the Arabic language.

During the trial, I saw him twice, upon his request, outside of court. Once, he remained in the courtroom after the session ended. I asked him why he didn't leave. He said he had something to say to me. I asked, 'Here?' He said, 'No. Just me and you.' I asked him, 'Concerning?' He said, 'My brethren, Barzan and Atban.' I said, 'All right, I'll call you tomorrow at 11.'

The next day, even though he was under US custody, we met. We would sit outside of the courtroom, and this was recorded. A guard would be present, and we sat and he spoke to me about his situation. I told him to leave it in the hands of God. He said he wasn't there to speak to me about himself. I said, 'Your brethren?' He said, 'Yes. In regards to Barzan, he is sick. And Atban, he is this and that ... In regards to Taha Ramadan, he's closer than a brother, he's my friend.' I said, 'I know. Don't fear for Taha, he's a strong man. Don't worry about him.' He laughed when I said that. This was the first time.

The second time, he asked for me and I saw him. He complained about the guards, the place and their food. He asked me if I could give him papers, for him to write on. 'A journal?' 'No,' he said, 'for my soul's explorations.' He used that term. I agreed, so long as he would give me copies. He said it was personal. I said, 'Well, anyway.' They gave him papers, and he wrote. Later on, I found a few of his notes: existential inquiries, thoughts and poetry. But he wasn't remorseful. He was someone who didn't regret anything.

A judge should understand the character of his defendant. If a judge understands the character of his presented defendant, then he can control that defendant's attitude and actions appropriately. Saddam's personality could affect people around him and, in this way, he wanted to control the court and those in it. And he did. At some point, he did have control over the court. This was his way.

When he was president, he gives a speech, regardless of anyone's opinions; he says whatever word comes to his mind, without hesitation; sometimes he would curse. Controlling or disciplining someone like that is difficult. You deal with him according to his ways. Saddam Hussein got his way by controlling others, he was controlling, so he had to be dealt with the same way. He gets upset when he sees that his opponent can't be controlled by him. Sometimes I would see him, after we would speak, his expression changes and he looks very, very sad.

I remember a time we judges were sat, I in the middle, and two to my left and two to my right. One of the judges was laughing, or maybe smiling, while Saddam was talking. Saddam warned him, raising a hand. I warned him, told him to address the head judge. He told me, 'Tell the honourable sir –' I can't remember his exact words, but he meant that the judge fix his posture, his way of eye contact.

Brandon Barfield

One day, he didn't feel like going to court. We were like, 'Dude, you have to go to court,' and he refused to go. He was like, 'I'm tired, I didn't sleep good, I'm not going to court.' Our lieutenant was like, 'You have got to go, man, it's the judge saying you have got to do it.'

We always took him up the back way, and one of my jobs was I had to open the door a certain way so that nobody could see because the camera was pointed directly into that room, and they didn't want us to be seen. I always counted down, 3, 2, 1. I think I was at 2, he goes, 'Watch this.' As soon as I opened that door, he started yelling, shoving his finger up, calling the judge all kinds of names. The judge started trying to go through opening the court, and Saddam started screaming again. He was in there maybe three and a half minutes, and the judge was like, 'Get him out of the court room.'

So he got back to the door, and I opened it and he walked in, and he took a deep breath and said, 'I think I will have my cigar now.' And I was like, 'Dude, this guy is *running* the court, man.' We took him downstairs, he got his cigar, and he wanted all his buddies to come round. So they cancelled court that day and gave that man a cigar with all his buddies.

Mowaffak al-Rubaie
If the judge sentenced him to imprisonment – even life imprisonment – there would have been a popular uproar. A popular uprising against the court, against the order, against everything. People were waiting for this death sentence to be passed on him. But he wasn't, if you like, presentenced, the sentence was not passed before the court, or before the trial.

There is no shadow of doubt in my mind that Iraq as a nation wanted him to go and to pay for the price. There are so many bizarre wishes among ordinary Iraqis. For example, 'Why did you hang him, doctor? You should have put him in a cage in Tahrir Square in the centre of Baghdad, ten dollars entry to look at him.' It's part of the healing process. It's part of the people venting anger on him.

Judge Raouf Rahman
The Special Tribunal Committee, made up of nine judges, reviewed the case. The preliminary decision was made by the first tribunal panel, which was made up of five judges led by Raouf Rachid. Then it reached the discriminatory body, made up of nine judges, led by Jamal.

It is difficult for a judge to sentence someone to death, but this is duty, law. Custom and duty – a lawyer can't ignore these obligations. Taking a person's life is very, very difficult. I didn't want to be a judge who sentences anyone with the death penalty, but this was my duty to the law. I felt like I applied the law I was meant to apply, and it wasn't an independent decision. I just announced the decision we all made. A huge responsibility. A judge has a big responsibility, mostly towards the law and the body that allowed him to apply it, fairly and justly. This is a greater responsibility than pleasing people. A judge's duty is applying the law justly and fairly, with a clear conscience.

Mowaffak al-Rubaie

When the judge was reading the sentence, Saddam stood up, or half stood up, and he started a slogan: 'God is great, God is great, Iraq is great, long live Iraq.' He was trying to distract the judge and not listen to the judge and not allow the voice of the judge to be heard by people in the court and people outside. I think it was all pre-planned.

I said to my people around me, 'This is a page we have to turn once and for all, and this is going to have a huge demoralising effect on the insurgency.' I was right for myself – it was a great relief – but I was wrong in thinking that it would badly influence the activities of the insurgency.

Judge Raouf Rahman

According to all laws, international or national, the defendant should be standing when sentenced. That way, we are properly practising the law. Saddam, firstly, wanted to challenge the court and, secondly, pride and vanity remained in his heart or mind. That's why he refused to stand for the verdict.

As I was reading, Saddam was shouting. He stood up from his place and started exclaiming on Arab nationalism, Iraq and the fall of spies. I told him, 'We aren't agents or spies; we are judges. We work for no one; we are agents of the law. You're delusional.'

Once the verdict is read, judges are meant to leave the courtroom. We left the room, and I told the head of the guards to accompany him gently. He was having a psychotic fit as the guards were trying to take him out. They told me that he kept shouting. He hit one of them.

'That's the End of Him'

John Nixon

It was a topic that I never really wanted to get into with him, but I knew, in my mind, that there would be some sort of a trial and it would most likely end with a guilty verdict and an execution. But one day when I was talking to Saddam, he just brought it up. He said, 'I know where this is headed. I know I'm never getting out of here. And I know that this is going to lead to my death.' But then he said, 'I am at peace with my God, and everything I did, I did for the Iraqi people, and basically I'm OK with that.' I didn't say anything to that.

I was fairly certain that this would end in execution, but I thought his execution would be, if you will, a more dignified affair. More of a pageant than the mob justice it was. Something that would be more ceremonial. There would be a trial, verdict pronounced and the verdict executed, and that he would be led into a room and that he would be hanged and that there would be witnesses. If anything, what it really was, it was just mob justice in the middle of the night.

I was sickened by it. I was part of the 'execution watch' – basically, I was on call if anything happened such as a commutation of his sentence or if somebody tried to rescue him and there was a shootout or whatever. If something happened that needed to be written up for the President, I was on call. I heard the news that he had been executed and shortly thereafter I learned that there was some videotape of it. Naturally I went to the videotape, and I remember watching it and putting my hand to my mouth: 'Oh my god, this is terrible.'

We went there to create a new Iraq. At least we were going to create rule of law. Things would be different. And instead, I saw this hanging in the middle of the night, this prisoner being taunted and, rather than rule of law, it's just mob justice.

I think when we talked about how Saddam knew that it would end on his execution, in my head I had an execution a certain way – more ceremonial, in a sense. His was the more accurate version. I think he knew exactly what was going to happen. It would end in him being surrounded by his enemies being taunted and it being done in the middle of the night and then having his body dumped somewhere.

He was the most dignified person there. He handled it exactly the way I thought he would. He didn't show any fear. In fact, he kind of gave it back to the people who were taunting him. It shouldn't have been like that: the dignified ones should have been the executioners. They were supposedly bringing justice from this man's rule. And it just was horrible. We were all disgusted with it.

Mowaffak al-Rubaie
After that sentence was passed on Saddam Hussein and then the appeal confirmed that sentence, we were given one month. During that one month, there were a lot of activities trying to stop us from carrying out the execution.

A few Arab leaders called me directly, and one of them said to me, 'Doctor, doctor, this is wrong. Don't do it, because people will have the courage against their own masters, that's kings or presidents.' My response was, 'I'm sorry, this is the sentence from an Iraqi court, and this man has committed so many crimes against humanity, against Iraqis, against Arabs everywhere, so this sentence has to be carried out.'

There was a lot of pressure from departments in the United States of America. The State Department were not that keen to execute Saddam Hussein, and I believe the CIA was not that keen as well, while the White House and the Pentagon wanted him to go.

A case filed against the government of Iraq in the state of New York tried to delay the execution. The excuse for that was that he was an American prisoner of war; the Iraqi government cannot try him and execute him. And that was all delaying tactics, because there is a section in the Iraqi legal code of practice that if you get to 70 you might be exempted. Saddam was approaching 70.

Inside Iraq, we needed the Minister of Justice in the chamber of execution. The Minister of Justice had travelled abroad and he was in Paris. We needed a judge there who has experienced more than five years; we had to bring, if you like, a second-hand judge to be present there, with the Prosecutor General, myself and the manager of the prime minister.

And he was not in our physical custody. The physical custody of Saddam Hussein was with the Americans. We had only legal custody of him. When we asked them to hand over Saddam Hussein to carry out the execution, the general who was in charge of him said, 'This is a list of requirements. You have to tick each and every box in this.' The most difficult one was presidential approval. According to the old Iraqi law before 2003, which was still valid then, if anyone was sentenced to death, this had to be approved by the president. The president was now Jalal Talabani. He refused to sign, because he had already signed a European declaration saying that he doesn't believe in the death sentence. I worked all night, playing with words in the statement and, at the end of the night, with a lot of modification in it, Jalal Talabani signed it. He signed the statement saying that he had no authority to say yea or nay, but I don't think the Americans got that translation. They wanted any signature from the president.

Brandon Barfield

Right before he died, like a couple of days before, something like that, he told us that he wanted all of us – because we were the nicest ones that guarded him, we didn't hurt him in any way, we were respectful to him – he wanted to smoke a cigar with us. And the Colonel said, 'We can't allow them to smoke with you because they guard you. It wouldn't be right.' I remember thinking, 'I have never smoked a Cuban cigar before, but you all come up here every day, several times a day, and smoke with this man.'

It was night time and he was asleep, and Sergeant Coleman came and called me to the office and said, 'Hey, it's time.' So me and Sergeant Coleman were standing next to the cell, and I tapped on the cell and told him, 'You got to get up.' He got up, and Sergeant Coleman said, 'Sir, it's time.' He literally threw the covers off and said he wanted to go take a shower so he could be clean when he went to see Allah. We told him, 'You ain't got time. This is a last-minute thing, like literally wheels up. You have just a few minutes to get ready, we are leaving.'

He had a bucket in there, about a gallon-size bucket. Man, he loved oranges, and he would throw his peelings in that bucket. He emptied that bucket out on the floor and filled it up in the sink and he got stripped down, butt-naked like the day he was born, and just took the full thing of water and just poured it all over and started washing his self. After that, he put his clothes on with his long black coat and his scarf, and then he stood up and he goes, 'I am ready.' The Colonel came out, and Saddam asked again if we could smoke cigars with him. Of course he said no. And Saddam had a box of them, and he said, 'I want them to have these.'

He came up and shook everybody's hand. Some of them he gave hugs to, but I didn't hug him. I shook his hand and everything, and I stood up and looked at him face to face and he shook my hand and told me I was a good soldier, and then he gave me some money with his picture on it. He gave everybody the same thing and he talked to each one of us about how he appreciated us. How the other ones hurt him and we called him sir and how we basically treated him good. Then he got to the front of the bus and he started crying and said bye to everybody. He didn't bawl, you know, but you could tell he was crying, he wiped his eyes. Held his hand up and waved bye to everybody and said bye and got off the bus.

Mowaffak al-Rubaie
The Americans handed over Saddam Hussein before the sunrise of Eid.

Anyone who is sentenced to death needs a death certificate, and I'm a doctor. More important is I am a national security adviser, so I was representing the government of Iraq, along with the Minister of Justice, a judge and the Prosecutor General, with the manager of the prime minister's office. We went by helicopter, we were flown by the Americans from the Green Zone to the prison, and we went into the chamber. We said our Fajr prayer, the dawn prayer, and we waited until the Americans brought Saddam to the doorstep. He was bound and he was holding the Qur'an in his hands. They stopped there, and I signed for him, that I received him. I was holding his left arm, and I led him to the execution chamber. Somebody from behind said, 'Doctor, doctor, no – he has to listen to the judge, and the Prosecutor General has to read the statement.' So I had to bring him back, sit him on a chair.

The judge started to read the statement, and Saddam started to say, 'Long live Iraq, long live resistance, down with Israel, down with Iran, down with this, down with that, long live that, long live that and long live this ... ' The usual rants of Saddam Hussein. I was really fed up, and I reached the end of my tether. I said, 'Shut up. We've been living with this for 36 years, just shut up.' He said, 'I'm sorry,' and he carried on, he carried on and on and on.

Then we took him to the room. When he went into that room, he looked up to the rope. He looked me in the eye. I did not blink. I did not blink. I stayed, I stayed looking at him. After a while – two minutes, three minutes or even one minute, but it felt like long time – he said, 'Doctor, this is for a man.' A sign of manhood. This is not for a chicken, if you like. I didn't reply to that. I untied his arms, then tied them behind him. It was little bit tight, and I loosened it up. We made a mistake: we tied his feet. You do not tie his feet, because he has three or four steps to go up. And then he went up.

I'm a doctor. I'm meant to revive life and relieve pain. That's the irony. The whole room smelt death, felt death, the whole room you can see death. For me, it's a very strange feeling. I've done hundreds of CPU cardiopulmonary resuscitation. Trying to prolong life for people. Now I'm causing death to this guy. OK, he's a criminal, but then let somebody else do it. Why do I have to do it? It was not a funny feeling, it was a strange feeling.

He was supposed to wear a hood on his head. He refused to do it. He wanted to show that he was brave, courageous. And then he stood and we asked him to say, 'There is no god but Allah, and his messenger is Mohammed.' This is something you do before you die. We had to remind him – he did not say this voluntarily or spontaneously. If you don't remember this, in this critical moment of the last second of your life, when will you remember it? It shows to me that Saddam never believed in the Qur'an, in Islam, religion. His religion was himself.

I tried to pull the lever to bring him down. It was hard. I don't know whether it was jammed. I pulled the lever. With honour and pleasure, yes. I am proud that I have carried the justice of the Iraqi court on this brutal, ruthless beast who has inflicted unbelievable atrocities throughout the years of his war.

I pulled the lever. It didn't go. So we had to ask him a second time to say, 'There is no god but Allah, and Mohammed is his messenger.' Before he completed it, this time it went down. And here he is. With his cervical spine cut, and his white shirt stained with blood.

Brandon Barfield
I was standing outside. He walked up casual, like he always did, dragging his heels, because he never did pick his feet up, he always dragged them with little flip-flops he had on him. He walked right on up there, and they put the noose around him. He had his wife's scarf on that she made him, so they put the rope around his neck right there. They were just talking junk to him and he was talking junk back. There was a huge crowd of people outside, and we were

guarding them all because they were going insane trying to get him. They hated him – man, they hated him. Then he did pray, and in the middle of his prayer they pulled the switch. There was a loud snap, and then you could see his shadow fall and then he would swing back and forward, and then everybody in that crowd just started cheering and going crazy.

Mowaffak al-Rubaie
I said to the guards, 'Let's have the white bag, the plastic bag to put him in.' The guy said, 'No, no, doctor, we have to make sure that he is dead.' Well, you know, brain-stem death is instantaneous, so it was obvious. I went myself with another guy, put him in the white plastic bag and put him on a couch.

Unfortunately, people around dealt with Saddam in an unhuman and Islamic way, in humiliating Saddam Hussein after he was dead. I believe this is in the basic principles of our religion: if you are alive and a criminal, you belong to the government. They do whatever they want. But once you're dead, the government does not own you, you don't belong to the government. You are owned, the remains, by the family. That's it. If you don't own the thing, you don't do this to the remains.

Brandon Barfield
They brought his body out and it was underneath a complete white sheet. They were supposed to just view the body, but the whole crowd somehow grabbed him, and they were holding his body up, passing it over their heads like a rock concert – like they do when they dive into the crowds and they just send them through a wave. The sheet came off, and I remember the women reaching up. They were grabbing his arms and his private parts, trying to rip them out.

They were refusing to give the body back. I remember looking at Mike and I said, 'Man, we are going to have a day on shootout right here.' There had to be two, three hundred people. I was like, 'We haven't got enough ammo. I don't know what the heck we are going to do, man. How are we going to get his body back out of this crowd?' When we walked up there to try to get it, they moved his body in the middle of the crowd, so we couldn't get to him. But we pushed through the crowd, got his body back, and we dragged him on the bus.

I remember sitting there, watching, while he was lying in the middle of the aisle of this little school bus. I just sat there thinking, I wonder if he ain't really dead, he is going to move or wake up or whatever. Every time you hit a bump his head would flop around. The way his neck had broke, the only thing holding it on was the skin basically, so like his head like, man. I had to put my foot next to his head so his head wouldn't flop around.

We took him to the airport, and there was two black helicopters waiting. They had brought their medics over, and we handed him over to them. The medics checked his heart rate and his pulse, and took a little needle thing and stabbed him in the foot and the finger to make sure he was dead, and then they loaded his body up into the helicopter while two Apache helicopters circled around making sure nobody was coming, and then we watched it fly off.

Mowaffak al-Rubaie

Unfortunately, the fact that we were going to bring the remains of Saddam Hussein was not counted in the number of passengers in the helicopter. He didn't have a seat. Where do we put him? Where do we put this stretcher? On the laps of these people sitting in the helicopter? That's a problem. Well, we put it somewhere, OK. The helicopter went up, and I was holding the stretcher from one side and the seat on the other.

And then I saw the rising sun in Baghdad, and said that this was going to be good luck. This is a new sun on Iraq. God willing.

Brandon Barfield

We came back, and that Colonel and a major was standing there, and each one of them had a box of cigars. They called us into formation, and I was thinking, 'They are going to hand us a cigar.' The Colonel said, 'He wanted you all to have these, but we can't give you all these, because these are considered war treasures so we are just going to take them and confiscate them.' And he put one underneath his arm. You know, this dude is going to take these cigars and they are going to be selling them as the last box from Saddam. That guy's last wish before he died was for us to have a cigar and you are refusing him his last wish. I always thought that was a little weird, but I don't know. I mean, I'm not an officer, I just follow the rules, I just do what I'm told. But I don't know.

The only thing that I remember him complaining about was he did not want to be hanged – he said that was a coward's way to go out. He wanted to be killed by a firing squad, because that is the way he said soldiers were supposed to die. He was upset because he was being hanged and being treated as a traitor, and that is the main thing he complained about.

Judge Raouf Rahman

I saw it on TV and I gave my opinion on it. I said the way he was executed demeaned the significance of the law. The method was primitive, unprecedented. The way he was executed was uncivil. Executing someone sentenced to death is difficult enough, but when it's in the streets, and crowds gather, and a mob forms ..?. For one thing, this is against the rule of law. For another, it's uncivilised. Barbaric. That's what people in the villages do. Like any other Iraqi, he deserved humane treatment, until his soul meets God, and he travels the skies.

Samir Al-Jassim

I always knew he was going to be executed. I knew he was going to be executed, no matter what, because he is guilty. I mean, he committed so many crimes against Iraqi people. How could he get away with that? I mean, how? Attacking the Kurds, killing thousands of innocent civilians, killing a lot of people from the south, from everywhere – he is guilty. He did a lot of crime, he is responsible for destroying the country, he is not going to get away with it. I knew he was going to get executed.

I watched the video when he was hanged. It shows when they put the rope around his neck, and when his body was dropped. Dead. That's the end. That's the end of him. It's over. It's done. He is dead. That's a good thing. He deserved it. He really deserved it.

A lot of people were celebrating in the street. There was a big celebration for his death, for sure. A lot of people were happy seeing Saddam being killed and hanged, they were celebrating. Yeah.

I'm glad they did it on a day that is a holiday which is a big deal in the country. A lot of people don't like that. But he deserved it. Fuck 'em a thousand times. A person like him should have no mercy. I think he wanted to be executed as a soldier, shot by a bullet. I think I'm glad that they chose the hanging with a rope. It means like you don't deserve the real death penalty – you were just killed because you are a piece of shit.

Waleed Nesyif
Saddam's execution happened in 2006, and it coincided with the very first day of Eid, which is a Muslim celebration after the fasting of Ramadan. Saddam was not supposed to be executed, not on that day. Nobody would have believed that this was going to happen because it's unprecedented to kill someone – execution or otherwise – in Eid. In the Islamic faith, during such times, no war, no killing, no nothing. I managed to find the video of Saddam being walked onto the podium on which they put the noose around his neck. They had a black hood that they would put on his face. He was like, 'I don't want you to put that on,' but they forced him to.

And he was saying his *Shahada*: 'I witness that there is no god but Allah and Mohammed is his prophet or messenger.' As a Muslim, you're supposed to say this before you exit this realm. He said it the first time, and he was about to say it the second time, and then they yanked it, man. As I watched his body drop uncontrollably, I just broke out in tears. Partly because, no matter who you are or how evil a person you are, seeing someone die is not something that should be easy on anyone. But the other thing was

– and I think this was the thing that just hit me – that it almost all came together to me at that time. Like I understood what just happened you know, from 2003 till now. Through executing this guy in this manner on this day.

Whether we like it or not, this man represented us. For 30-odd years, he was Iraq for the world; the world knew us through him, and we knew the world through him as well. To see him in that fashion, it sealed our deal in a sense: we don't count for shit. Because it wasn't just an execution. This was probably the biggest slap we can get as an Iraqi people. That is as blatant as possible an analogy of who's the boss. This is who you are really, right now.

Of course, the news afterwards is showing some Iraqis celebrating, some of them demonstrating, and I was there literally curled up in a ball crying because I was just thinking, 'We're just game over.' If there was an ounce of hope in me at that time it was just *poof*. My girlfriend walks in on me and she sees that I'm crying, she's asking me what's going on and I can't even speak. I couldn't take it.

I didn't cry because of any affinity I felt towards the guy or his character. I was under no illusion of what this man has done and whether or not he was deserved of death. See, my issue with this is not that he was executed, it's that he was executed under such circumstances. And not by us, even though it was claimed to be by us. Yeah, the guys who led him to the execution chamber were Iraqis, but this whole thing was concocted not by us. America. Specifically, the guy who pretty much gave the order, his name is John Negroponte. John Negroponte had visited Iraq the day before and had a secret meeting, a closed cabinet meeting with no press allowed. And the next day Saddam was executed.

Now there is another nuance to this particular day he was executed on. Traditionally, Sunnis and Shias celebrate Eid on the same day, but typically it happens that Saudi Arabia announces Eid and all of the Sunnis will follow that, but the Shias will wait for when Iraq announces Eid, and usually it is a day apart. So they executed him on the first day of Eid for Sunnis. Whether they intended it or not, this is how it was interpreted: it was a further definition to the division intended between the Shias and the Sunnis. Up until that time, they were still standing in solidarity together, because the civil war didn't really start until 2006. That was one of the catalysts. Saddam's execution marked one of the major turning points in Iraqi society which eventually led to the civil war in 2006. The bloodiest years we've had, and it didn't stop until 2010. Iraq blew up. We were holding it together, trying to, against all odds, against everything, and that was one of the punches that, when it came, the wound just opened up. It just opened up. It was a clearly divisive move and at the same time it was a clear message to Iraqis. This is the guy that represented you, and this is where he's at: dangling from a rope. And I say this as a man who stood against Saddam in every ounce in me, my family was executed by Saddam. And we've been hurt by him in ways that I cannot recount. But that's one thing, and his execution was another.

Brandon Barfield

We came home right before Halloween, and I remember my ex-wife said she wanted to throw a Halloween party. We went down to the Halloween shop and they had this skeleton guy dressed exactly like Saddam, and as soon as you walked in the door he started flopping around, screaming. It freaked me out for a second. My ex-wife swears that she called me by my name twice before I said, 'Huh?' She said I was just staring at it. She was, like, 'Where are you at? You are in your own little world.' I said, 'I'm just looking at it, that's kind of creepy.' But I never told her I guarded Saddam.

Mowaffak al-Rubaie

I felt immediate closure myself. But unfortunately, after the death of Saddam Hussein, he's remembered on a number of corners, unfortunately not only in the Sunni community but also some of the Shia community. It's very important that people will not forget. We should never, ever forget Saddam Hussein and his two sons and what they have done in Iraq. Probably we should forgive some of his followers because they were forced to follow him. But not forget Saddam Hussein, because if you forget Saddam Hussein, what will happen? This is a recipe for disaster. We will grow another Saddam Hussein. It's a cycle, it's a vicious circle.

There is hope here now. There is hope that people will be enlightened, aware of something, they will choose the right member of parliament, then they will choose the right prime minister or the right president, and rectify the system. During Saddam's time, there was no hope. A friend of mine, a doctor, said, 'I did not even allow myself to think differently. To think any different from the government, from Saddam Hussein. Just in case it will show on my face and they will recognise this.'

The millennials will not do this.

Just and Fair

John Nixon

He was quite sane. People asked me when I worked for CIA, they asked me when I debriefed him, and they asked me for years afterwards ... People still ask me: 'Was he a madman?' No. He was a very sane person. He had some brutal methods that he used. He certainly had views that were different from ours, but I never got the sense that he was mentally ill or deranged or that he was delusional. He was a lot saner than some of the people I met at CIA. Let me put it that way. And in our government.

I had participated in hundreds of briefings on him and wrote hundreds of memos and wrote hundreds of reports and did everything I could. And I came away with the realisation that we actually never knew who he was. That many of the things that we thought about him were actually wrong. There was a whole lot of information we didn't appreciate, or we didn't even know about.

His words resonated far beyond my last day: 'just and fair'. We thought this whole process was about justness and fairness. We thought the whole war – going to war, removing him from power because he was going to use WMD against us – was about justness and fairness. And yet, from that moment on and throughout the entire war, the justness and the fairness and the justifications for the war became less and less, certainly when it came to his trial and when it came to his execution. There was no justness, and there certainly was no fairness. It was mob justice. For me, that was very, very hard to swallow. It was at that point in time that I began to really feel complicit in an almost criminal action. And I began to come to the belief that we shouldn't be there and that we had no reason to be there. If Saddam Hussein needed to be removed from power, that should have been for the Iraqis to do, not for the US.

Our analysis had always been that Saddam called all the shots, especially on the big-picture items, like going to war or relations with another country, weapons of mass destruction. One of the things that we discovered during the debriefings, and also subsequently talking to some of the other detainees, was that really Saddam had become kind of aloof in the last few years of his regime. He was getting older, he had other interests at heart. Chiefly, he wanted to write and thought of himself as a writer. That's not to say that he wasn't still president – he felt very strongly that he was the president, he was the leader of Iraq – but he had turned over a lot of the day-to-day running of the government to his loyal allies, people like Taha Yasin Ramadan and Izzat Ibrahim al-Douri and Tariq Aziz. At that time, in this post-9/11 world, when Saddam should have been paying closer attention to what was going on, he's actually paying less attention. At the time of the invasion, instead of getting ready for this bone-crushing invasion which is coming to remove him from power, he's sending drafts of a novel to Tariq Aziz – like, a week before the invasion – asking him what he thought, a critique of his novel. And in terms of weapons of mass destruction, I think Saddam's fiction is way up there. His is some of the worst writing you'll ever encounter. But Saddam thought he was a great writer. It just shows you this complete lack of understanding between the US and Iraq. At a time when Saddam thinks the US is going to move closer to Iraq, the US decides the opposite: it's going to remove him from power, it's coming to get him. And at a time when we think Saddam is still running the show the way he's always done it, he's basically off writing a novel.

It's not the picture that the US intelligence community and the US administration had given to the country and to the world. In a sense, we had really not done our job well. We created this caricature that we felt comfortable with, a caricature of bloodthirstiness and cruelty, and then we disseminated it to the rest of the world. Everybody bought into it and it was not reality. It was easier to believe in the caricature than to actually do the hard work and try to come to a clearer understanding of who this person is and what it is they're trying to do and what are the pressures on them.

One of the things that I think that our intelligence community and our government does very poorly is deal in empathy. Now, I'm not saying sympathy – there's no reason to sympathise with a guy like Saddam Hussein. But when you're trying to figure out who someone is and what they're up to and what they want, sometimes it's good to look at it from their vantage point and try to see how they view things, because it makes it a little easier to figure out what they want. That's very hard to do. When you go to a policy-maker and try to do that, they oftentimes are not interested at all. And they sort of see someone trying to do that as almost being disloyal. Who are you loyal to? Are you loyal to the US or are you loyal to Saddam Hussein? A little more empathy might have saved us three trillion dollars and four thousand American lives and hundreds of thousands of Iraqi lives, and all of the fallout that has affected the region since.

Nothing was gained. Nothing was gained from toppling Saddam. Nothing.

Chapter 5
'Those Who Are Wet Aren't Scared of the Rain'

Timeline

10 January 2007	President Bush announces the deployment of an additional 21,500 US troops in Iraq, in what becomes known as 'the surge'.
10 June 2007	The Awakening: US forces start to arm Sunni Arab groups that promise to fight al-Qaeda.
29 August 2007	Radical Shi'ite cleric Muqtada al-Sadr announces a six-month suspension of his Mahdi Army's operations.
23 March 2008	US military casualties in Iraq pass 4,000.
18 April 2007	Five car bombs kill 198 people in Baghdad.
16 September 2007	Blackwater private security contractors open fire on Iraqi civilians in Baghdad, killing 17 and wounding 20.
25 March 2008	The Battle of Basra begins.
1 September 2008	US forces formally hand control of Anbar province to the Iraqi army and police.

17 November 2008	US Ambassador Ryan Crocker and Iraqi Foreign Minister Hoshiyar Zebari sign the *Agreement Between the United States of America and the Republic of Iraq on the Withdrawal of United States Forces from Iraq and the Organization of Their Activities during Their Temporary Presence in Iraq*, stating that all US forces will be withdrawn from Iraq by 31 December 2011.
20 January 2009	Barack Obama succeeds George W. Bush as US President, and swiftly issues a presidential memorandum ordering the withdrawal of US forces from Iraq.
28 May 2009	The UK withdraws the last of its combat forces from Iraq.
30 June 2009	The USA withdraws its forces from Iraqi cities.
7 March 2010	Iraq holds a general election.
18 August 2010	The USA withdraws the last of its combat forces from Iraq.
31 August 2010	President Barack Obama announces the end of the US combat mission in Iraq.
15 December 2011	US forces formally end operations in Iraq.

Introduction

The war in Iraq, far from being a short and easy victory for America, proved to be messy, complicated and protracted. It was a war consisting of numerous false dawns, such as the initial conquest of Baghdad, defeating al-Qaeda in Fallujah, and the capture and execution of Saddam Hussein. It was hoped that any one of these events might swing the war back towards an American advantage. All, it would transpire, failed to do that.

From whichever angle the war was looked at, it appeared to be a disaster. Post invasion, Iraq had turned from a secular, educated, ordered society into an ultra-radicalised, sectarian, divided culture, splintered between competing religious sects and the ever-increasing dominance of al-Qaeda. Huge areas of the country were under Sharia law, enforced by extremist Islamic groups. For everyone involved it was hard to see a successful way out of this situation.

In 2007, President George Bush decided, in opposition to the dominant opinion of the American public, to increase rather than decrease the number of US troops in Iraq. At the same time, America started paying Sunni tribal leaders to join them against what was now considered to be a shared enemy, al-Qaeda. The combination of these two strategy initiatives radically altered the landscape of the Iraq War. Almost immediately, the violence decreased. Many Sunnis, sick of living under the arcane rules of Sharia law, turned on al-Qaeda and pushed them out of the cities. It had taken many years, but eventually Iraq was establishing something close to peace, albeit incredibly fragile.

It wasn't long however, before disaster would strike again. In 2009, America elected a new president, who had campaigned to end the war in Iraq. When Barack Obama took office, his instincts were to untangle America from the situation which had bogged them down for the last nine years. For many Iraqis, the end of American occupation was all they wanted but, when America did eventually leave, the country they handed back was broken and deeply wounded. Iraqis were scarred and traumatised by the years of fighting, aerial bombardments, kidnappings, executions, torture, revenge killings and suicide bombs. The healing may have started, but only just. Not enough time had elapsed to fully bury the memories of the recent sectarian horrors. It would not take much to expose the metaphoric corpses from their shallow graves. And that is, unfortunately, what happened. When America pulled out, Iraq collapsed.

Omar Mohammed, a professor of history at the University of Mosul, and Tahany Saleh, a student there, were living in Mosul with their families when, on 4 June 2014, a new Islamic group entered the city. Unlike previous radical sects who had established a presence in Mosul, this group seemed different. They wore distinctive black uniforms, kept their hair long, drove expensive SUVs and were extremely well-armed with new, high-tech weapons. It wasn't long before the group declared their intentions to establish the caliphate in Northern Iraq and set about enforcing their draconian laws. This is how the people of Mosul, and soon the rest of the world, first heard of ISIS.

It might not be possible to state definitively that the American invasion gave rise to the Islamic State. There are a number of factors in play. It is fair to say that one of those significant factors was the invasion of Iraq in 2003 and the disposing of Saddam Hussein. It's doubtful the Neoconservative architects of the initial invasion could have predicted the consequences of America's involvement in Iraq. One man who did predict what was to come was Saddam Hussein. The trouble was, when he warned the world of the risks, the world did not listen.

'If You Only Smile'

John Nixon
When I was talking with Saddam, we talked about sectarian problems and he said to me, 'What is Saddam Hussein, Sunni or Shia?' I said, 'You are a Sunni.' And he said, 'Yes. And do you think that I care who is Sunni and who is Shia? As long as they are Iraqi, that is what I care about. But now that you are here and now that you've removed Saddam Hussein from power, Iraq will become a playground for these forces that are looking to build hatred and to unleash terrorism on Iraq and on the region.' He was dead right about that. He knew more about his country than we did and, when I look back on it, he was under no illusions as to what was going on.

Tahany Saleh *was a university student in Mosul, who watched as her city fell into the hands of al-Qaeda.*

If the American soldiers wanted to walk down a street, they would block it and stop the civilians from walking alongside them. They feared us, they didn't trust us, so naturally we didn't trust them. They saw us as strangers, as enemies. I remember, I was in my first or second year at university. I was on my way there, but they'd blocked the road. I had to cross because I had an exam. So they said, 'It's impossible, they'll kill you if you cross.' 'But I'm a girl, carrying my books – how are they going to kill me?' He replied, 'They don't trust anyone. You might be a suicide bomber, explode yourself.'

So this thought was stamped in our minds: they see us as enemies. They didn't try and understand that we are just regular people. I have dreams, thoughts, I have plenty of things and, despite the person in front of me being armed and foreign, I didn't consider him my enemy. But he considers me his enemy. They feared us and considered us enemies before getting to know us, so it's natural for us to hurt them, and be hurt by them. On the one hand, if you smiled to an American soldier you'd be killed, because the 'freedom fighters' won't accept that – if you only smile. And if you *don't* smile at an American soldier, or opposed an American soldier, or you created some kind of tension, or if you tried to object to anything, the American soldier would kill you, because he'd consider you a 'freedom fighter.' And you're just a civilian.

That is something that I used to think about a lot: how is it that these people came calling themselves liberators while being scared of the people they came to liberate? That is one of the reasons that has planted fear and worry in the hearts of the Iraqi and Mosuli people – it's the Americans. Because they didn't treat us normally, as civilians, they treated us all as people who kill them. 'We have the right to shoot at anyone' – or any animal that is walking down a Mosuli street because animals might be rigged with bombs too. So, yes, I was very scared of being around them. I'd always avoid them; I'd just stop in my place. I remember one time, where I just stood in my place for half an hour. I didn't move, because they were close by to us. Because if it's not them who shoot, then a car bomb might go off. The 'freedom fighters' might arrive, and a battle could start. So we had to live with these things on a daily basis as civilians.

All the youths who felt that there was an occupation – that our land should be defended, that we should defend our cause, that we shouldn't allow them to stay in Mosul, that they have to get out of Mosul – began to join the resistance. All these issues made a lot of young guys get dragged into the cause. They felt that they were freedom fighters, and should carry weapons. Iraqis have a very strong relationship with weapons, extremely strong. If you were to give an Iraqi child a nice little colourful toy and a toy weapon, he'd leave the colourful toy aside, not even think about playing with it, and take the weapon. A young guy has access to weapons made easily available to him, and he's had a dream of carrying weapons for his entire life, and now he's defending – to use Iraqi terminology – 'your women, your honour, your land'. Defending them from the occupier. They never think to themselves, not even for a moment, 'Let me just be a regular simple person, and not get myself killed and kill those around me.' When IEDs killed children and women, they used to call them martyrs. Didn't those who died have dreams? Those who died, have they not left a mother behind? A sister, a lover, a wife behind? Don't they have this thought? Why are you making decisions for us when it comes to death and killing? On what basis?

Al-Qaeda was there. They were called the freedom fighters, or 'the brothers' or 'the community' – they used to always use the term 'community'. So we used to know 'community' meant those people. Zarqawi himself, I don't think so. He might be at the end of the world, but his followers were around, they were present, and they increased in numbers. They bombed. All they needed was 'a cause', and they'd have a lot of loyalty. Zarqawi's cause, al-Qaeda's cause and the community's cause were very present. It had a lot of popularity in Mosul via their soldiers, people he delegated to spread these things. They didn't have a specific goal. They were against the army, against the police, against the civilians, against those who'd greet the soldiers, against those who would greet an American soldier, against those who would greet an Iraqi soldier, against those who would build, against companies, against investors, against doctors. They were against everything. Against everything that brought life, against everything they felt threatened their existence. They didn't have a specific enemy, where they would only kill specific people, or a certain group of people. No. Everyone was targeted. All people were targeted. For example, Christians. I used to know a lot of students who left Mosul for the countryside and would travel in and out every day to go to university. If a Christian friend of mine would want to go to the market, she'd be forced to wear a hijab. She'd keep a hijab in her backpack.

The closest explosion to me was in our neighbourhood market. We found out that many children were killed in that explosion.

And this person told me, 'They're lucky to have died. They're martyrs, and they will now go to their God, and He will take them to paradise.' But before paradise, perhaps this child was a student who was going to an exam and had a dream. His mother dreamt that he would become a doctor, an engineer or a teacher, but he's now gone to paradise, and the mother and the child's dream were left behind. How can you give yourself the power to take someone's life away, to kill citizens in this way, so that you could hurt just one American, or hurt an apostate Iraqi soldier, and you make the excuse that the citizens are going to go to God and paradise. Those who have stayed behind, the mother, the daughter, the wife, the children – those who have stayed behind, will you knock on their door one day and ask them what help they need? 'Your son is in paradise, and he called me to ask me to come to you and help out.' No. They will remain in fear. They will be broken. They will remain shaken, scared, poor and hungry; nothing will compensate them at all. There will be orphans, mothers who have lost their sons, women who are widowed.

What's wrong is that we live in a society where men give themselves the power to either take or give life. Not men in general, but religious men in particular. They used to say things like, 'Blow yourself up, and you will go to paradise.' What about those who die along with you? OK, you want to go to paradise, but what about those who aren't dreaming about going to paradise? They have a life they were meant to live. How are you going to deal with their cases? This is something I didn't understand: I didn't understand how they give themselves the right to kill. People from all sides, I'm not talking about a specific group. Some killed because their religion told them that they should fight the occupier; some killed because they had to defend themselves; some people killed simple citizens, who didn't want to die and go to paradise. I didn't understand this. I was a child and didn't have any experience, but I used to ask, 'Why?' That was a question that was always with me. 'Why do you give yourself the right to ruin another's life?'

Mark Kukis *was a journalist for* Time *magazine, who reported from Iraq from 2006 to 2009.*

I came back from Afghanistan in 2002, and kind of kicked around in Washington hoping to go to Iraq. I couldn't find a big organisation to hire me in 2003. I asked around and finally got invited by *Time* in 2006. When I arrived in Baghdad, sectarian violence was at its height and the country appeared to be breaking up. At that time, I imagined I would cover the break-up of Iraq, much as we saw the break-up of Yugoslavia. There was talk of partition: the Kurdish part of the country had already been its own nation in all but name, there were pretty clear sectarian divides that would allow the country to cleave. You would have the Sunni west, you would have the Shia east, and Baghdad would be the centre. And there would be some sorting out of Baghdad that would be bloody and horrible, and eventually there would be some partition of Baghdad that reflected the general partition of the country. That's what I thought I was going to cover, and that the Americans would stand by ineffectually, and watch this bloody process unfold. That's what I thought I was getting into.

I got there in October 2006. At the time that I arrived, the proceedings for Saddam's trial were ongoing. Honestly, by the time I got there nobody cared – there were so many other major problems in Iraq that Saddam and his drama was very distant in people's minds. He ruled for so long, he was such a prominent figure, and his trial seemed to generate such little interest from Iraqis at that point. They just didn't care because there were other things going on. The main question on people's minds at that point was whether they should stay or go. People were concerned about 'Do I leave Iraq? Can I stay here? Is my family going to be killed? Am I going to be killed?' The situation was so chaotic that really Saddam Hussein was kind of a sideshow, it was not big on people's minds. It was striking how little Saddam and his fate meant to the country at that point in time. You have to keep in mind, more than four million people had left the country and the people that stayed were wondering whether they could stay and survive.

I do remember the day that he was executed. We got word that he was being transferred and that he was about to be executed, and that took everybody by surprise. We didn't get any advance warning about this. What we heard was the Americans had handed him over to Maliki and Maliki's forces. We turned on the TV and waited, and then we saw the footage of him being hanged, and the place erupted in gunfire. And by the place, I mean all of Baghdad. It seemed like everybody in Baghdad went to their roof and fired a gun. I've never heard so much gunfire in my life, and it went on and on and on and on – roaring gunfire from all the rooftops for miles in a city of seven million people. And then it went quiet and that was it.

I remain a little bit puzzled by the gesture. I think, as an outsider, the relevance of it didn't fully register, but what I took it to mean was that people fire guns at weddings – people fire guns, you know, to celebrate a lot of things – so it's meant as a sign of celebration. It's not necessarily a negative thing, but so much gunfire surrounded the death of Saddam Hussein. Obviously there is a celebratory element to it, but I think it also said something deeper about the violence that Saddam and his years brought and about the violence of the moment, that the only way to express happiness about the demise of such a violent person and such a violent regime that emitted such turmoil and violence in the city itself was this cathartic expression of gunfire. But it really seemed like a momentary interruption to a bigger crisis. It didn't really have this sort of closure sense to it. It didn't really seem like some sort of threshold or anything like that. Iraq was really still disintegrating. The city was in chaos and many people feared for their lives on a daily basis, and so frankly it seemed like a momentary distraction to a much bigger, more pressing matter which was the fate of the country.

A student at the time of the invasion, **Omar Mohammed** *was now a professor of history at the University of Mosul.*

Who is Nouri al-Maliki? He's a member of the Dawa party. The Dawa party is an extreme Shia party in the opposition against

Saddam before the 2003 invasion. When the Americans came, the Dawa party came with them, and they were based either in Britain or in Iran. They took power. They said the former government, pre-2003, was Sunni; now it's time for the Shia to take rule of Iraq. Maliki believed that this is a Shia right and that he should work to serve the Iman of the Shia. He didn't believe in the state. He said that we are not here because we believe in politics or we believe in democracy; this is not about democracy, this is about the right of the Shia people to rule Iraq. He is the one who established this idea that the Ba'ath was a Sunni party that ruled Iraq for 30 years. From this base, from this idea, Maliki applied his politics. He is directly involved with the Iranians, he is backed by them. The United States can work with its enemies, which is considered to be Iran, when it comes to the interests of the United States. They don't care about Iraq, they don't care about democracy, they care about who can serve them best, so they brought Maliki. Maliki himself, with his think tanks, with his lobbies in Europe, in the United States, you can see people writing profiles about him in *Le Monde* and the *New York Times*, in *The Times*, in other major newspapers, writing about Maliki that he is the hope to stabilise Iraq. But what kind of hope is this? They gave the Americans the idea that you cannot rely on Kurds or Sunnis, so rely on the Shia. They are the only people that can provide you with what you need in Iraq.

When Maliki came to power, Ayad Allawi was supposed to be the prime minister and then the Americans pushed for Maliki. Allawi was also Shia, but people didn't care because he was a secular candidate. Maliki led to the disaster now, the sectarianism he started. He started the collective punishment of Sunnis on behalf of Iran, with the support of America. Yeah. He is the one who later sent troops to Kirkuk, to Hawija, when they killed the protestors. He is the one who sent them to Mosul, and he is the one who ordered the military to withdraw from Mosul when ISIS came. And he delivered Mosul to ISIS on a golden plate. The man is sectarian. His agenda is a sectarian agenda. He is speaking against a group of people, the Sunni people. He's accusing them of terrorism. He sends Sunni politicians to prison. He sentenced one to death and one to life, and they had to flee. He arrested a Sunni PM. So the man is a disaster. Yet the Americans brought him because they believed that he can deliver what they couldn't. He can achieve what they couldn't – to stop terrorism.

When Maliki understood that he is backed by both Iran and the United States, he then started cleansing and clearing the Sunni cities, destroying them, doing the collective punishment of the Sunnis. He started arresting the Sunni leadership. He sentenced the Vice President to death, who was living outside Iraq, now retired. He arrested a Sunni MP with all his staff. He created another sectarian-based government.

John Nixon

Maliki was a compromise candidate after the United States lost confidence in the prime minister, Ibrahim al-Jafari. There was a period of government formation in which they were trying to find a new prime minister, and eventually Maliki was chosen. Maliki was a member of the Dawa, which is really one of the more successful, important of the Shia parties in Iraq. He had been an exile: he had been in Iran for about a year and then in Syria, and I think also in London, but he came back and became prime minister and initially hated the job. I remember this one *Wall Street Journal* interview he did where he said, 'I hate this job, I can't wait to leave it.'

Then he was instrumental in making sure that Saddam was executed right on the eve of Ramadan. Once that happened, he changed. He became much more assertive and much more mercurial, harder to predict. Over time, he became much more sectarian in pursuing strictly Shia interests, particularly the interests of the Dawa party. And in his second administration he began to go after Sunni politicians and Sunni leadership. He went after the leadership of the Iraqi Islamic party. It was a big deal. There were a series of things that Maliki did where we started to see rippling again in Ambar province, which is the Sunni heartland. They're very upset with the way the government is treating them and denying them funds. It's shortly after this that what becomes ISIS sort of infiltrates the elements that were al-Qaeda in Iraq that had gone underground. They begin to take form again and become powerful, and this is how you get the beginnings of ISIS. When ISIS explodes in 2014, it's largely through the wrong-headed policies of the Maliki government.

One of the ironic things about Maliki's time as prime minister is that it is a mirror image of Saddam. He used a lot of the same tactics that Saddam used to maintain his authority and his rule on the country. He began to build up his own security service within the office of the prime ministership. He began to reach out to various Shia tribes and tried to kind of buy them off and gain their support throughout the country. It was kind of amazing how it really began to resemble Saddam's government. The office of the prime ministership really became very, very powerful under him. Eventually he lost power and, to this day, he's still trying to take it back.

America had good relations with Maliki, but our criticisms of him grew and our wariness of him grew. When he was running for re-election, Ayad Allawi was really America's man. He was created by us in a sense, and he had won the election. But it became very clear through the statements emanating from the Iranian government that Iran would not tolerate Ayad Allawi as Prime Minster of Iraq. Ayad Allawi is a Shia, but he has very good relations with the Sunnis. He had a very longstanding relationship with the American government and with the CIA, and Iran simply said this was a red line. The Obama administration just decided that we should somehow overturn the election, and we should ensure that Maliki be given a second term. Through the process of government formation, it was agreed that Maliki would return as prime minister and Ayad Allawi would be given a security role in the new Maliki government. Allawi saw that there was no way to fight this and kind of accepted it, but he never was given the role that he thought he was going to get. He was completely marginalised. I don't know why the Obama administration acquiesced to this.

It was a terrible precedent – number one, because this was a relatively free and fair election, and number two this was a person who probably would've had good relations with the Sunni community, who might have been able to help diminish tensions rather than ratchet them up the way Maliki did. And three, it showed a level of influence that Iran had that was unhealthy.

The Shia groups don't really want to share power. And the other entity that doesn't want to see power-sharing between Sunni and Shia is Iran, to which many of these Shia groups have close ties in one form or another. Iran does not want to see a revitalised Sunni community. Iran does not want to see the Sunnis be given any ministry in the Shia government, especially any ministry that is going to have any role in terms of military force or security, because what Iran wants is a relatively weak Iraq – maybe an Iraq that can police most of its interior, but it doesn't want to have an Iraq with a strong military, and it doesn't want to have an Iraq that has security forces that might be able to threaten Iran. And it certainly doesn't want to foster anything that's going to bring the Sunnis back to taking the power away from the Shia government.

Mark Kukis

It was just chaotic. *Time* had its compound outside the Green Zone, and in that compound we shared resources with the *Washington Post*, NBC and a few other organisations. I arrived at a scene where our little compound was ringed by blast walls. It had already been hit twice by car bombs, so one side was collapsed in rubble. There was rarely electricity in the city, although we had electricity through generators. I had to venture out with six armed bodyguards in order to remain safe.

On any given morning in Baghdad I would wake up to the sound of multiple car bombs echoing through the city. Car bombs were made chiefly by Sunni militants, and they were deployed early in the morning to maximise casualties during rush hour. After a round of car bombs and sirens and smoke curling over the city, you would see and hear these explosions going on in the city.

There would be the response, there were sirens, sometimes there would be gunfire and then, through the day, all the time you would hear the presence of the American occupation overhead: fighter jets and helicopters and more sirens and more sporadic gunfire.

And then at night things would go eerily quiet because there was a curfew. In practice, the curfew fell at about 8 o'clock and so things would go really, really quiet except for the American war planes and helicopters. They would continue bombing various areas through the evening. What you didn't hear so often was the extraordinary amount of murders that went on in the middle of the night – the Sunni militants were active mostly during the morning hours with car bombs and then, at night, after the daytime chaos, the Shi'ite militants would take to the streets to fight the curfew and go into communities and kill people. That was a cycle of violence that just went on day after day after day after day.

The Sunnis were attacking Shi'ite civilians and Shi'ite militias and Iraqi government and American forces. Initially the Sunni insurgency arose as almost a kind of a nationalistic resistance movement to the American occupation, and in their early days they were mostly concerned with attacking American forces. But the Sunni insurgency in the period from 2003 to 2006 began to change, and those changes went along two lines. One, the insurgency began to attract a lot of criminal elements. In the old days a lot of the Sunni insurgents, particularly the organisers, were military men who considered themselves Iraqi nationalists and were generally professional people. But as the insurgency endured and had to live in the shadows and had to find its own forms of money, it became also a criminal enterprise, so there was a general sort of chaotic criminality to the Sunni insurgency. At the same time, it became infused with sectarian ideology, so the insurgent elements began to see their cause not so much as getting rid of the Americans, but basically Sunni versus all, right? So Sunni versus Shi'ite, Sunni versus the government, Sunni versus the Americans – anybody who wasn't radical Sunni became an enemy, and so they were lashing out in all directions.

The Shi'ites were also lashing out in many directions. There were two main militias: the Mahdi Army and the Badr Brigade. The Mahdi Army and the Badr Brigade fought each other at times, and the Mahdi Army and the Badr Brigade fought the American forces at times, they fought Sunni militants, and they fought the Iraqi government.

There was a fairly standard intimidation. If you were thought to be associated with the Americans, you would get anonymous threatening phone calls and then, if things developed, people would come to your house and kill you. It was that simple. Sometimes you didn't get the courtesy of the call. Sometimes gunmen would appear, sometimes in broad daylight, and drag you and your family away.

Amid all of this violence, you have all these different factions, the Sunnis, the Americans, the Iraqi government, the various Shia militias all fighting in cross-directional ways, and at the same time there's rampant criminality in Baghdad. People are being abducted left and right and held for ransom. It becomes an industry – people just get taken off the streets. They're held for days or weeks on end and a ransom is demanded, and they're handed back over. Or they're not. So there's just general anarchy in the city. I'd never seen anything quite like it.

What it's like to be there and living in that environment day to day is to sort of be aware of violence all around you, and any given moment be steps away from a scene of carnage and witness that. And then that just keeps unfolding again and again and again. There's multiple times where, you know, you'd be at the end of a day or find some calm moments where you could just have a cup of coffee or a cigarette, just take a moment and just try to relax, and then all of a sudden there'd be the riff of an explosion very near, or gunfire would send everybody scrambling to the ground. Oftentimes, if the gunfire was very close all of the bodyguards in our villa would arm themselves. And so any time you thought you might calm down there would be some sort of scare, some sort of scrape that would put you back on edge.

Waleed Nesyif

The thing that made me leave the country [in 2004] was the final death threat that I received and what happened after, which made me think, 'If I stay, this time the danger is not only upon me but it's upon the family.' I was a translator / fixer for the media. You are associated for better or worse with the West, and the West is associated with America and you almost automatically have a target painted on you as a sympathiser or a collaborator of an agent. So I was receiving death threats almost on a constant basis. I remember the first one: I was in the Palestine Hotel, and one of these bearded, Islamists walked into the foyer, and he asked if I was an Iraqi. I said yes, and he asked if I was a translator, and I said yes. And then he held me by the collar. He was trying to get into a fight with me, and we got into a physical altercation, and then he was removed. As he was removed, he kept screaming, 'We will get rid of you, one by one.' Then it kept happening and happening and happening.

One day, I go to visit my family and there was a letter waiting. A piece of paper saying, 'We will remove your stench from the holy soil of our country ... you are filth ... infidel ... we shall cleanse you ...' I didn't come back home, not until two weeks after. Another friend of mine received similar death threats almost at the same time. He also ignored it, but they kidnapped his brother. A few days after, they sent him his brother's head in a garbage bag.

This is when the kidnappings had started happening, and journalists were being assassinated. It's just one story after another. I had already lost two or three friends, who were executed point blank. One of them was Alan; he was executed alongside an American and co-worker called Marie. She was part of Civic America to Iraq. They did an official body count, which the American army was supposed to do and they didn't, so this lady came for this organisation that basically does a body count as well as casualties. They were stopped on the road, and they executed them both. Kidnapping was really big business. Terrorism was big business.

So the decision was very clear. They know where I live. I have three younger brothers, my dad was in the Iraqi army, which makes him a target already, and there is my mum. I couldn't have lived with myself if something happened to one of these people because of me. It was the hardest decision that I had to make in my life because I couldn't tell the family that I was leaving, because I didn't want to alert anyone to the fact. I had no idea who it was. In my profession, I had connections with the Mahdi Army, I had connections with the Fallujah resistance, and I was not on the American side – I was clearly on the Iraqi side, because I was a huge critic at that time of the American action and aggression against Iraq. Have they mistaken me for someone? Or is there something that I have done that they are after me? But those were the wrong questions. You don't ask those questions when you are under that threat. The question is when and where. So, yeah, three days after that I was in Jordan.

They gave me a visa for three days, and I was illegal in Jordan for a few months. Got accepted to a school in Canada, but they wouldn't give me a visa because I didn't have a passport. At the time, I only had this piece of paper, a travel document issued by the Coalition Provisional Authorities. And the Canadian Embassy just looked at it and was like, 'Sure, yeah …' 'But I've got full scholarship.' 'No, no, no. Get us a passport.' At that time, the first interim Iraqi government was established, and one of their first actions was to produce a temporary Iraqi passport. So I went back to Iraq to get a passport. I got my passport, left, went back to Jordan. I gave them the passport and they were like, 'We don't recognise this one. It's not an official passport.' I was like, 'Well, the government gave it, it was under occupation recognised by the international community.' I met with an immigration officer, and they were explaining that this is not a recognised document. I asked why? 'It's temporary.' And I was like, 'Yeah, I understand, but you watch the news, right?' And she was like, 'Do you have an old Iraqi passport?'

I almost lost my shit, but I kept my cool somehow. 'Do you mean to tell me if I bring you an Iraqi passport that has Saddam's photo right at the very front page, you will accept that and you do not accept this? Which was issued by the Coalition Provisional Authorities that liberated us from Saddam?' And she was like, 'Yeah.' One of the questions she was asking was 'Why do you want to leave Iraq?' And I told her, 'If you listen quietly right now, from Jordan, probably you can hear the bombs still. All the way from Baghdad.' Anyhow, that was a few months' process of back and forth with the Canadian consulate, back and forth, back and forth, back and forth. Towards the very end there was almost like a James Bond operation – I felt either I was making it or I'm being sent back home or in jail, I don't know. They called post-working hours, and they asked me to come to the Consulate. I go to the Consulate. The Consulate is closed. And there is a guard waiting for me: 'Are you Waleed? Come with me.' Lights are off, I'm walking into this empty, echoey, big marble building, and I'm like, 'What the fuck is going on here?' We go up to the third floor, and nobody is there. There is just me and the guard, that's it.

So we walked into this room, and all of the visa officers that have interviewed me were all sitting in one row, behind this bullet-proof glass. I'm like, 'OK, this is not good.' I said hello. Nobody answered. They weren't even looking at me in the eye. They kept quiet for a few minutes, whispering to each other. Finally, he opened up my passport, closed it, gave it to me and said, 'Here is your passport.' Then he gave me this piece of paper and he was like, 'And here is your temporary student permit.' I didn't understand: 'I'm sorry, what does that mean?' He was like, 'Due to your circumstances, we don't recognise this passport, so we cannot issue you a visa on the passport itself, but this piece of paper would be the equivalent and would allow you go to go Canada and study.' And I was like, 'I'm sorry, hold up, do you mean I can go to Canada now?' 'Yeah.'

Omar Mohammed
The insurgency against the Americans didn't come as a surprise. First, they have dismissed a trained army who have been fighting for

years; the first response for those people is to fight the Americans. Second, for those who considered Americans as occupiers, they wanted to fight back; they called themselves the resistance against the Americans. Third, the growth of extremism didn't come first. The way the Americans treated the people, the way the Americans treated this fight, created more extremist groups. And also the way the politics of Iraq were made: supporting or creating a sectarian system; accusing the other people of being pro-Saddam, which is the collective punishment of the Sunnis; opening the borders for Iran to enter Iraq; abandoning all the other economic resources of the country – with all of this, the Americans themselves allowed it to happen. It's the result of their mistakes.

The turning point for Iraq was in 2003 when the Americans came, and the jihadists came with them. From Jordan, from Palestine, from Saudi Arabia, from Syria ... Attacks happened before that, but to be something happening on a daily basis, to see videos of them, to see them in the city – by the beginning of 2004 this had become the official scene of the city. We started feeling wherever there is an American Humvee or Hummer, we are expecting a bomb. It became something normal.

Syria used to send devices to Iraq, and these devices were what the jihadist groups used to connect the bomb to the remote bomb. You can read on this device, in Arabic, 'To be used only against the Americans. A gift from the Syrian people, to the Iraqis.' The first person to take charge of one of the jihadist groups came from Afghanistan. Abu Talha, he was known as. He came from Afghanistan and stayed for a while in northern Iraq with Ansar al-Islam. So did Zarqawi, who came from Afghanistan through Iran to Iraq, and then he established al-Qaeda in Iraq. And it wasn't just Sunni jihadism, it was the Shia jihadism as well, against the Americans. Muqtada al-Sadr, for example, and his army called the Mahdi Army were fighting against the Americans. And you would also find Iranians fighting with them against the Americans.

There were many attacks per day. They also started killing the police. They did a horrible thing in 2004: the first beheading in the city. They beheaded a young Christian man, because they accused him of spying for the Americans, and they distributed the video. This man is still remembered in the city now; whenever you talk to people from Mosul now, they tell you, 'We lost the city when Remon was beheaded.' And the Americans were there. The city was kind of delivered to the jihadists. We started paying taxes to the jihadist groups. Sometimes you would pay to this group, then another group would come, take more money. So we didn't know what to do. If you don't pay, you can't tell them, 'I paid the other group.' They will say, 'It's not us.' So this is how death became normal in Mosul from that point. Death became normal in the city. I saw fingers of civilians, half of the head of a woman, part of the body, flesh, all around. My uncle found a leg on his rooftop after a bombing. When I say normal, I mean it became something that, if you don't see it every day, you feel something is missing. In 2008, we had two months where there no attacks – we really felt like something bad was happening. 'Why are there no attacks?' We see the violence every day. We see dead bodies, corpses, in the street almost every day. Executions every day. And the Americans are in Mosul.

In 2008, Baghdad sent troops: the Golden Division. At that time, they were called 'the dirty troops' because they were arresting everyone, putting people in the prison. They were known for raping the prisoners. These troops arrested almost 200,000 people: women, men, young, elderly. Those who were arrested at that time, I saw many of them in the street after 2014 – they were senior leaders and fighters with ISIS. Those monsters were created in prisons when the Americans were in control. So this is how daily life looked.

One of the major developments that the jihadists brought to Iraq is the car bomb. The borders of Iraq were open so to import things into Iraq was easier, so they imported many used cars from UAE, from Kuwait, from other countries, and mainly they brought a Swedish or German car. They imported these cars, and this car became the car of choice for the jihadist car bomb. And then you would see the development of the literature of jihadism: they called the car 'the horse of the jihad' and the driver is 'the knight' of this 'horse'. They valued this car because it was something that they could easily use and it was cheap – you could buy it easily with no licence. They would just leave it in the street, or next to a building where the Americans would cross by, or they would attack a building and civilians would be there. There were always civilian victims, civilian casualties. The jihadists, the Americans – both of them didn't care about the civilians.

The security forces were a disaster. Monsters. They were monsters. Just like the jihadists, but they were wearing uniform. Tribal men joined the security forces, Shia extremists. They would say, 'You are Sunnis, you are Ba'athists,' because they identified the Sunnis as Ba'athists. That's why sectarianism was growing more and more and more. The factory of creating sectarianism wasn't just in Baghdad; they were creating more sectarianism in Mosul. But because it was more under the control of the jihadists, the jihadists could produce a more destructive narrative that was feeding jihadism in other cities of Iraq and that was feeding the sectarian war. The security forces in Mosul were creating more monsters, they were crushing the people of Mosul, and that led to the creation of ISIS as we know it. Many people joined the jihadists – we are talking here about village, uneducated people, workers who lived on daily salaries. When they got arrested, insulted, on a daily basis, they couldn't go to the government and tell the government, 'Look at your security forces, what they are doing to us.' They couldn't, because the government was part of this. So they decide to take the other side, which was the jihadist, who could provide them with power, give them weapons and money.

I was lucky to have my father encouraging me to focus on my study. I finished my secondary school with good grades. I wanted to be a chemist, I wanted to go to the college of chemistry, then I changed my major from chemistry to history. I don't know why, but I couldn't find answers in the chemistry, to be honest. I had lots of questions about the Americans: why they were here, what they were doing here. Did they even know what they were doing? This kind of thinking led me to read more books, which led me to start focusing on my education, to go as fast as I could to college. From the first year, a professor who was teaching me at the university started to give me access to more books. He gave me access to what's called the *Encyclopaedia of Islam*, a big encyclopaedia written by hundreds of orientalists. So I started reading, and I was exposed to a different narrative of history and Islam, and this helped me to continue my life safely, away from the violence. I was running from that violence. Then I became more critical of the situation and also the roots of terrorism and how religion is providing this kind of terrorism. At home, when my uncle said something about history, I'd say, 'This is not true.' And then he started saying, 'You are corrupted because you went to college. You started thinking about parts of our history that we should respect, without questioning.' I told him, 'I can't. I have to question everything.' So this gave me more strength to continue away from the violence.

In my third year of college, I launched a small initiative with my friends at the university: it was meant to teach non-violence to children in one of the most affected neighbourhoods in the town, Rashidiyah in north-west Mosul. It was once mixed and had diversity, but then it became only for Sunni Turkmen. So, in collaboration with a sociologist, we found a place to teach the children. Some of them were children of jihadists or soldiers from the Iraqi army. Their fathers had been killed, or some of them had their fathers imprisoned, so with my friends we would teach them non-violence. I happened to know some people from Baghdad who were running an NGO to help orphans, and they asked me to take the responsibility of doing this in Mosul. I used to visit the orphan house from time to time, to deliver things to them – people would donate clothes etc., and we'd give them to families.

Tahany Saleh
In 2005, 2006, Mosul fell into the hands of al-Qaeda. They totally controlled all aspects of the city. Iraqi soldiers then lived in complete horror, because they could be targeted at any moment. Citizens were also targeted by explosives. There was killing, there

were lots of explosions. I remember one time, we got up in the morning, and in front of our house there was a dead body. I remember Dad really worried for us that time, he didn't even tell us that there was a dead body. It was daily. In all parts of Mosul. Not a day would pass without a car bomb. Not a day would pass without an explosive belt, or a suicide bomber. Not a day would pass without death in Mosul. Not at all.

The sound of a car bomb is different depending on the size of the explosion, and the distance it was from you, whether you were at home or walking the streets. Sometimes it would make you forget yourself. You'd stop thinking, moving, everything. We'd stop for some seconds, and then we'd start worrying about siblings that might have been outside the house, and that the explosion might have hurt them. You wouldn't only be overwhelmed by fear because of the sound of the explosion but because you might lose someone in just one moment, it's very easy. You might hear the sound of the explosion, and your entire life might change after that, or it will be destroyed, and lose its value. So, with the sound of an explosion, not only were we scared of dying but that this explosion has hurt people you love.

But there was an evolution. These explosives and these sounds evolved from one year to another. The first explosion we heard wasn't like the explosions we heard a year later with car bombs. They became stronger, more violent. Instead of destroying a space that four houses took up, it would destroy bigger areas, so even the sound of killing evolved in Mosul. ISIS or al-Qaeda used to develop their modes of killing, they were continuously developing them. They didn't use mortars until 2014. They would use explosive belts and car bombs, or armed confrontation, but they would put all their effort into car bombs. Sometimes they'd have dual explosions. A car bomb alongside an explosive belt, with a person in the car. They'd use techniques to increase the killing. For example, explosives that were carrying metal shrapnel so that, when it exploded, it would kill people, not buildings. I remember I once saw an explosion right in front of my eyes. The explosion led to a ball of fire that rose to the sky, it was fascinating. I stood in my place, and I was amazed. A ball of fire that was rising to the sky ... And after that the shrapnel started falling. It wasn't just from the explosion. It was from the shrapnel they used in the bombs, so that they would kill a maximum number of people. They'd use metal, glass, other things. So in that way they evolved. It's indescribable.

After the collapse, around 2005, 2006, the situation was more or less controlled, but the assassinations started. They'd assassinate shopkeepers, doctors, engineers, students, people from all groups. So not a day passed without killing, not a single day. Killing was easy, it was simple. There was nothing easier. That is why 2005 was full of terror for all citizens; it was total horror. It was very possible that you'd never return home if you went out – that was something completely normal. You could be assassinated. If you were opposed to any person, he could kill you, and blame terrorists. There were successive breakdowns for all life's values. Everything that existed broke down completely. Most of the streets were blocked, there were explosives everywhere. Explosive factories turned up, that was something normal. The army would know that they were explosive factories and they were building IEDs, car bombs, but they didn't have the courage to raid these factories. When they used to arrest terrorists, people who were proven to be planting bombs or carrying weapons, they would get paid and release the terrorist.

The prisons reinforced the terrorists and their power, because it allowed them to meet terrorists that were even fiercer than them. So hate was sown in them, a hate for life. They were thinking, 'We're imprisoned because we have a cause, we're imprisoned because we're defending our land, we're imprisoned because we refuse the occupation.' All this built up a hate in these prisoners, and that got them to be even more violent when they came out of prison. They became more brutal, they wouldn't differentiate between civilians or children. They were blinded by their cause. That is what led to ISIS becoming such a big power in 2014, a giant power.

The New Bogeyman

Mark Kukis

When I first went out with the military, the Bush administration had not yet announced the surge in their strategy. They hadn't declared their intention to try to save Iraq. So in the early days I would go out with US military forces, and the soldiers that I was with were confused and frustrated by the situation. They were confused because they didn't quite understand the violence – there's multiple factions killing each other for multiple reasons and multiple dimensions on any given day, and often many soldiers didn't quite understand the full complexity of it. They also felt really frustrated because there were no weapons of mass destruction, they felt lied to about the war. They had been there for far too long, many of them were just getting to the point where they felt betrayed. I don't know if betrayed is the right word, but they felt frustrated by the fact that they had been led to a conflict for reasons that turned out to be unjustified and that they remained in this country, fighting a war that they didn't understand. They weren't clear what they were doing there.

What should have been thought through more carefully by policymakers is the fact that American military presence for years before 9/11 had drawn terrorist attacks – the Khobar Towers bombing in Saudi Arabia, attacks against American forces in Lebanon. Unlike in Germany and Japan, where the presence of American forces tended to create stability, if you look at the long span of the presence of American forces in the Middle East what you find is that they tend to attract violence. To me it follows that if you put a whole bunch of troops right in the middle of the Middle East, you're going to get a whole bunch of violence, and that didn't seem to occur to anybody in the Bush administration.

When you get a whole bunch of violence directed at a whole bunch of American troops sitting in the middle of the Middle East, what you also get is primary and secondary effects. Basically, that violence creates a whole system of politics, right? The violence of the resistance creates more violence and induces radicalism. What you have is American troops being attacked by nationalistic insurgents. That action creates ripple effects: it draws militants together, those militants have varying ideas, those ideas morph, then violence begins to multiply. And so to me it seemed very clear that putting a bunch of troops there was a terrible idea. Putting a whole bunch of American troops in the heart of the Middle East seemed like a terrible idea because it would create a lot of violence and generate a lot of violence.

And to see the terrible effects on the Iraqi side ... Our bodyguards were all Iraqis. Everybody had stories about relatives being killed. It was hard to find anybody in Baghdad who didn't have someone in their family abducted or murdered. The violence was seen to be affecting everybody's life. Everybody seemed to have either personal experience or a family member who had been touched by the violence. To see all of that unfold day after day after day, it was just heartbreaking. Iraq to my mind in this period was collapsing into anarchic violence, and it didn't seem like a civil war, it just seemed like mass violence.

As the violence rose, it became very hard for me to do any kind of reporting outside. I faced a major dilemma that if I wanted to go into the streets of Baghdad and do reporting and interview somebody, I would put myself at risk – which is scary enough – but my drivers, my bodyguards, all of them are at risk too. Say we go to a market to interview a shopkeeper. I emerge as a conspicuous Westerner with six bodyguards, I get a couple of quotes, I get back in my car, we drive away safely. Somebody has now seen my bodyguards and my driver with me. They lived out in Baghdad without the comfort of an armed compound, and so they could be targeted by militants. This was not an abstract threat, this happened many times. An Iraqi manager had been killed. One of our drivers was abducted and held hostage for many days; he managed to escape and alerted us. It was very real that the people working around me would be targeted because they worked with me, and so I felt trapped in the Bureau. My own safety's one thing, but then I'm going to risk the lives of seven, eight people, you know, for some quotes – it didn't make sense. So I did a lot of embedded reporting. I was very, very aggressive about getting out with the troops.

The operations that I went on day to day, before the surge, really boiled down to two types of missions. One, they would go to places where they thought insurgents were either hiding or hiding weapons, and they would kick down doors and interrogate people and look for arms. The other form was to actually go out and try to support Iraqi security forces. They'd go to police stations where security forces were supposed to be and look for what they called national police and try to round them up and go on patrols with them – essentially, go around the streets and make a show of force in areas where there was violence. What they would often find is they'd go to police stations and they would be either abandoned or mostly abandoned, and the security forces were just not around. Security forces were in a state of collapse in the fall of 2006, so police stations would just go abandoned.

We would go up in a convoy of American Humvees, and you'd go inside and the building would be bullet-scarred and there'd be charred vehicles in the parking lot. A couple of times we went in and there would be dead bodies lying around. The few police that were around, one of the jobs that they did is they would go and collect the corpses that would turn up in the streets during the day from the sectarian murders. So you'd walk into these horrible police compounds, there'd be dead bodies, there'd be charred vehicles, there'd be clear signs of fighting, there'd be only a few people around sometimes, and the Americans were tasked with trying to put together a patrol with this. It just wasn't working very well.

The other remarkable thing is that, even amid all of this violence, the city still continued to have – I don't think you could call it normalcy, but people went about their normal daily routines as best they could. Schools were open, people shopped ... I mean, you can't hide in your house all day long, you know, you have to get out there to go get your groceries, you've got to pay your bills. So people were out and about in the streets doing the things that they do in any given city and the markets were full. On any given day, people were out trying to go to their jobs, make a living and get their kids in school, and they did as best they could amid high levels of violence.

Obviously, the Iraqi people did not enjoy the presence of the Americans. If you're living as an average Iraqi during the occupation, it's impossible not to feel what I would consider the suffocating presence of the American military occupation. All day long there are Black Hawk helicopters roaring over rooftops overhead, you hear fighter planes roaring overhead, anywhere you go in the city there's a traffic jam caused by an American military convoy. If you get close enough to see one of these American military convoys, you'll see a group of Humvees and maybe other heavy vehicles with their guns trained at street level, looking for threats. So you just couldn't go anywhere without seeing, hearing or feeling the American occupation anywhere in the city, and that alone is enough to make people unhappy. Add to that the fact that Americans are coming round kicking down doors in various neighbourhoods, and people get further unhappy. One of the things that people got really unhappy about was that the Americans would kick down doors and they'd be looking for weapons, and people would have like old hunting rifles and stuff like that and the Americans would take them. So you've got Americans taking property that clearly wasn't, you know, a militant activity. But the Americans had their orders and so they took them and people got really frustrated at that.

The strong impression that I had in the period before the surge was that the Americans were not being very effective at finding insurgents or finding weapons or stopping the violence. Every time I was out with them it seemed like they were kicking down doors and nothing was there, right? It seemed like they were responding to violence and they had just missed what had happened. The Americans would be on a base somewhere, and they would get a call from one of their informants or intelligence networks, and they would say there's a shooting or a car bombing or something going on. The Americans would respond, and they would not be able to find anybody or anything really related to an incident that had just happened. It always seemed like they were coming too late to the scene of violence to make a difference, and where they were trying to intervene beforehand they wouldn't find anything, so the whole enterprise just seemed hugely ineffective to me. Levels of violence were rising without any clear resolution. It didn't seem like the American forces were capable of containing the increasing levels of violence and the seeming disintegration of the country.

I mean there is an intense anger, confusion and frustration among Iraqis. It's hard to generalise because Iraq is a big place, the people are sophisticated, they have a lot of thoughts about what happened to them. But in 2006 I think there was a fair amount of surprise among Iraqis that things had gotten that bad. Most intelligent observers in Iraq wouldn't say that toppling the Saddam regime was going to lead to a lot of good outcomes, but the fact that the country, particularly Baghdad, was so far gone in terms of the violence subsuming the society, I think there was a genuine sense of surprise that violence had risen to the levels it had in 2006.

It didn't have to come to this. It's difficult to overstate the significance of disbanding the Iraqi army – that loomed in people's minds more than the invasion itself as the reason why things had become so bad, because the Iraqi army as an institution in society was really the glue that held a lot of it together. One of the things that's important for people to remember about Iraq is that probably the height of unity for the Iraqi nation was its war with Iran and the relationships that were formed in that experience. The nationalistic relationship that was formed in that experience really did endure through Iraqi society, through not just one generation but multiple generations, and the generation that fought that war was still around. In living memory, people in Iraq could associate a real strong sense of national unity with the army, and then the army was gone. That, I think, more than anything left Iraqis really feeling like the Americans had caused a whole lot of problems and did not have solutions to offer.

The American military was primarily concerned with establishing a government and a security force that could maintain some sense of stability in the country, so if there was any good guys to be had it was in the government. That said, I would never suggest for a minute that any of the military commanders looked at the Iraqi government and thought, 'This is a good crowd.' There was plenty of scepticism and alarm and frustration with the Iraqi government that the American forces were tasked with supporting.

John Nixon

I returned to working fulltime in Iraq in late 2005, and one of the first things I began to work on was Muqtada al-Sadr. Muqtada al-Sadr was a cleric in Iraq who was the son of Mohammad Sadeq al-Sadr, one of the most influential Shia theologians inside Iraq in the late twentieth century. [Mohammad Sadeq al-Sadr] had developed a large and devout following, but was assassinated by the Saddam Hussein regime in 1999. Subsequently, after the fall of Saddam, Muqtada emerged and basically replaced his father and became the focal point of the Sadrist movement. Muqtada had a significant following and was now a major force in Iraqi politics. One of the things that I found when I was studying him and writing about him, and interacting with my fellow colleagues in the intelligence community, was this hostility that people had about Sadr – because Sadr was an opponent of the occupation and his forces were killing American troops. He was the new bogeyman. The old bogeyman was Saddam Hussein. He's gone now, and we need to have a focal point, a focus of our government to find that person that we revile and becomes the poster child for everything we're trying to defeat. That was Muqtada, and he fit the bill perfectly. He was a cleric, he wore a turban, he was kind of pudgy ... It was almost like he was out of Central Casting for a Hollywood villain.

Waleed Nesyif

Muqtada is an incendiary speaker, very charged and good in mobilising the people. I think his colloquialism was intentional, you know? To relate to everyone. We are dealing with a predominantly blue-collar individual, working class. They were educated, but the education was not, you know, of higher degree, so you can't really use flowery rosy language with them to try and describe something simple. He was to the point, and he spoke their language and was able to mobilise them through that – not unlike Trump. So his popularity started rising and then the Mahdi started becoming, like, a known player.

In the beginning, the Mahdi Army was more a formation that was meant to kind of instil order inside Sadr City first and help out where they could. Or at least that's what they were claiming, you know? Having interviewed so many of them, the individuals who were part of the army actually believed this is what they were doing. It is not that they were fighting only for an ideology. There was some resemblance of unity and patriotism. This was for Iraq, for Iraqis. But, of course, they had their own angle, as led by their leader. Them going against the Americans started coming through. Some of their clerks started being arrested by the Americans. There was a couple of guys from the Mahdi Army that were arrested. They organised a massive demonstration, and it was a peaceful demonstration – I was there – where they went outside of the Green Zone and there was hundreds of thousands of people and they were just praying. Just praying. But I can see the look in the American soldiers' eyes: they were terrified. Terrified because they did not think that somebody can mobilise Iraqis after all of this disorder has ensued. But this guy was able to.

Something interesting happened in that demonstration as well: the Iraqi police at that time joined in with the people. They marched together. When that happened, I think the Americans started going, like, 'OK, their loyalty is not to the institution that they belong to, rather to their creed.' Right? They are Shia and the leader of their creed was Muqtada al-Sadr, and I think that's when they started taking him ever so seriously. Before, I think he was kind of dismissed. He put himself on the map in the best way possible. It was a civil and a passive demonstration, but he just showed the sheer numbers that he is able to mobilise. That was very, very powerful. At the same time, it helped getting some, let's say, brownie points from other Iraqis. This guy is anti-Iran and anti-America, which automatically put him as the best of the worst.

Soon after, attacks on Sadr City started happening. Of course, the claim was 'terrorist activities' and all of that. But they weren't an insurgency. That, I think, is a very important distinction to make here. They couldn't say that they were an insurgency because they were public, and they have demonstrated already that they are willing to go the passive way. And they have also demonstrated that they have got the numbers and that they have no problem being transparent. They had a media division, they had a public relations division, they had a financial sector. You know, we are talking like an actual organisation. So that was the genesis of the Mahdi Army.

John Nixon
I worked very hard on trying to figure out who this guy was. And while I disliked Muqtada and thought he was our enemy, I felt like I had learned something from my experience with Saddam, and I could see that Muqtada was operating under certain constraints and also certain pressures that would force him to sometimes do things that we didn't like. And sometimes he did those things willingly. But what was important was that Muqtada was the bane of the Bush administration's existence. For five years, he was a thorn

in their side. Trying to get Iraq to quiet down and have a functioning government and create a new Iraqi civil society was very difficult with Muqtada's armies fighting (the Jaysh al-Mahdi), his militia and then the special groups who were nominally under him with their alliances in Iran. This made life very, very difficult for the Bush administration.

Finally, in early 2007 – right before the surge begins where the US brings in several thousand more forces to try and get control in Iraq – Muqtada flees to Iran. He stays there for several years. But by 2008 I had written a paper for President Bush, basically telling him Muqtada al-Sadr is having a very difficult time in Iran and he is unsure of what his next moves are. He is uncertain as to the movement and some of the challenges that he is now facing in trying to keep control of his movement while he is in Iran. This paper was the first bit of good news the Bush administration had really gotten about Sadr. So when I went to brief it to the President, it was met rapturously.

President Bush, when he was in office, would often be accused of being an idiot and a simpleton and, from my interactions with him, I would not agree with that. He was a clever person. He was smart to a certain degree. He could be very knowledgeable about Iraq in terms of the information that was coming into the intelligence community, he read that stuff and he remembered it. Where I think his shortcoming was is that he couldn't make sense of it. When there were conflicting viewpoints, he got confused. He didn't know which one to believe and he would, at that point, go back to these kneejerk reflexive views of his, which were safe. Early on, before the war, the CIA had sent down an expert in Islam to talk to the President about Iraq and about Islam in the Middle East. And he was explaining the history of the Prophet Mohammed, and the schism between Sunni and Shia. Reportedly, the President's response was, 'I don't get it, I thought you said they were all Muslim?' I think he didn't have a good understanding of the outside world when he became president. I'm not so sure he had a real sophisticated understanding of the outside world when he left office. He believed what he wanted to believe and was comfortable with that. He kept criticising our analysis on the Jaysh al-Mahdi and Sadr and he said, 'Are they good people or bad people?' I said, 'Mr President, the Middle East is a place where you can't put things in nice, neat convenient boxes. Because sometimes things are good but they're also bad.' Oh my god, it was ... the response was being coldly stared at; it was sort of like when I angered Saddam. In hindsight, I wish I had chosen my words a little bit better but, on the other hand, I'm glad I said what I did.

The President asked me, 'So what's up with Sadr?' and I told him the truth. I said, 'Well, Muqtada al-Sadr has taken a beating in Basra.' The Maliki government had just done the Charge of the Knights campaign into Basra. I said, 'It has hurt the special groups but, in a sense, what Maliki has done has probably removed a problem for Sadr. And I've come to the conclusion that, despite the fact that Sadr is still in Iran and still doesn't like being there, he is eventually going to come back someday to Iraq. He will probably play an important role in the political system in Iraq for years to come. He's a young man with a following that is in the millions and they will do almost anything for him.' Once I'd said that, Bush got this very confused look on his face. And then he started asking questions: 'What about the Jaysh al-Mahdi? I mean, those guys are thugs.' I said, 'Yeah, they are thugs and they do things that are counterproductive at times and they kill people. But Sadr is the living example of his father, he's all that these people have from his father, and religion matters to these people. Their religion matters a great deal.' I couldn't believe I had to tell George Bush, the ultra-Christian, you know, that religion matters.

Mark Kukis

Maliki represented basically the political arm of Shia militias who were consolidated in control of Baghdad and southern Iraq. Maliki was allowing Shia killings to happen. Maliki and the people around him were OK with this, they were encouraging of this. That was the widespread perception in Iraqi society, to my experience, and certainly that was my perception. What evidence do I base that on? Well, the fact that the security forces are involved in the sectarian killings, and national police are allowing Shia militias to run around at night; and there's a whole series of towns just on the edge of Baghdad towns that are ostensibly under the control of the national police and these places became notorious. Areas where government forces were ostensibly in control were the scenes of massacres led by Shi'ite militants, so either the security forces are complicit or they're actively involved.

The Sunni militant community by and large saw Maliki as just a stooge of the Americans and the embodiment of a Shi'ite power grab. The general attitude from many Shi'ites was that Maliki was a good thing and that the Maliki administration would effectively help consolidate power and resources for the Shi'ite communities. I think the question that people had in mind was 'Can he help consolidate Shia power in Iraq and ultimately get rid of the Americans?' because one of the big things that was on people's minds was how long these Americans were going to stay. The Shi'ites didn't want them around, and Maliki was very explicit that he didn't want them around. No one really wanted the American presence to go on much longer than it had to.

There were foreign fighters, but they were in the low thousands. The number of Iraqis who were fighting, participating in the violence on the side of the Sunni militants and the Shi'ite militias, was in the multiple thousands. My understanding, based on what the military told me, was that the presence of foreign fighters did not have a significant influence, at least on the scale of the violence. Maybe in terms of the nature of the ideology that surrounded some of the Sunni violence, but in terms of, like, material impact on the violence the foreign fighters did not have a significant effect. The presence of foreign fighters was minimal; the violence that was being perpetrated in Iraq was mainly being done by Iraqis.

What became clear to me was that a lot of Iraq's problems were being blamed on the presence of foreign fighters, yet nobody seemed to have seen any foreign fighters lately. And so I began to suspect that the foreign fighters were something of a scapegoat, that if you actually examined the violence what you find is that it's Iraqis victimising other Iraqis and that in the aftermath of this violence they point fingers at these elusive, ghost-like foreign fighters. And that serves two things: one, it allows people to escape culpability, and two, it allows blame to be shifted so that there is some sort of healing process after this violence, that you don't have to reckon with on an interpersonal level. I became convinced that way too much was being blamed on the presence of foreign fighters generally in Iraq, so I started to ask whoever I could, 'How many are there, have you seen any lately, can you show me proof?' And what I found was scant evidence of foreign fighters. I got some statistics that suggested that they were in the hundreds in Anbar Province, but the people fighting in Anbar Province numbered in the thousands.

The military officials that I talked to did not seem to have that political idea in their mind, the idea that 'Hey, if we pin this on the foreign fighters it's better for perceptions back home.' They seemed genuinely interested – like me – in how many foreign fighters are there, how many Iraqi fighters are there, so they seemed pretty clear-headed about it generally. I should also stress that it wasn't just al-Qaeda and foreign fighters on the Sunni side that were of particular concern in terms of infiltrators into Iraq. One of the major assertions that the Bush administration was making at this time was that Iran was sending fighters into Iraq. We heard this explicitly from many areas of the Bush administration. I even went out on an embed along the Iranian border looking for these infiltrators. And what I heard again and again from American military officials is 'We have some evidence, but nothing conclusive.' They were fairly candid about it in terms of if the violence is an overall social phenomenon, the presence of foreign infiltration from Iran and elsewhere in the Middle East on the Sunni side is marginal to the overall picture. Virtually, to a one, every military official that I talked to had that attitude. In my mind, al-Qaeda in Iraq became a label for fighters in Iraq who subscribed to a type of violence that had this highly sectarian quality to it.

That was Sunni-based. One of the things that's important to understand is that al-Qaeda in Iraq was Iraqi fighters. Not to say that there weren't other people involved, say from countries like Jordan or Saudi Arabia, but in the end the killing and the dying came from Iraqi nationals. When sectarian violence was at its height, somewhere in the neighbourhood of 250 to 300,000 people died and four-point-something million people fled Iraq. There's all these bodies, but there's no real evidence that foreign fighters were there. They became an excuse for a lot of the violence that Iraqis themselves were perpetuating. When I interviewed multiple sheiks who took part in the Awakening, I never heard any of them mention about foreign fighters; they were mostly concerned with Iraqis. It's true that there were foreign fighters who infiltrated Anbar Province and helped form al-Qaeda in Iraq, but it should not be overstated. Their presence had a marginal effect on the overall violence in the conflict. They amplified some of the ideology but in terms of material resources – you know, guns, money, people being involved in killings – that was Iraqis confronting other Iraqis. The foreign fighters come in for a lot of blame for a lot of things, and it's not to suggest that they weren't there, but to put the focus on them and ignore the fact that this was essentially an Iraqi internal conflict is to misunderstand it.

Tahany Saleh

Really, the Americans never tried to help the people in any way at all. For example, when there was an unsafe area in Mosul, they'd leave it unsafe; they'd block it off. They wouldn't address the politics. They wouldn't study the factors that made certain areas unsafe, and think about how to solve the problems. No, on the contrary, they used to reinforce the fear. When they used to arrest one of those terrorists, they'd keep him in jail. And when that terrorist was released, he'd be more barbaric, more monstrous, where he'd built a hatred towards all of humanity. If it was religion-driven, initially – that he had to fight an occupier on his land, and he had a cause that was linked to religion – when they were released from American prisons they came out with a full-on hatred towards humanity.

I don't think that the Americans had well thought-out politics that would help treat the problems in Iraq. On the contrary, they increased the chaos. On what basis would they completely destroy the infrastructure, like when they dissolved the Iraqi army? Iraqi soldiers weren't Saddam Hussein soldiers, they were Iraqi soldiers. When they fired them from their jobs, they didn't compensate them. For many long years, there were plenty of families with no income. Many families that were in need of an income didn't get it, because the father was in the previous Iraqi army. So there were no real solutions being brought forward. I don't know if American policies had other issues, or outlooks or other solutions – I didn't feel that as a citizen. When it comes to the reality on the ground, Americans did not help Iraqi citizens at all. They didn't invest, they didn't calm the security situation so that investors could come in. On the contrary, there was constant tension, fear, chaos. Chaos from weapons, from corruption. If you want the truth, they fuelled the terror in Iraq, and the civil war too.

They could have ended it in very simple ways. They could have simply got leaders that Iraqis respect from every region. A person that local people trust, and get them to take responsibility over a certain area. What do you need? What does your area need? Young people from the area could protect it, and that didn't happen. That is what led to all this fighting. Being a supreme authority, as a 'great country', they could help the people in one way or another. It was unnecessary for them to just stand by and watch as people were getting killed according to their sect. At that time, I used to only see the Americans standing and watching, while the people burned. As civilians, we used to always ask ourselves why

American policy didn't limit the extremism that was spreading, the sectarianism too. Why were they just standing and watching?

Waleed Nesyif

While I was in Canada – trying to assimilate and live, and not go past where I have come from, but like make do with where I am right now – civil war in Iraq started intensifying and taking a different shape. Before it was covert, now it became overt. It was public. People were being murdered by literally the hundreds on a daily basis. Now I'm the oldest of three brothers, so I have two younger brothers that I treated like my own children because I helped raise them, and my father and my mother plus obviously friends and cousins and all of that and everybody was at home. I come from a mixed family. I got the news of my uncle getting kidnapped. You get the news, what do you do? I've never felt this helpless in my life as I was during those dark fucking years, particularly from 2005 to 2009. Because you call and, when my mum picks up the phone and finally we connect to speak for the seven or ten minutes, all she wants to do is basically comfort me and tell me, 'Everything is all right, don't worry, continue, keep going.' And all I was telling her was, 'Everything is all right, don't worry, continue, keep going.' Lying to each other willingly so we can give each other the comfort we both needed. While deep inside, we knew shit had hit the fan. I started checking with friends so I can tell what is the truth of what my family is telling me versus what actually had happened. My friends were telling me 'So-and-so got murdered, so-and-so got killed, so-and-so got killed, so-and-so got kidnapped ...' I'm going through the record in my head of all of my high school friends and the people that I knew, and they are just dwindling down. You know, fizzling out.

I got the news about my uncle. My mum is telling me, 'Don't worry, your uncle got kidnapped,' a quandary of a statement that should not really be put together. I'm like, 'Come again?' She is like, 'We think these guys wanted someone else, but your uncle happened to be there so they kidnapped him. They want 70,000 dollars, so we are trying to gather the money from everyone. Hopefully we can send the money and then they will let him go.' The style of that time was they would kidnap you, ask for ransom; you pay the ransom, they still send you a dead body if you are lucky. Thankfully, this uncle, they released him. I think we negotiated a price for him from 70,000 to 15,000 or something like that. Money we didn't have, everybody was poor at that time.

And then they kidnapped his son. He was on his way to university, and he was taking public transport. It was him and two other students. They hopped on, the driver started driving, and they were asking the ticket man, 'Do you not want the fee?' and he was like, 'In a bit.' They started noticing that they were driving somewhere different, and finally the ticket man turned around with a gun. They asked them for IDs. My cousin happened to be Sunni, another guy was Sunni, and one of them was Shia. The Shia guy was standing between my cousin and his friend. The ticket man just shot this gun in his head, right between them, and he was like, 'Oh, you are Sunnis you are good.'

If you can imagine, you are off to boarding school, and your family is in literally the most dangerous place on Earth. Every goddamn phone call you receive could be it. That is why I hate fucking phones. I hate phones, I hate the phone ringing, I never have my phone on the ring, it's always on silence and vibration, because I can't listen to that goddamn sound because of the number of phone calls that I received: 'This one is dead, this one is dead, this one is dead, this one is dead ...' It just becomes relentless, month after month after month. You mourn the first one, the second one, the third one, the tenth one, the fifteenth one ... and then what?

The Awakening and the Surge

John Nixon
I worked on the hunt for Zarqawi. He was found and killed in early June, and I was in Baghdad right after he was killed. Bush came out to the Green Zone, that day. He basically came out and said, 'This is great, we've turned a corner with this. You people are making a difference.' I remember thinking, 'We've gotten *one guy*. I don't know how many hundreds of millions of dollars we've spent trying to get this guy for the last two years.' I would see the GIs coming out, waiting to get on the helicopters and do their night raids, and I remember thinking, 'Who is going to go broke here first – Zarqawi or us? This is requiring so much effort.' One of the things that I saw in the war in Iraq was this belief, and you see it in the military and you see it in the White House and you see it even in the CIA as well, we work ourselves up into this lather and we start believing it: 'If we just get *this* guy ... We gotta get him ... If we get him, everything's going to be great, everything will work out ...'

Then we got him, and the day after, it was back to work, and we've now got to get the next target and they're going to find somebody else, and al-Qaeda and Iraq lived on. Now, to be fair, it was at that time, shortly thereafter, the surge started, which was a good move, and also the Awakening had begun. The Sunni tribes had basically turned against al-Qaeda in Iraq for a variety of reasons. These are the things that calmed down Iraq, and these are the things that are real success stories and changed the security environment dramatically.

The Awakening was a realisation amongst the Sunni tribal community that their interests were being harmed, not helped, by al-Qaeda in Iraq. Suddenly the Awakening turned to the Americans and said, 'Maybe we have a common enemy in al-Qaeda in Iraq, and maybe we can work together.' Basically, they switched sides and began to help the American and coalition forces attack and dismantle al-Qaeda in Iraq. It worked, and it couldn't have been done without Iraqi help. Once the tribes saw this happening, once they had had enough of al-Qaeda on their territory, killing their people, taking their women, stealing their money, they realised the Americans can be an ally at this point. Al-Qaeda in Iraq was worse than the Coalition presence, and if the relationship had been carried forward – if somehow the United States had been able to force the government in Baghdad to keep this relationship going – I don't think you'd have the rise of ISIS. I was in Baghdad in 2009, and I could not get over how quiet it was. It was really the first and only time that I was there where, if I heard an explosion, it was very far away and very infrequent – maybe once or twice or three times in the course of a week. I was amazed. I was stunned.

Omar Mohammed
The Awakening movement, which was supported directly by Bush, was mainly in Anbar. It wasn't in Mosul, but we were aware of it. They call them *Sahwah* – tribal fighters. They were armed by the US army, they were given weapons and money. They asked them to kill the jihadists. That was it. Nothing else. After the many things they had tried, the American army in Anbar thought that the only way to stop the violence, to stop the jihadists from growing, was to have the people themselves, the tribes, take down their own people. They were giving money and weapons to the tribes, something they didn't expect. Bush himself visited Anbar and met with the person who created the Sahwah.

This is the impact of the Awakening: a civil war that still has its effects in Anbar. Instead of supporting civil society, they used the tribes just the way Saddam used them. And this is also how ISIS used the tribes after 2014. And now the tribes are being used by the militias. It's the same circle of violence.

Mark Kukis
The Awakening was a movement that arose in Anbar Province chiefly around the town of Ramadi, and it was a group of Tamil sheiks who up until 2006 had either actively supported the insurgency, passively supported the insurgency or been neutral. The way multiple sheiks characterised it was that, in the early days of the American occupation, many of the tribal leaders in Anbar Province sympathised with the insurgents on a nationalistic level. They wanted the American occupation to end, they were supportive of violence aimed at the American occupation, and they further believed that the insurgents didn't have an interpretation of Islam or politics that was incompatible with the way that they lived their lives. That began to change.

An insurgency that goes on as long as al-Qaeda needs money, like any other organisation. So where do they go when they need funds? Well, they start taking from people. Some tribal leaders were willing to cooperate with them and give to them, but at times when in need of resources, cars, land, hideouts and the like, al-Qaeda would go and take it from people. And eventually they took from the wrong people. They took from too many sheiks and too many communities, and they angered too many tribal leaders. Eventually some people decided that they didn't have to be victims of insurgence, they didn't have to take it passively, and they weren't willing to take it any more, and they began to fight back.

It's fair to say that no community has a wide acceptance of this kind of imposition of violence and strict interpretations of Islamic Law – I hesitate to call it Islamic Law because that's not what it really is. It's not. It's a form of terror. When you think about how al-Qaeda came into communities, they did not impose a strict interpretation of Islamic Law; they terrorised these communities. They made people fear them because they were men of violence, and they were there to take what they needed for their cause. The idea that you could impose these kind of draconian restrictions on a society was more about power than it was religion, and more about terror than it was religion.

'THOSE WHO ARE WET AREN'T SCARED OF THE RAIN'

We heard about the Awakening – Sheik Sattar and his cooperation with the American troops – because local journalists had reported on it. The Americans were keen to talk about it; they were seeing this as an emerging success story. So it was a development in the war that seemed significant. If, in fact, there was to be an organised resistance among tribal sheiks in Anbar aligned with the Americans, then it seemed that the Americans were hoping it would become a reasonable thing. Their strategy here – we take the tribal sheiks, we galvanise them, we eliminate al-Qaeda as part of our broader counterinsurgency strategy – that seemed like a plausible plan.

Going into Ramadi, I heard a lot about Sattar and his brother, Ahmed. The Americans clearly saw Sattar as a leadership figure, as someone who could be a public face of the Awakening. His brother Ahmed was more or less the thinker and the strategist behind them. Sattar was the public persona of the Awakening but, in order for the Awakening to work and be organised and be effective as a mobilised force, you really needed both brothers working together. The Americans were very explicit about this. But they were also very aware that Sattar had this sort of star quality to him: he looked like a swaggering Arab chieftain, right out of Central Casting. So we went to take a look.

Sattar had his compound very near the American military base, and I was primarily embedded with American military. I would go out on American patrols, and any number of patrols would go out to Sattar's compound and check in with him. At one point I was over in Sattar's compound, and the American commander who gave me a ride over there said, 'Hey, we're going to take care of some other stuff. Are you OK to stay here with Sattar?' And my answer to that was, 'Absolutely not, this is not a safe situation.' I didn't know Sattar or his people. You go into Sattar's compound and it's full of gunmen and everybody seems polite, but it's not clear who is who, at least to me as a person new to this. There was a nice moment with Sattar and his brother: they could see my alarm and they very quickly said, 'You don't have to worry here. We're secure here, it's fine, there's no threats to you. You can just stay here with us.' So I spent a long evening with Sattar and his brother, totally in their care, and what I took away from that was that, at least in that moment, in that particular spot, the Awakening was able to pull some ground. They were making some gains. I was struck by how clear-headed they were about the Americans, about the fault that the Americans had for creating the problems, about the limits of the American ability to support them, and I think that they were clear-headed about what needed to be done. They were fighting a very dirty conflict, and they were not shy about acknowledging that.

Sattar lived up to all the hype. He played the part perfectly. A very determined man, very gracious, warm ... at the same time, he had a steely quality to him. He was a remarkable individual. I don't want to in any way lionise Sattar and his brother – I mean, these were men who fought for practical reasons, and we should also be aware that there were many atrocities committed in Anbar at this time. The Awakening was not above targeting civilians, they were not above executional killings, they didn't take prisoners, they were not bound by the laws of combat that the American forces were bound by. As one sheik put it to me: 'The reason why we defeated al-Qaeda was because we fought like al-Qaeda. We wore masks, we terrorised them. If they killed one of our fighters, we killed one of their fighters.' They were engaged in a murder campaign, and to my mind there was no way that they could systematically evaluate who they were killing. I find it difficult to imagine that every person that they killed in the name of defeating al-Qaeda was really an al-Qaeda operative. I'm sure that many atrocities were committed by the Awakening and its forces, and so I don't mean to in any way regard Sattar and the others associated with him as being heroes in the story.

He was very media savvy. He knew what the image meant. He was image conscious. He makes an interesting character, but the thing that really mattered was his ability to deliver results. He delivered hundreds of recruits for security forces to man police stations in Ramadi, to go on patrols, and no one had ever done that, so his ability to mobilise people was what really mattered. Not the image but his ability to say, 'All right, you need 300 men for this area; we'll deliver them.' And then they did. And that's what made the difference. According to Ahmed, they rounded up 4,000 police volunteers. You have to keep in mind that the security forces in Ramadi had totally collapsed: whatever sort of policing there was, was gone. People were too afraid to put on a uniform and go down any kind of police station, so there were no security forces. The Americans would fight the insurgents, and they would get no help, and then the insurgents would melt into the civilian population. So Sattar and his brother were able to manifest 4,000 fighters who the Americans could trust to be reliable, competent and not harbouring insurgents. That's a gain. That's a huge development.

I don't think even the most Pollyannaish of American officials had a notion that violence would disappear from Iraqi society if the Awakening was successful. What they did see was an ability to essentially drive the insurgency to the margins of the political trajectory of Iraq, and make the place safer for civilians. Maybe bring some of those four million people back who fled the country. What they saw was a bunch of tribes linking together, making success against insurgency — that's what we want. Iraq is full of tribes, here's a great solution for this. For a while, it allowed the Awakening fighters and the American forces to push Sunni insurgents to the margins of places like Ramadi and Fallujah and elements of Baghdad. The success the Awakening had was a significant achievement for the Americans and their hopes of pulling the country from the abyss. It was one of the first signs of hope that they had since the place had gone into this seemingly endless downwards spiral. Finally in Anbar, with Sattar and the Awakening, they had signs that some form of victory could be had.

This was all before the surge. The surge was basically the Bush administration re-invading Iraq. I think it was somewhere in the neighbourhood of 120,000 troops in Iraq before the surge, and then they added an additional 30,000 troops, so it brought up the total number to roughly 150,000 American troops in Iraq. The 30,000 troops that came were largely dedicated to combat activity, basically fighting the insurgency; before the surge, US forces that were in Iraq had a mix of duties – supporting Iraqi forces, trying to keep general order and the like. The 30,000 troops that arrived with the surge were largely intended to directly confront militants, to be more active in seeking them out and finding their hideouts and eliminating them. In addition to this influx of troops, there was a reconfiguration of the troops, so the forces that had been up in Mosul and out in Anbar and the like, many of them were drawn back into Baghdad. It was widely believed that the way to stabilise the country was to stabilise the Baghdad area first, and then much of the insurgent activity that was manifesting itself in other parts of the country could be quelled. They had to win the battle of Baghdad in order to sort of defeat the insurgency generally. The way I took it was that it was a last-ditch effort to save the country while they still had control of the White House. If they wanted to actually make a sincere effort to resolve the problems that had materialised following the invasion, this was their way to do that. They saw a military problem and they crafted a military solution for it.

Omar Mohammed
The Golden Division was small units of Iraqi soldiers, well trained by the Americans. Some of them were trained in the United States and sent back to lead the division. It was a Shia unit, trained to fight against terrorism. They were sent to Mosul prior to 2008 and the goal was to clean the city from terrorism. But when they came, they cleaned the city by arresting everyone. This was their way of finding terrorists: arrest ten, one of them could be a terrorist. This is how they dealt with the city. The Sunnis were seen as terrorists. They explained this: 'Al-Qaeda is Sunni, the other jihadists are Sunni, so you are also terrorists.' This is how they saw us.

The people felt oppressed. The people felt targeted, directly, by the government. Not because the government here is fighting against terrorism, but because they are Sunni. The government used the argument that the people didn't collaborate with the security forces. How could they collaborate with the government if they were all considered as terrorists? It has always been like this. It was a battle between the government and the jihadist, and we were in the middle. If we got closer to Baghdad, we would be beheaded by the jihadists. If we got closer to the jihadists, Baghdad would behead us. So we had no options. We stopped being productive. We stopped believing in the state. We are no more trusting the state to protect us. We are targeted. The Americans also saw us as terrorists because we were Sunni. They created this identity and gave it to us: the Sunni identity, which we didn't have before. We had Iraqi identity. We had national identity. With all that they have done, they created the Sunni identity that felt oppressed.

The consequences of imposing or creating the Sunni identity is that you are no more trusting the state, and then it will be easy for any extremist group to use this identity. It will always be justified by the extremists that they are here to protect the Sunni because they are targeted by the Shia government. And it will be used by the government to say, 'You see, you say you are Sunnis, you don't say you are Iraqis.' So this kind of discourse started coming, which created more problems between the Iraqi societies against the city of Mosul. And the city of Mosul lost its real identity, which was a mixed identity, which had coexistence and diversity. The Christians started identifying themselves politically as Christian. The Sunnis had this political identity, Sunnism. The Yezidis started identifying as Yezidis, it became a political identity. So the city is no more one city.

Mark Kukis
One of the things that they did differently after the surge was they began to more forcefully target militants, and they became more effective at finding and confronting them. Probably the most significant thing that I found was that the troops were much more determined with a counterinsurgency mind-set than the troops I'd embedded with before. When I was out with troops in the Baghdad area previously, they were concerned mostly with stabilising an urban environment, almost like police work; they would

try to go into neighbourhoods and make sure insurgents weren't active, coordinate with security forces and generally kind of keep peace as much as they could. Troops that I embedded with during the surge were much more counterinsurgency-focused: they had clear pictures of militants and their networks and how they operated; they seemed to have better intelligence and they seemed to know where the insurgents were. When they went out to confront insurgents, they had more luck finding them and engaging with them than I had experienced with previous embeds. They seemed much more determined to fight them and they seemed much more sophisticated in their awareness about how they operated.

The surge and its effects I think were somewhat limited. Yes, they did fight the insurgency in more sophisticated and more effective ways during this time period, but to call it a success is I think to misunderstand the larger picture of what was happening in Iraq at this time. It's true that the Americans eliminated many insurgents with their new strategy; it's also true that a variety of other factors helped lower the violence and that American operations can only account for a fraction of the lowering of violence. I would point to two other main factors.

One is that there was a surprising unilateral ceasefire by the main Shia militia, the Mahdi Army. There had been a series of confrontations within the Shia militia community – basically Shia militias were at odds with one another. This culminated in a bloody exchange in front of the key Shi'ite shrine in southern Iraq. After this, the leader of the Mahdi Army, Muqtada al-Sadr, seemed genuinely sickened by the idea of Shi'ites killing Shi'ites right in front of one of the most revered shrines, and at that point he called a unilateral ceasefire. Importantly, it was not a ceasefire just to include Shi'ites fighting Shi'ites – it was a total ceasefire. So no Shi'ites attacking American forces, no Shi'ites attacking al-Qaeda, just a ceasefire. That had a huge impact on the balance, as any American official will tell you.

The other major factor that I'm convinced had a significant impact on the reduction of violence was the fact that much of the sectarian violence, in Baghdad in particular, had played out in such a way that things grew quiet. Neighbourhoods that had once been a mix of Sunni and Shi'ites became all Shi'ites and vice versa. The fight for certain areas, certain neighbourhoods in parts of Iraq had been fought and won, and quiet prevailed in these areas, more so than it had in previous times. That was not a function of the American intervention; that was a function of the dynamics of the conflict among Iraqis. Based on my observations and the conversations I had with various military officials, I would say that American surge efforts contributed roughly to about a third of the reduction of the overall violence that Iraqis were experiencing at this time. I think you could assign roughly the same percentage to the Mahdi Army ceasefire, and to the fact that certain areas of Iraq had become quiet because of their own internal dynamics.

One of the major misconceptions about the American experience in Iraq is that, with the right counterinsurgency strategy, you can prevail and achieve your political aims in these kinds of conflict environments. If you do a clear-headed analysis of the American counterinsurgency strategy, what you find is that it did have a significant impact on the reduction of violence – it eliminated a number of insurgents – but overall there were other factors and greater forces that shaped outcomes more decisively than the American presence did. That's very difficult for American military thinkers to swallow, the idea that there are greater forces than them out there in Iraq shaping events, but it's true. In the end, Iraqi society and the violence in that war had its own trajectory. The traditional narrative says that Iraq was falling apart, we added more troops and a better strategy and we fixed Iraq, and that's just not what happened. What happened was that Iraq was falling apart, Americans employed more troops in a different strategy and they had a significant impact, but not a decisive impact, on the trajectory of Iraq, and Iraq as a society and as a country remains on its own trajectory driven by its own internal forces. The American efforts there have only shaped them at the margins.

Withdrawal

John Nixon
To be fair, Obama had a lot on his plate in 2009, in terms of the financial meltdown that had occurred, and trying to dig the United States out of that. However, it couldn't have come at a worse time, because it was the first time since the war started in 2003 where there was quiet. Iraq had calmed down a great deal. It was a perfect time to try to place pressure on the Malaki government and maybe place pressure on these issues – these very, very hard issues – of reconciliation and power sharing. We had leverage now, and it was a missed opportunity on Obama's part. If he would've seen this not as something that he inherited, but as an opportunity to advance American interests in rebuilding Iraq. There are a series of turning points in the whole fiasco of the Iraq War, and I think this is one of those crucial turning points where we had an opportunity to solidify the gains of the surge and also perhaps set Iraq on a different path forward. It was going to be hard work, and it required engagement on a level that the Bush administration had invested in this war, which was pretty all-consuming. Obama clearly showed that he viewed this as an unwanted inheritance, and that didn't change at all, I think, over time, certainly as Iranian nuclear capabilities became the focus. Al-Qaeda in Iraq had reached their apogee and were on the down slope by the time Obama came in. They were very much defeated and on the run, a diminishing force. I just think we let victory kind of slip away.

Waleed Nesyif

I remember being on the plane home [in 2011]. I've never felt this scared to return to the thing that I love the most, which is my family. Emotions were so strong at that time that I couldn't even understand it so I took my notebook and I just kept writing, stream of consciousness, just writing. I found one of the things that I wrote recently, and there was this big passage where it literally just says 'war drums war drums war drums war drums war drums war drum war drums.' How my mind was functioning at that time.

Got on that plane, and I could hear my people for the first time, loud and clear, with their complaints, with their nuances, the goods and the bads and the uglies, you know, and I was like, 'This is actually happening, I'm going home.' Landed at the airport, got mistreated by the police, and I was like, 'Finally, I arrived!' If you don't get insulted at the airport, you know, it's like you haven't really made it yet – this is Baghdad.

I knew my brothers were waiting for me at an area where passengers can go and basically go and meet their loved ones; the airport was a security district, so if you are not flying you cannot go and welcome people, you cannot enter the airport. I got in a cab and we were driving, and it just hit me: I left my brothers, they were kids. The youngest was nine years old, he used to sleep on my arm every afternoon, I put him to bed. It's almost like I was in a dream and I just woke up; life was frozen in my head while it continued over here. And then when we finally made it and I saw them, I was so shocked that I locked the doors. They were trying to open the doors and it's like, 'What the fuck is wrong with you?' I was like, 'This is not real.' Finally seeing my brothers ... My youngest is taller than me, number three looks like the spitting image of me, and the second oldest looks older than me, that's how beaten by life he was.

They took me to my mum, to the house, and she was looking at me, touching my face, she was like, 'Are you real?' It was an insanely happy moment. The only way that I can describe it, it's like somebody just put my feelings in a blender and now try to understand what you feel. And I'm like, this is the worst fucking smoothie I've ever had in my life. Nevertheless, it was a joyous occasion to be with the family and then I noticed – where's Dad? And they were like, 'Oh, he had to go do something for his unit in the army,' and I was like, 'Yeah, but he retired two months ago so why would he go back to the unit?' And they were like, 'We don't know, you know your father never speaks about his work.' Something was itching at me so I started picking at it. 'All right, let's cut the bullshit – where is Dad? You tell me right now.' And as I was flying he had had a heart attack, and he was at the hospital being operated on as I had arrived. The doctor had advised him that he cannot get emotional so they were like, 'You can't go see him, he will get emotional to see you because he will be very happy and this will be quite dangerous for the operation he's just had, you need to give him a few days.' Thankfully, he made it through, everything is OK.

Mark Kukis

Baghdad's a big place and, even in the most violent of days, mini-markets were open and people went about their life, people went to school. Even amid a lot of gunfire and explosions, life went on in Baghdad. You don't just shut down a city of seven million people. Much of Baghdad had been really torn up by the explosions and the general levels of violence. There was a lot of war damage around, plus all the war damage that had happened when the Americans first attacked the place during 'shock and awe'. The city was scarred – and visibly scarred – and there was life on the streets, but it was slow to emerge. In that time period, life was tentatively resuming in the streets of Baghdad amid this picture of war destruction. Meanwhile, there was this really pervasive sense of anxiety about the future that stuck with people as they tried to resume a bit of normal life and take advantage of the relative calm.

During this time, actually, there was a moment late in 2008. My Iraqi colleagues came in and they were like, 'We were just outside and one of the American patrols went by and they had their guns up rather than pointed down.' They were like, 'That's a good sign. The troops are feeling more relaxed, they don't feel like they have to aim their guns everywhere they drive. They're just kind of roaming around and that's a good thing.' The American occupation during this time was still as pervasive. I never saw a lessening of the American presence – I left in mid-2009 and they only started drawing down troops after that, so the entire time I was there, there was a very robust presence. I mean, if you went outside you saw American convoys, you didn't go more than 20 minutes without hearing an American helicopter or an American jet overhead, so the occupation was everywhere. It was horrible.

The other thing is, there's these practical inconveniences, these everyday inconveniences. You want to go to the market, but the roads are shut down because a convoy has come through and all traffic stops. I mean, just the sound and the clatter – this is another dimension of the Iraqi experience that I sense but cannot fully grasp. I've never lived in an environment where a foreign force has occupied and I've then felt that kind of existence politically and personally. Many Iraqis have tried to describe it to me and I just think that's one of those things that you can't quite get. An Iraqi general tried to explain it to me: 'Look, it's not easy, a foreign army occupying your country day after day, you know. You go into the streets and you feel –' he didn't say emasculated, but this is what he meant. Like, 'I'm out with my wife, and my wife is afraid and I can't do anything about that. She's afraid when she sees the Americans and I'm afraid.' These were people who had everything to gain from the fall of Saddam Hussein, and yet the presence of these American forces sort of created a sense of menace and foreboding in their lives, for every day, year after year. You can understand the psychological and emotional significance of that, how that must make people individually in that society feel. It must be awful.

Waleed Nesyif
I realised I'm no longer Iraqi. I started slowly exploring what had happened, first to the family then to each and every individual,

and then slowly verging out into the streets and then finally seeing it: the Iraq I've had in my head all these years, churning and churning and churning, and the pictures did not match. At all. The change was so drastic from the Iraq that I had left, and I want to illustrate it with a simple small story. How I kissed my friend on the mouth. See the Iraqi kiss is known to be right, left, right; that's how we kiss in Baghdad, you greet someone right, left, right. First friend I see, I kissed him on the right, switching. He didn't switch. We ended up kissing on the mouth. We took it with a laugh and we hugged. Second one, same thing happened. Third one, same thing happened, and I was like, 'Hang on a minute over here, when did we change the way we kiss and greet each other?' They were like, 'It's always been like this.' I was like, 'No, no, no, it's not that I left 100 years ago, it wasn't even 10 years ago. We kissed right, left, right.' And they couldn't remember, they couldn't remember how we were. Life was so intense and all of these changes were happening so rapidly that people resorted to absolute survival mode which means you only keep in mind the things that can help you survive and get by and move on to the next step. No looking back, no looking to the side left or right. Forward drudging only.

And here I am, the hopeless romantic who has been reminiscing, writing and talking about our history and how we used to be, and now I'm trying to reconcile the two goddamn worlds, and it's a completely different country. I remember having this lunch with the family and finally spoke to my father. It's the same household, but each individual of us had lived in a completely different country. You see, the Iraq my dad lived in and grew up during his most formidable years was completely different than the one he raised me in, and the one I grew up in, it's completely different than the one that my younger brother had grew up in. Yet we are still in the exact same physical location. Try to reconcile that.

Then the unfolding begins of what actually had happened, because this was all just the family stuff. One of the things that really shocked me was how old my friends looked. I looked like a

'THOSE WHO ARE WET AREN'T SCARED OF THE RAIN'

goddamn kid. Literally, I was a scrawny little guy barely weighing about 70 kilos. They were looking at me, laughing at me: 'Do they not feed you in Canada? What's wrong with you?' All my friends are fat, bald, wrinkles so deep you can put your finger in it, you can rest a cigarette in it. I saw this guy, I swear to God I thought it was his uncle, and he was one year younger than me. I saw him and I didn't recognise him, and he was like, 'Waleed!' because apparently I looked almost the same. I looked at him and I was like, 'What happened to you?' and he was like, 'What do you mean?' I was like, 'You look 50.' And he was like, 'Welcome to Iraq.'

I started exploring the streets and one of the first things that I started noticing: I have never seen such ungodly crazy hairstyles as I have in Iraq. Oh my god, man, some people were taking that shit into the next level, they looked like aliens. One of them, I stopped him in the street: 'I've got to ask you, who the fuck told you you looked good?' He had painted his beard with I don't know what, so it looked like somebody had slapped some tar on his face. His hair – one part had a circle, the other part had a circle, and the back was shaven completely. He was like, 'It's all like this outside – you know, in the West.' I was like, 'What if I were to tell you I just came from Canada, and you look fucking nuts?' And then there was this biker gang, Hells Angels wannabes, you know. They're wearing half tracksuits, half jeans with slippers, and they had bandanas but then the part of the hair that was showing outside the bandana they had gel on it, and just ... wow. Wow.

Something that I never thought that I would see in Iraq, because when I left we're not fat because we are poor. Poverty does not produce fatness, you're always trim, whether you like it or not. This is how people recognise that you're rich – if you have a belly. Because you can eat. One of these individuals had to profile-walk through the door because his shoulders were too wide. And these were not muscles, just extra layers of fat. One of these guys I went to high school with, we used to call him Starving Ali, because you could see his veins, that's how thin he was. I saw his belly, and I flat-out asked him, 'What happened?' He was like, 'I'll tell you what happened.

When you have a period from 2006 to 2010 you cannot walk out of your house as a man and if you do you do it as fast as you can … For four years, we did not move. You move, you get shot. So what do you do? You play Xbox and you eat. And you eat and you eat and you eat.' Imagine four years of sluggishness that is forced upon you, because it's either that or you go outside and you get killed.

But there is a silver lining there as well. Iraq is a very patriarchal society. Now you cannot go to work, you cannot open your shop if you're a man because literally you will get killed according to your ID. If you're Sunni you'll get killed by Shia; if you're Shia you'll get killed by Sunni. So what happened? The wives, the mothers, the sisters started going to work. And all of a sudden you had this female work force that was introduced into the street. Now, OK, the civil war has ended, the men want to go back, but these guys now have their own customers, clientele, they've developed their own sales style and all of these things and now they're fighting. Obviously, I'm simplifying, but feminism had actually taken a very interesting, unintentional helping hand in Iraq during those dark periods.

Mark Kukis
There was a lot of confusion about how long the Americans would stay involved in Iraq. If they're going to go, are they going to go in full, are they going to go in parts, and when will that be? I think that was the main idea on people's minds and, for Iraqis, that was really critical. Whether the Americans were staying or going affected calculations they had about their daily lives. If the Americans left all of a sudden and stability decreased dramatically, then maybe they've got to move to Egypt or Jordan or face something worse. Sunnis felt like, as long as the Americans were there, then the Maliki administration and the Shi'ite militias were held more in check than they would be if the Americans were gone. So if you're Sunni and you're thinking about an imminent American departure, you're terrified, right. If you're Shi'ite, and particularly if you're Shi'ite militia, and you're thinking about an imminent American departure, you're optimistic about your political and

economic fortunes. So there's basically two attitudes: a camp that was eager to see the Americans go so they could consolidate power and resources, and a camp that was eager to see them linger, because they felt like it provided, not full security, but more security than you might have if they were gone.

John Nixon
I had high expectations of Barack Obama when he became president. I thought his instincts on the war had been correct. I had hoped that he would do something about Iraq, one way or another, and also that he would take advantage of this point in time. He's coming into office in 2009, things have quietened down greatly, the surge has worked, the Anbar Awakening has really paid dividends in terms of putting al-Qaeda on the run and bringing stability and quiet to some of the Sunni areas, and things are looking up in Iraq. I think Obama had a real opportunity to shape things. And again, instead of seeing this as an opportunity to further American interests in the Middle East, Obama just ignores Iraq and treats it as though it's not his problem. He didn't create it, he didn't put the troops there, and he doesn't want anything to do with it. We went from an office that was sending analysts into the Oval Office to an office that, in the first two years of the Obama administration, sent an analyst into the Oval Office once. It's kind of a joke.

I used to think that if, as an intelligence analyst, you bring this information to those in power, they will know what to do with it and they'll use it wisely. And it's at this point that I realise it almost doesn't matter what we say, the politicians will do what they want to do. They're going to believe what they want to believe and what they'll do is do whatever serves their own self-interest. The message that [Vice President] Joe Biden brought to Nouri al-Maliki right before Obama's inauguration in January 2009 was: 'You've got a free hand to do whatever it is you want to do, just keep Iraq off the front pages of the US media. Just make sure that this kind of just goes away and isn't a problem for the Obama administration.' That's as a clear a plan I think we had. And once Maliki heard that, he turned into a very staunch sectarian player – the people that were harmed, severely harmed, by this were the Sunni tribes.

I thought we should try to help Iraq in terms of getting their political system going. We had now a window of time in which things had quietened down and the political conflict was kind of at a minimum. I thought this would be a good time for them to have an election, to let the Iraqis choose their leader, and then let's work with that leader and see if we can get some elements of reconciliation in a country that really has no tradition of reconciliation. It was worth a try. We had already spent a lot of time, money, effort, lives in trying to get to this point. It seemed worth continuing on. I didn't want to give up on Iraq.

Omar Mohammed
This was Maliki's fight against terrorism: allowing a terrorist group to come from Syria to establish its own state in Iraq. To occupy three cities and to lead to the genocide against Yezidis and cleansing of Christian and Sunnis and destroying a city. It's the responsibility of Obama, after the responsibility of Bush, and before them Bill Clinton and Bush the father. It's not something disconnected. It started with them and they continued, they did more disasters. Supporting Nouri al-Maliki, bringing him to power, was their disaster. If you see the *Time* magazine when on the front cover Obama is delivering the key of Iraq to Maliki, Maliki is looking at a destroyed country. Obama is saying bye. Like, 'Take over the country. I don't want it any more.' They just disappeared. The end of the American occupation happened in 2011. First they disappeared from everywhere. They stayed in certain places, but we knew that they disappeared from everywhere else.

Tahany Saleh
In the last phase, Americans really isolated themselves away from Iraqi streets. The soldiers who were in the cities stayed in their army bases – we rarely saw them in the streets. It didn't matter whether they stayed, or whether they retreated, we were already

in the midst of the fighting. Their presence is the same as their absence, because they never offered anything tangible. They didn't try to solve the problems, they didn't do anything. That is why I didn't give their withdrawal much significance. I don't even remember the date, or the time, because it has no value to us as citizens. The fight had changed, we were being killed. The war started targeting us; it wasn't targeting soldiers, or a certain group. Everyone was embroiled in it, and civilians will pay the price. But we have an Iraqi saying that goes: 'Those who are wet aren't scared of the rain.' And we were already completely drenched.

Omar Mohammed
The violence almost stopped at the beginning of 2011, but not everywhere. The second division of the Iraqi army came to Mosul and established their camp in the eastern part of the city. They were in control of the main streets. There was kind of an understanding between the local government, the Americans and the second division of the Iraqi army. So the violence went down, just a few months before the Americans left. It was a very peaceful period, although there were some car bombs from time to time. People started going out. The shops started opening to a late hour – when I say late, I mean 9pm, this is the latest they could stay open. But then things completely changed.

When Obama made the decision that he is going to withdraw from Iraq, two things happened – Iraq became an Iran-dominated country, although the Americans were still there, and the rise of extremism, whether it's on the Sunni side or the Shia side. I still don't understand how the United States, under Obama, delivered Iraq to Iran. Withdrawing from Iraq wasn't just to take the Americans from Iraq; he used it for his propaganda and the agenda in domestics, but at the same time he delivered Iraq to Iran in return and he created another conflict in the country. And the only obvious winner of that decision was Iran. Iran is in Iraq, and Iraq is no more a state, it's kind of an extension to Iran.

It wasn't about wanting them to leave the country any more. It was about what they did, they should fix. They should fix the problems they made. No, I wasn't happy when they left. Not because I wanted them to stay, but because there is no trust in the government, there is no trust in the security forces, there is no belief in the state, so there was nothing. Things have changed completely after the ten years of this terrorism, corruption, problems, killing. After thousands of people were killed in the sectarianism. The mission that was accomplished in Iraq when the Americans came and after they left, they brought to Iraq terrorism and a corrupted state. A permanently corrupted state.

Just a few days after Obama's announcement that they are withdrawing from Iraq, you can't imagine how many attacks happened in the city. We even started seeing the slogan or the title of ISIS, the Islamic State in Iraq, and on other walls you could see the Islamic State of Iraq and al-Sham. Then it became more like the bloodied time of Mosul after a few months of peace. ISIS became stronger. As if someone gave them the kiss of birth. They rose from nowhere. They came from nowhere.

'Deal with your problems.' This is what the Americans told us. 'Now it's your problem.' And now Trump also is saying, 'We don't want to do anything in Iraq.' Yeah. Was it just about the oil? I'm not sure. All I know is that the Americans left me with no country. When you say the name of Iraq, you wonder what is it? What's Iraq? Which Iraq do you mean? Iraq of the north? Iraq of the south? Iraq of what? Ask the minorities, do you know what is Iraq? Ask the Shia themselves now in southern Iraq. What the Shia government brought, what the Americans brought, they brought corruption and death. You have groups of people who do not trust each other, who do not want to live with each other. This is all thanks to America. The moment America left Iraq was the moment of declaring the birth of the most extremist group the world had ever known. The so-called Islamic State.

'THOSE WHO ARE WET AREN'T SCARED OF THE RAIN'

Waleed Nesyif

I grew up in an Iraq where we were Iraqi first and anything else second. I wanted to put this high school reunion together, so I was going to my friends, 'Hey, I want to book us a restaurant and we all get together. Let's just relive those days, they were fucking awesome.' And some of my friends started coming up with excuses. I was like, 'Why? Our friends, when was the last time you saw them?' He was like, 'It's been a while,' wanting me to change the subject. I was like, 'No, you've got to tell me why.' And he was like, 'Because you fucking invited –' you know, one of our friends. Of course I invited him, how else would a reunion be? And the guy was like, 'He is Sunni.' I've never been slapped this hard in my face by reality before. 'Do you mean to tell me you don't speak to him because he's Sunni?' And he was like, 'Yeah. And let me tell you something, Waleed: the Iraq you left is no more, this is the new Iraq.'

Mars and Earth. That's how alien this concept was. I grew up in a household where my mum is Sunni, my dad is Shia. Islam was seldom mentioned in the household, let alone affiliation or denomination. I went to a high school where you had all different types of people and you never spoke of goddamn religion. We were largely secular, especially in Baghdad. I mean, it says on your ID that you're Muslim, you might go to the mosque every now and then, but really at our core we were really a secular society where it didn't really matter what you do. The only religion we really knew was don't speak shit about Saddam.

My biggest wish is that I do something that could help at least the immediate friends and families bury this shit and move forward, and maybe it will trickle down to some other people. Because without it there is no future in Iraq. And I'm happy to say that things are changing. People are waking up to the purposeful divide that was implanted in Iraq between Sunnis and Shias, Arabs and Kurds, Muslims and Christians. Unfortunately, the pace is not as rapid as the country needs it to be in order to mend itself. You still have the pockets of people led by politicians, political parties trying to influence this, and you can see it so clearly during election times.

I thought – once I saw some of my friends being still fervent about that divide, unable to forgive each other due to the party or denomination that they belong to – that maybe the process of trauma is going to take them a little bit of time until they overcome it. But I kept seeing spurts of evidence that something is going to give and they could just fall back into it very easily. Because they weren't allowed the period of time to heal. In Iraq it's been from one thing into another, one thing into another. It's like being hit on your head multiple time by a hammer, and every time you want to raise your head somebody is hitting you from a different direction.

I went and I started filming all of the people that had been forcibly removed from their places in the south and they took refuge in Baghdad and were now living in squalor in literally shanty towns. And I filmed and I filmed, stories that make your heart bleed, the situation that these people were living in, because it's squalor and you still have to pay rent. The Iraqi army had been intensifying their operations in the Sunni triangle. The way they had been doing so was through mass arrests, and when they're arresting those individuals there are sessions of torture and there is absolutely nothing that is called due process. So your son gets taken, your husband gets taken, you don't know where they are. It's not that you're imprisoned in the same city so that you can have visitation rights or anything like that. None. This was going on for years. We had just walked out of a civil war that was Sunni-Shia. Predominantly the Sunni triangle is Sunni, and the government is predominantly Shia. So even if it was not meant to it was interpreted that this is Shia against Sunni.

People started demonstrating. It was peaceful demonstrations, no weapons. After 20-odd days of that, I decided to go see for myself what is going on, go and talk to people about it. So I went to Ramadi, and sure enough people have not been going to their jobs or to the schools, and they're all camping on a major highway in Ramadi and each tribe had its own massive tent. I started interviewing people, and the sentiment was very clear: 'The Iraqi

Government is Shia, we are Sunnis. They think we're not up to a challenge. Here we are. This is a peaceful demonstration, but we are going to get our rights back.' They started telling me about all of the female arrests on their families, so if an informant had informed on me and I was not at the house then they would take my mother or my sister or my wife. And for an Iraqi this is the end of days. So seeing hordes of tribes coming in, I was like, 'Civil war is not only probable, it's probably imminent.' We made it through the last one. This one is going to do us over.

And then I was seeing massive lorries unloading sheep, live sheep, and I was counting and I reached 200 and then lost count. I was asking one of these tribal leaders, 'What are these for?' and he was like, 'Oh, for food, you know, you've got to feed people.' I was like, 'How many times do you do this?' and he was like, 'Three times a day, breakfast, lunch and dinner.' And I was like, 'So every meal, you're slaughtering anywhere between 200 to 300 sheep? Who's coughing up the money?' And he was like, 'Oh, us collectively.' I was calculating each sheep was about 250,000 dinars, which works out to be about $200. I was like, 'Do you mean to tell me that tribal leaders are donating 50 million dinars a meal every day for 26 days now and indefinitely?' And he was like, 'Yeah.'

I started asking other people: 'Say they didn't meet your demands, they did not release the prisoners, they did not stop the informant law, what will happen then?' And he was like, 'Then we'll move on to a different phase.' And he left it at that.

I thought civil war again. Or Iraq will be divided for real this time because they've been talking about the division for a while: you have the north, the south, and then the centre right. Which was how the Ottomans ruled us – they separated us into three parts, and each part would have a representative or a ruler that reported back to Istanbul. I didn't know what at that time, but I knew something bad was about to happen.

That was back in 2014. I was back in Canada in May and my brother called me: Da'esh just took over a city in Anbar, they broke through the border, Mosul is next ...

A New Law in Town

Tahany Saleh

In 2014, I was taking my MA exams, so I was really focused on how I was going to pass them. I wanted to pass my exams, and get them over with. I remember, in the last days of April or May 2014, the roads were always blocked, always. We were always forced to walk a distance of five kilometres to get to university. We couldn't attend because of curfews sometimes. That would happen very often. On the last day I had an exam, we walked about seven kilometres; the bridges were completely closed off between the western and eastern sides. Our exam was scheduled for 9am and I got there at 10am, and they hadn't started yet because I wasn't the only one who was late. All the students were forced to come walking. We waited till 1pm, and the lockdown hadn't subsided. The bridges were still blocked. Our classmates who were on the eastern side couldn't cross over because it was completely forbidden. So the exam was postponed. Imagine, I had left at 7am and I only returned home at 5pm. I was incredibly tired. Emotionally tired, because I studied and couldn't take the exam. Tired because of the situation, which really got worse, it was incredibly bad. I got back home, I slept for a little, there was no electricity.

At 11pm on the 10th or the 9th, I was asleep and a friend of mine called. She said, 'Tahany, don't be scared, but "the Group" have crossed the bridge.' 'What do you mean they crossed the bridge?' She said, 'The army has completely retreated from the eastern side, and they are now on the western side, and the armed men are now heading towards the western side, because they have completely taken the eastern side.' I couldn't believe it at all. How can this happen? How did the army retreat? It was 11pm, everyone was probably sleeping, there was a curfew, and there was chaos. My sister was up. There was the sound of faraway gunfire, and they were getting closer. By the bridge on the eastern side, there was an incredible amount of fire and smoke, but there weren't many explosions. The explosions were far, we couldn't hear them. My younger brother wasn't at home, so we worried a lot about him. We waited for him till 1am and we couldn't wake Mum and Dad up to let them know. We didn't know what was really happening anyway. So he got home at 1am and explained that he was helping families who were fleeing from the eastern side to the western side. The armed men took the eastern side, and the families got scared so they came to the western side. And there was no army. They left their vehicles, their bases, their weapons. Can this be possible? No one understood what was going on. We didn't sleep that night because we didn't know what was going on.

At dawn, I heard megaphones. It's impossible to forget this. The sound I heard was: 'We are the Islamic State in Iraq and the Levant. We're coming according to the prophecy. We're going to govern you.' I heard words: 'The King of the believers.' What Islamic State? What does this mean? We didn't understand what was happening. 'We're going to govern you fairly.' All our neighbours tried to escape the area. We stayed because we didn't understand what was going on. It might only last a few hours, maybe days, and the army will return.

There was an incredible amount of smoke in Mosul, it's impossible to describe the quantities. Mosul was entirely covered in the colour black. We later found out that the smoke came from the army and police vehicles that were burnt, the warehouses, the weapons, houses were burnt, the armed men put fire to them. But we didn't know what Islamic State was, what ISIS was. We didn't know if they were freedom fighters, revolutionaries. We didn't know any details. We went out, and saw burnt cars as far as the eye can see. Army vehicles that were burnt, army bases that were open. People carrying weapons. Anyone could go take any weapon they wanted from police stations, they were completely open. The roads were open. People were walking the streets, but we didn't know what was going on.

This went on for days. We didn't know what was happening for days. Only that the Islamic State had come to govern under the prophecy. Many people in that time didn't understand what was going on – so much so that they clapped for them. They welcomed this new group that appeared. Because, as citizens, we wanted a break from the killing, the explosions, IEDs and all that.

Omar Mohammed
The rise of ISIS happened all of a sudden. We woke up in the morning and, from that morning, we started paying taxes to ISIS. After the American withdrawal, the extremists brought themselves to the surface, they came from underground, now they are on the ground, now they are active. We started witnessing the attacks – the daily attacks – of the terrorists against civilians, against security forces. The car bombs on a daily basis. In my neighbourhood, there was a checkpoint; there was an attack on this checkpoint every Friday. ISIS would destroy this checkpoint, the security forces the next day would bring a new checkpoint. The next Friday, ISIS would come and destroy it.

People were paying taxes to ISIS directly. They would come to all shops, businessmen and employees, everyone should pay. The domination of all the financial resources in the city, everyone should pay. Even if someone wants to do a project in the city for reconstruction, for the government. Building a school is not possible without paying ISIS. They would come to the shop, or to someone's house, they would leave a paper, on this paper written the money you should pay and they give you a phone number of the Islamic State. You have to pay, because if you don't pay they would kill us. People started paying this. They were waiting for the withdrawal, to fill the gap. There was a new law in town, a new power ruling the city. It's no more the Americans, no more the security forces, it's under the rule of the Islamic State. You would feel this because we stopped going to certain places because they became unsafe. We stopped driving through certain streets because they became unsafe, no more security forces there. Even the university became unsafe. We were ruled by ISIS after the withdrawal, and in 2014 it became official.

When the attacks happened in June 2014, we thought this is another attack that would take one to two days, that the terrorists would take control of the city, at most for the three days. The terrorists would come, they would fight against the security forces, the security forces would leave, it would be under the control of the terrorist groups two or at most three days, then the security forces would come back, fight back, and the terrorists would leave. It's like kind of a game, someone would take power, the other would leave, and then they would go back and the terrorists would leave. So we thought this is also another game, there is nothing unusual about it. This time, they were different. They were well organised, they were this time putting on a uniform, the black coats. They had new cars, and these cars had local names, and they have new weapons. They weren't fighting using AK-47s or small weapons, it was something heavy. It was put on the pick-ups.

The attack happened 3am on 6 June, it was a Friday. They took control of the city which was full of almost 60,000 soldiers from different divisions, including police, security forces, a special unit called the SWOT. The anti-terrorism police, the 2nd division of the Iraqi army, 9th division of the Iraqi army, and another special unit, the Iraqi Federal Police, intelligence, the helicopter division – all of them, all of a sudden, they all left the city. All of a sudden, they collapsed. The army have disappeared. The city is empty of everything, just 300 ISIS fighters. They didn't move to any other parts, they were just in the north-west of the city. It was another day of judgement.

A governor appeared at night. He was carrying an AK-47. He said, 'Don't worry, everything is OK. We will take back power. Those are our brothers who took back power, and they will give us our rights that were taken by the central government.' This is how he addressed the situation. He didn't say ISIS. We received information that the Turkish Consulate didn't leave and the General Consulate is still in Mosul. Then people started talking to each other. 'If the Consul is staying in this town, why should I leave?' People started returning back to their houses. By 10 June, it was a moment of silence: no more security forces, you even don't see ISIS in the street, everything was open. Streets were open, streets we never believed we could drive through again.

The next day I went with my mother to Albid to find a house. We wanted to rent a house in Albid. The security said, 'You have to get confirmation from the rental office, then I will give you security approval.' The office said, 'I can't rent you unless you bring confirmation from the security.' So they were playing it this way – it was impossible to get a house. Then next day, which was 12 June, we returned back to Mosul. We had a discussion. We said, 'Let's go back. The courts are here, the Turkish Consulate is still there, it means things are working. We shouldn't worry.' We turned back. And on 13 June, things changed. ISIS distributed a document in the street. And this document has a title – the *Charter of the City*, or the *Constitution of Medina*. Once I read this I said, 'This is something different. These guys are here to stay. It's something dangerous.' They were claiming the narrative of the prophet, that they were here as an Islamic State, and they gradually applied their rules, one by one. It's the Sharia Law or ISIS Law. It would read, 'You have tried the republican government, you have tried the rule of the American invasion, referring to them as Crusaders, you have tried all of these rules, now it's time to live under the rule of the Islamic State.'

Tahany Saleh

On the third or fourth day, on the Mosul University podium that used to be a stage for celebrations, where they'd hold the Spring Festival, they declared the caliphate. It was the 'King/Emir of Mosul' or 'Ruler of Mosul' – not sure about the name. He spoke with the people that were present, the young people, the families that were around the podium, who'd gathered. He told them that they were going to make a caliphate, one that follows the same rules as the prophet, it will rule by justice etc. But we don't have an army, we don't have a state, we don't have a government, we didn't know where these armed men came from, and they were in control of the city. We were scared and wary about what was to come. The army will come back at any moment – that was all I was thinking, waiting for them to come back, so that I could continue with my exams.

Some days passed, and there was still no army to be seen. The 'city document' constitution was published by ISIS. And that is when we understood that the city's circumstances had completely changed. Mosul is in the hands of people who don't have a name, 'Islamic State'. OK, we are Muslims – we live in a city that is majority Sunni or Muslim – what does Islamic State mean? Are you the same people who used to plant explosives? 'Yes, we blow things up so that we could control the apostates.' Who are the apostates? That was a new word we started hearing: 'rejecters'. Who are 'rejecters'? Nasiris, Christians, these terms started appearing.

And then they published the 'city constitution'. Women couldn't go out without being accompanied by a man or boy from the family; women could not go out on their own. You were obliged to adhere to Islamic dress codes, the burqa or the niqab. There were no salaries, all the services stopped working. As civilians, we didn't know what happened, how in one moment, in *just one moment*, more than 31,000 soldiers retreated from the city of Mosul. They suddenly retreated, and left the city. Where did they get the orders? How did they allow this group in, who were in very small numbers? They weren't more than a thousand people. How did they hand the city over to a group that have no global presence or any regional establishment? And who since 2003 till 2014 had been bombing and killing. It's the same people.

They started killing people, entering people's houses where they'd arrest people. They looted and robbed Christians' homes: they are sinners. The ways that ISIS used to kill were absolutely innovative. Every person died in a whole new way. It was rare for ISIS to kill two people in the same way. They had to innovate the way of killing, whether it be burning, burning parts of the body, cutting parts of the body off, shooting. All these things that the world watched, we lived. And to scare civilians, they'd hang people's bodies in the streets. To warn you that your fate will be just like that if you transgress their rules.

Then Sinjar happened. When they took Sinjar and they displaced the people of Sinjar, everything changed. It was settled in the first three days. That was it. Everything was over, everything will change with these people. Everything was on its way to destruction and devastation. Ultimate destruction. It was done in a way that was very clear. Everyone in Mosul was trying to leave the city, there was not a single person who wasn't trying to leave the city in one way or another. They were just trying to find a way. All the entrances were closed. Because if ISIS opened any exit, then not a single person would have stayed in Mosul.

Omar Mohammed

They didn't apply any rules in the first two months, until they started deporting the Christians. When they deported the Christians and then committed the genocide against Yezidis, they then came back to the city, and they started applying the rules. They had, from day one, what they called the media outlet. A white caravan with a big monitor and a window. There is a guy inside this caravan, putting ISIS videos, propaganda, fights, battles in Syria in Mosul on the TV. You would see this everywhere in the city. And this is how I knew that this is not something unorganised. These people were well organised. These people were ready. It would read 'ISIS occupied', even on empty buildings. They knew what they were doing. What we used to see as the police station now is the Islamic police station. What used to be the Iraqi flag is now the Black Flag of ISIS. Checkpoints in the street have laptops with them, checking for names. They also opened a centre to receive people who think they have made some mistakes and they want to apologise, who want to ask for mercy. The way they can do it is to go there, hand over their weapon and to return back to Islam. They would give them a card, and on this card it would read, 'He is Muslim.'

The first month, they didn't do anything publicly. I mean, we knew there were people they had executed, but it wasn't public. They didn't ask the people to follow the rules directly in this month. Even the mosques, they didn't take over the mosques. They didn't force the people to go to prayer, in the very first few days. Then things directly and essentially changed. Now everything should follow the rules of ISIS. They started doing public executions. They started surveying the houses to know whose house belongs to who, and if you own the house or are renting the house. They went to the bank and they asked the people who had deposits in the bank to go to the bank to check their deposits, because if you have a deposit in the bank and this deposit is connected to some work you did with the government, you can't take it back. You have to clear where did your money come from. They opened the police stations. They forced women to wear the niqab. Everything changed.

The first thing they did – apart from executions, arresting people, seizing houses – was the systematic destruction of the historical sites of the city. A Syrian historical site such as Nimrud, Nineveh which is on the east side of Mosul; the museum, where they destroyed artefacts; then they started destroying the historical shrines of Mosul, one by one. They began with the most important site, the Shrine of Prophet Jonah, or Nabulus as it is known locally, then they destroyed other shrines, seized the church, took down the crosses from the church and put up the flag of ISIS. They destroyed almost everything in less than a month. They destroyed the statues of men in Mosul, mostly the prominent musicians of Mosul from the Ottoman period.

ISIS wanted to impose its own history on the city, and they understood the first step to change history is to remove everything from the other history. We were dying gradually, witnessing the destruction of our history, and with each piece they take out we die again and again and again. So it was kind of ISIS was killing us, but cutting small pieces day by day. To make sure that we remain alive until we see the end of the destruction and then comes the final stage of death. This is what ISIS did, and this is how I felt when I saw this. They were destroying history that had survived for centuries. But ISIS destroyed it, dismembering and dismantling the city. And the world was watching, and they were able to stop ISIS but they didn't. They preferred not to stop them.

ISIS distributed a document. In this document they offered the Christians three options: to convert to Islam; to pay taxes for non-Muslims to live under protection of the Islamic State; or to fight. ISIS added another option: to be deported from the city. After this was distributed, they started forcing them to leave, but with one condition – they leave with only their clothes on them, they should take nothing with them. They established checkpoints on the borders of the city to check the Christians who were fleeing the city, to check if they were taking anything with them. They went to their houses, they seized everything that belonged to them. In one day, in less than 24 hours, the city was completely empty of the Christians.

According to their law, the law they use, in dealing with non-Muslims, the Christians are considered as the people of the book, which means they have a holy book just like the Muslims, the Bible. Whether they agree with the Bible or not, in Islam Jesus is a prophet and the rule in dealing with this they should be given options, and that is why ISIS gave them the three options. The Yezidis are considered non-believers, because they think that the Yezidis are worshipping the devil, so for the non-believers, who have no holy book coming from God like the Christians, Muslims and Jewish, they have no options – the only option is converting to Islam or death. So ISIS forced many Yezidis to join Islam, and of course fear led them to convert to Islam. Those who refused were killed. Their women were enslaved because they considered them spoils of war. They were given to the fighters. The children were also given to the fighters, because they also consider the children as slaves. The men were killed. Many Yezidis were executed in Sinjar. Thousands.

Tahany Saleh
After 2014, the fear that we lived in from 2003 till 2014 was nothing at all in comparison. A car bomb – that is something normal. An explosive belt – again, normal. 2014 was so different that it made us completely forget all the fear of the times that preceded it. So much so that we really wished our lives would end as soon as possible. We wished to die, that's it. We had had enough.

Omar Mohammed
On 22 April 2015, they brought two men wearing orange execution clothes. They put them in the middle and they had three cameramen. They were trying to find the best angle of shooting the video. They were asking the executioners to wait, talking to each other – 'Is this the best angle?' It looked like they were policing a film, not executing humans. They were carefully trying to find how to shoot the video, not thinking about the people who were going to lose their life. It looked like Hollywood producing a film. Moving the victims. 'Is the light good now?' And then they executed them. They were beheaded. And shot with a 4K camera.

At the moment of the execution, it was impossible to make any movement. I didn't feel anything. I know that my eye was going to the source of the blood, how the blood was flooding, but I was unable to close my eyes. I was unable to prevent myself from watching this because I felt nothing. As if I am the one that just died. And my body had frozen. Only my eyes were moving. I'm talking to you now, but I can still see their blood. I just returned home. I walked. It was so far from my house. I walked. I still saw this blood. And this happened again and again and again and again. Beheading, lashing, stoning, cupping of hands.

The difference between the violence ISIS did after 2014 and the violence before 2014 – whether it's ISIS, the Americans, the militias, the Iraq security forces – is that it was kind of disorganised before 2014. It was not well prepared. There was no stage to bring the actors who are going to behead. After 2014, it looked like something essential to ISIS, something they think about before they do it. Something theatrical. Something they discussed carefully. Because if they have the time to think about the best angle to shoot the video, it means they don't even understand they are beheading humans. It's part of their system. They deal with the beheading just the same way probably as they do to have to provide food to their soldiers.

I don't know how I am still OK, or how am I still sane. And I don't know if I have feelings or not. But what helped me is that at least I was doing something against them. And this gave me the strength to continue. To care about the victims, to make sure that I record their names so that they will be remembered. To make sure that they will not be forgotten. That the people will know that this happened to them and they will know who did this to them. To have this responsibility of fighting the history and holding another prophet, with all the consequences but knowing that you hold the narrative against ISIS, that ISIS with all its weapons couldn't manipulate the narrative, that there was someone who challenged ISIS – this helps me to humanise my feeling again.

'We Are Life'

At this point, **Omar Mohammed** *began an online blog, determined to record the truth of what was happening in his city.*

The birth of Mosul Eye was something that happened in the first moment of that attack. From that moment, I started writing about what was happening in the city. There were many rumours: the government says that his brothers took over the city and they will hand back to the righteous people; the Shia in southern Iraq were saying that Mosul should be collectively punished because they gave the city to ISIS; others were saying that the people of Mosul helped ISIS to attack the military and security forces. All of these rumours and all of this chaos. I found myself obliged to say what I thought. So I started writing on my personal account, on Facebook. This happened, this happened, this is how things happened, saying that there is an attack outside, there is still fighting, because I was watching from my window. I didn't understand the consequences in the beginning. I didn't understand how dangerous it was because I thought this is just something similar to the other attacks that happened a few days ago, it will finish in two days. But then things changed.

After I saw the *Constitution of Medina* that ISIS distributed, things changed in my head. Mosul Eye came to be a platform not just to document the history of Mosul, but also to protect the narrative of the city and to protect Mosul for now and for the future. The process – writing what's happening in Mosul since 6 June, writing every day, documenting every day – led to the creation of what is known to the world as Mosul Eye. That was my sense of history and understanding how dangerous and important the history was and the way ISIS were recognised by history. Which all began with the title of that document, the *Constitution of Medina*.

From the very beginning, I felt the responsibility and the importance of exposing what was happening, putting everything online. I felt the importance of making this history public. I also felt that, when ISIS came, they brought a mission that produced history with them, and this mission should be stopped, should be destroyed. The only way to stop ISIS from making this machine eat everything in the city was to make this history public, as it happened. I was the only source inside the city. There were no journalists – they were hiding, because they were a threat. There was no single person writing about what was happening. When I put this online, when people noticed this in the early days of the occupation of ISIS, you would see global media reporting 'Mosul Eye ... ISIS have done this ... Mosul Eye ... ISIS have executed people ... Mosul Eye .... according to Mosul Eye ...' They started sending me requests for interviews. I said, 'I can't do a foreign interview. The only way is send your questions.' I would answer the questions directly, and you would see it in the *Wall Street Journal*, the *New York Times*, *The Guardian*, BBC, other media outlets. And then in different languages, German newspapers, Russian newspapers, TV, even on Iraqi TV. And this became the voice of Mosul.

It was so important for me to be heard. Comparing the consequences of what could happen to me and the risk, what I am doing is worth doing, because the people are hearing what I'm saying. For the first time the city had its voice, and this time against the brutalist organisation of the Islamic State. It made me feel satisfied that I should continue. It gave me the strength to organise myself, to make sure that I can stay alive to continue this mission, and it also helped me evolving Mosul Eye. Doing this anonymously was essential. I kept my personal Facebook account working – I wanted to show the people that knew me that might suspect that this person is Omar, because I put the title of Mosul Eye, an historian from Mosul, documenting what's happening. Sometimes, in order to keep the lion from eating you, you stand in front of or in the mouth of the lion. Saying 'historian', there are thousands of historians in the city. I also kept my normal communication with people to the extent that they were criticising me – 'Why don't you care what is happening in your city?' – because I used to put music or pictures or writing about things not related to the city on my Facebook account so they would know that Omar is not doing this. Just normal Omar, who is interested in research, in posting pictures, or commenting on someone's post that has nothing to do with what's happening in the city. The same with my family. I just kept myself normal in the house: talking to my family, sitting with them, doing the normal stuff. When I would have a conversation with my friends, I would avoid – or prevent myself from – discussing anything that's happening. I started to have different personalities at the same time. Another life became my real life. The real life was Mosul Eye.

Tahany Saleh

If you 'liked' the Mosul Eye page, then ISIS might find and punish you. People who followed Mosul Eye were apostates and should be killed. So that page really scared me. Because when I read what was published on it, the daily posts ... I don't know how to describe. I'd visit it from time to time. I wouldn't use my account, I made a fake account so that I could read what was happening, read Mosul Eye's writing. Mosul's news, my city's news, and what we were living through. It was very hard.

When the writings first started appearing, he called himself Maurice Milton. He used to document what was happening in Mosul city on a daily basis. I followed this page, and had suspicions about who the person was. There is just one specific person that thinks in this way, and there can't be two of him. But I can't take the risk and ask him, or ask someone else. With every day that passed, I started becoming more and more certain that I figured out who it was. One day I copy-pasted one of Maurice's posts, and sent it to the person who I suspected could be the publisher and asked, 'Do you know this person?' He said, 'No, I don't know him.'

The person who was running Mosul Eye was putting his life in so much danger. How he was writing in that way, and could've been caught at any moment. One time I heard that the person who finds him out would get a prize. They used to call him 'the Black Devil', I think that was the name they gave him. The courage Mosul Eye's founder had to write in the most intense war, suffering, fear and death used to amaze and scare me at the same time. The tension came from asking myself how he had the ability to keep going. He documented what was happening in a particular way that gave me a lot of courage to continue. The existence of Mosul Eye in that time, for people who refused the reality that ISIS brought, was very meaningful. It was the peak of fear and death, and I felt that there was still hope for life. He's sure that the caliphate would end, so surely the caliphate will end. The hope that Mosul Eye's founder gave us was immense.

Omar Mohammed
I used to get threats almost on a daily basis. After the killing of the Jordanian pilot Muath al-Kasasbeh, who was burned alive in a cage, I received a threat from ISIS, and they said they would beg us to be killed like Muath al-Kasasbeh: 'We will kill you in an unknown way.' And they were able to do it, they could invent a new way to kill me. But what this specific thread told me was how strong I was. How much damage I had done to ISIS so they would tell me this. It didn't freak me out. On the contrary, it told me: 'Don't stop, continue, they are hurting, they are bothered.'

So I took Mosul Eye to a higher level. Keep doing it, put more pressure on ISIS. One of the threats mentioned that they knew me and they were coming for me. They mentioned lots of information, so I started analysing the threat. I found out that everything mentioned in the threat had been collected from the posts on Mosul Eye – they had just played with the words. I told them, 'Try another time, hard luck, this threat is based on information I have published.' I had lost the fear, at this stage. I'm not alone. I have the whole narrative of Mosul with me. I knew that ISIS feared my writing. ISIS feared what Mosul Eye was doing, so they were in a position of defence. I was the one that attacks. They were targeted, not me. The only fear I had was if something happened to my family I would never live with it. I was always looking at my mother, almost looking at her as if I was looking for the last time. My mother and some of my sisters kind of noticed: 'Omar, you are saying goodbye to us every day.'

I was speaking in their language, I was speaking out, saying what people couldn't say. I was telling the world what they felt, because I was one of them and what I felt was what everyone was feeling in the city. At the same, I didn't just talk about what was ISIS doing in the city, I made sure to bring new elements into the narrative. I started saying, 'I am listening to music now and that music is helping me to survive,' but I made sure that the music I chose was something that ISIS didn't like. 'Jewish Town' was one piece of music: the Jewish town is in Poland, and it's the town where the Jewish resistance against the Nazis happened. And I was sending a message through all of this.

Tahany Saleh
Mosul Eye kept publishing things intensely, in big numbers. Posts about daily life, posts that documented life in a way that made you think that it was impossible that it was just one person. It's impossible. It must be an entire organisation. It might even be the government. Because the things he talked about would penetrate ISIS really deeply. He really was able to penetrate them. How did he get to them?

To me, Mosul Eye's existence is what allowed me to think of what things will be like post-ISIS. It was a long time, and yes many days were difficult, but I dared think about these days, what will happen after ISIS. So I always held the motto 'We are life', and that is why, after liberation, I got a whole group of people to carry the motto 'We are life' – because this is the sentence that kept me grounded, at a time when it was very difficult for one to stick to principles, to certain ideas, to a thought.

Omar Mohammed

At the time of doing this, I started talking to the young people of Mosul, using Maurice Milton, giving them instructions on how to protect your identity online and asking them to do the same thing. Start exposing what's happening in the city, ISIS is afraid of you. The only one that responded to me was a young woman. She was 19 years old. I don't know why she trusted me, but she did. She said, 'I want you to tell me how to protect myself online.' She didn't tell me her name. I told her my golden rule: trust no one and document everything. Then I asked her to start describing things in the city before she put them online, so I could help her to hide herself when she wrote – sometimes when you write you don't know that you are exposing yourself in your own words. I gave her instructions that if she witnessed something she had to change at least some parts of the event, and to make sure that she was not writing about things that could only be within an identified area that could lead to her. And then I identified her through her words, then I helped her developing how she can deal with the words, and then she started posting.

Tahany Saleh

The army were close to where we lived for 85 days without entering. We were occupied by ISIS, there were mortars being shot, indiscriminate shooting. Either ISIS was going to stay, or the army would enter. We decided that we were going to make a move, because we could no longer handle it. We had no emotional strength whatsoever. That's why we decided to flee from the house, towards the security forces.

It was 7pm in the winter time, it was raining heavily the day before, it was extremely cold. We decided, along with our neighbours, that me and my two sisters were going to go. Mum and Dad stayed, and my brother stayed at home too. We didn't take anything with us, just a backpack with nothing in it. We walked at night, towards the sand barrier. The army was just behind it. It was night, very dark, the ground was muddy, it was very cold.

People were fleeing on a daily basis from Mosul city towards the security forces. The procession we walked with in the night was mainly women and children. The children were of all ages, I was surprised: were they not scared? Don't they want to cry? There was so much danger around us. We could have been fired at, at any moment. Because there was a huge procession of families, it could be seen by planes – ISIS could target it too. And it was in a place that wasn't far from residential neighbourhoods; it was on the outskirts of Mosul, but not far from residential areas. Everyone had to stay quiet.

The planes located us, so they would strike close to us. When the planes would fly over, we would sit on the ground, or in the mud or bogs that we were crossing. All the people were walking barefoot, because their shoes got really muddy, made them too heavy – they had to leave their shoes behind. I don't know how we managed to walk all that distance barefoot. I wasn't barefoot, I'd prepared myself. I'd followed the news, I was wearing strong shoes, but I felt so bad for the kids walking barefoot. We walked for about 16 hours. We got lost because it was very foggy. So we sat down and said, 'That's it. When the morning comes, we will either be with the army, or in ISIS's hands.' We were completely spent.

It was 6am and the shelling on us started. We were in a no man's zone, between ISIS and the army, so when battles flared we were right in the middle. The mortars started, the army was bombing, and ISIS were bombing. We heard the mosque, the call to morning prayer, and my sister said that she wanted to pray. I told her that it wasn't the time for that, leave it for later. She insisted to pray. You really can't refuse someone's requests in these situations. I told her to just do it quickly. We had to put our heads down, so that the shrapnel from the mortars doesn't hit us. So, she started praying, and she took her time. I asked her, 'What are you doing?' She kept quiet. My sister is used to praying every day, in her morning prayers, she does her 'thank you prayers', thanking God we're alive.

I noticed that she was praying an extra prayer. So, in a moment of intense anger – we were practically dead, the shelling was continuous, a mortar was going to fall on us, and that would be the end of us – I held her by her clothes hysterically, and shook her wildly, and told her, 'How are you thanking God for this ordeal! We are going to die, this is it!' She was crying, and I was crying, and the people around us were crying.

This father who was with us told his children, 'I'm sorry. I'm sorry that I brought you to this world, and couldn't take care of you. I apologise for being the reason that you have to walk barefoot in this cold, I'm sorry you live in this country. I'm sorry that everyone abandoned us. I'm so sorry.' With all that, we started feeling that we were going to die, and that was it.

The shelling subsided, and ISIS came. They surrounded us. They returned us to the city. They told us that they weren't going to hurt us. 'We aren't going to kill or arrest you. But if you do this one more time, you're going to be killed.' So we returned to the residential areas, which were close by.

We had told Mum and Dad that we'd call them when we'd crossed. It was 11am, and we called them. Dad said, 'Oh, you've crossed!' and we said, 'No, we're close by, can you come get us?' 'So you didn't cross?' And at that moment, Mum said, 'Thank God, you've returned, but we have to stay. Either we move when the army comes, or that is it.' We started coming to terms with the idea: the army is close by and we might be liberated at any moment.

A few days before the army entered, there was indiscriminate shelling on our neighbourhood. A family close to us was struck by a mortar. The father and the son died. The daughter, [other] son and mother stayed alive. So they brought the injured mother, daughter and son to our house. The girl was called Ammouna, her leg was injured, she was in shock because she saw her father killed in front of her. Her brother too. So she didn't say a single word, and I had to take care of her. I had no idea about first aid or anything, and there were no doctors. She was very beautiful. She had blue eyes, and I took care of her. I held her hand, but she wouldn't answer me at all, neither was she expressing her pain or anything. Ammouna wouldn't react to anything at all, and she had her eyes open most of the time but wouldn't interact with the person holding her hand, or even react to her injured leg. She was in that state for about three days. It lasted till the day of liberation.

On the day of liberation, at 12 in the afternoon, our neighbours knocked on our windows saying that ISIS snipers were on their roof, and that they had to escape from their house to ours. So now there were more than 35 people in our house. We all stayed in one room. Our house got struck, with some rockets, and smoke filled the house. Ammouna was holding my hand and she spoke for the first time. She said, 'There's Dad, and my brother, there they are.' I got really scared. I was thinking that that was it, and we were going to die.

The fighting lasted from 12 to 5.30pm, continuous shelling. We knew that the battle was over when there were only bullets fired. The mortar rounds stopped, and the planes stopped too. Just automatic guns, and that signified that the army was entering and securing the area. It meant that ISIS had withdrawn. We were able to tell this because we had lived through many battles.

We heard shots fired, but we didn't believe it. Mum left the room and then quickly returned. She was scared to say that the army had arrived – she worried they might be ISIS. She stayed quiet. We were completely broken, we had no hope whatsoever, nothing. And after that, we heard the sound of our neighbours, they were knocking at our door. They were all sure that we had died. They thought it was impossible that anyone from our family had survived.

When they announced that the army had entered our area and ISIS withdrew, the kids who were with us went out to the streets, running towards their home barefoot. There was glass everywhere, everything was bombed. They ran on the glass as if it were nothing. We tried to be happy, but what stopped us was Ammouna's mother. When she saw the soldier, she told him he was too late, and she was screaming and crying. 'My son was waiting for you to come, and you were late! You could have come before my son died!'

Everyone stayed quiet. We didn't celebrate or anything, but we were done with ISIS. And on that day, it got dark, and there was no electricity, but we felt safe because the army was on our street. I wanted to go to sleep that day, but I couldn't fall asleep. My sister and I had promised ourselves that on the day we get liberated, we would go out for a walk and wear our most beautiful clothes, because all that time had passed where we hadn't walked down a single street. We just had to do it. So we got dressed. It was a real celebration for us. We got dressed up, fixed up, wore nice clothes, and went out for a walk. Whenever we saw soldiers, we'd say hello to them. We were so happy, and throughout that entire walk we were saying, 'We are victorious.' She and I had won, because not a day passed where we bowed down to ISIS, or the killing that they practised. Nor did we accept their presence. Not at all. So it was *our* victory.

It's impossible to forget the feeling. It was a personal victory, after having gone through all these battles, all the despair and fear. I was still alive, and I'd overcome all these things. And Mosul Eye's prediction that we will live came true. That was the most beautiful thing.

A Clean Mirror

Mark Kukis
I think Iraq's future is really uncertain. It's unclear whether a stable political system can arise out of this environment and out of the legacy of this war. It's just not clear whether Iraq can be a functioning country. Even after all this time, it still faces major hurdles in terms of being able to provide some basic public goods, like security in the streets of Baghdad for its citizens. After all these years, after all this money spent, after all this bloodshed and fighting, we live in a world where today Baghdad is still an unsafe place. There's no real reason for hope that that will change any time soon. To me, that says that Iraq's ability to function as a country remains an open question.

The way I see Iraq is that it's caught up in a larger series of forces that are driving events across the region. To distil it, what you have is a massive demographic shift where Shi'ites are becoming more numerous and they're claiming more economic power across the region. Iraq is a centre of gravity for that conflict: the claims that they are making mostly disenfranchise a Sunni power structure that's prevailed for many, many centuries. What this boils down to, ultimately, is that we are seeing a transformation of the region where Iraq is at the leading edge of a restructuring of the economic and political power that will affect not just Iraq but the entire Middle East. As that process unfolds, you will see from year to year a series of events: there will be the rise of Shi'ite political power structures; there will be a lashing out by Sunni communities against those structures; and those structures over time will become more enduring and deeply rooted. In the end, they will claim what riches there are to be had across the Middle East.

That's what's happening in the Middle East, and American efforts to intervene will not change that. American intervention will not change the demographic realities in the Middle East. Long term, what we are seeing unfolding is happening quite rapidly and it's happening in a transformative way that will not be reversed by anything that America tries to do. At the same time, when you look realistically at Iraq and contemplate its future, you will see the rise of a new political power and economic structure there, but you will not see the disappearance of the old structure, and therefore you will not see the disappearance of the violence against the new structures. So violence in Iraq as we know it today is not going anywhere, and there is no intervention that Americans can do to solve that.

John Nixon

One of the great shames of the Iraq War is the extent and level to which Iran has a say in Iraq's foreign affairs, domestic policy and its security policy within the country. That can't be underestimated, and that is also a major grievance with the Sunni community. It does set the stage for why ISIS initially did so well. And it sets the stage also for why ISIS will probably come back in some other form, at some point in time. They have lost their caliphate, elements of it are on the run, they have taken a beating, but they are not defeated, and they are reconstituting as we speak. They will be back, and they will be back largely because the grievances that the Sunni community had, and has till this day, have not been addressed and will not be addressed. And that's fertile ground for ISIS to attach itself and grow again.

Tahany Saleh

ISIS can come back in a number of ways. A person is ISIS-like when one stops another's life. ISIS can't come back with its 'prophetic policies', the caliphate, Abu Bakr and all these labels.

But there might be some groups that will benefit from the chaos and take control of some parts of the city. It can take control of the markets, its economy, it can take control of people's lives, their salaries, their help. And that's something very difficult. It's very harsh. That they can take control of simple people's lives. This is probably because of the corruption in Mosul, because of the lack of government, the chaos, because of the intensity of the shock – people aren't thinking about the future in a normal way. We might think about the future in a way where they will give Mosul its rights. For example, the economy: they could give Mosul its right in balances, investment. We would like this. But with the chaos that Mosul is seeing because of political reasons …

Omar Mohammed

The battle to retake Mosul was led by the Iraqi security forces with the support of the international coalition, mainly led by the United States under Donald Trump, with the Secretary of Defense, James Mattis, who said that the tactic to take the city of Mosul from ISIS was to take it at any cost. The cost was the death of almost 40,000 civilians and the destruction of the city. If this is the safest and best the Americans have ever done, what is the most dangerous it could be? If the safest battle is to take a city with 40,000 civilians killed and 80 per cent of the city destroyed … if this is the meaning of 'safe' in the American military or political language, what is a dangerous battle?

I wanted the city to be liberated, but I was afraid that this was going to lead to the destruction of the city because they were under-prepared. The way they fought in the city it was clear that they didn't care about the civilians, it was a fight to finish ISIS. There is a huge difference between a battle to liberate a city from ISIS and a battle against ISIS. The second was what happening in Mosul, which means that civilians weren't taken into consideration. Trump wanted ISIS to be defeated at any cost and that was it. The Iraqi security forces didn't care about the civilians there, because their militias blocked the west borders of the city. I don't know if I can call it a liberation. It was the end of the battle between the Iraqi security forces and the international coalition and ISIS. It wasn't a liberation, because they left a destroyed city behind them, with two million people internally displaced, with hundreds of people in the prison because they are suspected of being ISIS with no trial, with camps full of families, mainly women and children, accused of being ISIS families. They are being punished for things they didn't do, with a city that's full of militias. If anyone has a good reason to tell me that this is a liberation, I would say it's a liberation, but it's not. They didn't even try to save the people.

What happened to Mosul was a punishment. It is to say this is the fate of any city that can allow, in the future, to have organisations like ISIS. It's to make an example out of Mosul, to make an example to any other city – you want ISIS, this is what you get. This is what they did with Berlin: the Nazis were defeated, Hitler committed suicide, the brutal regime was defeated, yet the bombing didn't stop. Now, if you talk to anyone, the example they give you is Mosul: 'Look at Mosul, what happened to the city, do you want your city to be like this?' Recently, there were demonstrations in Basra, people asking for their basic rights – they were asking for clean water because the city doesn't have clean water, there are not enough factories to produce the drinking water. The argument in the media was: 'Keep your head down. Do you want your city to be like what happened to Mosul?' This is dark, and they made us an example.

This is why, when you say you are a citizen from Mosul, they directly identify us as ISIS suspects or ISIS supporters or accepted ISIS. Choose whatever you want, they can go with you to different levels. If you didn't support them, you stayed. If you stayed – and they would agree you didn't have a choice to leave – then they will say, 'Why didn't you try …?' When they name the victims, we are not considered as victims. Who were considered as victims are the Christians. Anybody else. But not us, not the people of Mosul. After the fall of Saddam, they called us

Ba'athists, then they called us al-Qaeda, then ISIS came and they are using this label now.

Tahany Saleh
I've heard them saying that Mosul is not yet settled. How is it not settled? You mean, you're going to allow ISIS in on us again? You're going to open the borders, let ISIS in, and abandon us again? A fourth, a fifth, a millionth time? They might not let armed groups in, but they'll control people's livelihoods. I hope it doesn't happen. I hope that Mosul will be under international protection so that we can overcome this chaos, because this chaos might lead to clones that are more violent than ISIS. They would take people's livelihoods away from them. The Old Mosul markets wouldn't be rebuilt, neither its homes. Maybe a warmongering ISIS or military ISIS won't come back, but there are still some ways in which they endanger Mosul …

John Nixon
You have a situation that is calmed down but is still unstable. It's still feeling its way toward making itself whole, but no one entity can create stability and control, especially in this new era of democratic institutions. Then suddenly the guiding hand that is nurturing this gets pulled away – yes, a vacuum is created. The problem with vacuums is the things that can come in to a vacuum are not always good, you know. It would be great if Thomas Jefferson and the founding fathers of Iraq had kind of stepped in and said, 'Let us reason together and figure out an enlightened future which all Iraqis are a member of.'

Unfortunately, that didn't happen. What did happen was a very strong-armed Shia administration came in and asserted its role in a very harmful way with the approval and the support of their neighbour Iran. You have a sizeable community that had once run things in the country that now feel disenfranchised, alienated and humiliated by the role that they are given in what they perceive as their country. You have the makings of a calamitous grievance and a feeling that the centre does not listen to our needs and what it is we want. Into that mix comes this element that has been dormant for years but now sees its opportunity to rise up again. And that is exactly what happened in 2013 and 2014: large demonstrations in Ambar province, ISIS coming in, infiltrating like fish into the sea, infiltrating in classic Mao fashion, infiltrating these protest movements and these demonstrations, and basically feeding off that and becoming stronger. And then launching this attack on the centre and, in the process, grabbing some of Iraq's larger cities, showing the weakness of the centre and how it deals which a situation in which Iraqi soldiers are throwing down their weapons and ripping off their uniforms to escape from ISIS. It was so disheartening to see. I remember watching the images of this happening and thinking, 'Oh my god, this is even worse than I thought could happen.' It has shown us that we're dealing with a force that is much more pernicious and much more insidious than I think we originally thought.

The sad thing is – and I hate to say this – if you have a Saddam Hussein in power, if a Sunni politician or a Sunni military figure had somehow wrested control of the government, had basically created a new regime, you don't have the rise of a group like ISIS. You would've had a Sunni-led Iraq and you would've had an Iraq that still has stability, and an Iraq where Iraqis had made the changes themselves and they had not had this intervening hand from the United States and various other countries, including the UK – who have artificially transformed the landscape and have had all these opportunists and exiles come back and divide up the spoils and take corruption to even higher levels than what Saddam's government did.

There is most definitely a shared responsibility. When I hear these people, whether it's Blair or Bush, say, 'What we did was the right thing,' the thing that gets me most angry is whoever is interviewing them never says to them, 'Why?' They just let the statement stand for itself. And you know something? It's not true. There is a shared responsibility, and we have done everything and the Brits have done everything to forget about this. They don't want to face up to it. They don't want to face their responsibility because they know it's there.

Omar Mohammed
I don't see any hope. We are going to another kind of conflict. This time it's between the militias. All the signs are leading to a conflict, a bloody conflict between the Shia militias, and there are many parties will be happy to fund this conflict. I hope it will not happen, but everything happening now is telling us that another bloody conflict is coming to Iraq.

Waleed Nesyif
Now Da'esh has gone, and everyone in Iraq is waiting for what's next. It's not like, 'Oh my god, thankfully we got rid of Da'esh.' No, it's 'What's next?' It definitely happens in two- to three-year intervals. You get two years, three years of shit being patched and then something else happens. And every time it seems to be bigger than the other. Da'esh made us look at al-Qaeda like they were just a bunch of jokers, and they were, in comparison. Actually, even al-Qaeda denounced Da'esh.

I think the only chance in hell that we have is for the Iraqi government to be a government and not a bunch of clubs, because they're not even political parties any more – they're just a bunch of clubs. If you follow Iraqi politics, it's kind of like a comedy show. Nouri al-Maliki was enemies with one of the guys that he ended up making a block with, right after Maliki's party lost seats and this guy lost seats. They're like, 'Oh, let's make a political block,' so they made a block so now they have power. I don't think anyone in the Iraqi government has the interest of Iraqis in mind at all. At all. The only guy that kind of came close to it, Awadh Al-Badi, he tried. I'll give him that, he tried. He really, really tried, but god did he fall short.

If you look at our world today, you have the rise of Islamic global terrorism. You have the rise of white nationalism in its rawest and most disgusting form. You have millions and millions of refugees. You have Da'esh. You have nations hating nations, and you have a world that is completely governed by fear. And you want to know why? I guess this is a question that everybody is asking right now. Why? To me, you don't need to look any further than 2003. That, to me, was the genesis of it all. Scholars can continue to theorise, but the reality is this is our world and it's happening now.

I'm trying to figure out a way right now where I can actually give an impact that will help change our image, you know, to ourselves first. I want to clean that mirror, you know, so when we look at ourselves it's not full of blemishes and you don't know if you have an eye or a nose but rather you see yourself. And hopefully this mirror will turn into a window into the world where you see the world through a clearer glass as opposed to the dust. And I'm happy to say that there is strong evidence of that in Iraq, funded by the people, done by the people without the help of anyone.

There are some people that are doing phenomenal projects in Iraq right now. I have this friend who's a volunteer, he's a Shia guy from Baghdad, his name is Ali. I knew him as this like really funny, jokey kid. Now he's like one of the biggest freaking activists in Baghdad. This guy takes truckloads of help to Mosul, almost on a weekly basis, collecting it mostly from Shia. And he's by no means a singularity, you know he is representing another group of young Iraqi individuals that are trying to overcome this. And I want to be one of them.

There's this duality in Iraq where you have people trying to do good things and trying to overcome. But at the same time you have this lingering thought that something is going to happen that is damning, that could be a preventative to that good thing. That has happened so many times before. Now whether people are going to be able to prevent the contamination, continue on this path and quash this one, I don't know. But I'm happy that the positive exists. Let's get through this and come out of it alive and well together. It's fantastic to see, you know, and I hope it continues.

I really hope it continues.

Contributors

Ashley Gilbertson
In 2003 Ashley Gilbertson's photo of a soldier sliding down the bannisters in one of Saddam's palaces made the cover of *Time* magazine. He then embedded with 1/8th Infantry Marines, Bravo Company in Iraq for the American attack on Fallujah in November 2004. Ashley suffered from PTSD on his return to the USA and has struggled to come to terms with Billy's death.

John Nixon
A CIA analyst who spent years studying Saddam Hussein. Nixon was called upon to make the official ID. Given the endless 'body double' rumours, Nixon looked for tell-tale scars and tribal tattoos and asked a list of questions only Saddam himself could answer. He spent the following month with Saddam, 'interrogating' him, learning more about the complexities of the man and the regime he ruled over.

Dexter Filkins
Pulitzer prize-winning author of *The Forever War*, Filkins was present for the fall of the Two Towers. He followed the action to Afghanistan and, when Bush declared war on Iraq, he crossed from Kuwait and spent much of the following three years in Iraq, leaving in 2006, returning on a number of occasions after 2009.

Waleed Nesyif
Nesyif was born in 1984. His father was a Colonel in the Republican Guard, but Waleed chose a completely different career path and by

the age of 12 had formed his first heavy metal band. His fluency in English allowed him to start working for the Americans as a translator, and he went on to build a career as a journalist working for both Iraqi and foreign agencies. Waleed was eventually forced to leave Iraq and found refuge in Canada, where he is now married and has a young baby boy. He returned to Iraq for the first time in 2012, having not seen his family for nearly nine years.

Paul Bremer

Bremer was appointed by President Bush as Presidential Envoy to Iraq on 9 May 2003. His appointment declared him subject to the 'authority, direction and control' of Secretary of Defense Donald Rumsfeld. On 11 May, he replaced Lt General Jay Garner as Director of the Office for Reconstruction and Humanitarian Assistance in Baghdad. In June, the Office was transformed into the Coalition Provisional Authority, and Bremer became the country's chief executive authority. As the top civilian administrator of the CPA, Bremer was permitted to rule by decree. Among his first and most notable decrees were Coalition Provisional Authority Order 1, which banned the Ba'ath party in all forms, and Coalition Provisional Authority Order 2, which dismantled the Iraqi army.

Steve Russell

Russell was a Lieutenant Colonel in the US army. During Operation Iraqi Freedom, Russell commanded the 1st Battalion, 22nd Infantry 'Regulars' and conducted combat in Tikrit, Iraq from the spring of 2003 to the spring of 2004. His taskforce was a part of Colonel James Hickey's 1st Brigade, 4th Infantry Division. He was central to the hunt for Saddam Hussein.

Rudy Reyes

Reyes was a Sergeant in the 1st Reconnaissance Battalion. He spearheaded the attack on Baghdad and met fierce resistance, particularly from foreign fighters. He fought at Fallujah in April

2004 and then at Ramadi. His tour over, he returned to the USA and left the army and has now started an NGO with some other veterans, putting their skills to good. He also portrayed himself in the TV series *Generation Kill*.

Omar Mohammed
Mosul Eye is a news blog created and maintained by historian and citizen journalist Omar Mohammed. For more than two years, Mohammed used the anonymous blog to report conditions and events in the Iraqi city of Mosul during the occupation of the Islamic State of Iraq and the Levant (ISIL). Mosul was liberated on 10 July 2017 after a battle that had lasted for nine months and four days. Omar's blog is frequently cited as one of the few reliable sources documenting life under ISIL rule and has been called a critical source of information for journalists and scholars.

Christian Dominguez
Dominguez was a Lance Corporal Marine in Bravo Unit. He fought in the Battle of Fallujah in November 2004 and was with Billy Miller, who was shot as they ascended the minaret in search of the photo of the dead Iraqi sniper for Ashley Gilbertson. He returned from Iraq with PTSD.

Sam Williams
Williams was a US Marine in the 1st Battalion, 8th Marines in Fallujah. In total he served four tours in Iraq. He was one of the first Marines to be deployed to Mosul at the start of the invasion and then on his second tour he was part of Bravo Company in Operation Phantom Fury in Fallujah November 2004. He was the leader of the patrol that went into the minaret with Ashley and Dexter when Lance Corporal Billy Miller was killed.

Suzy, Lewis and Sabrina Miller
The parents and sister of Billy Miller, who was killed by a sniper in Fallujah in November 2004. Billy was the Marine who led

the way up the minaret in the search for a photo of a dead insurgent sniper for photographer Ashley Gilbertson. Suzy and Lewis live in Pearland, St Louis. They believe their son died fighting for freedom and that the Iraq War was a right and just war.

Mowaffak al-Rubaie

Also known as 'Dr Mow', al-Rubaie fled Iraq in the 1970s after being imprisoned and tortured under Saddam's regime, and settled in the UK where he studied to become a neurological surgeon. Mow was an active member of the Iraqi exiles, working with Chalabi and the Americans to bring down Saddam. Following the invasion in 2003, he returned to Baghdad and worked within the CPA helping to create the foundations of a new state. He was also assigned the role of National Security Adviser under the guise of which he oversaw the execution of Saddam Hussein in 2006. Dr Mow has become a controversial figure in Iraqi politics after serving two terms under Prime Minister Nouri Maliki. He still holds an advisory role in Iraqi politics today.

Issam Al Rawi

Al Rawi now lives in Jordan. He was part of Saddam Hussein's inner circle working as Special Adviser, and was named 'moustache man' by Saddam. He was detained by the Americans following the invasion but was released within 18 months. He rose through the ranks of the Ba'ath Party alongside Saddam Hussein from the coup in 1979 to the last days of the regime. He refers to Saddam as 'the Martyr'.

Nick Popaditch

A Marine for 15 years before his deployment to Iraq, tank commander Nick Popaditch was at Firdos Square when Saddam's statue was brought down in 2003. In Fallujah the following year, he lost one eye completely and all but eight per cent of the vision in the other.

Sally Mars
Mars was six years old and living with her family in Baghdad when the invasion began. She became a young musician, determined to have a voice, despite high-profile 'westernised' women in Iraq having been targeted and murdered by extremists.

Nate Sassaman
A Combined Arms Infantry Battalion Commander based in the heart of the Sunni Triangle in 2003, Nate Sassaman built a reputation as the 'Warrior King', one of the most aggressive US officers in Iraq at the time.

Mustafa Ahmed Abed and Um Mustafa Nidhal
Um Mustafa Nidhal and her eldest son Mustafa Ahmed Abed were both severely wounded during the attack on Fallujah in November 2004 – Mustafa, just 2 years old, suffered horrific and life-threatening injuries that ultimately required treatment in the USA.

Brandon Barfield
Deployed to Iraq in 2006, Brandon Barfield was part of the platoon guarding Saddam Hussein from his capture to his execution.

Judge Raouf Rahman
Judge Raouf Rahman was the chief judge of the Supreme Iraqi Criminal Tribunal, who sentenced Saddam to death by hanging in 2006.

Tahany Seleh
Now part of the volunteer force rebuilding Mosul, Tahany Seleh and her sister spent 944 days as virtual prisoners in their own home throughout the city's occupation by ISIS.

Mark Kukis
Kukis is a journalist for *Time* magazine, and was embedded with US forces in Iraq between 2006 and 2009. He reported on the

height of the civil war in 2006 and the Anbar Awakening of the following year.

Abu Mohamed
Fallujah resident Abu Mohamed joined the local resistance against the Americans with his father and brother, wanting to defend their country and resist the occupation.

Samir Al-Jassim
A refugee from the aftermath of the first Gulf War, Samir Al-Jassim returned to Iraq in 2003 as a civilian translator for the military, and was eventually sent to work with the special forces hunting for Saddam.

Um Qusay
Um Qusay lives in Al Alam, close to Tikrit. She became a well known public figure in Iraq following her role in saving 64 Shia survivors of the Speicher Massacre – she sheltered them in her own home while ISIS were in control of Tikrit.

Colin Marks
Colin Marks was a major in the Royal Irish Regiment, serving in Iraq.

INDEX

Abu Ghraib prison, Iraq 153, 155, 173, 176–8
  Battle of (2005) 227
Abu Hishma, Iraq 96, 109
Abu Risha, Abd al-Sattar 325–7
Abu Risha Ahmed 325–6, 327
AC-130 Spectre 198
Afghanistan 3, 8, 9, 14, 15, 18, 24, 25, 29–30, 31, 62, 73, 158, 161, 181, 289, 300
Agreement Between the United States of America and the Republic of Iraq on the Withdrawal of United States Forces from Iraq and the Organization of Their Activities during Their Temporary Presence in Iraq (2008) 282
Al Alam, Iraq 20–1
Al Duloiya, Iraq 103
Al Jazeera 78, 122
Allawi, Ayad 291, 293, 294
Amin, Judge Rizgar 253–4
Anbar Province, Iraq 185, 281, 292–3, 317, 318, 323, 324, 325–7, 328, 339, 345, 372
Anderson, Nathan 200
Anfal genocide (1986–9) xix, 257
Apache helicopter 114, 132, 270
al-Askari Shrine/Mosque, Samarra, bombing of (February 2006) xxii, 228
Aziz, Tariq xix, 256, 277

Ba'ath Party:
  Ba'athist revolution (1968) (17 July Revolution) xvi
  de-Ba'athification process and xvii, xxi, 77, 97–9, 101, 102, 106–7, 218
  Iraqi Civil War and xxii
  Maliki and 291
  overthrow of celebrated within Iraqi population xiv, 55, 99
  rise to power 139
  Saddam Hussein and ix, xix, 126, 253, 258
  sectarianism and xxii, 258, 291, 302, 371
Badr Brigade 296
Baghdad, Iraq vii–viii, xv, xviii, xx, 334–5, 367, 374
  Bush visits 78, 322
  car/suicide bombings in viii, 78, 79, 174–5, 281, 294–5
  changes in over course of conflict 335–8, 343–5
  first days of US occupation/lack of reconstruction within 56–73, 81, 83–117, 146–50
  Green Zone xxi–xxii, xxiv, xxvi, 252, 255, 267, 294, 312, 322
  Saddam execution, reaction to within 290
  Saddam flees 56, 58, 63, 64, 121–2, 229
  sectarian violence in 79, 294–6, 307–9, 310
  US invasion of/airstrikes on (2003) 5, 27, 28–9, 30, 33, 40–1, 44–8, 49–55, 283, 334
  US troop 'surge' and 327, 328, 329–30, 331
Bakr, Abu 368

al-Bakr, Ahmed Hassan 243–4
Balad, Iraq 96, 109
Barfield, Brandon 239, 241, 244, 247–50, 260–1, 265–6, 268–71, 274
al-Basheer, Ahmad 58, 61–2, 66
Basra, Iraq xxiii, xxv, 5, 32, 64, 370
  Battle of (Operation Charge of the Knights) (2008) xxiii, 281, 315
BBC viii, xxvi, 29
beheadings xxii, 300–1, 329, 355–6
Biden, Joe 339
bin Laden, Osama 3, 10, 13, 16, 20, 78
Blackwater 79, 82, 145–6, 153, 159, 160, 162–4, 174, 189, 228, 281
Blix, Hans 4
Bremer, Paul xvii, 77, 84–8, 93–4, 97–101, 102, 127–8, 138–9, 142–3, 144–5, 146–7, 160, 218
Brown, DeMarcus 209
Bush administration (George W. Bush) x, xvi, xviii, xviii, 7, 16–17, 73, 155, 238, 306, 307, 313–14, 317, 327, 332
Bush, George H. W. 16–17, 230, 340
Bush, George W. xiii, xv, xvi, 4, 119, 121, 134, 138, 238, 282, 372
  Awakening and 323
  'axis of evil' speech 3
  Baghdad visits 78, 322
  Bremer, appoints 77, 84–8
  de-Ba'athification and 98
  Fallujah and 146
  Gulf War and 16–17, 230
  ISIS and 340
  'Mission Accomplished' speech xiii, 5, 67, 68–9, 95, 155
  Muqtada al-Sadr and 314
  origins of Iraq War and 16–17, 18, 19, 25
  Saddam Hussein and 16–17, 18, 19
  start of Iraq War and 26
  'surge' (2007) and 281, 283, 306, 308, 309, 314, 327–31, 339
  'war on terrorism' and 3

Camp Speicher massacre (2014) xxiii

car bombings viii, 78, 79, 103, 107–8, 156, 174–5, 229, 281, 286, 294–5, 301–2, 304–5, 310, 341, 348, 355
Central Bank of Iraq 26, 88, 89–90
Chalabi, Ahmad xviii, xix, 16, 84
Charge of the Knights, Operation (or the Battle of Basra) xxiii, 281, 315
Charter of the City, or the Constitution of Medina (ISIS document) 350, 357–8
Cheney, Richard 17
Chin, Eddie 53
Christians, Iraqi xviii, 84, 165, 287, 301, 329, 340, 343, 351, 352, 354, 370
CIA:
  Ayad Allawi and 293
  Blackwater and 162
  Bremer and 85, 87, 98
  Bush and 314–15
  de-Ba'athification and 98
  9/11 and 9–10, 14, 18
  post-war planning and 85, 87, 98
  pre-war activities in Iraq xix, 9
  Saddam Hussein capture and 231–2, 322
  Saddam Hussein execution and 263–4, 292
  Saddam Hussein pursuit and 118–19, 121–4
  Saddam Hussein questioning and 229, 232, 233–5, 236–8, 239–40, 241–7, 263–4, 276–8, 285
  start of Iraq War and 26
  see also Nixon, John
civil war, Iraqi (2006–2008) xi, xv, xxii–xxiv, 230, 274, 281, 296, 298, 300, 307–31, 338, 344, 345
Clinton administration xiv, 16, 73, 340
Coalition Provisional Authority (CPA) xvii, xxi, 77, 87–8, 112, 142–3, 145, 146, 147, 160, 298, 299
  Blackwater and 160
  Bremer and *see* Bremer, Paul
  'de-Ba'athification' process (Order 1) xvii, 77, 97–102, 106–7

INDEX

elections and xxi, 112
establishment of xvii, 87–8
Iraqi army and security infrastructure, disbands (Order 2) xvii, 51, 77, 91, 99–102, 104, 106–7, 147–8, 310–11, 319
Iraqi Governing Council, establishes interim 77
Muqtada al-Sadr and 144–5
street vendors, outlaws 147
contractors, private military 79, 82, 145–6, 153, 159, 160, 162–4, 167–8, 174, 189, 228, 281
Crocker, Ryan 282

Da'esh *see* Islamic State of Iraq and Syria (ISIS) 'danger close' (dropping a bomb within couple-of-hundred-yard radius) 198
Dawa party xviii, 290–1, 292
de-Ba'athification process xvii–xviii, 77, 97–102, 104–5, 106–7, 147, 218, 310–11
Diyala river, Iraq 44–5
Dominguez, Christian 156, 183–8, 190, 191, 193, 196, 197–8, 199–201, 203, 205–7, 208, 213, 219
Dominus, Carlos 199
al-Douri, Izzat Ibrahim 277
Drew, Kevin 142
Duhok, Iraq viii, 254

elections, Iraq xx, xxi, 87, 112, 340, 344
(2005) xx, xxv, 227, 228
(2010) 282, 293–4
(2018) xxv
electricity supply, Iraqi xv, 24, 27, 70, 81, 91, 92, 147, 179
Enduring Freedom, Operation (NATO invasion of Afghanistan) 3
Exodus (television series) viii–ix

Fallujah, Iraq 67, 145–6, 156, 283, 298, 327
First Battle of (April 2004) 153, 157–75

four Blackwater contractors killed in (31 March 2004) 79, 82, 145–6, 159, 160, 162–4, 167–8, 174
ISIS in 156
Second Battle of (November 2004) 153, 156, 179–224
US forces killing of civilians in 67, 79
FBI 125, 237
Fedayeen Saddam 64, 108, 109, 125, 130, 165
Feith, Doug 16
Filkins, Dexter:
Afghanistan and 15, 25, 62
Fallujah and 156, 159–60, 161, 162–4, 172, 174–5, 182–3, 188, 189, 190–3, 195, 196–7, 204, 205, 206, 207, 210, 211, 213, 215, 216, 217, 219–20
invasion of Iraq and 25, 29–30, 31, 33, 44, 46, 51–2, 56–7, 62–3, 64–5, 67
9/11 and 9, 14
origins of Iraq War and 15–16
foreign fighters 316–18
Freres, Lance Corporal 170
'Future of Iraq' study (2002) 85

Garner, Jay 83–4, 87, 98
Geneva Convention 203, 204, 244, 248
Gilbertson, Ashley:
Billy Miller death and 203–4, 205–6, 207, 210, 211–12, 213–14, 217, 218
Fallujah and 156, 159–60, 188, 189–90, 192, 193, 194–7, 198–9, 201–2, 203–4, 205–6, 207–8, 210, 211–12, 213–14, 217, 218
Greenstock, Sir Jeremy 88
Gulf War (1991) 11, 16, 31, 85, 92, 123, 134, 135, 230, 240

Haditha, Iraq 126, 130
Battle of (2005) 227
Haiti xvi, 86, 93
Halabja, chemical attack in (1988) ix, xiv, 243, 245–6, 257
Hilla suicide bombing (28 February 2005) 227

Hussein, Qusay (Saddam's son) 64, 77, 121, 123
Hussein, Saddam xxiv, 4, 8, 84, 94, 228, 278, 335, 370–1
  Al Alam, attacks the village of 20–1
  Anfal genocide and xix, 257
  Arab nationalism and 258, 262
  Ba'ath Party and 97
  Bush and 16–17, 19
  'Elvis sightings' of 123–5, 127, 128
  FBI interviews 124, 237
  Halabja attack and ix, xiv, 243, 245–6, 257
  hanged (30 December 2006) 228, 263–75, 283, 290, 292
  insurgency and 119
  Iraqi people fear possible return of 63–4, 65–6
  ISIS and 372
  Kuwait invasion (1990) and xiii–xiv, xix, 16, 99
  Islamic extremism and 148, 155, 161, 284, 285
  9/11, link to/push for removal of within Washington ix–x, 7, 13, 16–20, 148, 155, 161, 238
  nostalgia for within Iraq xv–xvi
  palaces 64–5, 81, 89, 90, 92
  power vacuum within Iraq after removal of 155
  president of Iraq, becomes ix, xiii
  questioned/debriefed by CIA 233–50, 276, 285
  rebuilding of Iraq after Gulf War 92
  release of criminals before war 70
  search for and capture 78, 81, 95–6, 118–40, 142, 229–30, 231–5, 283
  sentenced to death 228, 230, 261–2, 263
  Shia 1991 uprising and ix, 31, 99–100, 136, 229–30
  statues toppled in Baghdad 5, 49–55, 57–9
  writing ambitions 258, 259, 277
  trial 227, 251–62, 289
  tribes and 323
  US invasion of Iraq and 4, 5, 8, 21, 25, 26, 29, 31, 34, 35, 41, 43, 45, 49–55, 56–9, 61, 62, 63, 64, 65, 66, 68, 70, 121–3, 229
  WMD (weapons of mass destruction) and x, 19, 139, 234–5, 237, 276, 277
Hussein, Sajida (Saddam's wife) 129, 244, 268
Hussein, Uday (Saddam's son) 24, 56, 77, 121, 123, 129

Ibn Ali, Hussein xxiv
IEDs (improvised explosive devices) 107, 110, 158, 173, 189, 287, 305, 348
insurgency, Iraqi xxii–xxiii
  Fallujah and 153–224
  origins of 69, 74–150
  al-Qaeda and *see* al-Qaeda
  Sunni Awakening and xxii–xxiii, 281, 318, 322–31, 339
  'surge' and (2007) 281, 306, 308, 309, 314, 322, 327–31, 332, 339
International Criminal Court (ICC) 251, 254
IRA 166
Iran xiii, xvi, xxii, 3, 17, 45, 64, 72, 148, 158, 238, 240, 267, 291, 292, 293, 294, 300, 313, 314, 315, 317, 332, 341, 368, 371
Iran-Iraq War (1980–88) xiii, 21, 24, 100, 124, 140, 310–11
Iraq:
  civil war (2006–2008) xi, xv, xxii–xxiv, 230, 274, 283, 285–31, 338, 344, 345
  constitution xxi, 146, 227
  elections *see* elections
  electricity/water supply xv, 24, 27, 51, 58, 59, 68, 70, 81, 91, 92, 147, 148, 179, 370
  future of 367–74
  gross national income per capita (GNI) xv

INDEX

government *see* Iraqi government
Iraq War and *see* Iraq War
9/11 and *see* 9/11
oil wealth xxiv, 72, 81, 90, 92, 148, 342
partition of considered xxii, 289
poverty in 68, 71, 89, 91, 101, 105, 344
Saddam Hussein and *see* Hussein, Saddam
sanctions against xiv, xix, 10, 17, 89, 92
sectarianism in xv–xxiv, 66, 84, 230, 258, 274, 283, 284, 285–31, 338, 340, 342, 343–5 *see also* Kurds; Shia Islam; Sunni Islam
WMD (weapons of mass destruction) and x, 4, 19, 78, 118, 119, 139, 148, 227, 234–5, 237, 276, 277, 306
see also individual area or place name
Iraqi Army 298, 303
  Awakening and 326–7
  disbanded by CPA xvii, 51, 77, 91, 99, 100, 101–2, 104, 106–7, 147–8, 310–11, 319
  Fallujah and 157, 158, 164, 223, 224
  Golden Division 301, 328
  ISIS and 348–50, 355, 357, 362, 363, 369–70
  sectarianism and 294, 301, 302, 308, 316, 328–9, 341, 344
  US hand control of Anbar to 281
  US Invasion of Iraq (2003) and 30, 31, 33, 34, 41, 46, 48, 51, 58, 63–4, 70, 71
Iraqi Aviation Club, Baghdad 149–50
Iraqi Broadcasting Corporation 24
Iraqi Freedom, Operation (2003–11) *see* Iraq War
Iraqi Governing Council 77, 79, 84, 251
Iraqi government:
  constitution and xxi, 146, 227
  CPA as *see* Coalition Provisional Authority (CPA)
  de-Ba'athification and 100–1
  falls after US invasion 62
  formal sovereignty handed to interim (28 June 2004) xvii, 146, 153, 298

muhassasa (scheme for power-sharing) xx, xxi, xxv
  remoteness of leaders xxi–xxii, xxiv
  sectarianism and 228, 290–4, 295, 296, 315–16, 338–40, 373
  trial of Saddam and 257, 265
  see also Allawi, Ayad and al-Maliki, Nouri
Iraqi National Accord (INA) xviii
Iraqi National Congress (INC) xviii, xix, xx
Iraqi National Guard 184, 186–7
Iraqi National Library, Baghdad 88, 89–90
Iraqi Olympic Committee, The 56–7
Iraqi Transitional Government 228
Iraq Survey Group 78
Iraq War (2003–11) x–xi
  Baghdad, bombing of ('shock and awe') 28–9, 32, 40, 41
  battles *see individual battle and area name*
  Blackwater and 79, 82, 145–6, 153, 159, 160, 162–4, 174, 189, 228, 281
  CPA and *see* Coalition Provisional Authority (CPA)
  de-Ba'athification process xvii–xviii, 77, 97–102, 104–5, 106–7, 147, 218, 310–11
  handover of power (28 June 2004) xvii, 146, 153, 298
  insurgency *see* insurgency
  Iraqi civilian support for xiv–xv, 7, 22–4, 27–9, 54, 55, 57, 58–9, 155
  Iraqi civil war and (2006–2008) xi, xv, xxii–xxiv, 230, 274, 283, 285–31, 338, 344, 345
  lead up to/Washington pushes for 3–4, 14–25
  looting during xvii–xviii, 31, 49, 56–7, 65, 67, 71, 81, 88, 89–91, 93–4, 351
  'Mission Accomplished'/'end of' (May 2003) xiii–xvi, 5, 67, 68–9, 95, 155
  post-invasion phase (2003–11) 56–345
  reconstruction/planning, lack of US xiii, xv, 24, 27, 56–73, 81–117, 124, 141, 143–4, 146–50

385

Iraq War (*continued*)
   Saddam Hussein and *see* Hussein, Saddam
   start of 26–48
   statues of Saddam toppled in Baghdad 5, 49–55, 57–9
   Sunni Awakening xxii–xxiii, 281, 318, 322–31, 339
   'surge' and (2007) 281, 306, 308, 309, 314, 322, 327–31, 332, 339
   US forces take control of Iraq 49–55
   US invasion of Iraq 29–51
   US withdrawal of forces 282, 284, 332–45
al-Islam, Ansar 300
Islamic Law 324
Islamic State of Iraq and Syria (ISIS) (Da'esh) xxvi, 346–66, 369–71, 372
   Camp Speicher massacre (2014) xxiii
   Charter of the City, or the Constitution of Medina (ISIS document) 350, 357–8
   destruction of historical sites 353
   development of modes of killing 304
   executions 355–6
   Fallujah and 156, 174
   future of 368–9, 371
   Maliki and 291, 293, 301, 302
   Mosul and viii, xxiii–xxiv, 284, 291, 301, 302, 304, 305, 342, 345, 346–66, 369–71
   Mosul Eye/online blog and 357–62
   Obama and 342
   origins of 107, 284, 291, 293, 301, 305, 323, 342
   al-Qaeda and 293, 373
   Saddam Hussein and 284, 372
   sectarian narrative of xxiii–xxiv, xxv
   tribes and 323
   Trump and xiii, 370–1

Jabar, Faleh Abdul xxv
al-Jafari, Ibrahim 292
al-Jassim, Samir 134, 135–8, 229–30, 232, 252, 256, 271–2

Jordan 22, 78, 102, 120, 126, 156, 161, 298, 299, 300, 318, 338, 360

Karbala, Iraq xxiv, 79, 144
al-Kasasbeh, Muath 360
al-Khazali, Qais xxiii–xxiv
kidnappings xxii, 161, 284, 297, 308, 320–1
Krongard, Buzzy 231
Kukis, Mark 289–90, 294–6, 306–11, 315–18, 324–8, 329–31, 334–5, 338–9, 367–8
Kurdistan Alliance (*al-tahaluf al-Kurdistani*, or KA) xx
Kurdistan Democratic Party (KDP) xviii
Kurds ix, xiv, xv, xviii, xix, xx, xxi, xxiv, xxv, 35, 84, 95, 99, 162, 165, 252, 254, 257, 271, 289, 291, 343
Al Kut, Iraq 41–2, 44
Kuwait 5, 24, 25, 29, 30, 102, 158, 166, 185, 301
   Iraqi invasion of (1990) xiii–xiv, xix, 16, 21, 99, 248

Law of Administration for the State of Iraq for the Transitional Period (8 March 2004) 79
League of the Righteousness xxiii–xxiv
looting xvii–xviii, 31, 49, 56–7, 65, 67, 71, 81, 88, 89–91, 93–4, 351

Mahdi Army (Jaysh al-Mahdi) xxii, xxiii, 281, 296, 298, 300, 312–13, 314, 315, 330, 331
Mahmud, Abid Hamid 123
al-Maliki, Nouri xxiii, 228, 290–4, 315–16, 332, 338, 339–40, 373
Marks, Colin 11, 15, 21, 71
Mars, Sally 27, 54, 59–60, 61, 65–6, 103, 107–8, 115–17, 155, 161–2, 177–8
Masood, Ahmed Shah 9
Mattis, General James 31–2, 369
Miller, Lewis 179, 180, 181, 215

INDEX

Miller, Sabrina 179, 181, 214, 215, 216, 217
Miller, Susie 179, 180–2, 215–16, 217–18
Miller, William 'Billy' 179–82, 183, 193, 205–18, 219
Ministry of Oil, Baghdad 81, 90
Mohamed, Abu 164–5
Mohammed, Omar:
   Awakening, on 323
   future of Iraq, on 373
   Golden Division in Mosul, on 328–9
   insurgency, on origins of 299–303
   ISIS in Mosul and 284, 291–2, 301–2, 323, 340, 341–2, 348–50, 352–6, 357–62
   ISIS origins, on 290–2, 299–303, 328–9, 341–2
   Maliki, on 290–2, 340
   Mosul, battle to retake from ISIS and 369–71
   Mosul Eye/online blog and 357–62
   9/11 and 10, 19–20
   Obama withdrawal decision, on 340, 341–2
   US forces in Iraq, on interactions with 60–1
   US invasion of Iraq, on 54–5
Mosaddegh, Mohammad xvi
Mosul Eye/online blog 357–62
Mosul, Iraq viii, 10, 123, 254
   Awakening movement in 323
   Battle of (8 November 2004) 153
   future of 371, 374
   insurgency in 300–5, 318–20
   ISIS in viii, 284, 285–8, 291–2, 342, 345, 346–66, 368–71
   liberation of xxiii–xxiv, 361–6, 369–71
   al-Qaeda in 285–8, 303–5
   surge and 328–9, 341
   US invasion of Iraq and 55, 64, 77
muhassasa (scheme for power-sharing) xx, xxi, xxv
Mujahideen Shura Council xxii, 162

Mukhabarat (Iraqi intelligence services) 97, 100, 233
Al-Musslit, Adnan Abid 129
Musslit family 128–30
Al-Musslit, Mohammed 129, 130, 131–2, 133, 135
Al-Musslit, Omar 129, 130
Al-Musslit, Rudman 130
Mustafa, Abu 157, 165, 221, 222, 223–4
Mustafa, Mustafa 157, 221, 222, 223, 224
Mustafa, Nidhal 156, 157, 179, 188, 221, 222–3, 224
Al Muwaffaqiyah, Iraq 39–40

Najaf, Iraq 145, 153
Nasiriyah, Iraq 36–7, 39
National Assembly of Iraq 227
National Security Council (NSC) 87
NATO 3
Navy SEALs 12, 46, 192
Nazi party 97
Negroponte, John 273
neoconservative group 16, 17, 284
Nesyif, Waleed 7
   Abu Ghraib, on 176–7, 178
   Bremer, on 83–4, 101–2, 146–7
   build up to war and/pro-war stance 18–19, 22–5, 155
   Canada, leaves Iraq for 298–9, 320–1
   disbandment of army, on 101–2
   Fallujah, on 145–7, 155, 159
   George Bush 'Mission Accomplished' speech, on 68–9
   leaves Iraq 297–9
   Mahdi Army, on 312–13
   9/11 and 10–11
   origins of insurgency, on 143–4, 146–50
   post-war situation in Baghdad, on 70–1, 72, 81, 83–4, 88–93, 101–2
   return to Iraq 333–4, 335–8
   Saddam execution and 257, 272–4
   Saddam trial and 257

Nesyif, Waleed (*continued*)
  Saddam, on search for 119–21, 139–40
  sectarianism and 343–5
  present-day Iraq, on 373–4
  US invasion of Iraq, on 27–9, 37–8, 40–1, 45–6, 47–8, 50, 51, 54, 58–9, 63–4
New York Times 94, 188, 197, 213, 215–16, 291, 358
9/11 ix–x, 3, 7, 9–13, 14, 15, 16, 17, 19, 20, 134, 144, 148, 181, 238, 277, 306
Nixon, John:
  Awakening, on 322–3
  Iranian influence within Iraq and ISIS, on 368
  Maliki, on 292–4
  Muqtada al-Sadr and 311–12, 313–15
  9/11 and 9–10, 13, 14, 16–18
  Obama, on 332, 339–40
  post-war planning, on lack of 73
  present-day Iraq, on 371–3
  Saddam execution and 263–4, 292
  Saddam link to 9/11, on 16–18, 19
  Saddam, questioning of 233–5, 236–8, 239–40, 241–7, 263–4, 276–8, 285
  Saddam, search for and 118–19, 121–4, 229, 231–2
  start of war and 26
  Zarqawi, role in hunt for 322
Northern Alliance 9

Obama administration 282, 283–4, 293–4, 332, 339–40, 341, 342
Obama, Barack 282, 283–4, 332, 339–40, 341, 342
Odierno, General 96
Ottoman Empire 143, 345

Panchot, Dale 114–15, 141
Patrick, Sean 36, 37
Patriotic Union of Kurdistan (PUK) xviii
Pearl, Richard 16
Pentagon 3, 10, 13, 17, 18, 85, 87, 218, 264
Petraeus, General David xxii–xxiii

Popaditch, Nick 11–12, 30–4, 38, 41–5, 49–51, 52–4, 57–8, 69, 158, 164, 168–72
Popular Mobilisation Units (*al-hashd al-shaabi*) xxiii–xxiv
Powell, Colin 86
prisons xxii, 153, 155, 161, 176–8, 301, 303, 305, 319, 345, 370

al-Qaeda 317, 330, 371
  Awakening and xxiii, 3, 281, 283, 323, 324, 325, 326, 328, 339
  Fallujah and 156, 161–2, 165, 174–5, 188, 222, 283
  foreign fighters in 317, 318
  funding of 324
  ISIS and 293, 373
  Mosul falls to 285–8, 303–5
  9/11 and ix, 3, 9, 10, 13, 148
  al-Qaeda in Iraq xiii, xxii, 156, 161, 174–5, 293, 300, 318, 322, 323, 332
  Saddam Hussein and x, 20, 161, 230, 238, 252
  sectarianism and xxii–xxiii, 318, 328, 330, 331
  support within civilian population of Iraq 161–2, 165, 324
  al-Zarqawi and 161, 174–5, 228, 287, 300, 322
Qusay, Um 7–8, 20–1, 34, 105–6, 110

Rahman, Raouf 253–6, 257–60, 261–2, 271
Ramadan 110, 113–15, 221, 256, 259, 272, 277, 292
Ramadan Offensive (27 October 2003) 78
Ramadan, Taha Yassin 256, 259, 277
Ramadi, Iraq 159, 224, 324, 325, 326, 327, 344–5
  Battle of (2006) 228
Rather, Dan 95
Al Rawi, Issam 8, 22, 26–7
Red Crescent (International Red Cross and Red Crescent Movement) 47, 146
'regime change', concept of xvi, xix

INDEX

Republican Guard 34–7, 47, 54, 64
Revolutionary Command Council 243
Reyes, Rudy 8, 12–13, 34–7, 39–40, 46–7, 68, 166–8, 172–4
Rice, Condoleezza 19
Richmond, David 88
Royal Marine Commandos, British 166
RPGs (rocket-propelled grenades) 107, 114, 127, 163, 169
al-Rubaie, Mowaffak 251–3, 256–7, 261, 262, 264–5, 267–8, 269, 270, 274–5
Rules of Engagement (ROEs) 93, 111, 188, 189, 203, 204, 213
Rumsfeld, Donald 16, 17, 19, 85, 86, 87, 104–5
Russell, Steve 125–7, 128–34

Sadr City, Baghdad 89, 312, 313
al-Sadr, Muqtada xxii, xxiii, 144–5, 146, 218, 281, 300, 311, 313, 314, 315, 330
Safavids xxii
Safwan Hill, Iraq 30–1
Al-Sahhaf, Mohammed Saeed 45–6, 47, 48
Sahwah (tribal fighters) 323
Salafi-jihadi organisations xiii, xxii, xxvi
Saleh, Tahany 284
   future of Mosul, on 371
   ISIS in Mosul, on 346–8, 350–2, 355, 359–60, 361–6, 368–9, 371
   al-Qaeda in Mosul, on 285–8, 303–5
   US policy in Iraq, on 318–20, 340–1
Samarra, Iraq xxii, 96, 124, 132, 141–3, 153, 159, 228
   Battle of (2004) 153
Sassaman, Colonel Nate 82, 94–7, 103–5, 106–7, 108–15, 124, 141–2
Saudi Arabia xxii, 16, 72, 148, 238, 273, 300, 306, 318
Sawyers, Sir John 88
Schwarzkopf, Norman 145
Second World War (1939–45) xvi, 97, 183
Sharia Law 283, 350
Shia Islam xiv, xv, xviii, xix, xx, xxi, xxii, 134, 289, 344, 345, 371
   Allawi and 293
   Awakening and 330, 331
   civil war and xxii–xxiii, 289, 290–1, 292, 293–4, 295, 296, 300, 302, 311, 313, 314, 315–16, 321, 328, 329, 330, 338, 344
   Dawa party and 290–1, 292
   future of Iraq and 373, 374
   Iraqi ethnic distribution and 84
   ISIS and xxiii–xxiv, xxv, 357
   League of the Righteousness xxiii–xxiv
   Mahdi Army and xxiii, 218, 281
   Maliki and xxiii, 228, 292, 293–4, 315–16
   Middle East region shifts in influence and 367–8
   Popular Mobilisation Units (*al-hashd al-shaabi*) xxiii
   al-Qaeda and 156
   Saddam and 21, 94, 95, 99–100, 245, 252, 257, 273–4, 285
   uprising (1991) ix, 31, 99–100, 136, 229–30
   US invasion and 94, 95, 99–100, 143
   US withdrawal and 338–9, 341, 342
Shinseki, General 104–5
Sinak bridge, Baghdad 50
Sinjar, Iraq 352, 355
snipers 46, 173, 174, 183, 188, 191, 192, 197, 203–4, 205, 209, 210, 365
al-Sistani, Grand Ayatollah Ali xxi
Somalia 125
State Department, US 13, 85, 87, 97, 264
Sufism 20
suicide attacks 78, 79, 194, 227, 236, 284, 285, 304
Sunni Islam xv, xviii, xix, 103, 109, 289, 314, 343
   civil war and *see* civil war, Iraqi
   de-Ba'athification and 99
   Fallujah 159, 165, 166
   insurgency *see* insurgency
   Iraqi ethnic distribution and 84
   ISIS and xxv, 351, 368
   Maliki and 291–4, 316, 338

Sunni Islam (*continued*)
  Middle East region shifts in influence and 367–8
  post-invasion Iraqi government and xxi–xxii, 95, 96, 345
  Saddam Hussein and xxi–xxii, 95, 126, 143, 238, 252, 257, 273, 274, 285, 372
  Sunni Awakening xxii–xxiii, 281, 283, 318, 322–31, 339, 340
  Sunni triangle 96, 159, 166, 344
  Sunni Umayyad Caliphate xxiv
  US withdrawal and 341
Supreme Council for the Islamic Revolution in Iraq (SCIRI) xviii
Supreme Iraqi Criminal Tribunal 253–6, 257–60, 261–2, 271
'surge, the' (US troop deployment) 281, 306, 308, 309, 314, 322, 327–31, 332, 339
Syria 18, 72, 97, 120, 123, 126, 148, 292, 300, 340, 352, 353

Talabani, Jalal 265
Talha, Abu 300
Taliban 3, 8, 9, 15
Tigris river 96, 103, 104, 109, 131, 32
Tikrit, Iraq 5, 64, 78, 110, 123, 125, 127, 128, 129, 130, 131, 132, 159
Time magazine 289, 294, 340
timelines 3–5, 77–9, 153, 227–8, 281–2
Trump, Donald xiii, 64, 312, 342, 369
Turkey viii, 24, 72, 142, 148

UN (United Nations) 78, 84, 85, 143
  Resolution 1441 3, 4
  Security Council 3, 4
United Iraqi Alliance (*al-itilaf al-Iraqi al-muwahad*, or UIA) xx
US Army:
  Afghanistan and *see* Afghanistan
  battles, Iraq *see individual battle and area name*
  casualty numbers, Iraq 153, 227, 228, 281
  contractors and 79, 82, 145–6, 153, 159, 160, 162–4, 174, 189, 228, 281
  force numbers, Iraq 85–6, 104–5
  insurgency and *see individual battle and area name*
  invasion of Iraq (2003) (Operation Iraqi Freedom) 26–73
  Marine corps 8, 11–13, 30–1, 33–7, 39, 40, 46, 64, 93, 99, 145, 156, 158, 163, 166, 172, 174, 179–80, 183, 184, 186, 189, 191, 192, 193, 194, 195, 196, 197, 198, 199, 200, 201, 204, 205, 206, 208, 210, 212, 213, 214, 215, 216, 217, 219, 220, 227
  Rules of Engagement (ROEs) 111, 188, 189, 203, 204, 213
  Special Operations Forces 132, 133, 134
  'surge' and 281, 306, 308, 309, 314, 322, 327–31, 332, 339
  training and deployment 179–82, 183–8
  withdrawal of forces from Iraq 282, 284, 332–45

Vietnam War (1955–75) 36, 39, 156, 183, 218
Village People operation, Al Duloiya 108–10

Wahhabism xxii, 20, 238
water supply, Iraqi xv, 24, 51, 58, 59, 68, 70, 81, 91, 92, 96, 147, 148, 179, 370
white phosphorus 47, 48, 192–3
Williams, Sam 156, 205, 208–11, 212, 213–14, 216–17
WMD (weapons of mass destruction) x, 4, 19, 78, 118, 119, 139, 148, 227, 234–5, 237, 276, 277, 306
Wolfowitz, Paul 16, 17

Yezidi people viii, xix, 84, 329, 340, 352, 354, 355

Zebari, Hoshiyar 282